该丛书译著受西安翻译学院2019年度双一流建设项目资助
The translation works in the series are funded by the Double A-class Development Project of the Xi'an Fanyi University, 2019.

西安名胜游

THE SIGHTS AND SOUNDS OF XI'AN

刘莹 张睿 著

图书在版编目（CIP）数据

西安名胜游：汉文、英文/刘莹，张睿著 . —北京：中国书籍出版社，2019.12
 ISBN 978－7－5068－7673－5

Ⅰ.①西… Ⅱ.①刘…②张… Ⅲ.①旅游指南—西安—汉、英 Ⅳ.①K928.941.1

中国版本图书馆 CIP 数据核字（2019）第 294314 号

西安名胜游

刘 莹 张 睿 著

责任编辑	张 幽 刘 娜
责任印制	孙马飞 马 芝
封面设计	中联华文
出版发行	中国书籍出版社
地　　址	北京市丰台区三路居路 97 号（邮编：100073）
电　　话	（010）52257143（总编室）　（010）52257140（发行部）
电子邮箱	eo@chinabp.com.cn
经　　销	全国新华书店
印　　刷	三河市华东印刷有限公司
开　　本	710 毫米×1000 毫米　1/16
字　　数	323 千字
印　　张	18
版　　次	2020 年 5 月第 1 版　2020 年 5 月第 1 次印刷
书　　号	ISBN 978－7－5068－7673－5
定　　价	75.00 元

版权所有　翻印必究

前　言

古都西安作为国家级历史文化名城，历经风雨十三朝，以其悠久的历史、深厚的文化底蕴、得天独厚的自然景观以及丰富的旅游文化资源吸引着无数中外游客。作为生活在西安并从事旅游英语教学的当代外语人理应肩负起讲好中国故事、传播中国文化的历史重任。为了让更多的外语学习者更高效地进行旅游英语学习，让外国游客通过旅游更深入地了解中国的历史和文化，让英文导游在与外国游客的交流中树立大国文化自信，《西安名胜游》应运而生。

本书运用中英双语全面介绍了陕西西安及周边著名景区，涉及西安市简介、博物馆文化、古帝王陵墓、古寺庙、宫苑园林、非物质文化遗产、地方小吃以及红色旅游等十二部分内容，力求做到语言表述准确、内容资料翔实、篇幅长度适中、中英双语表述对应，最大地发挥其实用价值，对中英文导游、英语学习者以及中外游客、旅游爱好者起到一定的指导作用。本书对于即将从事中英文导游的人士来说也是一本必备参考书。此外，本书也可作为各大高校旅游英语专业的教材使用。

书中难免存在一些不足之处，敬请社会各界朋友提出宝贵的意见，深表感谢！

本书共有12个部分，共计320千字。其中第一部分至第六部分由刘莹撰写并翻译，共计170,000字；第七部分至第十二部分由张睿撰写并翻译，共计150,000字。由于作者才疏学浅，阅历有限，书中差错难免，敬请社会各界朋友不吝赐教，深表感谢！

作者

2020年4月10日

Foreword

As an ancient city with a long history and profound culture, Xi'an, the capital of 13 dynasties, has rich cultural heritage, unique natural scenes, as well as abundant tourist and cultural resources, which attract numerous tourists at home and abroad. As instructors living and working in Xi'an and engaged in teaching ESP in tourism, we would like to tell well Chinese stories and bring overseas tourists closer to the unique Chinese culture through this book. *The Sights and Sounds of Xi'an* (bilingual) is compiled with the purpose of meeting the market demand for a bilingual version by tour guides in Xi'an, of encouraging the second language learners to have a better mastery of English in tourism, of helping overseas tourists know more about China's (particularly Xi'an's) history and culture, and of letting English – speaking tour guides build up their cultural confidence in their motherland when communicating with overseas tourists. That is why this book has come forth.

The Sights and Sounds of Xi'an bilingually introduces to tourists from various places in the world famous tourist attractions and historical sites in Xi'an and those in its vicinity. A brief introduction to Xi'an, the local culture and museums, ancient mausoleums of emperors in different dynasties, ancient temples, royal palaces and gardens, intangible cultural heritage, local snacks, sacred memorial places with historical significance to Chinese Communist revolutions are included in the book. The bilingual introduction is expressive and laconic in language, accurate and reliable in contents. Hopefully, this book offers useful references for bilingual tour guides, English language learners and those engaged in tourism. In addition, the book can be used as a textbook for university students majoring in English for tourism.

We'd like to thank all those who offer us any valuable suggestions.

The book consists of 12 parts with a total wordage of 320,000. Part 1 to Part 6 were written and translated by Liu Ying, totaling 170,000 words; Part 7 to Part 12 were written and translated by Zhang Rui, totaling 150,000 words. Inevitably, there might be errors in either diction or wording in the book due to the author's limited information and confined experience. We would like to thank friends from all walks of life for their admonitions and suggestions.

Author

April 10, 2020

目　录
CONTENTS

第一部分　陕西省概况 ······················· 1

第二部分　西安市概况 ······················· 5

第三部分　博物馆 ···························· 10
　陕西历史博物馆 ···························· 10
　西安碑林博物馆 ···························· 30
　秦始皇兵马俑博物馆 ······················ 48
　西安半坡博物馆 ···························· 58
　茂陵博物馆 ································· 71
　昭陵博物馆 ································· 76
　乾陵博物馆 ································· 82

第四部分　古陵墓 ···························· 84
　黄帝陵 ······································· 84
　秦始皇陵 ···································· 88
　汉阳陵 ······································· 91
　茂陵 ·· 94
　霍去病墓 ···································· 98
　昭陵 ·· 101
　乾陵 ·· 105
　杨贵妃墓 ···································· 110

1

章怀太子墓	112
懿德太子墓	115
永泰公主墓	117

第五部分　西安地标性建筑　121

西安钟楼与鼓楼	121
城墙	124
大雁塔	127
大雁塔北广场	134
大唐不夜城	137
小雁塔	140

第六部分　古寺庙　145

法门寺	145
化觉巷清真寺	150
兴教寺	154
青龙寺	158
香积寺	160
草堂寺	163
楼观台	166

第七部分　宫苑园林与国家森林公园　173

华清池	173
大明宫	182
大唐芙蓉园	187
曲江池遗址公园	191
兴庆宫公园	192
西岳华山	196
太白山国家森林公园	205
楼观台国家森林公园	206
秦岭北麓风景名胜区	208

第八部分　红色旅游 ········· 210
　　八路军西安办事处纪念馆 ········· 210
　　延安革命纪念地 ········· 213

第九部分　陕西非物质文化遗产 ········· 222
　　秦腔 ········· 222
　　陕西锣鼓 ········· 224
　　唐乐舞 ········· 225
　　民间剪纸 ········· 227
　　皮影戏 ········· 228
　　户县农民画 ········· 229

第十部分　地方小吃 ········· 231
　　樊记腊汁肉夹馍 ········· 231
　　牛羊肉泡馍 ········· 233
　　老童家腊羊肉 ········· 234
　　葫芦头泡馍 ········· 235
　　荞面饸饹 ········· 236
　　甑糕 ········· 236
　　凉皮 ········· 237
　　岐山臊子面 ········· 237
　　乾县锅盔 ········· 238

第十一部分　地方土特产 ········· 239
　　富平柿饼 ········· 239
　　临潼火晶柿子 ········· 240
　　黄桂柿子饼 ········· 241
　　黄桂稠酒 ········· 242
　　水晶饼 ········· 243
　　临潼石榴 ········· 244
　　中华猕猴桃 ········· 245
　　陕南核桃 ········· 245
　　陕南青茶 ········· 246

洋县黑米	247
陕北红枣	247

第十二部分　旅游纪念品 … 249

秦兵马俑复制品	249
唐三彩复制品	250
碑刻拓片	251
布贴绣	252
凤翔彩泥偶	253

附录 … 255

关中八景	255
陕西珍禽异兽	267

CONTENTS

PART ONE　A General Introduction to Shaanxi Province … 2

PART TWO　XI'AN IN BRIEF … 7

PART THREE　MUSEUMS … 18
- The Shaanxi History Museum … 18
- The Museum of Stone-Forest Tablets … 37
- The Museum of the Terra-cotta Army … 52
- The Banpo Museum … 63
- The Maoling Museum … 73
- The Zhaoling Museum … 78
- The Qianling Museum … 82

PART FOUR　ANCIENT TOMBS … 85
- The Mausoleum of Yellow Emperor … 85
- The Mausoleum of the First Qin Emperor … 89

The Yangling Mausoleum in the Han Dynasty ……………………… 92

The Maoling Mausoleum ……………………………………………… 95

Huo Qubing's Tomb …………………………………………………… 99

The Zhaoling Mausoleum ……………………………………………… 103

The Qianling Mausoleum ……………………………………………… 107

Lady Yang's Tomb ……………………………………………………… 111

The Tomb of Crown Prince Zhang Huai …………………………… 113

The Tomb of Crown Prince Yi De …………………………………… 116

The Tomb of Princess Yong Tai ……………………………………… 118

PART FIVE LANDMARKS IN XI'AN …………………………… 122

The Bell Tower and the Drum Tower in Xi'an …………………… 122

The City Wall …………………………………………………………… 125

Dayan Pagoda …………………………………………………………… 130

The North Square of the Dayan Pagoda …………………………… 135

The Grand Tang Sleepless Plaza ……………………………………… 138

The Xiaoyan Pagoda …………………………………………………… 142

PART SIX Ancient Temples ………………………………………… 147

The Famen Temple ……………………………………………………… 147

The Mosque in Huejue Lane ………………………………………… 152

The Xingjiao Temple …………………………………………………… 156

The Qinglong Temple ………………………………………………… 159

The Xiangji Temple …………………………………………………… 161

The Caotang Temple …………………………………………………… 164

The Louguantai Temple ……………………………………………… 168

PART SEVEN GARDENS AND NATIONAL FOREST PARKS …… 176

The Huaqing Pool ……………………………………………………… 176

The Daming Palace …………………………………………………… 184

The Grand Tang Paradise ……………………………………………… 188

The Qujiang Pool Site Park …………………………………………… 191

The Xingqing Palace Park …………………………………………… 194

Mount Hua ········· 199
The National Forest Park at Mount Taibai ········· 205
The National Forest Park at the Louguantai Temple ········· 207
The Scenic Resort at Qinling Mountains ········· 208

PART EIGHT REVOLUTIONARY MEMORIALS ········· 211
The Memorial of the Eighth-Route Army—Xi'an Liaison Office ········· 211
The Revolutionary Memorial Sites in Yan'an ········· 216

PART NINE The Intangible Cultural Heritage of Shaanxi Province ········· 223
Shaanxi Opera ········· 223
The Drum and Gong Performance ········· 224
Music and Dance Performances in Tang Style ········· 226
The Paper-cuts ········· 227
The Shadow Play ········· 228
The Huxian Peasant Paintings ········· 229

PART TEN THE LOCAL SNACKS ········· 232
The Fan's Cured Pork in Pancakes ········· 232
The Shredded Pancakes in Mutton or Beef Broth ········· 233
The Tong's Cured Mutton ········· 234
Shredded Pancakes and Chitterlings in Broth ········· 235
Buckwheat Noodles ········· 236
Rice-date Paste in a Steamer ········· 236
Cold Rice-flour Noodles ········· 237
The Qishan Wheat-flour Noodles ········· 237
Pancakes Baked in Wok ········· 238

PART ELEVEN THE LOCAL PRODUCES ········· 239
Persimmon Cakes in Fuping County ········· 239
The Fire-Crystal Persimmons ········· 240
The Persimmon Pancake ········· 241
The Rice Wine ········· 242

The Grystal Cakes ········· 243

Pomegranates ········· 244

The Kiwi Fruits ········· 245

The Walnuts in Southern Shaanxi ········· 246

The Shaanxi Green Tea ········· 246

The Black Rice ········· 247

Dates/jujubee ········· 247

PART TWELVE TOURIST SOUVENIRS ········· 249

The Replica of Terra-Cotta Figures ········· 249

The Replica of Tri-color Glazed Pottery ········· 251

The Rubbings of Stone Tablets ········· 252

The Applique Articles ········· 253

The Painted Clay Figurines ········· 253

ADDEDUM ········· 260

The Eight Famous Scenic Attractions in Central Shaanxi ········· 260

Rare Birds and Animals of Shaanxi Province ········· 269

第一部分　陕西省概况

"陕西"得名始于西周。西周初年，周武王的胞弟周公和大臣召公的封邑以"陕原"为界，分陕之东、陕之西而治。"陕原"位于河南省陕县西南，后人称"陕原"以西之地为"陕西"。陕西在春秋战国时为秦国辖地，因此现在陕西省简称为"陕"或"秦"。陕西省省会是西安。

陕西位于黄河中游、西北地区东部，与山西、甘肃、四川、湖北、河南等5省、内蒙古自治区和宁夏回族自治区及直辖市重庆接壤，是中国大西北的门户，为连接中国东、中部地区和西南、西北的交通枢纽。全省面积20.58万平方公里，占全国土地面积的2.14%。

陕西地势狭长，南北高中间低，由北向南依天然地形形成陕北黄土高原、关中平原和陕南秦巴山地三个各具特点的自然区。秦岭是陕西境内最大的山脉，呈东西走向，是我国南北方的天然分界线。秦岭也是黄河、长江两大水系的分水岭。秦岭以南的秦巴山地属亚热带气候，主要出产水稻、玉米、油菜等。生漆产量居全国首位。盛产茶叶、蚕茧、核桃、板栗、中药材等土特产。关中平原是陕西的主要产粮区，也是全国的小麦、油料、棉花生产基地之一。关中平原降水充沛，土地肥沃，素有"八百里米粮川"的美称。陕北高原煤炭、天然气、石油储量丰富，天然气储量约占全国已探明储量的15%，属世界级特大气田。在国家的大力扶持下，正在形成"西煤东运""西气东输"的格局。

陕西是中华文明的发祥地之一和文物古迹荟萃之地。我们的祖先很早就在关中平原一带繁衍生息，辛勤劳作。考古发现有距今约115万年的蓝田人和6000年以前原始社会的仰韶文化遗存——半坡遗址，以及被誉为"世界第八大奇迹"的秦始皇陵兵马俑。从公元前11世纪起，先后有西周、秦、西晋、前赵、西汉、东汉、新朝、前秦、后秦、西魏、北周、隋、唐等13个王朝和国家在陕西建都，历时1200多年。陕西人文资源极为丰富，古遗址、古墓葬、古建筑、国家级文物数量在全国各省中居于首位，是名副其实的"文物大省"和"天然历史博物馆"。因此，人们常说"看中国五千年要到陕西"。

陕西的自然资源也十分丰富，有素以"奇拔俊秀"冠于天下的五岳之一——华山、连绵起伏的黄土高原、黄河第一大瀑布——壶口瀑布及以奇特的自然地貌和多样的森林景观而著称的太白山国家森林公园等。

现在，陕西的旅游资源初步形成了以西安市为中心，向东西南北辐射的四条旅游热点线路，并以点线结合形成了不同内容、不同风格的十大旅游区，具体如下。

1. 古都西安旅游区
2. 骊山风景名胜旅游区
3. 长安古寺庙旅游区
4. 华山旅游区
5. 咸阳帝王陵墓旅游区
6. 宝鸡法门寺旅游区
7. 延安三黄一圣旅游区（三黄指黄河壶口瀑布、黄帝陵、黄土风情，一圣是指延安革命胜地）
8. 榆林塞上风光旅游区
9. 黄河旅游区
10. 柞水溶洞旅游区

陕西现在是我国的重要旅游省份之一，旅游业已经成为陕西经济的支柱产业。

PART ONE   A General Introduction to Shaanxi Province

The name of the province "Shaanxi" first appeared in the Western Zhou Dynasty. In the beginning of the dynasty, Master Zhou and Master Zhao had their own manors built respectively to the east and west of Shanyuan Tableland, which lay in the southwest of Henan Province. People named the region to the west of the tableland "Shaanxi", which means "west of Shanyuan Tableland". Then during the Spring and Autumn Period, Shaanxi fell under the jurisdiction of the Kingdom of Qin, so it is now also called "Shan" or "Qin" for short. Today the capital of Shaanxi Province is Xi'an.

Lying in the Middle Reaches of the Yellow River, and in the eastern part of the northwest region of China, Shaanxi Province borders in such a geographical location neighboring Inner Mongolia, Ningxia, Gansu, Sichuan, Hubei, Henan, and Chongqing. Therefore, it serves as the gateway to the northwest of the country, and offers a link of communication between the Southwest, Northwest, Central and East China. With an area of 205,800 square kilometers, Shaanxi Province takes up 2.14% of the country's total territory.

Topographically, Shaanxi Province is long and narrow in shape, with a higher altitude in both the south and the north but lower in the middle. Therefore it canbe divided into three regions: Plateau in the south, Mountainous Region in the north, and Plain in between, each with its own distinctive features. The Qinling Mountain Range, the largest mount in the province, extending from east to west, is not only the natural dividing line between South China and North China, but also the watershed of the two greatest water systems in China—the Yellow River system and the Yangtze River system. The Qinba Mountainous Region to the south of the Qinling Mountain Range is dominated by subtropical climate, which contributes a lot to the growth of some agricultural produces such as rice, corn and rapeseeds. Its production of raw lacquer ranks first in China. Apart from this, this region is also famous for its production of tea, cocoons, walnuts, chestnuts and medicinal herbs. With an abundance of rainfall and a stretch of fertile land, the Plain has become a corn production base of Shaanxi Province as well as one of the nation's bases of wheat, oil-bearing crops and cotton. So it is well-known as the "800-Mile Grain Basin". The Plateau possesses a large quantity of coal, natural gas and petroleum deposits. Since its gas reserve amounts to 15% of the nation's verified total, this region ranks among the biggest gas fields in the world. With the help of the central government, a new pattern of "coal transported from the West to the East" and "gas transported from the West to the East" is gradually taking shape.

Shaanxi is one of the cradles of the Chinese civilization, so places of historical interest can be found almost all over the province. Archaeological findings reveal that ancestors of Chinese people have lived and labored in this region from a very early age. The greatest excavations in Shaanxi include the Lantian Man 1.15 million years ago, the 6,000-year-old Banpo Village of the primitive Yangshao Culture, and the "Eighth World Wonder" —terracotta warriors and horses of the First Emperor in the Qin Dynasty. From the 11th century BC, onwards, 13 kingdoms or feudal dynasties established their capitals in this province, with a span of 1,200 years. The major ones are the Zhou, the Qin, the Han, the Sui and the Tang. Shaanxi also boasts a variety of cultural resources. It ranks first with regard to the number of its historical sites, ancient tombs, ancient buildings and artifacts of great significance, so it is worthy of the name "a province with rich relics and ruins" and "a natural history museum". This well explains the saying that "A visit to Shaanxi is a must for the acquaintance of 5,000-year-old Chinese history".

Apart from this, the natural resources of Shaanxi Province are also abundant. Here, one can find the precipitous and splendid Mount Hua, one of the five Holy Mountains in China, the rolling Loess Plateau, the Hukou Waterfall, the biggest waterfall on the Yellow River and the National Forest Park at Taibai Mountain, which is famous for its unique geographical features and its various forest scenes.

With Xi'an in the center and four most popular tourist routes extending in different directions, the tourist attractions in Shaanxi Province are distributed in 10 tourist zones which bear different subject matters and distinctive styles:

1. Xi'an—the ancient capital;
2. Mount Li—places of historical interest and natural scenery;
3. Chang'an—ancient temples;
4. Mount Hua;
5. Xianyang—mausoleums of emperors;
6. Baoji— the Famen Temple;
7. Yan'an— "Three Yellows" (the Hukou Waterfall on the Yellow River, the Mausoleum of the Yellow Emperor, and the Yellow Loess Plateau) and "one sacred place" (a sacred revolutionary place);
8. Yulin—frontiers scenes;
9. The Yellow River;
10. The Zhashui Karst and Caves

Shaanxi Province is now one of the major tourist destinations in China and tourism has become the mainstay in its economy.

第二部分　西安市概况

西安古称长安，取长治久安之意。长安是著名的"丝绸之路"的起点。公元1369年，长安更名为西安。它是我国八大古都之冠，从公元前11世纪起，先后有周、秦、汉、隋、唐等13个王朝在此建都，历时1200多年，是我国历代建都朝代最多、历时最长的都城。它与意大利的罗马、希腊的雅典、土耳其的伊斯坦布尔并称为"世界四大古都"。

西安位于黄河流域中部，地处有"八百里米粮川"之称的关中盆地，海拔412米，年平均气温13摄氏度，年平均降水量604毫米，多集中在七、八、九三个月。西安市辖新城、碑林、莲湖、灞桥、未央、雁塔、阎良、临潼、长安、高陵、鄠邑等十一个区和蓝田、周至两个县，面积10752平方公里，2018年末，西安人口达1000.37万。

西安境内仅国家级重点文物保护单位就有56处，如新石器时代母系氏族社会的半坡遗址，被列入《世界遗产名录》的秦始皇陵，唐代的大雁塔、小雁塔，明代的城墙、钟楼与鼓楼和有近千年历史、有"石质书库"之称的西安碑林等。漫步西安，如同走进一座上下数千年的历史博物馆，因此，人们常说："不到西安，不算真正到过中国。"

西安是陕西省省会，也是西北地区政治、经济和文化的中心。它是西北各省通往西南、中原及华东的门户与交通枢纽，亚欧大陆桥陇海铁路线上最大的中心城市。现在，西安已经建立起了门类齐全、庞大的工业体系，成为西北地区最大的现代化工业城市。优越的地理位置使西安成为中西部最大的商品流通中心与物资集散地。

西安的高等教育规模仅次于北京、上海和武汉，名列全国第四。西安是全国高等院校和科研事业的重要基地。正在兴建、初具规模的长安大学城将吸引全国各地几十万学子到此学习。西安的民办教育也处于全国领先地位。改革开放以后，全国第一家民办院校就诞生在西安，现在西安拥有万人以上学生的民办院校就有五家。全市大专以上学历人口比例和成人接受教育比例均居全国第一。

西安是科技之市。拥有各类科研技术机构3000多个，科研综合实力居全国第三，拥有许多中国乃至世界第一流的科学家。全市每年有近3000项科技成果和发明专利问世。中国第一台计算机、第一架民用飞机、第一块集成电路、第一台高速摄影机、第一台清晰数字化彩色电视机，都是在西安诞生的。西安聚集了中国航天三分之一的力量，西安阎良航空基地集飞机设计、制造、试飞于一体，是"中国的西雅图"和亚洲最大的飞机城。

西安目前建立了"五区一港两基地"，即西安高新技术产业开发区、经济技术开发区、曲江新区、浐灞生态区、沣渭新区、国际港务区、航天基地、航空基地。西安是一座名副其实的知识城、科技城和人才城。

截至2005年，西安已经与世界近150个国家和地区建立了直接贸易关系。到西安投资的国家和地区已达57个。全球500强企业已经有83家在西安投资。其中有日本的日立、富士通、东芝，德国的麦德龙、汉高股份，美国的IBM、微软、惠普、可口可乐、百事可乐等。

西安是全国旅游热点城市之一，旅游业发展迅速，旅游环境日益改善。西安有星级饭店上百家，国际旅行社几十家，国内旅行社众多，旅游业已经成为西安市的支柱产业。西安市在全国诸多城市中首批入选"中国优秀旅游城市"行列。

西安交通便利，航空、铁路、公路运输四通八达。西安—咸阳国际机场拥有国际、国内航线300多条，与日本的东京、大阪、福冈、名古屋、广岛、新潟，韩国首尔实现直航。西安火车站不仅是中国的特等客运站之一，也是欧亚大陆桥在中国境内的重要站点。西安市的公路交通十分便捷，从市中心通往各旅游景点的道路有40多条，其中旅游专线9条。

近几年来，西安城市建设与人居环境明显改善。城市新增水域面积近万亩，新增绿地18万平方米，全市森林覆盖率达到48%。城市饮用水质达标率为100%。在市区看到蓝天，看到秦岭，呼吸到新鲜空气的时间越来越多了。

西安是一座底蕴深厚的城市，是一座充满生机的城市。有人曾经这样比喻：中国是一棵参天大树，到了北京看到了大树的树冠；到了西安看到了大树下的树根。在改革开放的今天，西安这座古老的城市正焕发出青春的活力，以其独有的魅力吸引着国内外宾朋。

西安永远是您的第二个家。

PART TWO   XI'AN IN BRIEF

Xi'an was once called "Chang'an". The connotation of this name is "permanent peace". Xi'an marked the starting point of the world famous "Silk Road". It obtained its present name in the year 1369. Xi'an ranks first on the list of China's eight largest ancient capitals. From 11th century BC, onwards, Xi'an has been established as the capital city by 13 kingdoms or feudal dynasties successively, including the Western Zhou, the Qin, the Han, the Sui and the Tang. It serves as an ancient capital city of the most dynasties and the longest span of time in China. And it was regarded as one of the "Four Great Ancient Capitals of the World", together with Rome, Athens, and Istanbul.

Xi'an is situated in the middle of the Yellow River valley and at the center of the Central Shaanxi Plain. 412 meters above sea level, Xi'an has a average temperature of 13℃, and an average precipitation of 604mm annually. The rain season always falls on July, August and September. Xi'an City has jurisdiction over eight districts (Xincheng, Beilin, Lianhu, Baqiao, Weiyang, Yanta, Yanliang, Lintong, Chang'an, Gaoling and Huyi), and two counties (Lantian and Zhouzhi), and it occupies an area of 10,752 square kilometers. By the end of 2018, Xi'an had a population of 10,003,700.

Within Xi'an one can find a large number of historic attractions, 56 of which have been listed among the national monuments, such as the remains of Banpo Village, a Neolithic matriarchal clan community, the Mausoleum of the First Qin Emperor, which has been enlisted as one of "The World Cultural Heritages", Dayan Pagoda and Xiaoyan Pagoda built in the Tang Dynasty, the Bell Tower, Drum Tower and City Wall built in the Ming Dynasty, and the time-honored Forest of Stone Tablets. Walking around this old city is like going through thousands of years back in history. So there is no wonder why people always say "He who has not visited Xi'an can not be said to have visited China".

As the capital of Shaanxi Province, Xi'an is the political, economic and cultural center in the northwestern region of China. It provides a link of communication between the Southwest, the Middle and East China. It counts as the biggest central city along the Eurasia Continental Bridge, which runs parallel with the artery railway line from Lianyungang to Urumqi. Up to now, a vast industrial system has been established, so Xi'an has been changed into the largest modern industrial city in the northwest of China. With its geographical advantages, Xi'an has become the biggest commercial center in the Midwest of China.

With regard to higher education, Xi'an ranks fourth in the country next to Beijing, Shanghai and Wuhan. It is also an important base of scientific research center in China. The Chang'an College Town, which is now under construction, will be a great appeal to hundreds of thousands of students from around the country. The development of private education in Xi'an is also ahead of the other regions of the country. After the implementation of the opening-up and reform policy, the first private institute of higher education was founded in Xi'an. Till today there have been 5 institutes each of which keeps an enrollment of over 10,000 students. The proportion of people who receive continuation education and vocational schooling and plus ranks No. 1 compared with other cities in China.

Xi'an is a city of science and technology with 3,000 research institutions of various kinds. It is the third on the standing list in terms of colligated scientific strength, including many first-class scientists renowned both overseas and at home. Nearly 3,000 scientific innovations and patents come out every year in Xi'an, such as the first personal computer, the first civil aero-plane, the first integrated circuit, the first high-speed video recorder, the first high-resolution digital color TV set and so on in China. One third of China's spaceflight potency is congregated here in Xi'an. The air base of Yanliang district, Xi'an City located in Yanliang, the largest aero-plane city in Asia, is often termed as "China's Seattle", where aero-plane designs, manufactures and flight-tests are carried out.

Now "five zones, one port and two bases" are established in Xi'an, namely the Hi-tech Industrial Development Zone, the Economic Development Zone, the Newly-developed Qujiang Zone, the Chanba Ecosystem Zone, Newly-developed Fengwei Zone, Xi'an Internaitonal Logistics Park and two Bases of National and Civil Hi-tech Aerospace Industry. Xi'an is a place full of information, state-of-the-art technology and gifted people.

Up to the year 2005, Xi'an has established direct trade relations with nearly 150 countries and areas throughout the world. As many as 57 countries and areas have been investing in Xi'an; 83 out of 500 best enterprises in the world have their investments in Xi'an, including Hitachi, Fujitsu, Toshiba from Japan, Metro, Henkel from Germany, IBM, Software, HP, Coca-cola, Pepsi-cola from America and so on.

Xi'an has emerged as one of the most popular tourist cities in the country. With a rapid development of tourist industry and gradual improvement of the tourist environment, Xi'an now has a total number of over 100 ranking hotels, several dozes of international tourist agencies and many more domestic tourist services. In fact, tourist industry has become the mainstay in Xi'an's economy, and the city is honored as one of the "Popular Tourist Cities in China".

Xi'an possesses a convenient transportation with a completed network of airlines, railways and highways. Xi'an-Xianyang International Airport has established more than 300 domestic and international airlines, and opened up airlines directly bound for Tokyo, Osaka, Fukuoka, Nagoya, Hiroshima and Niynaya in Japan, and Soul in Korea. Xi'an Railway Station is not only a passenger transportation station of top class, but also an important spot of the Eurasia Continental Bridge in China. As for high way service, there are more than forty roads connecting the center of Xi'an City and various tourist attractions, nine of which are specialized tourist routes.

In recent years, the urban construction has been accelerating and residential environment has been greatly improved with surface water coverage of nearly 10,000 acres, greenbelt coverage of 180,000 square meters and forest coverage of 48% in the city at large. The table-water has been up to par 100%. Now we see much more of the blue sky and the Qinling Mountains afar, and inhale more fresh air than ever before.

Xi'an is a city of design and fashion, a capital of sights and sounds, a place full of life and drive. Just as the metaphor goes, China is like a sheltering tree, you see its crown in Beijing, but you witness its root in Xi'an. Today with the opening-up policy, Xi'an, an ancient city, is gradually taking on a new look. With its unique charm, the city poses a great appeal to tourists both from home and abroad.

Xi'an is forever your second homestead.

第三部分　博物馆

陕西历史博物馆

陕西历史博物馆由中国著名建筑师张锦秋女士设计，是一座国家级现代化大型博物馆，位于大雁塔西北1公里处。这座雄伟壮观的仿唐建筑群，占地约7万平方米，建筑面积5万多平方米。它汇集了陕西文化的精华，展现了中华文明的发展历程。鉴于陕西在中国历史上的地位，国家投资1.44亿元人民币，兴建了这座博物馆，于1991年6月建成开放。

博物馆建筑古朴典雅，别具特色。它将中国古典宫殿建筑和庭院建筑紧密地结合在一起，色彩协调，体现了中华民族的传统建筑风格，同时具有地方特色和时代精神。

博物馆珍藏陕西出土的文物精品11.3万件（组），展室面积达1100平方米。博物馆设有文物保护科技中心，具有先进的化验、测试技术和文物保护修复手段。为了加强中外文化交流，建有由电脑控制的六国语言同声传译的国际学术报告厅。

当游客步入博物馆大厅，首先映入眼帘的是一座巨狮雕塑，它原来立于唐代女皇武则天母亲的陵墓顺陵前。它塑造精美，造型雄伟，堪称"东方第一狮"。中国古代石狮及狮子雕刻艺术是由阿富汗传入的，因此，这座巨狮不但是陕西历史文化的反映，也是中外文化交融的产物。

陕西历史博物馆主要展示从陕西出土的历史文物，分史前、周、秦、汉、魏晋南北朝、隋唐、宋元明清七大部分，形象系统地展现出自170万年以前至公元1840年的陕西历史。在中国历史上，曾经有13个朝代在陕西建都，历时1200多年，陕西是我国建都王朝最多、建都时间最长的地区。因此，从某种角度来说，陕西古代史是中国历史的浓缩。

史前时期（170 万年以前—公元前 21 世纪）

陕西古代史的第一部分是史前史，从距今约 170 万年至公元前 21 世纪。陕西是亚洲重要的人类起源地。1964 年在陕西省蓝田县发现的头骨化石是目前已知的亚洲北部最早的直立人，最新测试数据证实，蓝田人生存的年代距今约 115 万年。

继蓝田人之后，1978 年在陕西省大荔县发现了一个相当完整的人类头骨化石，距今约 10 万年左右，处于人类发展的一个新阶段，即"智人"阶段。大荔人头骨化石是我国迄今发现最完整的早期智人化石。大荔人使用的工具特点是器形较小。

老官台文化是陕西境内已知最早的新石器时代文化遗存，距今约 8000 年左右。老官台文化因 1955 年首先发现于华县老官台而得名。新石器时代区别于旧石器时代的重要标志有三个：一是出现磨制石器；二是发明陶器；三是开始定居并出现了原始农业。博物馆里陈列的磨制而成的石铲、石刀等，说明我们的先民已不再单纯靠采集和狩猎来获取生活资料，已进入刀耕火种的原始农业阶段。

仰韶文化距今 7000 至 5000 年。博物馆里展出的尖底瓶、石球、陶网坠、骨箭镞、鱼叉和各种彩陶器说明，处于仰韶文化时期母系氏族社会的半坡人生产力已大大提高。在物质文明发展的同时，人们开始了精神文明的追求。从半坡出土的陶埙，是我国迄今发现最早的吹奏乐器。1985 年，我国一位民乐演奏家用它成功地吹奏乐曲，引起国际音乐界的极大兴趣。

距今约 5000 年前，中国进入龙山文化时期。这类文化遗址因首先在山东省章邱县龙山镇附近发现而得名。陕西境内龙山文化村落遗址分布广泛，其中以渭河流域最为密集。从龙山文化开始，人类进入了父系氏族公社阶段。随着社会经济的发展，男子开始取代女子在社会中占支配地位。制陶工艺采用了快轮，因而制作出的陶器陶壁厚薄均匀，造型多样。另外，灰陶取代了仰韶文化时期的彩陶。

黄帝陵位于陕北黄陵县。黄帝出生在大约 4700 年前，是龙山文化时期父系氏族社会华夏部族的杰出领袖。陕西是当时华夏部族活动的中心区域，以黄帝为领袖的华夏部族经过 52 场战争统一了中原，因而黄帝被视为中华民族的祖先。每年清明节，海内外的炎黄子孙都来这里寻根问祖，祭拜黄帝。

周朝（公元前1046年—公元前256年）

周朝包括从公元前11世纪在陕西形成的周族到周方国、西周王朝三个历史发展阶段。周族是龙山文化后期由生活在泾河、渭河流域的若干部落融合而成的，以善于农耕而闻名。考古学上把这一时期的文化遗存称为先周文化。博物馆里陈列的先周文化遗存主要出土于武功县和长武县。

博物馆里陈列的卜骨是牛的肩胛骨，保存完整。占卜是周人进行活动前必然的准备过程，可以说事事必先占卜。占卜方法是先在龟甲或兽骨上凿出小孔，然后点燃用艾叶搓成的绒条贴近小孔背面熏，根据龟甲、兽骨受热后裂纹的形状、方向等判断吉凶，以确定是否应该做某件事，事后再在卜骨上记录下结果。这些占卜纪录便是中国最早的成形文字——甲骨文。

公元前16世纪，为了躲避一些游牧部族的侵扰，周族迁移到今扶风、岐山县一带建立都城，设立官制，并得到商王朝的承认，封为"方国"，周方国都城即著名的周原。馆内有近年来在周原考古出土的各种建筑遗存，如空心砖、板瓦、筒瓦、瓦当、陶水管等。

公元前11世纪，商王朝灭亡，西周王朝取而代之，建都丰、镐。丰京、镐京隔沣河相望，丰、镐就是古代西安建城的开始。

西周是中国青铜制造繁荣鼎盛的时期。陕西迄今发现的西周青铜器达数千件，仅陕西历史博物馆就收藏有2000多件。馆内展出的有礼乐器、生产和生活用具，也有实战兵器。

编钟是中国古代的一种乐器。由几个或数十个大小不等、音阶不同的钟依次编排成组，悬挂在架子上。演奏时，通常小钟是以木槌或金属锤敲击，大钟则以木棒或金属棒敲击。编钟不但能演奏古曲，还能敲奏出现代一些民歌小调和简单的乐曲。

青铜器也是奴隶社会的礼制，即权力与等级的象征。鼎是古代的一种炊具，用来烹煮肉类。铜鼎是由原始社会的陶鼎演变而来的。在夏、商、周三代，铜鼎作为礼器在奴隶主贵族举行祭祀、饮宴等活动时使用。传说夏禹曾制九鼎，代表天下九州，作为政权的象征。所以，后世把取得天下叫"定鼎"。西周等级制度森严，鼎在当时有标志身份的特殊意义。西周的青铜器造型庄重，文饰精美。有些器物上还铸有文字，叫"铭文"，多的竟达500余字，是研究西周历史的珍贵资料。

随着农业和手工业的发展，商品交换日益频繁。当时用"贝"作为贸易的媒介。贝币是中国最早的实物货币，所以许多具有价值意思的汉字都用"贝"

字作偏旁。

青铜器纹饰是研究青铜器艺术的重要内容。青铜器纹饰有两大类：动物纹和几何纹。二者均神秘怪诞，很难看懂，这是因为制作的本意是用这些青铜器祭祀天、地、鬼神和祖宗。一般人看不懂，正说明其构思的巧妙和成功。

秦朝（公元前221年—公元前207年）

秦人原是活动在今甘肃天水一带的部族。公元前770年，秦襄公被周平王封为诸侯，在今陕西凤翔县建立雍城，作为都城。博物馆展出的秦朝文物，多出土于秦雍城遗址。

秦国的社会经济以农业为主，陕西出土了大量铁农具，说明铁器当时已经取代了青铜器并且被广泛使用。

雍城的宫殿、宗庙规模相当庞大。金缸是用于连接房屋木构架的建筑构件。金缸未发现前，学者们曾设想，我国早期木构架接点的加固，从开始的捆扎构造到后来的榫卯连接之间必然采用金属加固。金缸的发现证实了这一猜想。

秦国前期的国君陵墓也集中在雍城，共发现了13座，已发掘的秦公一号大墓是我国目前发掘的最大的一座陵墓。墓深24米，面积5334平方米，有166人殉葬。考古学家推断墓主可能是秦景公。尽管这座陵墓多次被盗，仍出土各种文物3500多件。

公元前350年，秦国迁都咸阳。秦始皇继位后，在十年时间内先后吞并六国，建立了中国历史上第一个统一的多民族的中央集权制封建国家——秦。秦都咸阳的宫殿规模空前。考古工作者在咸阳发掘了一号和三号宫殿，发现了大批珍贵文物。博物馆里来陈列了阿房宫一号宫殿的复原图。

秦始皇统一六国后，采取了统一货币、统一度量衡、统一文字等一系列改革措施，对促进中国封建社会经济和文化发展做出了重大贡献。以货币为例，秦统一以前，货币的形式、大小、轻重以及计算单位都纷杂不一，给人民生活带来很多不便。秦始皇统一全国后，命令全国通行圆形方孔钱。以后历代的铜钱都依照秦朝的式样，一直到清末，沿用了2000多年。

秦始皇陵及其兵马俑坑中发现的各式兵器、兵马俑、巨型瓦当及铜车马，集中展示出秦王朝在军事、经济、科技、文化等方面所达到的前所未有的水平。

汉朝（公元前202年—公元220年）

汉朝是中国历史上一个十分重要的朝代，构成中华民族主体的汉族也在这时期正式形成。汉王朝是当时世界上最强盛的国家之一，对中国历史上以后各朝代的发展有着深远的影响，所以今天世界上许多国家把"汉"作为中国人或中国文化的代称。

汉长安城是中国历史上第一座国际性大都市。它比当时西方的古罗马城还大两倍。从长安城遗址出土的陶水管道和今天的下水管道非常相似，说明当时长安城已有了完善的下水道系统。

汉朝的瓦当非常著名。和秦代瓦当相比，汉代的瓦当面积加大，边棱加宽，瓦质发灰，文字瓦当增多。瓦当上的文字除标明用途、使用范围外，还具有很高的书法价值。

汉代非常重视农业，牛耕已经广泛使用，并从中原地区推广到西北边疆。博物馆展出的从汉墓出土的铁制农具、陶仓及仓内的粮食，表明汉代农业的高度发达。发达的农业是汉代强盛的物质基础。

在农业发展的基础上，畜牧业也十分兴旺。当时的家禽、家畜数量大，品种多。博物馆展出的陶质牛、鸡、鸭、猪圈等都是从汉墓出土的随葬品。

汉代冶铁、纺织、制陶、造纸等手工业的规模和技巧上都超过了前代。当时冶铁规模很大。从汉代画像石上拓下来的冶铁图照片，形象地显示了东汉冶铁作坊中的操作情形。

汉代陶器有画彩和色釉两种。博物馆里有彩陶鼎、方壶、熏炉和釉陶壶。汉代彩釉主要有绿色和黄色两种。

1957年在西安灞桥一座西汉墓中出土了西汉纸。以前普遍认为纸是公元105年由蔡伦发明的，博物馆里陈列的西汉纸的年代不晚于公元前118年。灞桥纸的发现将我国造纸的时间向前推进了近200年。

横贯亚洲大陆的"丝绸之路"在汉武帝时开通。汉代丝织品种类繁多。在中国丝绸西传的同时，西域各国的良马、植物、乐舞等也源源不断地传入中国，长安成为亚洲最大的国际交流中心。博物馆展出的马体格健壮，是典型的西域良马；而求良马正是汉王朝开通丝绸之路的重要目的之一。

魏晋南北朝（公元220年—公元589年）

公元220年到公元589年的魏晋南北朝是中国历史上社会大动荡、民族大融合的时期。这一时期朝代更迭频繁，有时几个政权并存，因此这一时期的文物具有浓郁的军事色彩和地域特点。

马刺不管怎么扔都是三个尖着地，一个尖竖起，是对付骑兵的有效武器。据说这是蜀国丞相诸葛亮的发明。

十六国时期，在陕西先后有前赵、前秦、后秦、大夏等少数民族建立政权。

匈奴大夏政权在今陕北靖边县建立都城统万城，统万城坚固无比，雄伟壮观，是中国保存最完整的古城堡之一。

魏晋南北朝时期，陕西是各民族内迁的中心。博物馆里形态各异、族属不同的大量陶俑，是当时民族融合的有力证据。从《少数民族姓氏演化表》上可以看出许多姓氏当初的族源。现在陕西许多汉姓，实际是由少数民族姓氏演化而来的。

镇墓兽是放置在墓中镇墓驱邪，确保死者灵魂安宁的神兽。博物馆展出的人面兽身镇墓兽与埃及的狮身人面像具有相同的艺术构思，可见半人半兽是人类共有的神话观念。

宗教艺术是魏晋南北朝时期最具特色的艺术形式之一。佛教在汉代传入中国，魏晋南北朝时得到各少数民族政权的大力提倡，饱受战乱之苦的人民也希望在求神拜佛中得到解脱，于是，佛教及佛教艺术都有了极大发展。造像是佛教艺术的主要形式之一，造像材料有金、银、铜、石、玉等。博物馆展出的多种佛像中，尤其以一尊铁佛造像最为引人注目。据说这尊铁佛是按隋文帝杨坚的形象塑的。他出生在尼姑庵，由尼姑抚养长大，虔诚信奉佛教。他将自己装扮成佛的化身是为了宣扬自己是秉承佛的旨意统治天下。在隋文帝的大力扶持及影响下，佛教在隋唐时期走向鼎盛。

隋唐（公元581年—公元907年）

隋、唐两代是中国封建社会的鼎盛时期，也是陕西历史上的黄金时代。现在的海外华人自称为"唐人"，他们居住的地方称为"唐人街"，反映了唐朝对后世产生的巨大影响。

隋王朝于公元581年建立，第二年就开始修建都城——大兴城。大兴城是由少数民族建筑大师宇文恺设计并主持修建的，唐代改名长安城。唐长安城是在隋大兴城的基础上进一步修葺完善的。唐长安城气势宏伟，整齐划一，全城分为宫城、皇城和外郭城三大部分。以朱雀大街为中轴线，11条纵向大街和14条横向大街把整个长安城划分为108个区域，称为"坊"。这种布局对以后各朝代都产生过影响，也被亚洲一些国家如日本、朝鲜规划都城时所效仿。唐长安城面积达84.1平方公里，是东罗马首都拜占庭的7倍，阿拉伯首都巴格达的6倍，明代长安城的9.3倍。

我国瓷器起源很早，考古发掘证明，我国远在3000多年前的商代就有了原始瓷。唐代，瓷器成为重要的手工业产品，并远销国外，使中国有"瓷国"之称。唐三彩是盛唐时的一种以黄、褐、绿三种颜色为主要色釉的陶瓷工艺品，主要作陪葬品用，彩色釉的使用，把我国陶瓷工业推向一个新的阶段。三彩器流行的时间较短，烧制的地区较少，因此遗物不多，非常珍贵。

汉朝之后，中国铜镜在唐朝得到快速发展。唐玄宗李隆基常在八月五日他生日的这一天赐文武百官铜镜，以后民间也竞相效仿，更刺激了铜镜的生产。博物馆展出的四神十二生肖镜、孔子问答镜、八卦镜等式样新颖，纹饰图案活泼多样，是唐代铜镜的精品。

唐代金银器制作精美，是唐王朝的标志。这些富丽精致的金钵、银盘碟、石榴罐等大多是1970年从西安南郊何家村出土的，这次出土共发现各类文物1000多件，其中金银器有270件，是唐代金银器出土最多的一次。

博物馆陈列有从扶风法门寺出土的金银器，有饮食器、容器、药具、日用器皿等。式样众多，综合运用了浇铸、焊接、切削、抛光、铆接、镀金、鎏金等工艺手段，反映了唐代金银器制作工艺的最高水平。

唐代社会安定，人民生活富足，因而有更多时间从事文化娱乐活动。狩猎、打马球、荡秋千、拔河及杂技、乐舞等活动非常盛行。

丝绸之路在唐代更加繁荣，唐代时中外交流达到鼎盛，当时有300多个国家和地区与唐朝友好交往。博物馆展出的唐代丝绸之路线路图中，骑马俑、骑驼俑多为胡人形象。图中琉璃制品是由罗马传入，牛首玛瑙杯质地精良、造型优美，具有浓郁的波斯风格。

展柜中的白瓷胡人头、黑人俑和白瓷人形尊等实物都是唐王朝与中亚、非洲友好交往的见证。

宋元明清（公元960年—1911年）

宋以后，陕西失去了京都地位，但西安仍是封建王朝控制西北、西南的军事重镇，成为西北政治、军事、经济与文化的中心。

博物馆陈列有宋代铜质象棋子，它的数量和名称与现在的象棋完全相同。

还有陕西甘泉县出土的宋代秧歌画像砖，表明现在仍盛行于陕北的秧歌舞至少起源于宋代。

北方的金人灭宋时，兵分三路，其中一路攻占陕西。博物馆里的相扑俑砖和高钞铜板都是在陕西发现的金代遗物。我国相扑运动起源于汉代，当时并不作为体育竞赛，而是军队生活中强身健体、锻炼意志的格斗训练。高钞就是纸币，是金代最重要的货币，流通范围很广。铜板是用来印刷这种纸币的。

博物馆还陈列有在陕西发现的元代文物。蒙古族建立了元朝，蒙古人以游牧为主，善于骑马，所以遗物中马的形象较多，馆内展出了元代骑兵俑。

铁板幻方是1957年在元代安西王府遗址发现的，上面铸有36个阿拉伯数字。这36个数字排列成方阵，横、竖、对角的6个数字相加之和都是111。这在古代被认为是奇妙莫测，所以称作幻方。幻方被郑重地藏在石函里，压在房基下，作为避邪、防灾的物品。铁板幻方是我国数学上应用阿拉伯数字最早的实物资料。

公元1369年，明王朝攻占陕西，改奉元路为西安府，西安就是从此时得名的。馆内有一份明代丈量土地的记录，叫鱼鳞册，明代以此作为征收赋税的依据，这是目前所见到的年代最早的鱼鳞册实物。

馆内陈列有清代光绪皇帝时的一份乡试题。科举制度由隋代开始，历代皇帝都通过科举考试选拔各级官吏。清代乡试一般三年举行一次，但遇有特殊情况也有额外开恩加试的，叫"恩科"。这份试题上有"恩科"字样，是为庆贺光绪皇帝登基大典而举行的加试。

服饰是社会物质生产和思想文化的综合反映。馆内宋代至明代的陶俑各具时代特点，为我们研究当时的社会生活及习俗提供了宝贵资料。宋代崇尚程朱理学，因此服饰拘谨保守，式样变化不多，颜色也较单调。元代男俑的服饰窄袖紧身，袍服拖到膝盖上下，腰间束带，足登长筒皮靴，具有典型的蒙古族风格。

馆中展示的庞大的仪仗队是从明朝开国皇帝朱元璋的儿子朱樉墓中出土的，可以看到当时职务不同、身份各异的人的不同服饰。中国的陶俑艺术自唐代以后逐渐衰落，过去认为到明代已基本结束，这一大俑群的发现填补了中国艺术史上的一大空白。

宋代到清代是中国瓷器的繁荣时期。除官窑外，各种风格的民窑也纷纷兴起，形成了八大窑系，其中陕西铜川耀州窑是北方民间青瓷的代表，宋代最为兴盛。馆内展品中宋瓷使人耳目一新。这里陈列的有壶、罐、茶座、茶托、盒、碗等器物，釉彩以青为主，少量为酱红色。花纹装饰以莲花纹为最多，还有缠枝牡丹、飞鹤、飞凤、鱼鸭等，工艺高超，造型古朴，使人流连忘返。

宗教是古代社会生活的重要内容。宋代以来，陕西开窟造像之风盛行。馆内陈列的各种佛教造像都是从陕北各地石窟寺中发现的。

PART THREE MUSEUMS

The Shaanxi History Museum

Designed by Ms Zhang Jinqiu, China's well-known architect, the Shaanxi History Museum is a sizable national museum with a wide range of modern facilities. It is located one kilometer away northwest of the Dayan Pagoda. The entire building complex assumes the architectural features of the Tang Dynasty. It covers an area of 70,000 square meters with a floor space of over 50,000 square meters. It houses the cultural heritage of Shaanxi Province and shows the development of the Chinese civilization. The national central government invested 144 million yuan in the establishment of the Shaanxi History Museum. It was completed and open to the public in June, 1991.

The museum shows a great deal of elegance and originality in style. It assumes the architectural features of ancient Chinese palaces and courtyard. The harmonious tone of the museum reflects the traditional architectural style of the Chinese nation, as well as the local characteristics and the spirit of different times.

It houses 113,000 historical and cultural artifacts unearthed in Shaanxi. Its exhibition halls cover an area of 1,100 square meters. The museum has established a science and technology center for the preservation of cultural artifacts. The museum has advanced laboratory, testing technology, cultural relics protection and restoration technology. To meet the needs of cultural exchange, it has also built a computer-controlled international symposium hall where simultaneous interpretation can be conducted in six different languages.

When visitors enter the museum hall, the first thing they see is a statue of giant lion. It was originally erected in front of Shunling Mausoleum, the tomb of Empress Wu Zetian's mother of the Tang Dynasty. With its exquisite craftsmanship and imposing appearance, the lion is believed to rank the first in Asia. Stone lions and their carving skills were introduced to China from Afghanistan in ancient times. So this lion represents both the local civilization and the cultural exchange between China and other countries.

The Shaanxi History Museum chiefly displays the historic artifacts excavated in this province. The exhibition may be divided into seven major sections: the Prehistoric Age, the Zhou, the Qin, the Han, Wei, Jin, Southern and northern dynasties, the Sui and the Tang, the Song, the Yuan, the Ming and the Qing. All the exhibits vividly and systematically depict the history of Shaanxi Province, ranging from 1,700,000 years ago to the year 1840. Back in history, 13 dynasties established their capitals in Shaanxi Province, with the duration of more than 1,200 years. This area was established as the national capital by more dynasties and for longer periods than any other place in China. In a way, the ancient history of Shaanxi is a microcosm of Chinese history.

The Prehistoric Age (1,700,000 years ago—21st century BC)

The first section focuses on the history of Shaanxi Province during the Prehistoric Age, which ranges from 1,700,000 years ago to the 21st century BC Shaanxi is an important source of information on the origin of the human race in Asia. The fossil of a man's skull discovered in Lantian County, Shaanxi Province was the earliest known Homo erectus in North Asia. The results of the latest research program prove that Lantian Man lived about 1,150,000 years ago.

After the discovery of the man's fossil in Lantian, the fossil of a rather complete hominid skull was found in Dali County, Shaanxi Province in 1978. The hominid lived about 100,000 years ago, and belonged to a new stage of human evolution, known as the stage of "Homo Sapiens". The fossil of the Dali Man's skull is intact, compared with those of the hominid skulls excavated in China. The stone implements ever used by the Dali Man are relatively small in size.

The earliest Neolithic cultural heritage in Shaanxi is known as Laoguantai Culture, which originated about 8,000 years ago. Laoguantai Culture is so named because it was first discovered at Laoguantai, Huaxian County in 1955. The Neolithic Culture is different from the Paleolithic Culture in three major respects: the use of polished stone implements, the invention of pottery utensils, and the emergence of settled habitation and primitive farming. The polished stone spades and knives on display indicate that our ancestors made a living not solely by gathering and hunting, but by means of slash-and-burn.

Yangshao Culture dates about 7,000 - 5,000 years back. On display here are tip-bottomed bottles, stone balls, pottery plummets, bone arrows, harpoons and painted pottery utensils, which indicate that Banpo men lived in the matriarchal clan community and had a relatively high level of productivity during Yangshao Culture period. With the progress of material civilization, they began to strive for a spiritual civilization. The pottery wind instrument unearthed from the site of Banpo Village is the earliest musical instrument in China. In 1985, a Chinese folk musician played pieces of music on it, and aroused the wide attention of the international musical circles.

China went into the Longshan Culture period about 5,000 years ago. Longshan Culture was named after Longshan Township, Zhangqiu County, Shandong Province, where it was first discovered. The village ruins typical of Longshan Culture are scattered extensively in Shaanxi Province and chiefly centered in the area of the Weihe River. Starting from the period of the Longshan Culture, mankind moved into the age of patriarchal clan community. With social and economic development, men began to play a dominant role in social activities instead of women. With the invention of the fast potter's wheel, the earthenware ever made was uniform in thickness and varied in style. In addition, painted pottery wares gave way to their grey pottery counterparts of Yangshao Culture.

The Yellow Emperor's Mausoleum is located in Huangling County in Northern Shaanxi. The Yellow Emperor was born about 4,700 years ago. He was a legendary leader of Huaxia tribesmen in the patriarchal clan community society during the Longshan Culture period. Shaanxi was then the central area of their activities. Under his leadership, the Huaxia tribesmen unified the Huanghe River Reaches after fighting 52 battles. Therefore, the Yellow Emperor was worshipped as the forefather of the Chinese nation. Every year on the Qingming Festival, the people of Chinese origin come from different parts of the world to search for their roots and offer sacrifices to the Yellow Emperor.

The Zhou Dynasty (1046 BC—256 BC)

The Zhou experienced three different stages of historical development: the Zhou Clan, the Zhoufang State and the Western Zhou Dynasty. The Zhou Clan was formed by several small tribes that resided along the banks of the Jinghe and the Weihe rivers during the later period of Longshan Culture. The clan was adept at farming. Archaeologists call the cultural ruins of this period the Early Zhou Culture. The cultural relics in this museum are from the Early Zhou period. They were mostly unearthed in Wugong and Changwu counties.

There is a oracle bone in the museum which is a well-preserved scapula of an ox. Divination had to be practiced in preparation for all major activities at that time. The way to practice divination was to chisel holes into a tortoise-shell or animal bone, twisted mugwort into a thread, and applied the burning thread to the holes. The tortoise-shell or animal bone would crack under heat. The diviner would interpret the cracks in the bones according to their shapes and directions, and decide whether it was lucky or ominous to do certain things. A record of the divination results was then carved onto the tortoise-shell or animal bone, which formed China's earliest written script, known as "oracle bone inscriptions".

To avoid the nomadic tribe's invasion and harassment in the 16th century BC, the Zhou Clan settled down in the present-day Fufeng and Qishan counties, and established a capital, an official ranking system and a governing body. The Zhou Clan was acknowledged by the Shang Dynasty and appointed as the "Fang State". The capital of the Fang State was Zhouyuan. There are many building ruins in the museum, such as hollow bricks, plain tiles, roofing tiles, tile-ends and pottery sewer pipes.

In the 11th century BC, the Shang Dynasty perished and the Western Zhou Dynasty came into existence instead. It established its twin capital cities in Feng and Hao, which were separated by the Feng River. This marked the emergence of the ancient city of Xi'an.

The development of China's bronze culture reached its peak during the Western Zhou. Thousands of bronze vessels have been found in Shaanxi, and out of 2,000 are housed now in the Shaanxi History Museum. There are many cultural relics in the museum such as ritual and musical instruments, daily utensils, farming implements and weapons as well.

Chime bell is an ancient Chinese musical instrument—a set of bells of different sizes and scales. The bells are arranged in order and tied to the supporter. When it comes to performance, the musician taps the small bells with wooden or metal bars. Both classical and modern folk music can be played with the chime bells.

The bronze vessels represented the system of rites in the slavery society. They were the symbol of power and social strata. Tripod is a cooking utensil of ancient times. It was used for stewing meat. Bronze tripods were derived from the pottery ones in the primitive society. During the Xia, Shang and Zhou dynasties, bronze tripods were ritual wares only possessed by slave owners and aristocrats, and they were mainly used on sacrificial occasions or at banquets. Legend goes that King Yu of the Xia Dynasty once had nine tripods made, which symbolized his control over the nine kingdoms. The administrative power was then referred to as a "seizure of the tripod". The caste system was very strict in Western Zhou Dynasty, and the tripod was a symbol of privileged identity. Bronze utensils made in this period were elaborately shaped, decorated with various patterns, and inscribed with "epigraphs". Some of the epigraphs even had 500 characters. They are valuable data for the study of the history of the Western Zhou Dynasty.

With the development of agriculture and handicraft, exchange of goods was on the increase. This sort of "shell" was used as a medium in trade. "Shell money" was the earliest form of currency in kind. The Chinese characters that symbolize valuable things have the character "贝" (shell) as their radicals.

The bronze vessels with decorative designs and patterns provide an important source of information for the study of the art of bronze wares. The decorations can be classified into two major categories: animal designs and geometric patterns. Both of them generally look mysterious and weird, and difficult to understand. This is because the vessel makers intended to use these vessels to offer sacrifices to the Heaven, the Earth, God and their ancestors. Making them difficult for the ordinary people to understand proves the success of its artistic conception.

The Qin Dynasty (221 BC—207 BC)

The Qin people were an ancient tribal clan that used to live in Tianshui, Gansu Province. In 770 BC, King Ping of the Zhou Dynasty bestowed a favor on Qin Xianggong and appointed him an imperial duke. Later, Qin Xianggong established Yongcheng as his own capital in the present-day Fengxiang County, Shaanxi Province. The artifacts on display were excavated from the site of Yongcheng.

Farming was an important factor in the economy of the Qin Kingdom. The iron implements unearthed from the site of the kingdom indicate that iron wares were widely used instead of the bronze wares.

The palaces and ancestral temples in Yongcheng were sizable and spacious. "Jingang" was used as bronze woodwork joints in architecture. Before the discovery of "jingang", scholars believed that the evolution of China's early woodwork joints must have included the use of metal devices in its progress from the tying-up of woodwork members to the use of mortice and tenon joints. Their belief was justified by the discovery of the bronze woodwork joints.

The imperial mausoleums of the early Qin Dynasty were chie fly centered in Yongcheng. Up till now, 13 of these tombs have been discovered. No. 1 Tomb for the Duke of the Qin is the largest tomb excavated so far in China. It is 24 meters deep, and 5,334 square meters in size. Altogether, 166 people were buried alive with the dead. Archaeologists believe that the dead monarch may be Duke Qin Jinggong. Unfortunately, the tomb has suffered many serious robberies. But in spite of this fact, more than 3,500 cultural artifacts have been unearthed.

In 350 BC, the Qin kingdom relocated its capital Xianyang. After the First Qin Emperor rose to power, he annexed the six kingdoms in ten years' time, and founded the first multi-national, autocratic and centralized feudal empire in Chinese history. Hence, the Qin Dynasty came into existence. Xianyang, the capital of the Qin Empire, witnessed the construction of many magnificent palaces. The archaeologists have unearthed No. 1 and No. 3 palaces in Xianyang and discovered large quantities of valuable cultural artifacts. The museum displays a picture of the restored Palace No. 1 in E'pang Palace.

As a result of the national unification, the First Qin Emperor enforced a single currency, standardized units of weight and measure, and popularized a unitary written script, thereby making valuable contribution to the development of the feudal economy and culture in China. Take currency for example. Before the standardization, currencies of various forms, sizes, face values and weight had been in circulation, and the calculation had been quite difficult. All this caused a serious inconvenience to the people. Once in power, the First Qin Emperor issued a round coin pierced with a square hole in the centre as the national currency. The later dynasties and the imperial rulers followed the pattern of Qin's coins for the next 2,000 years until the Qing Dynasty.

The various weapons, terracotta warriors and horses, tile ends, and bronze chariots and horses discovered around the First Qin Emperor's Mausoleum show the unprecedented prosperity and progress of the Qin Dynasty in its military affairs, economy, science and technology and culture.

The Han Dynasty (202 BC—220 AD)

The Han Dynasty constitutes a very important episode in Chinese history. The

Han nationality took shape during this historical period. The Han was one of the most powerful empires in the world. It exerted a far-reaching influence on the development of the succeeding dynasties in Chinese history. That is why "Han" is often referred to as a synonym for the Chinese people and civilization in the world today.

The Han city of Chang'an (present-day Xi'an) was the first international metropolis in Chinese history. Chang'an was twice the size of Rome in the West. The ceramic drainage pipes are very close in shape to those of the present day. This indicates that there was already an advanced sewage system in Chang'an.

The eve tiles of the Han Dynasty are very famous. Compared with the Qin tiles, the Han tiles are larger and greyer with wider edges, and there was an increase in the number of tiles that were inscribed with characters. The characters on the tiles tell of their uses, and are also of great calligraphic value.

The Han Dynasty attached great importance to the development of agriculture. Oxen were widely employed across the Central Shaanxi Plain, and gradually introduced into the northwestern frontiers. The iron farm tools and pottery utensils with grain in them were excavated from the Han tombs. They indicate a high level of agricultural development in the Han Dynasty.

Animal husbandry was well developed too. Various domestic animals and fowls were bred in great numbers. The museum displays pottery oxen, chicks, ducks and pigsties which are all burial objects excavated from Han tombs.

The Han Dynasty outstripped the previous dynasties both in scale and skill in the fields of metallurgy, textile, pottery-manufacture and paper-making. Metallurgy was conducted on a large scale. This stone-relief rubbing vividly depicts the operations in an iron smelting workshop in the Eastern Han Dynasty.

The Han pottery includes two principal types: painted and glazed. The museum displays painted pottery tripods, square pots, incense burners and glazed pot. Green and yellow colors were commonly used at that time.

This sort of paper made in the Western Han Dynasty was discovered in a Western Han tomb at Baqiao, Xi'an, in 1957. It was previously believed that paper was invented by Cai Lun in 105 AD But this sort of paper may date back to 118 BC. Therefore, the discovery of the Baqiao paper indicates that paper-making started in China at least 200 years earlier than the generally known time.

During the reign of Emperor Wu Di, the Silk Road, which ran across the Asian continent, was formally opened. It enabled Chinese silk to be exported to various countries in the Western Regions. In return, horses of fine breeds, plants, music and dance were introduced into China. At that time, Chang'an became the largest centre of international exchange in Asia.

The museum displays a plump and sturdy horse which is a typically fine breed brought back to the interior of China through the Silk Road. Seeking horses of fine breeds was one of the important motives for the Han Dynasty to open the Silk Road.

The Wei, Jin, Southern and Northern dynasties (220 AD—589 AD)

China experienced a long period of social upheavals and national amalgamation from 220 AD to 581 AD. It was also a period of frequent dynastic changes when several regimes co-existed. The historical artifacts of these turbulent years obviously assume military and regional features.

No matter how you throw the cal-traps, they will fall to the ground on three of their studs, with a fourth one pointing upward. The weapon was effectively used to attack cavalrymen on the battlefield. It is said that the cal-trap was invented by Zhuge Liang, the Prime Minister of the Shu Kingdom.

During the Sixteen States period, a number of minority nationality regimes, such as the Former Zhao, the Former Qin, the Latter Qin, and the Daxia, established and exercised authority in Shaanxi Province. This is the domain where battles for power frequently took place.

The museum displays a picture of Tongwan City, the capital of the Daxia regime, established in Jingbian County in Northern Shaanxi. The city is as strong and firm as stone, and looks as splendid as ever. It is one of the best-preserved castle cities in China.

Shaanxi was a center of national amalgamation from 220 AD to 581 AD, as is evidenced by these pottery figures. From the "Evolution Chart of Minority Nationality Family Names" which displays in the museum, we can find many of the family names were derived. In fact, many of the Han family names in Shaanxi derived their origin from those of the minority nationalities.

Tomb-guarding animals were divine beasts of prey placed inside tombs to fend off evil spirits and ensure the spiritual tranquility of the dead. There are two tomb guardians with the face of a man and the body of the beast. Their artistic style is similar to that of the Sphinx in Egypt. This means that such semi-human and semi-beast objects reflect a common mythological conception shared by both the East and the West.

Religion-related art works were one of the most characteristic forms of art in the dynasties of the The Wei, Jin, Southern and Northern. Buddhism was introduced to China during the Han Dynasty, and was popularized by several ethnic minority regimes. Those who suffered greatly from the unceasing wars and upheavals wished to seek relief and comfort by worshipping gods and Buddha. Therefore, both Buddhism and Buddhist statues was a major form of Buddhist art which underwent tremendous changes. The making of Buddhist statues was a major form of Buddhist art. The statues were made of a number of materials such as gold, silver, bronze and jade. Among many of the Buddhist statues on display, the one made of iron is the most eye-catching. The statue of Buddha is said to have been modeled on Yang Jian, Emperor Wen Di of the Sui Dynasty. Yang Jian was born in a Buddhist nunnery, and was brought up by the nuns. He showed fanatic enthusiasm for Buddhism. He posed as the embodiment of the Buddha in order to tell his people that he was ruling the whole country just by the order of Buddha. Under his influence, Buddhism reached its zenith in the Sui and Tang dynasties.

The Sui and Tang dynasties (581 AD—907 AD)

The Sui and Tang dynasties were China's feudal society at the height of their power and splendor. They also marked a golden era in the history of Shaanxi. Chinese residing overseas today still regard themselves as the "descendents of the Tang" and the place where they live as the "streets of the Tang" (China Town). This, to some extent, reflects the enormous impact the Tang Dynasty has had on its descendants.

The Sui Dynasty was founded in 581 AD It began to construct its capital city, the Daxing City, in the following year. Yu Wenkai, the master architect of minority nationality, designed and oversaw the construction of the city. In the Tang Dynasty, its name was changed to Chang'an. The new city was built on the basis of Sui's Daxing City with further improvement and expansion. As a magnificent and well-planned city, Chang'an was divided into three areas: the palace city, the imperial city and the outer city. With the Scarlet Bird Street as the axis, the city was crisscrossed with 11 vertical and 14 horizontal streets, dividing Chang'an into 108 rectangular compounds known as Fang. This layout of Chang'an has had far-reaching influence on later, and has served as a model for capital cities in some other Asian countries such as Japan and Korea. The Tang's Chang'an City covered an area of 84.1 square kilometers, seven times the size of Byzantine, capital of the Eastern Roman Empire; six times the size of the Arabian capital Baghdad; and over nine times the size of the Ming city of the same name.

Chinese porcelain originated far back to ancient times. Archaeological studies have proven that China began her primitive porcelain manufacturing in the Shang Dynasty 3,000 years ago. In the Tang Dynasty, china ware was exported far away to foreign countries as major handicraft product. It is well-known that China was famed as a "nation of china." Here on display are Tang tri-colored glazed potteries, all being burial objects. In the prime of the period, the Tang Dynasty produced glazed pottery of brown, yellow and green colors. Colord glaze brought Chinese pottery craft into a new stage. However, the craft prevailed only in a rather short period in limited areas. Therefore, the small number of tri-colored glazed pottery is of priceless value today.

The Tang Dynasty marked another period of rapid development of Chinese bronze mirrors after the Han Dynasty. Li Longji, Emperor Xuan Zong of the Tang Dynasty offered bestowed bronze mirrors on his civil and military officials on the fifth day of the eighth lunar month, his birthday. The practice was soon imitated by the public, which further stimulated the production of bronze mirrors. The bronze mirrors, engraved with the designs of the four deities and of the 12 zodiac animals and those engraved with Confucius' questions and answers or with a design of the Eight Diagrams, are lovely and stylistically various. They are the most exquisite bronze mirrors in the Tang Dynasty.

Gold and silver ware was beautifully made and served as a symbol for the Tang Dynasty. These exquisite and gorgeous gold bowls, silver plates and pomegranate-shaped vessels were mostly discovered at Hejia Village in the southern suburb of Xi'an in 1970. More than 1,000 cultural relics of various kinds were unearthed. These relics included 270 gold and silver vessels, representing the largest excavation of Tang gold and silver ware.

The museum displays gold and silver ware which was excavated at the Famen Temple in Fufeng County. It included food and drinking vessels, containers, medical tools and daily utensils. They were of various shapes and were made with a combined technique of casting, welding, cutting, polishing, riveting, gilding, and gold-plating, etc. They depict a very high technological standard of gold and silver ware in the Tang Dynasty.

During the Tang Dynasty, people led a relatively plentiful and stable life and abided by social rules and orders. Consequently, they enjoyed more leisure and entertainment. Hunting, polo, swing, tug-of-war, acrobatics, music and dance became very popular.

The Silk Road enabled the Tang Dynasty to be even more prosperous. The Sino-overseas exchanges reached their peak during this period. Over 300 nations and regions had friendly relations with the Tang Dynasty. The museum displays a picture of the route of the Silk Road in the Tang Dynasty. These pottery figurines of horse and camel riders in the picture look like the Northern nomads. The vessel made of precious stones was brought into China from Rome. The ox-headed agate cup is made of high quality material and beautifully shaped, featuring strong Persian influence.

In the display case are the white porcelain statues of a nomad's head, the pottery of black man and white porcelain wine container of a human figurine, which strongly prove the friendly exchanges between the Tang Dynasty and Central Asia, and Africa.

The Song, Yuan, Ming and Qing dynasties (960 AD—1912 AD)

Since the Song Dynasty, Shaanxi lost its position as the national capital, but it remained a place of strategic importance for the feudal dynasties to maintain control of the Northwest and Southwest of the country. On the other hand, it was still the military, political, economic, and cultural centre in the Northwest.

The museum displays a set of bronze chess pieces of the Song Dynasty. They are exactly the same to their contemporary counterparts in both the number and name.

There is also a Song brick unearthed in Ganquan County, Shaanxi. It is engraved with a design of the yangge (folk dance). This verifies that the yangge dance, popular in Northern Shaanxi today must have originated at least from the Song Dynasty.

When the army of the Kingdom of Jin in the north swept southwards with the purpose of overthrowing the Song Dynasty, it advanced along three routes, one of which led to the capture of Shaanxi. These pottery figurines of Sumo wrestlers, the mouldboard to print jiao Tzu, a kind of money, are all Jin relics unearthed in Shaanxi. Chinese Sumo began in Han Dynasty. It was not regarded as a competitive sport at the time, but a combat exercise in the military, aimed at body building and willpower tempering. Jiao Tzu is actually a kind of paper currency, the most important currency in the Jin Dynasty that was circulated in wide area. The mould-board on display here was used to print this kind of currency.

The museum displays the Yuan cultural artifacts unearthed in Shaanxi. The Mongolians founded the Yuan Cultural artifacts. Displayed in the case are the pottery figurines of cavalrymen of the Yuan Dynasty.

The magic iron plate was unearthed from the ruins of the Anxi Palace of the Yuan Dynasty. This magic plate is engraved with 36 Arabic numbers. The magic about this plate is that the sum of any of the six horizontally, vertically and diagonally aligned numerals equals 111. This was regarded as mysterious in ancient times, and the plate was thus called "a magic plate". It was placed under the foundations of the palace to fend off evil spirits and disasters. This magic plate is the earliest material proof of the use of Arabic numerals in Chinese mathematics.

The Ming Dynasty took over Shaanxi in 1369 AD and changed Fengyuan Road to Xi'an prefectural government. This was the first time that the City of Xi'an used its present name. The museum displays a record of land measurements in the Ming Dynasty, called "fish-scale book" The Ming government collected taxes according to the book. It is the earliest fish-scale book that has been discovered thus far.

There is a provincial level examination paper during the reign of Emperor Guang Xu of the Qing Dynasty. The imperial examination system, which began in the Sui Dynasty, sought to recruit civil officials through examinations, which were normally held once every three years. There was always an exception. If such case arose, extra examination would be given. This is called "Bestowed Exam". This examination paper is from an additional examination in order to congratulate Emperor Guang Xu on his ascending the throne.

Clothing is a comprehensive indicator of the level of material production and ideological and cultural development during a particular social period. The museum displays a set of porcelain figurines from the Song and Ming dynasties which feature characteristics of their own times. They provide us with valuable data for the study of social life and social customs during that time. The Song rulers advocated Cheng Zhu's neo-Confucianism. As a result of its influence, clothing tended to be reserved and conservative in style, colors being simple and plain. In the Yuan Dynasty, the males wore narrow-sleeved and tight fitting clothes, the robes reaching to their knees. With belts at their waists, and boots on their feet, these clothes bear typical Mongolian style.

The massive guard of honor was unearthed from the tomb of Zhu Shuang, Zhu Yuanzhang's son. Zhu Yuanzhang was the founder and the first emperor of the Ming

Dynasty. Members of the guard wore different uniforms which indicate their different ranks and different responsibilities. The art of Chinese pottery figurines decreased after the Tang Dynasty. It was thought to have, more or less, come to an end by the Ming Dynasty. The discovery of this large number of pottery figurines filled a blank in the history of Chinese art.

The Song and Yuan dynasties saw rapid development of Chinese porcelain. Apart from the government-run porcelain kilns, privately-run kilns began to emerge to form a system of eight different porcelain kilns, among which the Yaozhou kilns at Tongchuan, Shaanxi Province are representative of the celadon vessels in the northern part of China. Chinese porcelain became most prosperous in the Song Dynasty. Among the exhibits the Song porcelain vessels offer visitors a new and fresh impression. On display are pots, jars, tea sets, boxes, bowls etc. Most of the glaze colors are blue, some dark reddish brown. The dominant designs and patterns take the shape of lotus flowers. Besides, peonies twining branches, flying cranes, flying phoenixes, fish and ducks, etc. are also employed. Their high technology and simple and unsophisticated modelings are so attractive and enchanting.

Religion was an important part in the life of the ancient society. From the Song Dynasty onward, the carving of Buddhist statues and construction of grottoes in Northern Shaanxi became popular. The Buddhist statues on display are unearthed from the scattered grottoes in Northern Shaanxi.

西安碑林博物馆

西安碑林博物馆是一座庭院式建筑，位于西安市三学街孔庙旧址。在唐代（公元618年—公元907年）这里是太庙所在地，宋代成为孔庙，1950年扩建为博物馆。

牌楼
牌楼是由古代的牌坊演变而来的一座装饰性建筑。中国古代很多地方都修有牌坊。在封建社会里，为某个人立牌坊被看作是一种很高的荣誉。

石拴马桩

牌楼后有泮池,一座石桥横跨池面。第一道门里中间的小径两旁共陈列了28个明清时代的石拴马桩,相向而立。石拴马桩是我国古代用于拴系、震慑牲畜的一种石刻,在陕西主要分布在渭北地区,其桩顶饰有动物和人物造型,具有浓郁的渭北民间特色。除了拴系、震慑牲畜这一目的外,拴马桩还具有镇邪、吉祥和装饰意义。新中国成立前,渭北地区富豪或官宦之家的院门外两侧,大都栽立有成排的拴马桩,供迎来送往时拴系客人代步的坐骑。

景云钟

第二道门里东面的亭子内陈列着唐代的景云钟。这口钟铸造于唐景云二年(公元711年),故名景云钟。当时挂在道教寺院景龙观的钟楼上(现址在今西安西大街)。据传每天撞击报时时,全城都能听到清亮悦耳犹如凤凰鸣叫的钟声。景云钟重约6吨,用5000多公斤铜,25块铜模铸造而成。钟上有18行铭文,共计292字,是唐睿宗李旦自作自写的,其内容是描述道教的神秘玄妙和对钟的赞誉。钟身上有32枚钟乳,是为了装饰和调节音韵的。在1964年的世界名钟展览中,景云钟被选为世界名钟。每年除夕,中央人民广播电台播放的辞旧迎新的"新年钟声"就是景云钟的录音。现在位于西安市北大街报话大楼的巨钟每小时都以悦耳动听的钟声向全市报时,这钟声也是景云钟的录音。

石马

西面的亭子内置放着刻于公元424年大夏时的一匹石马。它形象生动逼真,表现浑圆有力,马的两条后腿下还雕刻着一个被征服者的形象。大夏是匈奴贵族所建立的国家,属于东晋时期的十六国之一,这十六国大部分是各少数民族上层分子所建立的割据政权。由于当时战争连绵不断,各国统治的时间也较短,留下的文物极少,因此这匹战马显得尤为珍贵。

西安碑林博物馆占地面积3万多平方米,陈列内容分为"西安碑林"和"石刻艺术"两大部分,此外,馆内还经常举办各种专题文物展览。

碑林

西安碑林创建于1087年,是收藏我国古代碑石时间最早、数目最大的一座艺术宝库,保存有从汉到清的各代碑石、墓志共3000多块。这里碑石如林,故名碑林。

西安碑林内容丰富，它既是我国古代书法艺术的宝库，又汇集了古代文献典籍和石刻图案；记述了我国文化发展的部分成就；反映了中外文化交流的史实，因而驰名中外。到西安旅游，如不参观碑林，将会遗憾终生。

西安碑林是在保存唐代石经的基础上发展起来的。唐代人所称的石经，包括公元745年唐玄宗李隆基书写的《石台孝经》和公元837年刻成的《开成石经》。这些石经原来都立在唐长安城务本坊的国子监太学内（今西安城南文艺路一带）。唐末，朱温强迫唐昭宗迁都洛阳，对长安城进行了毁灭性的破坏，使宏伟的长安城变成一片废墟。驻长安的佑国军节度使韩建为了便于防守，将长安城进行了缩建，致使石经被弃于郊野。后来韩建将太学和《石台孝经》首先移进城内的文宣王庙内（今西安西大街社会路一带）。

公元909年，节度使刘鄩守长安时，又将弃于城外的《开成石经》也迁至文宣王庙内，文宣庙便成了西安最早的集中唐代碑石的地方。但文宣庙内地势低洼，环境不佳，对保护石经不利，于是全部石经及唐代其他重要碑石在1087年被移置到现在的碑林所在地，这就是最早的"西安碑林"。当时由于光线不好，又经常有人用墨拓印碑帖，致使碑石变得乌黑，人们就称这里为"墨洞"或"碑洞"。

公元1555年关中发生大地震，碑林遭到严重破坏。《开成石经》共114面，有40面被震倒折断。1588年，当时陕西学官叶时荣等人将《开成石经》上所有残缺的文字，都照石经原字样补刻在97块小石碑上，放置在石经的旁边，使《开成石经》成为一部完整的石刻书籍保存下来。公元1664年，又增刻了《孟子》。

"碑林"这个名字是清代初年才确定的。碑林现收藏从汉到清各代碑石3000余件，分别置于7个陈列室、6个墓志廊和1个碑亭展出。

1961年3月，国务院公布碑林为全国重点文物保护单位。

碑林第一陈列室前是专为陈列《石台孝经》修盖的碑亭。《石台孝经》是碑林最大的石碑，刻于公元745年，是唐玄宗李隆基亲自书写的。《孝经》是孔子的学生曾参将孔子所讲授的孝道加以整理、编纂而形成的一部儒家经典。前面一部分是李隆基为《孝经》作的序。玄宗为《孝经》写序的目的是表示自己要以"孝"治理天下。序文后面是《孝经》原文。石碑上的小字是玄宗为《孝经》作的注释。底座由3层石台组成，上面刻有生动的线刻画，有蔓草、狮子花等，是唐中期比较有代表性的雕刻艺术品。石碑顶端是浮雕卷云瑞兽。此碑由4块石头组成，底下有石台，所以称为"石台孝经"。

第一陈列室

碑林第一陈列室主要陈列《开成石经》碑，内容包括《周易》《尚书》《诗经》《周礼》《仪礼》《礼记》《春秋左氏传》《春秋公羊传》《春秋谷梁传》《论语》《孝经》《尔雅》等12部经书，计650 252字，用石114方，两面刻文。清代补刻的《孟子》17面3万余字也陈列于此，合称《十三经》。这些儒家经书是封建社会知识分子必读之书。因为当时印刷术不很发达，为了避免文人学士们在传抄经书时出现错误，并能永久保存，就把这些经书刻在石碑上，作为范本，立于长安城国子监内，供人们校对。我国自东汉开始，曾先后7次刻经。《开成石经》碑是目前仅存的一套完整的石刻经书。

第二陈列室

碑林第二陈列室主要陈列唐代著名书法家的碑石，这些碑石历来都是人们学习书法的范本。其中有唐初著名书法家欧阳询写的《皇甫诞碑》；有"小欧阳"之称的欧阳询之子欧阳通写的《道因法师碑》；颜真卿写的《多宝塔碑》和《颜氏家庙碑》；晚唐柳公权写的《玄秘塔碑》；长安弘福寺和尚怀仁集王羲之之字刻成、世称"千金贴"的《大唐三藏圣教序碑》以及中外驰名的《大秦景教流行中国碑》；等等。

《大秦景教流行中国碑》是研究唐代中外文化交流的宝贵资料。"大秦"是中国古代对罗马帝国的称呼。"景教"是基督教的聂斯脱利派传入中国后的名称。景教在公元635年传到长安。此碑刻于公元781年。碑文记述了景教的教义和教旨，在我国的传播及景教徒在唐代近150年中的活动情况。还有用古叙利亚文刻的记事和僧徒多人的名字。

此碑原立于唐大秦寺，公元1623年出土后被放置于西安西郊金胜寺。后来此碑拓片传到国外，并译成了拉丁文稿，遂引起许多国家注意。一些外国人认为，欧洲多基督教徒，像这样记载景教的碑石应当运到欧洲供人瞻仰。1907年，英国派丹麦人荷尔漠来西安，企图以3000两白银收买此碑。陕西巡抚得知此事，即将此碑移存碑林。荷尔漠只好复制了一通假碑运往伦敦。

第三陈列室

碑林第三陈列室保存有汉至宋代（公元前206年—公元1279年）各种书体的珍贵碑石，包括篆书、隶书、楷书、行书、草书等五种书体。通过这些碑石，可以了解我国书法及文字的演变过程。

陈列室里有一块宋代梦英和尚用篆书书写的碑。他把许慎《说文解字》中的540个部首和偏旁分别用篆书书写，并用楷书注释，为我国研究篆书及汉字演变提供了资料。

汉代的《汉曹全碑》是用隶书刻写的。字体刚劲优美、结构匀称，在汉隶中独树一帜，是我国著名的汉代书法名碑之一。隶书出现于秦末，和篆书相比，隶书简单易写。由篆到隶，是我国文字在形体上一次大的变革。隶书在汉代成为通行的书体。

陈列室中还有用楷书刻写的碑。楷书出现于三国时期（公元220年—公元280年）。到了隋唐时期，楷书更加成熟，成为普遍通行的书体。历代统治者都规定楷书为书写官府文书和科举文章的正式书体。

草书《千字文》碑是用1000个不重复的汉字编写的我国古代儿童的启蒙识字课本。《千字文》碑是唐代著名草书书法家怀素和尚写的。怀素的草书豪放有力，对后代有很大影响。

第四陈列室

第四陈列室保存有宋至清代书法名家的诗文真迹以及有珍贵史料价值的明清时期的碑石，还有一部分是宋至清代的各种线刻画。

陈列室中有两幅画分别是《达摩东渡图》和《达摩面壁图》。达摩是南天竺（印度）王子。他于公元520年来到中国，因和南朝梁武帝探讨佛理，语不投机，于是东渡入北魏，住在河南少林寺，终日面壁修行达9年之久。《达摩东渡图》刻画的是传说中达摩肩挑芒鞋站在一只芦苇上东渡时的形象；而《达摩面壁图》刻画的是达摩坐在蒲团上面壁的形象。画面以粗线条写意，颇为传神。刻工刀法也简洁有力，是两幅生动的人物画。

此外，还有一幅《集字魁星点斗图》。中国封建社会的科举制度以五经取士，每经首选一人称为"魁"，所以当时学府多筑有魁星楼或魁星阁，奉祀魁星点斗像。这幅图以儒家修养的标准"正心修身，克己复礼"八个字组成魁星形象，图中魁星一脚翘起托一个"斗"字，一脚立在"鳌"字上，取"魁星点斗，独占鳌头"的意思。这副线刻画形象生动，拼凑巧妙。

第五陈列室

第五陈列室主要陈列宋、元、明、清各代记述修庙、记功、修渠、筑城等史实的碑石，是研究当时社会和地方史的参考资料。

此外，还陈列有清代马德昭的"虎""寿""福"等一笔而就的大型题字碑石，题字运笔有力，气势磅礴，给参观者以美的享受。

第六陈列室

第六陈列室陈列的碑石都是元、明、清各代的诗文碑石。其中元代赵孟頫的《游天冠山诗碑》、明代董其昌的《秣陵旅舍送会稽章生碑》、清代康熙皇帝临米芾的《赐吴赫书碑》、林则徐的《游华山诗碑》等都很珍贵。

第七陈列室

第七陈列室建于1982年，专门保存宋《淳化秘阁帖》碑。《淳化秘阁帖》共10卷，前5卷是历代封建帝王和名臣及书法名家的楷、草、篆及古文各种书体，后5卷是王羲之和王献之的草书作品，是宋代以前中国书法家作品的汇集。《淳化秘阁帖》原本于宋淳化三年（公元992年）被太宗令翰林侍书王著摹刻在枣木板上，存在宫里。宋太宗令人将书帖拓印成墨本分赐给大臣。由于是在皇宫里刻的，所以叫"秘阁帖"；因刻于淳化年间，又称《淳化秘阁帖》。版刻成后不久即毁，由宋到清，公、私复刻本很多。西安碑林所藏《淳化秘阁帖》是1646年摹刻的，共145石，两面刻字。

墓志廊

在碑林徊转的6条长廊上陈列着由魏至清的各代墓志。魏晋时严禁厚葬和立碑，但死者的亲属为了纪念死者，便将褒扬死者的言辞刻在石上，悄悄放入墓内。这种石刻后来就演变为墓志，墓志上的铭文称为墓志铭。

石刻艺术

石刻艺术室建于1963年。它汇聚了散失在陕西各地的西汉至唐代的石刻70余件，分陵墓石刻和宗教石刻两大类，按年代顺序陈列。

石刻艺术是中国文化遗产的瑰宝。陕西是中国石刻艺术发展较早、遗存较丰富的地区之一。特别是汉唐石刻以众多的数量和高超的艺术水平驰名国内外，在我国雕刻史上占有突出的地位。

馆内有一对放在陵墓前的镇墓兽，叫"避邪"，是工匠们综合了狮子和老虎的特点雕刻的一种想象中的猛兽。它们四肢挺拔有力，形象威武活跃，充分体现了汉代工匠们高超的雕刻技巧和创造才能。

画像石是用刀凿在石面上的图画。它起源于西汉，盛行于东汉，出土于陕北，2000多年来，以显明的特色，显示着不朽的艺术魅力。西汉时期，厚葬风气极盛。在贵族阶层中，视死如生的观念很强。他们把生前的生活情景和崇信爱慕的东西雕刻于墓室，期望来世能够继续享受。汉代画像石便是在这种厚葬风气中产生的。石刻艺术室陈列的东汉画像石出土于陕北，内容除少数神话历史传说外，大部分取材于现实生活，如牛耕、狩猎、乐舞以及贵族生活等。这些画像形象生动，是汉代社会生活的缩影。因此，它们既是艺术创造，又是历史记录，为我们研究东汉社会提供了珍贵资料。

陕北共出土东汉画像石近500块，其中133块由碑林博物馆收藏。

《牛耕图》反映了陕北使用牛耕的实况，为研究中国古代农业生产提供了有价值的历史资料。画面线条虽然简单，但是中国古代以牛耕为题材的作品极为罕见，所以非常珍贵。

馆内保存有一套完整的墓门。门扉上刻有朱雀、青龙、白虎，门框下部有玄武。朱雀、玄武、青龙、白虎是古代象征南、北、东、西的四方之神，刻在门上有祈求吉祥和守卫的意思。

馆内存有唐高祖李渊的堂弟李寿的石椁（公元630年），由28块青石组成。他的墓志不是一般的方形，而是龟形。龟在唐代象征长寿和显爵。但是龟形墓志在此之前仅发现过一件，而且已经流失，因此这件龟形墓志在考古史上是非常罕见的。

馆内有一尊石犀原立在唐高祖李渊献陵前，刻于公元635年，重10吨。它是根据外国赠送的活犀牛的形象用一整块巨石雕刻而成的，是古代中外友好往来的一件纪念物。

"昭陵六骏"是唐太宗李世民为了纪念他征战时骑过的6匹骏马，在修建昭陵时诏令雕刻的，由著名画家阎立本作画。其中"飒露紫"和"拳毛䯄"两件骏马石刻在1914年被一个美国人通过勾结军阀运到美国，现存费城宾夕法尼亚大学博物馆。1918年，他又将其他四骏浮雕打成数块，企图再次装箱运走，被当地群众发现拦截下来。六骏浮雕造型优美，神态逼真，是唐代杰出的艺术珍品。

有一对走狮原放在昭陵前，造型生动且富有感染力，充分显示了狮子雄伟、豪放的气派。在唐代，驯狮跳舞很流行。狮子经过训练后，在宫廷内随乐起舞，供人们娱乐。这两只狮子是当时会跳舞的狮子，旁边是驯狮人的形象。

佛教是1世纪前后由印度传入中国的。魏晋南北朝时期（公元265—公元589年），中国佛教产生了一些不同流派，出现了一些专门讲授佛教的学者。隋唐时代是中国佛教发展的鼎盛时期，开始有了中国佛教的特有宗派。佛教传入以后，偶像雕刻也随之传来，促进和丰富了中国石刻艺术的发展。

馆内有一尊雕像是南北朝时期的作品，带有明显的印度犍陀罗雕刻的特点。犍陀罗雕刻是古代佛教雕刻艺术的一个流派，公元1—6世纪盛行于古印度的犍陀罗，其特点是姿态生动，线条简练，衣纹质感强。馆内保存的弥勒造像既继承了中国的传统技法，又吸取了外来艺术的优秀成分，从而丰富了中国的石刻艺术。

馆内有一尊隋代的弥勒菩萨像。他头戴宝冠，身饰璎珞，跣足而坐，整体比例匀称，雕工精致，是隋代风格的典型作品。隋代的雕刻仍然有南北朝后期的某些特色，但趋向写实。它们突破了外来艺术规范的束缚，形成一种丰满柔美的民族风格。

唐朝是中国艺术高度发展的时期，也是佛教造像日趋成熟的时期。其多变的风格、逼真的形象、纯熟的技巧，都是空前绝后的。

馆内有一尊菩萨雕像，造型秀美，神情肃穆，肌肉、璎珞、披巾和莲瓣都雕得极其精细，富有质感。整个造像比例均衡和谐，刀法熟练明快，是唐代石雕中的一件珍品。

还有一尊武士俑，在造型上气势威武，刀法流畅，其健壮的体格和全身的盔甲都采用了合理的夸张手法，是盛唐的一件佳作。

供养灯由9层组成，造型优美，结构和谐。工匠以丰富的想象力，巧妙地运用了虚实、松紧等对比手法，构成了一个优美的整体，充分显示了唐代工匠的高度智慧。

李耳的雕像，传说为西域名雕刻家元伽儿所作。整个雕像端庄、丰满，是唐代石雕中的一件珍品。道教是汉族信奉的一种宗教，创立于东汉末年，李耳是道教理论的创始人。

The Museum of Stone-Forest Tablets

The Museum of Stone-Forest Tablets, a courtyard-styled structure, is situated on the site of the Confucian Temple on Sanxue Street, Xi'an. It served as the Imperial Ancestral Temple in the Tang Dynasty, and later became the Confucian Temple in the Song Dynasty. In 1950, it was extended into the museum that greets us today.

The Decorated Memorial Arch

"Pailou" (decorated memorial arch) is derived from its prototype "paifang". Paifang was set up to honor men of attainments in ancient times, and could be seen almost everywhere in China.

The Stone Stakes

Behind the "pailou" is a pond with a bridge. On both sides of the central path inside the first gate, there are altogether 28 stone stakes that dated to the Ming and Qing dynasties. They stand facing each other. These stone stakes were used to tie and submit animals in ancient times, and they were mainly found in the areas north of the Weihe River in Shaanxi. They were decorated with animal and human figures, which reflect the local cultural traits. In addition to tying and submitting animals, they also served evil-repressing and decorative purposes. Before 1949, the rich and noble in the areas north of the Weihe River used to have such stone stakes installed on both sides of their front gates.

The Jingyun Bell

Jingyun Bell is housed in the eastern pavilion inside the second gate. It was cast during the 2nd reign of Jingyun (711 AD), hence its name. Originally, it was hung inside the bell tower of Jinglong Taoist Temple (in the West Street today). It's said that its clear and beautiful sounds could be heard all over the city when the bell was struck. It weighs six tons, and about 5,000 kilograms of molten bronze were poured into 25 casting moulds to make the bell. It bears an inscription of 292 Chinese characters in 18 lines. In fact, the text was written by Emperor Rui Zong (Li Dan) in the Tang Dynasty. It touches on the profundity of Taoism and gives praise to the bell. On the bell there are 32 nipples which were used for tuning and decoration. It was accepted as a world-famous bell at the World Bell Exhibition in 1964. Over the years, a recording of its chimes is played by the Central People's Broadcasting Station on New Year's Eve to usher in the New Year. The huge clock on top of the Post & Telecommunications Building on North Street strikes on the hour with clear and sweet sounds, which are also the chimes recorded from Jingyun Bell.

The Stone Horse

In the west pavilion there is a stone horse, carved in 424 AD during the Daxia period. The horse is vivid and true to life. Between its hind legs is a statue of a conquered man. Daxia, one of the 16 sovereign states in the Eastern Jin period, was established by the Hun nobles. Most of the states were separatist regimes set up by the members of the upper-class strata of the ethnic minority tribes. Because of constant wars, each of them only existed for a short time and left behind very few relics. The stone horse, therefore, is of particularly great value.

The Forest of Stone Tablets Museum covers an area of about 30,000 square meters. Its exhibits can be divided into two categories: stone tablets and stone sculptures. In addition, special exhibitions are often held in the museum.

The Forest of Stone Tablets in Xi'an

The Forest of Stone Tablets was originally set up in 1087. The treasure house comprises a large collection of centuries-old stone tablets. Over 3,000 stone tablets from the Han Dynasty through the Qing Dynasty are preserved. The museum houses numerous stone tablets, which look like a dense forest, hence its name the "Forest of Stone Tablets."

The Forest of Stone Tablets is not only a treasure house of ancient Chinese calligraphy, but also a rich collection of historical documents and stone carvings of various styles. The tablets bear evidence to the cultural achievements recorded in ancient China and the cultural exchanges between China and other countries. No tourists will take the risk of missing the Forest of Stone Tablets, once they visit Xi'an.

This place initially served to store the stone classics of the Tang Dynasty, including the *Classic on Filial Piety* in the handwriting of Emperor Xuan Zong in 745 AD and the *Kaicheng Stone Classics* engraved in 837 AD. They were originally erected inside the Imperial Academy (in the area of Wenyi Road, south of the urban district) in the Tang Dynasty. By the end of the Tang Dynasty, Zhu Wen forced Emperor Zhao Zong to move the capital to Luoyang and then brought Chang'an down to ruins. Han Jian, commander-in-chief of the garrison, reduced the size of the city for the sake of defense. As a result, the "Stone Classics" were abandoned in the suburban wilderness. Later on, Han Jian moved the Imperial Academy and the *Classic on Filial Piety* into the Confucian Temple (on the Shehui Road, Western Street, Xi'an) in the urban district.

In 909 AD, when Liu Xun defended Chang'an, he moved the *Kaicheng Stone Classics* from the suburbs into the Confucian Temple, which became the first place to store the stone tablets of the Tang Dynasty. Because of its low-lying location and poor environment, which were not fit for stone classics, all the stone classics and important stone tablets of the Tang Dynasty were relocated to the present place in 1087 AD. Owing to poor lighting and constant rubbing, the stone tablets became very black, people used to call this place "a dark cave" or "a cave of stone tablets".

A great earthquake took place across Central Shaanxi in 1555 AD. The Forest of Stone Tablets suffered serious destruction. *Kaicheng Stone Classics* were engraved double-sided on 114 stone tablets, and 40 stone tablets were fell down and lay broken after this earthquake. In 1588 AD, Ye Shirong, a scholar of Shaanxi, supplied the missing characters and carved them onto 97 small stone tablets. They were then placed here to supplement the stone classics. Therefore, *Kaicheng Stone Classics* could be kept in their complete form as "a book of stone carvings". In addition, the *Book of Mencius* was engraved onto stone tablets in 1664.

It was not until the early Qing Dynasty that the "Forest of Stone Tablets" was officially named. It now houses over 3,000 stone tablets from the Han Dynasty to the Qing Dynasty. The stone tablets are now on display in seven display rooms, six epitaph corridors and one tablet pavilion.

The Forest of Stone Tablets was declared an important National Historical Monument in China by the State Council in March, 1961.

In front of the first display room is the Tablet Pavilion specially built for the *Classic on Filial Piety*. The *Classic on Filial Piety* is the largest stone tablet in the Forest of Stone Tablets. It was engraved after the handwritten copy of Emperor Xuan Zong (Li Longji) in 745 AD. The *Classic on Filial Piety* was compiled by Ceng Shen, a disciple of Confucius, after he attended his teacher's lecture on filial piety. Emperor Xuan Zong wrote a preface to the classic in the hope that the country would be governed on the principle of filial piety. The preface is followed by the body of the classic. The small characters are Emperor Xuan Zong's annotations to the classic. The tablet is set on a three-layer base, with vivid carvings of trailing plants and lions. The upper part is decorated with clouds and auspicious animals in bas-relief. The tablet is made up of four pieces of stone, and a base under it, therefore it is literally called the "Stone-base Classics on Filial Piety".

The First Display Room

The first display room houses the "Kaicheng Stone Classics," including 12 Chinese classics, namely *The Book of Changes*, *The Book of History*, *The Book of Songs*, *The Rites of the Zhou Dynasty*, *The Book of Ceremonies*, *The Book of Rites*, *Zuo*

Qiuming's Commentary on Spring and Autumn Annals, *Gong Yang's Commentary on Spring and Autumn Annals*, *Gu Liang's Commentary on Spring and Autumn Annals*, *The Analects of Confucius*, *The Classic on Filial Piety*, and *Chinese Semantics*. The classics, with a total number of 650,252 characters, were engraved double-sided on 114 stone tablets. The display room also houses another classic entitled with 30,000 characters, which was engraved on 17 stone tablets in the Qing Dynasty. This Classic and 12 others are called the "Thirteen Classics". These 13 classics were required readings for feudal society intellectuals. Printing was quite backward in ancient times. The classics were engraved on stones as the standard copy so that they could be well kept and men of letters could avoid errors in copying them. The stone tablets were then erected in the Chang'an Imperial Academy for the proof-reading of handwritten copies. From the Eastern Han Dynasty onwards, the classics were engraved seven times. However, only the "Kaicheng Stone Classics" remain intact today.

The Second Display Room

This display room mainly houses the stone tablets of calligraphy written by famous calligraphers of the Tang Dynasty. Up to today, these tablets have served as models for learners of calligraphy to follow. Several examples are the *Tablet to Huangpu Dan* by Ouyang Xun, the *Tablet to Master Dao Yin* by Ouyang Tong, the son of Ouyang Xun, the *Tablet to Duobao Pagoda* and the *Tablet to the Yan's Ancestral Temple* by Yan Zhenqing, the *Tablet to the Mysterious Pagoda* by Liu Gongquan, *A Forward to the Sacred Teaching of Xuan Zang* (also known as the Priceless Tablet) by Huai Ren, the monk of Hongfu Temple in Chang'an who collected the characters written by Wang Xizhi for this tablet, and the world famous the *Nestorian Tablet*.

The Nestorian Tablet provides valuable data for the study of the cultural exchanges between the Tang Dynasty and other countries. "Da Qin" is an ancient Chinese term for the Roman Empire. Nestorianism is a sect of Christianity. When introduced into China, it got its Chinese name "Jing Jiao". Nestorianism spread its influence to Chang'an in 635 AD. The stone tablet was engraved and erected in 781 AD. It offers an introduction to the doctrines, rites and influence of Nestorianism, and the activities of its Chinese believers during the Tang Dynasty. It also bears the names of many missionaries and records some incidents in the Syrian language.

The stone tablet was originally erected in the Da Qin Temple. It was unearthed in

1623 AD, and then moved to the Jinsheng Temple in the western suburb of Xi'an. Later on, some rubbings of this tablet were found overseas, and they were translated into Latin. The tablet thus aroused wide attention in many countries. Some foreigners believed that it should be moved to Europe since there were many Christians there. In 1907, the United Kingdom sent a Danish man name Halmore to Xi'an in an attempt to buy the tablet at a cost of 3000 taels of silver. At the news, the governor of Shaanxi ordered that the tablet be moved into Forest of Stone Tablets. So, the Danish man had to make an imitation tablet and shipped it back to London.

The Third Display Room

The third display room houses the stone tablets that range from the Han Dynasty to the Song Dynasty (206 BC—1279 AD). They bear a wide variety of Chinese script forms, including seal script, official script, regular script, running script and cursive script. These stone tablets show the evolution of the Chinese writing system.

There is a stone tablet which was inscribed in seal script by Meng Ying of the Song Dynasty. According to Xu Shen's book *An Analysis of Chinese Characters*, Meng Ying wrote the radicals and basic structural parts of 540 Chinese characters in seal script and marked them with phonetic symbols in regular script.

The *Tablet to Magistrate Cao Quan* (the Han Dynasty) was inscribed in official script. The characters are made up of elegant, vigorous and well-arranged strokes. It is one of the famous tablets inscribed with characters in the Han style of official script. The official script appeared by the end of the Qin Dynasty. Compared with seal script, the official script is simple and easy to write. The evolution from the seal script to the official script is generally reckoned to be a dramatic change in the forms of Chinese characters. The official script became popular in the Han Dynasty.

A stone tablet inscribed with characters in regular script, which began in the period of the Three Kingdoms (220 AD—280 AD). It came to maturity and gained popularity during the Sui and Tang dynasties. The rulers of the successive dynasties all made it a rule that official documents and imperial examination papers should be written in regular script.

Tablet to Thousand Character Classic stone tablet was inscribed in cursive script. It comprises 1000 different characters. The stone tablet is said to have served as a primer for children in ancient times. It was written by the celebrated calligrapher Monk

Huai Su in the Tang Dynasty. Huai Su's bold and unconstrained style of writing was followed by other calligraphers in later periods.

The Fourth Display Room

This display room houses works of poetry in authentic handwriting of the well-known calligraphers from Song through Qing dynasties, tablets of historical significance in Ming and Qing dynasties, and some line engravings from the Song through the Qing dynasties.

Here are two line engravings: *Bodhidharma's Eastbound Journey* and *Bodhidharma in Meditation*. Bodhidharma was a prince of Southern Tianzhu (present-day India). He arrived in China in 520 AD. Because he had different views on Buddhism from those of Emperor Liang Wu of the Southern Dynasty, Bodnidharma left for the Wei Kingdom, another state in the east and settled down in Shaolin Temple, where he practiced Buddhism for nine years, facing the wall day in day out. This tablet describes the story of Bodhidharma. He crossed the river on a piece of reed, with a pair of shoes on his shoulders. The other is a portrait of Bodhidharma sitting on a cushion in meditation. These are two carved sketches of life-like figures. Their rough sketches reveal a vivid touch.

There is a drawing composed of characters ingeniously pieced together. It is called *JiTzu Kuixing Diandou Tu* (a portrait of Kuixing composed of characters). In the feudal society, the imperial examination system was used to select officials by testing their knowledge about the Five Confucian Classics. Those who won the first place in the examination would be honored as Kuixing (the star at the tip of the Big Dipper). It is not a surprise, therefore, that pavilions called Kuixing Lou or Kuixing Ge could be found in most colleges, where a portrait of Kuixing was often enshrined. In this drawing, the figure of Kuixing is composed of eight characters, meaning "restraining oneself and returning to the rites", which was upheld as the norm of mental cultivation for Confucianists. Kuixing himself stands on one foot over a character, meaning "turtle", with the other raised up and supporting a character meaning the "Big Dipper". The man's posture implies that he ranks first on the list of successful candidates. This picture is vividly and ingeniously constructed.

The Fifth Display Room

The fifth display room houses the stone tablets which record such historical facts as temple repair, canal digging and wall mending during the dynasties of Song, Yuan, Ming and Qing. They provide valuable data of reference for the study of feudal society and local history.

There are also some tablets inscribed with big characters written in a single stroke by Ma Dezhao in the Qing Dynasty. They include "虎" "寿" and "福" which literally mean "tiger" "longevity" and "happiness". The characters assume a vigorous style and offer much enjoyment to their viewers.

The Sixth Display Room

The sixth display room mainly houses stone tablets of poetry and verses that dated back to the dynasties of Yuan, Ming and Qing. Typical examples are *A Visit to Mount Tianguan* by Zhao Mengfu of the Yuan Dynasty, *Farewell to Zhang Sheng in Moling Inn* by Dong Qichang of the Ming Dynasty, *A letter to Wu He* by Emperor Kang Xi of the Qing Dynasty in Mi Fu's writing style, and *A Visit to Mount Hua* by Lin Zexu. They are all treasures of the country.

The Seventh Display Room

This last display room was built in 1982, and houses *The Secret Court Copybook of Chunhua* in the Song Dynasty.

The secret copybook is made up of ten volumes. The first five volumes contain the works of calligraphy in seal script, cursive script and regular script. They were created by famous emperors, ministers and calligraphers in anciet times. The other five volumes contain the works of Wang Xizhi and Wang Xianzhi in cursive script. They are a collection of the works of the Chinese calligraphers before the Song Dynasty. "The Secret Court Copybook of Chunhua" was originally engraved on a board of date wood by Wang Zhu by the order of Emperor Tai Zong of Song Dynasty in the third reign of Chunhua (992 AD). It was initially kept at court. Its rubbings were made and distributed to high-ranking officials. Because it was first engraved in the imperial court, it was thus named *The Secret Court Copybook of Chunhua*. Also because it was created during the regin of Chunhua, it was thus called "the Secret Court Copybook of Chunhua".

The original book was destroyed not long after it was engraved. However, many private and public copies of the wood carving appeared from the Song to Qing dynasties. The present copy, an imitation of *The Secret Court Copybook of Chunhua*, was engraved double-sided on 145 pieces of stone in 1646 AD.

The Corridors of Epitaphs

Along the six tortuous corridors, there are epitaphs from the Wei to the Qing dynasties. In the Wei and Jin periods, it was strictly forbidden to hold extravagant funerals for the dead and erect memorial tablets before their tombs, but to commemorate the deceased, their families and relatives engraved on the stone tablets words of compliment for the dead and placed the tablets secretly into their tombs. This type of stone engraving later gave rise to the emergence of epitaphs.

The Stone Scuplture

This showroom was built in 1963. It houses more than 70 stone sculptures which were collected from different parts of Shaanxi Province. These pieces of art are classified into two groups: mausoleum carvings and religious carvings. They are arranged in chronological order.

Stone Sculpture is the gem of the nation's excellent cultural heritage. Shaanxi is one of the places where many of the Chinese early stone sculptures and historical relics have been found. The province is particularly renowned at home and abroad for its large number of superb stone sculptures, which occupy a conspicuous position in the nation's sculptural history.

There is a pair of stone animals used to be placed in front of a mausoleum to protect it from the attack of evils. The craftsmen combined the physical features of lions and tigers, and created such an imaginary beast of prey. Both its forceful legs and its active appearance reveal the superb skills and creativity of the sculptors of the Han Dynasty.

The stone reliefs dated back to the Eastern Han Dynasty, and they were discovered in Northern Shaanxi. Reliefs are pictures chipped on stone surface. They originated from the Western Han Dynasty and became popular in the Eastern Han Dynasty. With the passage of more than 2,000 years, they still show their eternal artistic glamour in a unique style. During the Western Han Dynasty, extravagant burial was very popular.

The concept of "living again after death" dominated the mind of noble men. They engraved on the tomb walls whatever they used, loved and respected during their lifetime, so that they could still enjoy them in the nether circumstances. Besides some historical legends, the subject matter of the reliefs originated from the real life, such as plowing, hunting, music and dance and the style of noble lives. These reliefs, vivid and true to life, are the microcosm of the social life of the Han Dynasty. Therefore, they are not only works of art, but historical records as well. They provide valuable data for the study of the Eastern Han Dynasty.

About 500 stone reliefs that dated back to the Eastern Han Dynasty were unearthed in northern Shaanxi, and 133 of them are preserved at the Forest of Stone Tablets Museum.

There is a piece of stone carving shows how oxen were used for plowing in the fields in Northern Shaanxi, and provides us with a general understanding of the country's agricultural production in ancient times. Such a work of art about ancient plowing, though simple in style, is rarely seen and thus very valuable.

There is an intact gate to a mausoleum. Its leaf is decorated with the pattern of the Scarlet Bird, the Blue Dragon and the White Tiger, and its lower part, with the pattern of the Tortoise. The Scarlet Bird, the Blue Dragon, the White Tiger and the Tortoise were believed to be gods of the four directions in ancient times, representing the South, the North, the East and the West respectively. The appearance of such patterns on the door suggested good luck and safety in ancient times.

There is an outer coffin for Li Shou (630 AD), a cousin of Emperor Gao Zu (Li Yuan) of the Tang Dynasty. It is made up of 28 black stones. The epitaph is not in the traditional square shape, but in the shape of a tortoise. In the Tang Dynasty, longevity and high rank were symbolized by a tortoise. However, it was very rare to find a tortoise-shaped epitaph. There have been only two epitaphs of the sort found so far. Unfortunately, the one discovered before this particular one was lost for reasons unkonwn. So this tortoise-shaped tombstone is really valuable for archaeological research.

The stone rhino, 10 tons in weight, was carved in 635 AD, and initially placed in front of Emperor Gao Zu's tomb. It was modeled out of a huge stone after the living rhino that a foreign envoy sent to the Royal Court in the Tang Dynasty. It is actually a memento of friendship between China and foreign countries.

When the Zhaoling Mausoleum was built by the order of Emperor Li Shimin, six stone horses were also sculpted in memory of the six horses, which had served him in constant wars. They were actually created by the famous painter Yan Liben. Two of the bas-relief horses, known as "SaluTzu" and "Quanmaogua", were shipped overseas by an American under the cover of the war lords in 1914. They are now displayed at the University of Philadelphia Museum, Pennsylvania. The other four stone horses were broken into pieces when the Americam metioned above attempted to ship them away in boxes in 1918. The local people found out his evil intention and drove him away, the four stone horses were then left behind. The bas-relief horses are vigorous and graceful. They are regarded as rare treasures of art from the Tang Dynasty.

There is a pair of stone lions used to be placed in front of the Zhaoling Maosoleum. They were so vividly modeled to reveal the animal's imposing and mighty power. In the Tang Dynasty, training lions was very popular. Tamed lions could perform dances to the accompaniment of music in the imperial palace. The man standing by is a lion trainer.

Buddhism was introduced into China from India around the first century AD in The Wei, Jin, Southern and Northern dynasties (from 265 to 589 AD), different sects of Buddhism appeared in China. There were many scholars who specialized in Buddhism and gave lectures on the religion. Buddhism was at its zenith in the Sui and Tang dynasties. Different sects of Buddhism were developed in China. Idol carving also came to China with Buddism, and stimulated the development of Chinese sculpture.

There is a statue dates back to the historical period of the Southern and the Northern Dynasties. It is a typical example of Indian Gandhara, India between the 1st and 6th century AD. This kind of sculpture shows the beauty of postures, the terseness of lines and the authenticity of clothing. The statue of Maitreya incorporates the traditional Chinese craftsmanship with the features of foreign art.

The carving of Maitreya Boddhisattva belongs to the Sui Dynasty. With a jewel crown and jade lace trimmings, he is in the sitting position. The delicate carving is well proportioned, typical of the Sui sculpture, but still with certain characteristic touches of the Southern and Northern period. The statue shows a realistic style. The Sui Dynasty developed a unique artistic style, which was not restricted to any foreign forms of art.

The Tang Dynasty witnessed a high level of development of Chinese art. The carving of Buddhist statues attained maturity. Many unprecedented advances were made in the art of Buddhist statues in terms of style, figuration and workmanship.

There is a carving of Bodhisattva looking graceful and solemn. The meticulously carved muscles, jade trimmings, scarf and lotus petals are all real to the touch and well-proportioned. And its cutting shows a skillful, lucid and lively style. This masterpiece of the Tang sculpture is great in every sense.

The museum displays a statue of a vigorous warrior. It must have been sculpted with ease and grace. His strong physique and armor suit are somewhat exaggerated, but with reasonable accuracy.

The Sacrificial Offering Lamp was made of nine layers altogether. It is fine and compact in structure. The craftsman drew on his powerful imagination, and adopted a contrastive approach to work out such a well-knit structure. The marvelous craftsmanship is certainly an embodiment of its creator's superb wisdom.

There is a statue of Li Er, the founder of the theory of Taoism, a religion of the Han nationality. The religion originated from the late Eastern Han Dynasty. The statue was probably created by Yuan Jia'er, a famous sculptor from the Western Regions. This work of art is one of the masterpieces among the Tang Dynasty sculptures.

秦始皇兵马俑博物馆

1974年3月,陕西省西安市临潼县西杨村村民在秦始皇陵东1.5公里处打井时,意外地发现了许多碎陶人,经考古工作者探测,这是一个长方形的秦代兵马俑坑。1976年通过钻探,此坑的北侧20米和25米处又发现了两处兵马俑坑。考古学者按照它们被发现的时间把它们分别定名为兵马俑一号坑、二号坑和三号坑。三个坑的总面积为22 780平方米。

这一发现震惊中外。为了妥善保护这些罕见的、具有重要历史价值的文物,1975年国务院批准在一号坑原址上修建一座占地16 300平方米的博物馆,于1979年国庆节正式对外开放。兵马俑三号坑展厅也于1989年9月27日正式向国内外观众开放。二号坑展厅于1994年正式开放。秦始皇兵马俑博物馆被列为中国十大名胜之一,还被联合国教科文组织宣布为世界文化遗产。

一号坑平面呈长方形,东西长230米,南北宽62米,深5米,总面积14260平方米,为坑道式土木建筑结构。坑东西两端各有斜坡门道5个,坑道内有10道夯土隔墙,隔墙上架着粗大的横梁。横梁上铺有芦席、细泥和填土,底部以青砖墁铺。

兵马俑一号坑按实战军阵排列。俑坑的东端是一个长廊，站着三排面向东的战袍武士俑，每排70件，共210件。他们手持弓弩，是一号坑军阵的前锋部队。长廊南边有一排面向南的武士俑，是右翼；北边有一排面向北的武士俑，是左翼；西头有一列面向西的武士俑，是后卫。他们手执弓弩等远射兵器，担任整个军阵的警戒任务。在10道隔墙隔开的11个过洞里排列着38路面向东的纵队，每路中间都排列有驷马战车。陶俑全部身披铠甲，手执长兵器。他们是一号坑的主力部队。一号坑共有27个探方。根据每个探方里兵马俑排列的密度推算，全部发掘后可出土兵马俑6000余件，其中以步兵居多。

一号坑东端以北20米处是二号坑。占地面积6000平方米。它是由4个单元的4个不同兵种构成的一个曲尺形军阵，估计可出土陶俑1000多件，车马和鞍马500多匹。第一单元即俑坑东边突出的大斗子部分，是由334件弩兵俑组成的小方阵。第二单元即俑坑的南半部，包括1至8过洞，都是由64乘驷马战车组成的方阵，每乘战车有军士俑3件。第三单元即俑坑的中部，包括9至11过洞，是由19乘战车和100名步兵组成的方阵；第四单元，即俑坑的北半部，包括12至14过洞，都是由战车6乘、鞍马和骑兵俑各124件组成的骑兵阵。4个单元有机联系构成一个大阵，又可以分开构成四个独立的小阵，能攻能守，自我保护力强，反应快速。4个单元中就有3个单元布有车兵，战车占到整个军阵面积的半数以上，这表明在秦代车兵仍为作战的主要力量。木质战车因为年久已朽，但车辕、轮等却在泥土上留下了清晰的印迹，车上的铜质构件仍然存在。

三号坑在二号坑以西、一号坑以北25米的地方，平面呈凹字型，面积为520平方米，仅有1车4马和68个陶俑。它的东边是一条长11.2米，宽3.7米的斜坡门道；与门道相对应的为一个车马房，车马房两侧各有一个东西向厢房，即南厢房与北厢房。三号坑共出土陶俑68件。这些陶俑的编组与排列与一号坑和二号坑不同：一号坑和二号坑内的陶俑都是按作战队形排列，而三号坑内的武士则是环绕坑壁面朝里相向夹道式排列。三号坑内武士俑所持兵器也与一号坑和二号坑内的武士不同：后者配备的有远射程弓弩，近距离格斗的矛、戈、钺、剑等；而三号坑内只发现了一种无刃兵器叫作铜殳。铜殳在秦代是一种专门用于仪仗的兵器。在北厢房内还发现残鹿角1件，动物朽骨1堆，可能此处是专供战前占卜或祷战活动的场所。通观三号坑整个布局，它可能是整个地下军阵的指挥部即军幕。

考古挖掘发现，一号坑和二号坑均经火焚烧而毁。到底焚于何时，为何人所焚，史书没有记载，学术界也说法不一。但一、二号坑底部普遍覆盖约15至

20厘米厚的淤泥，坑内到处可见梁木被烧后残留的木炭遗迹，多数文物已经破损。这些都证明，兵马俑坑当时建好后不久便被毁掉。据史书记载，秦始皇死后四年，项羽入关，即"燔其宫室，掘其陵墓"。考古发掘也证明，现在秦始皇陵园建筑遗址内堆积着很厚的砖瓦残片、红烧土块以及炭迹、灰迹等。秦俑坑距始皇陵仅1.5公里，因此它可能与秦始皇陵园地面建筑同时被项羽所焚毁。

在我国，陶俑最早出现于战国时期，但那时制作火候低，陶俑体形较小，制作粗糙。而秦兵马俑不仅形体高大，而且制作精细，造型准确，工艺水平极高。陶俑最矮的为1.78米，最高的为1.97米；轻重也不同，最轻的不到110公斤，而最重的则达300公斤。为了使体形高大的秦俑保持平衡，站立更加稳固，秦代工匠在每个陶俑的脚下加上一个脚踏板。踏板全部用模子制作而成。陶俑的脚、鞋、腿、甲衣全部用手制作。腿有的实心，有的则空心。实心腿采取分段制作，空心腿则采取泥条盘筑法制作。体腔全部是空心；多数采用泥条盘筑法制作，也有采用几段范模制作的，然后再套接而成。

手臂也有空心和实心两种。空心臂采用泥条盘筑法制成，实心臂则分段制作。手的制作有两种方法：模制与手制。制作工艺最为复杂的是头部：先用两个模具分别模制出俑的脸部及俑头的大部分，然后将两部分粘合，再把单独模制而成的耳朵和鼻子粘上去，然后再根据每个俑不同的体形、性格等进行细部刻画，接着还要制作各种各样的胡须和发髻。经过秦代工匠精雕细刻，陶俑一个个栩栩如生、容貌不同、神态各异。据推测，这些陶俑都是秦代工匠按照秦兵雄姿如实塑造的。

陶俑制好后入窑烧制。为了防止陶俑陶马在烧制过程中变形、爆裂，陶俑、陶马制作时就在身上留有1至3个小圆孔。陶马烧成之后，身上的圆孔又用同样大小的陶饼堵住。由于大多数俑头都是烧成之后才安上去的，这些陶俑的颈部本身就是透气孔。这样，在烧制过程中陶俑、陶马体内的气体可以通过这些透气孔排出，不会因为气体受热膨胀而引起陶俑爆裂。陶俑出窑后还要精心彩绘。由于经过焚烧和自然的破坏，今天人们已看不到陶俑当年那色彩绚丽的原貌，但是绝大部分陶俑、陶马身上仍有颜色的残迹，个别的色彩甚至完好如新。颜色的种类有红、绿、黄、紫、褐、白、黑、朱红等十余种，均为矿物质原料，这表明2000多年前我国劳动人民已能大量生产和广泛使用这些颜料。这不仅在彩绘艺术史上，而且在世界科技史上都有着重要的意义。

兵马俑坑位于秦始皇陵东侧，象征着他们是保卫京都咸阳的近卫军。坑内所有的陶俑都执有实战武器，面向东方，表明秦始皇始终不忘消灭六国，统一天下的雄心壮志。从兵马俑坑中出土了数以万计的实战兵器，有刀、剑、矛、戈、戟、弓、弩、簇等，分为长兵器、短兵器、远射兵器和礼兵器四大类。这些兵器制作精良，在铸造工艺方面达到了相当高的水平。

兵器中最引人注目的是一把青铜剑。历经2000年，剑表面没有生锈，至今仍锋利无比，光亮如新，一次能划透20张纸。经鉴定，这把剑系铜锡合金，并含十多种其他稀有金属，表面有一层10至15微米的含铬化合物氧化层，表明曾采用铬盐氧化技术处理。镀铬技术是在20世纪30年代由德国人发明的，而我国在2000多年前就开始在兵器上镀铬，实在令人叹服。

在秦俑坑发现了数百件弩机，它们的栓、悬刀和其他部件全部可以通用互换，误差不超过1毫米。铜镞共分为4种类型，同类型铜镞3个面的轮廓线误差不超过0.15毫米。可见，在秦代由于战争的需要，在武器生产上已经实行了标准化。这充分显示了当时的冶金工艺和兵器制造技术已具有相当高的水平。

1980年12月在秦始皇陵西侧20米处，发掘出土了两乘大型彩绘铜车马，按照发现的顺序，编为一号和二号铜车马。当时皆被埋在7米深的坑里，外面用一个木椁装着。出土时，因木椁腐朽，土层塌陷，两辆铜车马都残破严重，其中二号铜车马已碎成1555片。经过考古工作者和各方面专家两年半的艰苦修复，二号铜车马于1983年10月1日正式对外展出。一号铜车马也于1988年正式展出。

这两乘车都是四马单辕，呈前后纵向排列。前面的一号车应为古代的"高车"。二号车叫"安车"，也叫"辒车京"，分为前御室和主人坐的后乘室。两室之间隔以车墙。赶车的人坐在前御室，主人坐在后乘室。后乘室前面及左右两侧有3个车窗，后面留门，门窗都可以灵活启闭。窗上的小孔可以用来调节空气，还可以从中外望。车上有椭圆形伞状车盖。此车通体施以白色为底色的彩绘。二号车配有1 500余件金银构件和饰物，显得华丽富贵。它可能是供秦始皇灵魂出游时乘坐的。一号车上配备有弓弩、箭头和盾牌，驾车者戴有官帽，这说明此车是用来保护后面二号车安全的。

铜车马处处依照真车、真马、真人制作，除尺寸约为真车、真马、真人的1/2外，其他都与真车、真马、真人无异。铜车马由大小3 400个零部件组装而成。车长3.17米，高1.06米。铜马高65至67厘米，身长1.2米。其重量也各不相同，最轻的为117公斤，最重的为212.9公斤。车、马和人的总重量达1 243公斤，主体由青铜铸造而成。车马的金银装饰品共计1 720件，金银器总重达7公斤。其制作工艺之高超，造型艺术之逼真，令人赞叹不已。如伞状车盖厚4毫米，车窗仅厚1毫米，还有许多透气孔。马璎络用细如发丝的青铜丝铸成，直径仅有0.1毫米。马的项圈是由42节金和42节银焊接起来的，考古学家们只有借助于放大镜才能看到这两种熔点不同金属的焊接痕迹。马的笼头是用一根金管和一根银管,采用子母扣连接的方式制成,笼头上有根销子,拔下销子就可将笼头完整地取下来。据初步研究,制作铜车马采用了铸、焊、铆、镶、嵌、錾、刻等多种工艺手段。

铜车马是我国年代最早、驾具最全、级别最高、制作最精的青铜器珍品,也是迄今为止世界考古发现的最大青铜器。它的出土,为考证秦代冶金技术、车辆结构、工艺造型等提供了极为珍贵的实物资料。

The Museum of the Terra-cotta Army

In March 1974, when several farmers were sinking a well about 1.5 kilometers east of the First Qin Emperor's Mausoleum, they came upon many fragments of terra-cotta figures. The results of archaeological excavation showed that it was an oblong pit with terracotta warriors and horses. Again in 1976, two more pits were discovered 20 meters and 25 meters north of the former one respectively. They were then named Pit 1, Pit 2, and Pit 3 by the order of discovery. The three pits cover a total area of 22,780 square meters.

The new discovery stirred up a sensation all over the world. In order to provide the historical artifacts with adequate protection, a museum with a floor space of 16,300 square meters was set up on the site of Pit 1 in 1975 upon the approval of the State Council. It was officially open to the public on October 1, 1979. The exhibition hall of Pit 3 was open to the public on September 27, 1989. The exhibition hall of Pit 2 was completed and opened to the public in 1994. The Museum of the Terracotta Army, one of the top ten places of historical interest in China, was also listed as the World Cultural Heritage by the UNESCO.

Pit 1 takes an oblong shape. It is 230 meters long, 62 meters wide and five meters deep. It covers an area of 14,260 square meters. It is an earth-and-wood structure in the shape of a tunnel. There are five sloping entrances on the eastern and western sides respectively. Inside the pit are ten earth-rammed partition walls, across which huge and strong rafters are placed. The rafters are covered with mats and fine earth. The floor is paved with bricks.

The terracotta warriors and horses in Pit 1 are arrayed in battle formation. In the long corridor to the east end of the pit stand three rows of terracotta warriors facing east in battle robes, 70 in each, totaling 210 altogether. Armed with bows and arrows, they constitute the vanguard. There is one row of warriors in the south, north and west of the corridor respectively, facing outward. They are probably the flanks and the rear guard. Holding crossbows and arrows and other long-distance shooting weapons, they took up the job of defending the whole army. The ten rammed partition walls divided Pit 1 into 11 latitudinal corridors where stand 38 columns of warriors facing east with horse-drawn chariots in the center. The warriors, clad in armor and armed with long-shaft weapons, are probably the main body of the formation and represent the principal force. There are altogether 27 trail trenches. According to the density of the formation in each trail, it is assumed that more than 6,000 terracotta warriors and horses could be unearthed from Pit 1, most of which are infantrymen.

Pit 2 is located 20 meters to the north of the eastern end of Pit 1. The pit is measured 6,000 square meters. The Pit is L-shaped and consists of four different mixed military forces in four arrays. It is estimated that there are over 1,000 terracotta figures, 500 horse-drawn chariots and saddled horses. The first array, the eastern protruding part of the pit, is composed of 334 archers. To the south of the pit is the second array, including the first through the eighth passage ways. It is composed of 64 chariots, each of which carries three warriors. The third array, the middle of the pit, including the ninth through the eleventh passage ways, is composed of 19 chariots and 100 infantrymen. The fourth array to the north of the pit, including the 12th through the 14th passage ways, is composed of six chariots, 124 saddled horses and cavalrymen. The four arrays are closely connected to constitute a complete battle formation and can be divided up to act independently, capable of attacking and defending and quick response. Three of the four arrays in Pit 2 have charioteers. The chariots took up most of the battle formation. This proves that charioteers were still the principal fighting forces in the Qin Dynasty. The wooden chariots have become decayed with age, but the shafts and wheels left clear traces in the clay. The bronze parts of the chariots remain intact.

Pit 3 is located 25 meters to the north of Pit 1 and to the west of Pit 2. The plane of the pit is of concave shape, totaling about 520 square meters. One chariot, four terracotta horses and 68 clay armored warriors were unearthed out of the pit. To its east there is a sloping entrance, 11.2 meters long, 3.7 meters wide, opposite which is a stable. On both sides of the stable, there is a winging room. 68 terracotta figures were unearthed from it. The arrangement of the terracotta figures is quite different from that in Pit 1 and Pit 2, in which the warriors are placed in battle formation. But those in Pit

3 are arrayed opposite to each other along the walls, in two rows. Even the weapons held by the warriors in Pit 3 are different from those in Pit 1 and Pit 2. The latter were armed with long-range cross-bows and bows and short weapons such as spears, barbed spears, swords and axes. Only one kind of weapon called "shu" was discovered in Pit 3. This kind of weapon had no blades and is believed to be used by the guards of honor. Pit 3 also unearthed a remaining deer-horn and animal bones. This is probably the place where sacrificial offerings and war prayers were practiced. Judging by the layout of Pit 3, this is most likely the headquarters directing the mighty underground army.

Archaeological excavations show that Pit 1 and Pit 2 were destroyed after a fire. When it was burnt down and who did it was not recorded in history. There are various opinions about its destruction in the academic circle. The floors of both Pit 1 and Pit 2 were covered with a layer of silt, 15 to 20 centimeters thick. The remains of cross-beams and logs burnt to ashes can be clearly seen and most of the relics remain fragmented. This illustrates that the pits were destroyed soon after they were completed. According to historical records, four years after the First Qin Emperor's death, Xiang Yu came, and "burnt the palaces and dug up the grave". Archaeological discoveries also proved that there are many broken bricks and tiles piled up inside the ruins of the ground structure of the mausoleum, with burnt clay, coal and ash traces. The pits are only 1.5 kilometers away from the mausoleum, so it was perhaps destroyed together with other structures within the tomb area by Xiang Yu.

Pottery figures first appeared in the Warring States Period in China, but they were small in size and roughly made with low temperature. The Qin terracotta warriors and horses were not only big in size, but also exquisite in craftsmanship. The height of the terracotta warriors varies from 1.78 meters (the shortest) to 1.97 meters (the tallest). Their weights are also different. The lightest is less than 110 kilograms and the heavies to 300 kilograms. In order to keep the balance of the terracotta warriors, the workmen in the Qin Dynasty added a pedal to each warrior under his feet, so that the warriors would stand more firmly. The foot pedals were made in molds. The feet, shoes, legs and armors of the warriors were made by hand. Some legs are hollow, and some are solid. The solid ones were made separately, but the hollow ones were made by the ring-building method. The bodies of the warriors are all hollow, made with the previously-mentioned method. Some were made separately and then joined together to complete the work.

There are also two kinds of arms: hollow and solid. The hollow arms were made by the ring-building method, and the solid ones were made separately. There are two ways of making the hands: molding and hand-shaping. The most sophisticated technique of processing is the heads. Two molds were used first of all to make faces and most parts of the heads, and the two parts were joined together. Ears and noses which were made separately were added later on. The roughly made models were carved exquisitely in detail according to their personal strata and characters. Finally, moustache and hair in various styles were made. After careful and detailed engraving, the terracotta warriors look vivid, different in appearance and expressions. It is presumed that these warriors were made according to the real valiant Qin army soldiers.

After the terracotta warriors were readily made, they were put into kilns to be fired. In order to prevent the warriors from deforming or exploding, one, two or even three small holes were made in the body of the warriors and horses. After the horses were fired, the small holes in the body were covered with terracotta cakes of the same size. Most of the terracotta heads were fit in the body after being fired, so the necks of the terracotta heads were natural ventilation holes. Thus, the air stream produced in the firing process of the terracotta warriors and horses could be expelled, and the figures would not explode. The clay figures were carefully painted with colors after they were baked. As the terracotta figures have been burnt and gone through a natural process of decay, we can't see their original gorgeous colors. However, most of the figures bear the traces of the original colors, and a few of them are still as bright as new. They are found to be painted with mineral dye stuffs of red, green, yellow, purple, brown, white, black, pink, vermilion, etc. This demonstrates that the Chinese people used these dye stuffs extensively over 2,000 years ago. It is of great significance not only in the history of color-painting art, but also in the history of world science and technology.

The pits are located to the east of the First Qin Emperor's Mausoleum, symbolizing the main defending force that guarded the Qin capital, Xianyang. All the terracotta figures in the pits face east with practical weapons. This shows that the First Qin Emperor would never forget his great ambition to conquer the six states and to unify the whole nation. Thousands of real weapons were unearthed from the pits, including broad knives, swords, spears, dagger-axes, halberds, cross-bows, arrows, and arrow heads. The weapons can be classified into four categories: long-shafted weapons, short weapons, long-range weapons and weapons for guards of honor. They were delicately made and enjoyed a high level of casting technology.

The most arresting among the weapons is a bronze sword, which still glitters in metallic luster without being rusting, though buried underground for over 2,000 years. Being very sharp, the sword can cut through 20 pieces of paper put together. Technical examination reveals that the sword is composed of an alloy of copper and tin, and more than ten other rare metals. It is plated with a thin layer (10-15 microns) of oxidated chromium, which proves that the weapon was oxidated with chromium when it was made. The technology of chromium coating was invented by a German in the 1930s, but in China chromium-coating technique was employed in the making of weapons over 2,000 years ago. It is really a wonder and compels admiration.

Hundreds of crossbow triggers were also discovered in the pits. Their bolts and suspending knives can be used interchangeably, with a tolerance error of one millimeter. The arrowheads are divided into four kinds. The outline of the three sides of the arrow heads of the same kind has a tolerance error of 0.15 millimeter. From this, we can see that weapon manufacturing was already standardized just to meet the war needs. This also shows that the metallurgical technology and weapon-making technique reached a high standard in the Qin Dynasty.

In December 1980, two sets of large painted bronze chariots and horses were unearthed 20 meters west of the First Qin Emperor's Mausoleum. They were labeled as Chariot No. 1 and Chariot No. 2 respectively by the order of discovery. They had been enclosed in a wooden coffin and buried in a pit seven meters deep. When excavated, the chariots and horses were seriously damaged due to the decayed wooden coffin and the collapse of earthen layers. No. 2 bronze chariot and horses were found broken into 1,555 pieces when excavated. After two-and a half years of careful and painstaking restoration by archaeologists and other experts, they were finally open to the public on October 1, 1983. No.1 bronze chariot and horses were also open to the public in 1988.

The bronze chariots drawn by four horses, with a single shaft, were placed one before the other vertically. The front chariot, No. 1 Chariot was named "High Chariot". The back chariot, No. 2 Chariot was named "Security Chariot", and also called "Air-conditioned Chariot". It has a front room and a back room, between which there is a partition. The front room is supposed to be for the charioteer and the rear one for the master (emperor). There is a window on either side with a door at the back. The windows and doors could close and open easily. The small holes in the windows were used for ventilation. On top of the chariot, there was an elliptical umbrella-like canopy. The chariot was color-painted against a white background. No. 2 Chariot was fitted with more than 1,500 pieces of silver and gold and other ornaments. Probably it was used for the First Qin Emperor's soul to go out on inspection. No. 1 Chariot was equipped with crossbows, arrowheads and shields. The charioteer wore a hat. This shows that it was employed to protect the No. 2 Chariot behind.

The chariots and horses are exactly the imitations of actual chariots and horses in half life-size. Each chariot with horses is composed of 3,400 components. The bronze chariot is 3.17 meters long and 1.06 meters high. The bronze horse is 65-67 centimeters high, 1.2 meters long. Their weights vary from 177 kilograms, the lightest, to 212.9 kilograms, the heaviest. The total weight of the chariot, the horses and the driver is 1,243 kilograms. The main body is cast in bronze. There are altogether 1,720 pieces of gold and silver ornaments on the chariots and horses, with a total weight of seven kilograms of silver and gold wares. The umbrella-like canopy on the top is only four millimeters thick, and the window is one millimeter thick, with many ventilation holes. The horse tassels were made of bronze thread as thin as hair, whose diameter is only 0.1 millimeter. The horse necklaces were welded together with 42 nodes of gold and 42 nodes of silver. Archaeologists can see the welding joints only with a magnifier. The horses halters, made up of a gold tube and a sliver tube, were joined with snap fasteners. In the halters, there is a pin. When the pin was pulled out, the halters could be removed completely. According to preliminary research, the making of the bronze chariots and horses involves different techniques such as casting, welding, riveting, mounting, embedding, engraving and carving.

The bronze chariots and horses were the earliest and most exquisitely and intricately made bronze valuables. They enjoy the highest class and have the most complete harnessing wares. They are also the largest bronze wares discovered in the history of world archaeology. The excavation of the bronze chariots and horses provides extremely valuable material and data for the research of the metallurgical technique, the mechanism of chariots and technological modeling of the Qin Dynasty.

西安半坡博物馆

西安半坡博物馆位于西安市东郊，距市中心9公里。它展出的是6000多年前的新石器时代母系氏族社会的一个村落遗址。这个遗址因发现于现在的半坡村而得名。

半坡遗址是一个典型的仰韶文化村落遗址。仰韶文化是中国新石器时代的一种文化，分布于黄河中下游。仰韶文化于1921年首次发现于河南渑池县仰韶村，它以红色彩陶为特征，所以，仰韶文化也称为"彩陶文化"。这类遗存仅在黄河流域的关中地区就发现了400多处，因此，黄河流域素有"中国古代文化发源地"之美称。

仰韶文化时期的生产工具以磨制石器为主，常见的有刀、斧、锛、凿等，打制石器仍占一定数量，骨器相当精致。日用陶器以细泥红陶和夹砂红褐陶为主。细泥陶上常有彩绘的几何形图案或动物形花纹。当时的经济生活以农业为主，渔猎为辅。仰韶文化属于母系氏族公社制的繁荣时期。根据碳-14法测定，整个中原地区的仰韶文化约存在于公元前5000年—公元前3000年。

母系氏族公社始于氏族公社的产生，终于父权制的确立，大体相当于旧石器时代晚期至新石器时代。此时妇女在氏族社会中居支配地位。母系氏族公社又分为早期和发展期，早期妇女从事采集，男子从事渔猎活动，实行族外群婚，子女只知其母，不知其父，世系以母系计；发展期已过渡到对偶婚，妇女经营原始农业，管理氏族事务和经济生活，丈夫居住于妻方，世系与财产继承以母系计。

半坡遗址是1953年春天偶然发现的，占地面积共50000平方米。从1954年到1957年，经过五次现场发掘，共发掘10000平方米，为总面积的1/5。1958年，在这里建造了中国第一座遗址性博物馆。

考古发掘证实，这座原始村落分为三个部分：居住区、制陶区和墓葬区。考古学家们在遗址内发现了10000件生产工具和各种各样的生活用具、46座房屋遗址、2座圈栏、200多个地窖、174个成人墓葬和73个小孩瓮棺。这里出土文物之丰富是前所未有的。

自然环境

人类要生存就必须有良好的自然环境。根据对植物标本的研究及出土动物骨头的鉴定得知，6000年前的半坡村一带温和湿润。那个时期，浐河和灞河水量很大，半坡先民从不为缺水而发愁。半坡村东有白鹿原，南接丛林覆盖的终南山。这里土地肥沃，水源充足，林木茂密，从而使半坡先民能耕种、渔猎、制陶、喂养牲畜、盖房，过定居的生活。

农业

半坡时期，男人外出捕鱼打猎，妇女采集。在这期间，半坡妇女通过对植物生长习性的长期观察和反复试验，发明了早期的农业。在家里，做饭是妇女的事，所以食物分配就自然成了妇女的责任。除此之外，妇女还要养育孩子、纺织和制陶，所有这些使得妇女在氏族的作用日益增长。

在地窖中还发现了炭化的粟种及装在陶罐中的菜籽。这说明半坡先民不仅种植粮食，而且还种植蔬菜，这极大地丰富了他们的物质生活。

半坡人砍伐树木，烧荒垦田。烧过的荒草树木成为自然肥料，从而使荒地成为可耕地。

狩猎

狩猎是半坡先民的一项主要活动。除了提供肉食之外，狩猎还能为先民提供其他生活用品，比如：皮毛、骨头、兽角和油。6000年前，这里到处都是动物野兽。从遗址上发现的动物骨头来看，斑鹿是半坡先民的主要猎物。那时候，人们集体出去打猎，打猎工具以箭、石球和石矛为主。

捕鱼

半坡遗址西边的浐河水量充足，鱼类成群，捕鱼是半坡先民的另一活动。在遗址上还发现了制作精巧的鱼钩和鱼叉。早期的鱼钩没有倒刺；后期的鱼钩和鱼叉上都有了倒刺。遗址上没有发现渔网，有可能渔网是用植物纤维编的，所以早就烂掉了。但是，考古学家们在一些陶片上发现了鱼网纹，除此以外，还发现了一些石鱼网坠，再次说明了6000年前人们已经用渔网捕鱼了。

制陶

在半坡遗址还发现了许多各式陶器。根据它们的用途，可分为饮食器、炊器和储藏器。

半坡的陶器以红色为主。那时，陶轮还没有出现，半坡先民制陶主要采用泥条盘筑法。什么叫泥条盘筑法呢？就是把泥搓成条，再一圈一圈地盘成器皿的形状，用骨刀刮平，再放到窑里烧制。

制陶区在半坡村的东边。这里发现了六座两种不同形制的陶窑：横穴式和竖穴式。横穴式建于早期，而竖穴式建于晚期。和横穴式陶窑相比，竖穴式陶窑更为先进。细看窑壁可以得知，烧陶时窑内的温度可达800℃—1000℃。

半坡遗址出土的陶器不仅外观很美，而且图案繁多。大部分彩绘图案都与鱼有关。由于居住在河岸边，半坡先民主要靠捕鱼为生。捕鱼时和鱼打交道多了，就对鱼有了直觉。除了鱼纹之外，还有鹿纹、山纹、麻织物纹等。大部分装饰纹位于陶器的上半部，而漂亮的印纹则在陶器的中部或底部。

编织

半坡遗址还发现了一些骨梭和81枚骨针。在一些陶器底部仍然留有麻织物的印迹。这些都说明这个时期已有了编织技术。这里出土的大量的骨针都有针眼，线可以从针眼里穿过去。这说明半坡先民已经掌握了缝纫技术。据考古研究，那时所用的缝纫材料可能是麻和兽皮。

居住区

半坡是仰韶文化中最大的村落，居住区就占了30000平方米。居住区周围有一条长300米的壕沟，可以防御野兽的袭击，还可以防洪。壕沟的北边是墓葬区，东边是制陶区。这里共有46座房屋。中央有一所160平方米的大房子，周围是较小的房屋。这些小房屋的门都朝着中间的大房子。这所大房子可能是用来开会讨论氏族内部事务的，同时也是老人及儿童居住的地方，宗教仪式活动如"成丁礼"等也在这里举行。

小房屋中有些是圆形的，有些是方形的；一些是半地穴式建筑，一些是地面上建筑。半坡先民在建造房屋时，先在地上挖一个坑，然后顺着坑用茅草搭起棚子做房顶。现在这些房屋看起来很原始，但它们却代表了从穴居向前迈出的一大步。为了出入方便，先民们在南边建了一条坡道，只能过一个人。然后建了一条高于地面的门槛，防止雨水进入。火是做饭、取暖、照明不可缺少的条件。可想而知，火对先民是多么重要。难怪每个房屋中央都有一个火坑呢！

房屋外边有200个地窖，它们是用来储藏工具和粮食的。地窖共有两种：一种是早期地窖，另一种是晚期地窖。早期地窖面积小，形状不规则；晚期地窖口小、底大、形式固定，而且窖大。这种地窖数量的增多及其形式的固定表明了生产力的提高和粮食产量的增加。

所有的地窖都是露天地窖。这说明半坡先民集体劳动，平均分配，当时的社会是没有阶级、没有剥削、没有私有财产的原始社会。

居住区周围有一条壕沟，宽、深各 6 米，其主要用途是保护半坡居民不受野兽的伤害，不受雨水的破坏，同时也能避免氏族之间的矛盾冲突。据估计，要完成这项巨大工程，必须移走 11000 立方米的土方。如果一辆卡车一次能载 3 立方米的话，那么，这么多的土方就需要 3666 辆卡车。现在用机器挖这样一条沟不算什么，可是，在 6000 多年前用原始石器来挖就太难了。

墓葬区

半坡的墓葬区在壕沟的北边，共有 170 座成人墓葬。考古发掘显示：半坡人无论多人合葬还是单人独葬，男女都是分开的，没有一座墓葬是合葬墓，这就是母系氏族社会的特点。当时实行对偶婚，男人被"嫁"给女人。白天男女双方生活在一起，晚上各自可以寻求其他性伴侣。其结果是，孩子只认其母，不认其父。母亲是一家之主，孩子随其母。只要女人愿意，男人随时有被赶走的危险。男人甚至死后还要被送回原母系家庭安葬。这就是为什么在半坡遗址没有一个墓是男女合葬的原因。

人死后安葬的姿势不同，有仰面葬、俯身葬、屈肢葬等。人死后常常要葬在一个地方，让其腐烂，然后骨头被收起来，正式葬在公共墓地。这种葬法也叫作"洗骨葬"，因为人们相信肉体属于人类世界，腐烂之后，人的灵魂才能到另一个世界去。人死后都面朝西安葬，大概因为古人们相信人死后要去另一个世界，而这个世界在太阳落下的地方。

每个墓里有 3 到 4 件随葬品，一般是碗、盘、瓶和其他一些烹饪用品。这些随葬品大多放在死者的腿部附近。这一点说明，6000 年前的时候，人们就已经产生了灵魂概念。他们相信人死后要去另一个世界，所以应该带上其日常用品。

小孩瓮棺

小孩死后，半坡先民把他们装入瓮馆安葬，这是当时的习俗。孩子死后不能葬在村子的公共墓地里，先在房屋周围的某个地方挖个洞，将瓮罐埋在那里，然后把尸体放入，再在口上盖一个碗或盆——这要看瓮罐有多大了。通常他们还在盖罐的碗或盆的顶部中央凿个洞，以便灵魂出入。大一点的孩子通常装在两个相连在一起的瓮罐里。

把孩子葬在房屋周围表示母亲对死去孩子的爱。她们认为孩子太小不能独立生活，还需要照顾；另一方面，也说明半坡当时有着严格的丧葬制度，既然孩子早早就去世了，那么他们就不能算作氏族的成员。

到目前为止，在半坡遗址共发现了 73 个瓮棺。显然，由于恶劣的自然环境，当时的婴儿死亡率是相当高的。

生产工具

半坡遗址属于新石器时代，生产工具通常是磨制的，比较光滑。钻孔在后期才出现。磨光的工具大多用来砍伐，像斧和凿子等。通常人们在制作一件工具时会将磨制和打制结合起来操作，例如，某件工具的刃部需要磨光，而其他地方只要打制就可以了。

在遗址上还发现了诸如石刀、陶刀和石镰等收割工具。在早期文化层发现的石刀、陶刀制作比较粗糙。而在后期文化层里，考古学家们发现了带把镰刀，这些镰刀和现在用的镰刀多少有些相似。生产工具的发展反映了人类智慧的不断提高。在半坡遗址上还发现了用来加工粮食的磨盘和磨棒，人们把粮食放在磨盘上，手里拿着磨棒通过挤压进行脱壳。

刻画符号

半坡时期文字还没有出现，但是在出土的陶器上却发现了 113 个刻画符号。如果将这些符号和商代（公元前 17 世纪—前 11 世纪）的甲骨文比较，就可以看出两者有相似之处。人们认为这些符号可能就是最早的汉字形式，是甲骨文的前身。

尖底瓶

尖底瓶是半坡出土陶器的代表作。它是一种符合重心原理，用来打水的工具。瓶子一挨水面，就会自然倾斜，因为重心发生了改变，当水装满后又自然竖起。这种瓶子有两个优点，一是可以背在背上，便于携带；二是从河里往家里背水时，水不容易洒出来。

人面鱼纹

人面鱼纹是在半坡遗址上发现的，它反映了早期先民们的艺术造诣。人面鱼纹线条明快、优美；头发换成了漂亮的发髻，口角含着两条小鱼。它表达了半坡先民和鱼的密切联系，可能是当时半坡先民的图腾。

陶甑的运用

半坡先民早已发现蒸汽可以用来做饭,所以他们制作了陶甑。这是人类历史上迄今发现的最早对蒸汽的利用。

圈栏遗迹

在发掘中还发现了两个圈和一些猪、狗、牛、羊、马、鸡的骨头。据一些专家的研究,6000年前家畜只有猪和狗,其他的动物正在驯化期。因为狗容易驯养,而且是狩猎的好帮手,猪生长快,又易于圈养,所以,它们是最早的家畜。

The Banpo Museum

The Banpo Museum is located in the eastern suburb of Xi'an, nine kilometers from the center of the city. It houses the site of a 6,000-year-old village, which belongs to a Neolithic matriarchal clan community. The site was named "Banpo" because it was unearthed near the present-day Banpo Village.

Banpo is a typical site of the Yangshao Culture which belonged to China's Neolithic Age. remains of the Culture were located mainly in the middle and lower reaches of the Yellow River. The Yangshao Culture first came to light in Yangshao Village, Mianchi County, Henan Province in 1921. With painted red pottery as its chief feature, Yangshao Culture is also known as "the Painted Pottery Culture." More than 400 sites of the Yangshao Culture have been discovered in Central Shaanxi Plain of the Yellow River Valley. Thus the Yellow River Valley has always enjoyed the reputation of being "the cradle of China's ancient culture".

Production tools, such as the knife, axe, adze and chisel, were mostly made of stone by means of grinding and polishing. There were chipped stone implements and bone objects as well. Pottery utensils for daily use were chiefly made from refined terracotta and red sandy clay. Some objects of refined terracotta were decorated with zoomorphic and geometric designs. Agriculture dominated the economic life of that age, while fishing and hunting came second. All these finds give evidence to the fact that matriarchal clan community came to its prime. Using the Carbon-14 dating method, we may come to the conclusion that the Yangshao Culture can be traced back to 5,000 BC to 3,000 BC in Central China.

It is believed that the matriarchal clan community began with the birth of primitive clan communes, and came to an end not long before patriarchal society was established. This happened in approximately the period spanning the late Paleolithic and Neolithic Ages. Women then played a dominant role in society. The matriarchal society falls into two periods: the early period and the latter period. In the early period women were engaged in gathering while men were occupied with fishing and hunting. As a result of the intertribal communal marriage, children were closely associated with their mothers. Yet their fathers remained somewhat like a stranger to them. They followed their mothers in the family pedigree. The latter period of the matriarchal society saw the transition to exogamy. Women took up farming, and managed the tribe affairs and the economic life as well. Husbands lived in the homes of their female partners, and they were also recorded together with their property in the family pedigree after their female partners.

Banpo remains were discovered by chance in the spring of 1953. It extends over an area of 50,000 square meters. Excavations were conducted in five phases between 1954 and 1957, opening up an area of 10,000 square meters, one fifth of the total. Banpo Museum was set up at the site in 1958, the first of its kind in China.

According to the archaeological survey, the village is divided into three sections: the living section, the pottery-making section and the burial section. By means of scientific excavation, archaeologists have discovered nearly 10,000 production tools and kinds of daily utensils, 46 houses, 2 pigsties, 200 cellars, 174 burial pits for adults and 73 burial jars for children. The discovery of so many artifacts is indeed unprecedented.

The Natural Environment

Favorable natural environment is essential to human survival and sustenance. The plant specimens and animal bones under study show that the area of Banpo Village was warm and moist 6,000 years ago. In those days, both the Chan River and the Ba River were affluent. The Banpo people never had to worry about the availability of water. To the east of Banpo Village is the Bailu Plateau, and to the south is the Zhongnan Mountain densely covered with vegetation. The Banpo people made this place their home because of its fertile soil, abundant water supply and dense forests. All this made it possible for them to conduct many activities, such as farming, fishing, hunting, pottery making, livestock breeding, house building, etc. therefore they lived a settled life.

Farming

In the days of Banpo, men had to go out hunting and fishing, while women made a living by gathering. Through the long-term observation and experimentation in their daily activities, the Banpo women developed primitive agriculture. With women doing cooking at home, the distribution of food became their responsibility, which, plus child rearing, weaving, and pottery-making, made their role in the clan increasingly important and dominant.

Some carbonized millet was discovered in the cellar, and Chinese cabbage seeds were discovered in pottery jars. This shows that Banpo people not only knew how to grow grain crops, but also vegetables, which greatly enriched their material life.

Banpo people opened up land by slashing and burning trees and wild plants, thus turning the ashes into fertilizer. In this way waste land was turned into cultivated fields.

Hunting

Hunting played an important role in the life of the Banpo people. It not only provided people with meat, but also supplied them with other daily necessities such as fur, bones, horns and oil. There were a large number of wild animals around the place 6,000 years ago. Judging from the animal bones discovered on the site, we can tell that the sika (spotted deer) was the principal game of the Banpo people. People then went out hunting collectively. The hunting tools they used were mainly arrows, pebbles and stone spears.

Fishing

Fishing was another occupation of the Banpo people. The Chan River to the west of the village had a large volume of water flow teeming with fish. Fish hooks and harpoons were found at the site, all of them exquisitely made. In the early period, they had no barbs on them; later on, barbs appeared on fish hooks and harpoons. Though it is impossible to find fish nets on the site, since they were then probably made of plant fibers, and had rotted along, long time ago. However, archaeologists found impressions of fish nets on pieces of broken pottery. What is more, some stone net sinkers have been discovered as another evidence proving that fish nets were used to catch fish 6,000 years ago.

Pottery Making

In Banpo remains, a large number of differently shaped pottery utensils were discovered. According to their usage, they could be classified into several kinds, such as food and water containers, cooking utensils, and utensils for storing things.

The pottery made by Banpo people was mainly red in color. The potters's wheel did not come into existence then. Pottery was still made by the ring-building method. What is the ring-building method? Well, people rolled the clay into long pieces, coiled them up into different shapes of untensils, smoothed their surfaces with bone knives and then fired them in the kilns.

The pottery making area is located in the eastern part of Banpo Village. In this area, six pottery kilns of two different types were discovered: horizontal and vertical. The horizontal kilns were used in the early stage, while the vertical kilns were constructed in the later period of Banpo. Compared with the horizontal kilns, the vertical ones were more advanced in structure. An examination of the wall of the kilns shows that the temperatures in the kiln could reach as high as 800℃ to 1,000℃.

The pottery utensils unearthed at Banpo were not only beautifully shaped, but also rich in the variety of colorful designs. Most of the designs had to do with fish. Because they lived by the riverside, Banpo people lived a lot on fish. As they often went fishing, they got a direct perception of fish. Besides designs of fish, there were also designs of deer, mountains and hemp fabric patterns, etc. The decorative patterns of the designs are found mostly on the upper sections of the pottery utensils, while the beautiful impressions are found either at the bottom or on the body of the utensils.

Weaving and Sewing

In Banpo remains, some bone shuttles and 81 bone needles with eyes were unearthed. Impressions of linen fabrics were found at the bottom of some excavated pottery vessels. All this may convince us that this period saw the emergence of weaving and sewing. The discovery of the large number of delicate bone needles, with eyes at their ends which made it possible to pass thread through them, shows that Banpo people mastered the skill of sewing. According to archaeological study, it is believed that the materials for sewing then were possibly linen and hides.

The living section

Banpo is one of the largest villages of the Yangshao Culture. The living section alone covers an area of 30,000 square meters. It is surrounded by a 300-meter-long moat which served the purpose of protecting the village against wild beasts and floods. To the north of the moat is the burial section, while to its east is the pottery-making section. In all, the remains of 46 houses were discovered. A house as large as 160 square meters was uncovered in the center of the living section with smaller houses built around it. The doors of the smaller houses were all open towards the large one in the center. It is believed that this large house was used as a meeting hall in which the Banpo people discussed their communal affairs, and at the same time, it served as a "dormitory" for children and old people. Religious and ritual activities of the clan were also held here, such as "adulthood ceremony".

As for the smaller houses, some were round and others were square in shape; some were built half under ground and others above ground in structure. In building these houses, Banpo people began with digging a pit and then along the edges of the pit, erected a framework for a roof with thatches. The houses may appear to us very primitive today, but they really represent a big step forward from cave dwellings. In order to get in and out conveniently, they built a sloping entrance in the south, which allowed only one person to pass. Then they built up a raised threshold to stop rainwater. It is not hard to imagine the importance of fire in the life to the primitive people, for fire was indispensable for cooking, heating and lighting. So no wonder there was a fire pit in the middle of every house.

There are altogether 200 cellars scattered outside the houses. They were mainly used to store tools and grain. They fall into two types: one from the early days; the other from the later days. The capacity of the cellars was small and they were of irregular shapes. In the later period, cellars were shaped like a pocket with mouth smaller than the bottom. They were of uniform shape and had large capacity. This growth in the volume of the cellars and the tendency in the latter period toward uniformity in shape indicated the growth of productivity and the increase in the output of production.

All the cellars were located in the open air, which shows that the Banpo people worked together, and enjoyed equal distribution. They lived in a primitive society without classes, exploitation or private property.

The entire living section is surrounded by a protective moat, six meters in both depth and width. Its main purpose is to safeguard the Banpo people from attacks of wild beasts and damage from heavy rainfall. At the same time, it served to prevent conflicts between clan members. It is estimated that to complete this big project, it was necessary to move more than 11,000 cubic meters of earth. Suppose a truck can carry a load of three cubic meters of earth each time. As many as 3,666 trucks would be needed. It would be so easy to do it today with machines. But what a job it would be with only primitive stone tools 6,000 years ago!

The Burial Section

To the north of the protective moat lies the burial section of Banpo Village. It was the place where adults were buried. Altogether 170 graves were excavated. Archaeological excavation has revealed that at the time of Banpo, males and females were separately buried either in groups or singly and there was not a grave where a man and a woman were buried together. This is precisely an indication of a characteristic matriarchal society when exogamy was practiced. At that time a man was "married" to a woman, during the daytime they lived together, but both could have sexual relations with others at night. As a result, their children only recognized their mothers instead of fathers. The family was always headed by the mother; children followed their mother; the man could be driven away any moment as the woman pleased. The poor man even had to be sent back to his matriarchal family for burial after death. This is why no graves with corpses of both sexes were discovered.

The deceased were found to be buried in various postures. Some were buried with their faces up and arms and legs straight and some were buried with their faces down and some were buried sideways. When a person died, his corpse would be placed somewhere for a period of time until it became decomposed. Then people collected the bones and buried them formally in the cemetery. This way of burial is also known as "washing bone burial". Perhaps Banpo inhabitants then believed that man's blood and flesh belonged to the human world, only when they became decayed could the soul go to another world. The heads of the deceased were directed to the west, probably because people then believed that the deceased would go to another world, and this world was in the direction of the sunset.

There were three or four pieces of burial objects in every tomb. They included bowls, plates, bottles and some other pottery cooking vessels. The burial objects were usually placed near the legs of the deceased. From this we can see that 6,000 years ago the primitive people already generated the conception that everybody had a soul. They believed that people would go to live in another world after their death. So they buried the dead together with his daily utensils.

Children's Burial Jars

To bury dead children in jars is a burial custom of the Banpo people. When children died, they were not supposed to be buried in the communal cemetery of the village. People first dug a pit somewhere near their house into which they placed a pottery jar, and then laid the corpse inside, and covered the mouth of the jar with a pottery bowl or basin, depending on the size of the jar. They usually chipped a hole in the center of the bowl or basin. This was probably a passage for the soul of the dead to come in and out. Older children were buried in two pottery jars jointly connected.

To bury the children near the house is probably an indication of the mother's affection for their lost children. Mothers perhaps thought that their children were too young to live by themselves, and they still needed to be taken care of. On the other hand, it is believed that there was a strict rule for burying the dead in Banpo. Since those children died very young, they were not considered as full members of the clan.

So far 73 children's burial jars have been excavated. Obviously, infant death rate was very high in those days because of tough natural conditions.

Production Tools

Banpo was a village of the Neolithic age, when tools were made by the technique of grinding and polishing and were comparatively smooth. Drill technique appeared in the later period. The polished tools are mostly for chopping such as the axe, and the chisel. Frequently polishing and chipping are combined in the making of a single tool. For instance, the edges of one tool need to be polished, while the others just need to be chipped.

Harvesting tools discovered and pottery knives found in the early layers were roughly made. In the later layers archaeologists found sickles which could be fixed to some handles. They were shaped more or less like metal sickles nowadays. The improvement in the farm tools reflected the constant development of human wisdom. Millstone and grinding stone which were used to process grain were also discovered. People put grain on the millstone and then they husked and crushed grain with the grinding stone in their hands.

Carved and Painted Signs

Characters did not come into being in Banpo days, but some 113 carved and painted signs were found on the unearthed pottery vessels. Comparing these signs with the inscriptions on bones or tortoise shells of the Shang Dynasty (17th—11th centuries BC), we may see a few of them bearing some resemblance to each other. It is believed that these signs were possibly the earliest Chinese script, the predecessor of the inscriptions on bones or tortoise shells of the Shang Dynasty.

Tip-bottomed Bottle

The tip-bottomed bottle is the characteristic of the pottery unearthed at Banpo. It is a water-drawing device which is in conformity with the law of the center of gravity. As soon as the bottle touched the water surface, it would automatically tilt. Then it would stand upright after being filled with water, due to the shifting of its center of gravity. It had two advantages for holding water. The first is that it was portable and easy to carry on the back. The second is that the water would not spill out when it was carried from the river to the living place.

Human-faced Fish Design

The design of a fish with a human face was a masterpiece painting discovered on the site, and reflected the artistic attainments of these early inhabitants. Its lines were clear and graceful. On its head the hair was well pinned and done into a knot, two small fish were held in the corners of its mouth. This design depicted the Banpo people's strong ties and special emotion with fish. It was most likely the totem of the Banpo people.

The Use of Pottery Steamers

Banpo people already found that steam could be used in cooking, and then they invented pottery steamers. This has been proven to be the earliest use of steam in human history.

Remains of the Sty

In the course of excavation, the remains of two sties and bones of pigs, dogs, oxen, sheep, horses and chickens were found. According to the study of some experts, the only domestic animals existed 6000 years ago could only be pigs and dogs, while other animals were being tamed. Because it was easy to raise dogs, and they were good helpers for hunting, and pigs were capable of quick breeding and easy to keep in sties, they became the earliest domestic animals.

茂陵博物馆

茂陵博物馆建在霍去病墓前，馆内陈列着原置于霍去病墓前的 16 件大型石刻和近年来在茂陵附近出土的珍贵文物。

我国从秦代开始就有大型石雕像，但遗存下来最早的作品却属于西汉时期，其中又以霍去病墓前这批石刻最具有代表性。这批大型石刻是我国目前保存的古代成组大型石刻艺术品种中时间最早的杰作，闻名中外。

霍去病墓前这组大型石雕，包括圆雕的马踏匈奴、跃马和卧牛，线雕与圆雕相结合的伏虎、卧象、野人、石蛙、石鱼等。它们原先有的置于墓前，多数置于象征祁连山的坟丘上。石刻按巨石自然形状顺势雕琢，着重突出内在神态，只在关键部位精雕细琢，大体轮廓则顺乎自然，风格写意浪漫。

马踏匈奴

马踏匈奴是霍去病墓石刻群的主像，高 168 厘米，长 190 厘米，宽 48 厘米，与真马大小相似，原先置于墓前。作者运用富于浪漫色彩的艺术手法，雕刻出一人一马，概括了霍去病抗击匈奴的功绩。石马昂首站立，肌肉丰满，尾长拖地。马腹下面仰卧着匈奴，两颊长满胡须，面容狰狞，手持武器，垂死挣扎。民俗学家认为，这一造型的含义是以正压邪，驱除鬼怪。东汉以后 2000 年间，种种镇墓辟邪神兽大约都发源于此，只是逐步演变得越来越模式化、象征化乃至神秘化罢了。

跃马
马的后腿跪在地上，前腿跃起。采用线雕与形体配合的手法，动态表情强烈。

卧马
马的躯体健壮，姿势自然生动。马头稍偏向左肩，右前腿稍屈，双目注视前方，使人由此想到西汉骑兵的勃勃英姿。

伏虎
匠师选用不规则的呈波浪形起伏的天然石料，运用线体相扭的造型手法，把虎的凶猛巧妙地表现出来。我国古代墓前放置石虎，以霍去病墓为最早。

卧象
雕刻风格重于写实。象鼻搭在左前腿之外，身躯匍匐在地，刀法秀丽娴熟，造出象体平滑、性格温顺可爱的艺术效果。

石猪
石猪作伏状，双耳较小，眼睛呈三角形，头部雕琢得相当精细。从形态看，这可能是野猪，或古代一种未完全驯化的家猪。

石鱼
匠师以精选的石料稍行加工，使之粗具鱼身外形。头部线条简洁明快，雕出嘴和眼的轮廓，看上去犹如在水中时隐时现的游鱼。

人与熊搏斗
石人牙齿外露，头稍前倾，双肩耸起，肌肉紧张，左腿屈膝，右腿跪地，腰间系带，胸前双手抱熊欲食。熊也不示弱，张口与人对咬。这件作品以线雕为主，运用扭曲的线条，夸张的手法，栩栩如生地表现出人兽殊死搏斗的场面。

牯牛
壮实的牯牛跪在地上，似乎正在歇息反刍。作品厚重圆润，线条清晰，动作自然。

猛兽食羊

这件作品主要采用高浮雕手法。猛兽方头大口,身短腿长,两只前爪撕扭小羊,小羊拼命挣扎。由于匠师选用了风化程度较重的石料,表面粗糙起伏,艺术效果更加强烈。

石人

石人比真人大,其眼和眉毛向上竖起,有身子却无腿。左臂剩下一少半,缺手;右臂完整无缺。石人手置腹处,五指分开,手心向外。这件石雕基本保持了石料原来的形状,情感表现比较突出,犹如一幅生动的漫画作品。

除了这批石刻外,茂陵博物馆还陈列从茂陵附近出土的各种文物,有青玉铺首、画像砖、各种文字瓦当等。其中最引人注目的展品,是被誉为"国之瑰宝"的鎏金铜马。鎏金铜马高62厘米,长76厘米,马身通体鎏金,光亮耀目。它的造型匀称,比例准确,肌肉筋骨完全符合解剖构造。鎏金铜马马颈显得细长,肩部较窄,四肢细长,体长略等于体高,是沙漠型马种,适于乘骑。它的外形特征与中亚土库曼斯坦南部的阿哈马十分相似,而土库曼斯坦的费尔干纳盆地正是汉代时的大宛国。

汉武帝酷爱名马。他听说大宛出产良马,便费尽心机,派兵远征,终于得到了这种马,命名为"天马"。鎏金铜马是"天马"的准确模型,它的额际双耳间有特意铸出的"肉角",与史籍上"大宛马有肉角数寸"的记载恰好相符。

The Maoling Museum

The Maoling Museum was built in front of General Huo Qubing's tomb. On exhibition here are 16 large stone sculptures originally placed in front of the tomb and other valuable historical artifacts excavated from Maoling, the mausoleum of Emperor Wu Di of the Han Dynasty.

Large stone carvings started in the Qin Dynasty, but the earliest works left belongs to the Western Han Dynasty. The stone carvings in front of Huo Qubing's tomb are the most representative works, which are the earliest and world-famous masterpieces of ancient stone carvings preservd in groups under state protection.

In this group of large stone sculptures, there are the "Hun under horse hoofs", a galloping horse and a crouching ox. There are also other sculptures such as a tiger lying in wait, a crouching elephant, a wild man, a stone frog, and a stone fish, which were made with the technique of line carving and circular engraving. Some carvings were originally installed in front of the tomb, while most of them were placed on the tomb, resembling the Qilian Mountain. The stone carvings were made according to the natural shape of huge stones with the emphasis on the inner spirit. Only some key parts were engraved with care and precision so as to lay stress on the momentous manners and an romantic style of carving.

The Hun Under Horse Hoofs

As the main statue of this group of stone carvings, "the Hun under horse hoofs" is 168 centimeters high, 190 centimeters long, 48 centimeters wide, and almost life size. It was originally erected in front of the tomb. With the technique of romantic art, the artist carved out a man and a horse, highly indicating the brilliant military success of General Huo Qubing. The stone horse is muscular, holding its head high, with its tail down to the ground. A Hun soldier is lying facing up under its hoofs, whiskered, looking ferocious and struggling desperately with a weapon on hand. Folklorists believe that the intention of the molding is to keep the evil under control and to get rid of the ghost. During the 2,000 years after the Eastern Han Dynasty, all kinds of tomb guardians erected before or inside tombs to exorcise evil spirits probably originated here, and gradually developed into pattern-like, symbolic and mysterious forms.

The Galloping Horse

This is a galloping horse with its hind legs kneeling down, and its forelegs rising up. The technique of straight-line carving along with its shape is used to show a strong sense of movement.

The Crouching Horse

The horse is healthy and strong in natural and vivid posture. Its head inclines to the left side. The right foreleg is a little bent. The eyes are gazing forward, which reminds us of the brave and bright cavalrymen in the Western Han Dynasty.

The Tiger Lying in Wait

The sculptor selected a piece of natural stone with undulations and created a ferocious tiger by means of straight engraving. This is the first stone tiger placed in front of a tomb in ancient times.

The Crouching Elephant

The crouching elephant carving shows the realistic style. The trunk is hanging over its left foreleg, and the whole body is crawling. The consummate skill made this sculpture looks smooth, and created a docile and lovely elephant.

The Stone Pig

The pig has a squatting position, with small ears and triangular eyes. The head was engraved with great care and precision. According to its appearance, it is possibly a wild pig (boar), or a sort of domestic pig not completely tamed in ancient times.

The Stone Fish

The sculptor worked at the selected stone and made a rough shape of fish. The bold engraving lines on its head show the outlines of its mouth and eyes. It looks like a fish in water now visible, now invisible.

The Man Fighting a Bear

The stone man baring his teeth, leaning forward his head, shrugging his shoulders, tightening his muscles, bending his left leg, kneeling down on his right leg, wearing a waist belt, holding a bear to bite. The bear is not to be outdone. It opens its mouth to bite the man. This carving shows a life-and-death struggle between the man and the beast mainly through the straight line engraving aside from cursive lines in exaggeration.

The Stone Ox

The strong ox is kneeling down as if it is resting and ruminating. The style of the statue is thick and round, and the lines are clear. Also, it is life-like and natural.

The Beast Eating a Lamb

This is a high relief carving. The beast has square head, a big mouth, a short body and long legs. Its two forepaws are clawing the lamb that is struggling. The use of a kind of stone material which has a rough and undulating surface because of weathering produces strong artistic effect.

The Stone Figure

The stone figure is larger than a real man. His eyes and eyebrows stand upright, his body remains legless. Half of his left arm is gone, but the right one facing forward is complete with palms on the stomach. The stone carving basically keeps the original shape of the rock. It looks like a piece of vivid cartoon work, and its emotions are expressed conspicuously.

Besides these carved stones, various cultural relics unearthed around Maoling are also on display now, such as the green jade door-knocker, brick reliefs, and eave tiles with inscriptions. The most striking one on exhibition is the gilded bronze horse which is honored as "the treasure of the nation". The gilded bronze horse is 62 centimeters high, and 76 centimeters long. It is gilded all over and still lustrous today. The bronze horse is well-proportioned, and the carving of bones and muscles accords with dissection theories. The neck is long and thin. The shoulder is narrow. The legs are slim and are almost the same length as the height. Apparently the bronze horse is of desert-type which is fit for riding. Its shape is quite similar to the Aha horse of the Southern Turkmenistan in the Middle East. The Fergana Basin which is located in Turkmenistan is exactly the Dawan State of the Han Dynasty.

Emperor Wu Di of the Western Han Dynasty ardently loved fine horse. As he heard that Dawan was famous for its steeds, he racked his brains in scheming of sending expeditionary force to get such a horse and named it "Heaven Horse". The gilded bronze horse is a typical example of it. On its forehead between the two ears, there was a "flesh horn" carved intentionally which tallies with the description in historical books— "Dawan horse has an inch-long flesh horn".

昭陵博物馆

昭陵博物馆依唐代三朝元老李勣墓而建。

李勣原姓徐，名世勣，字懋恭。17岁时，他参加隋末瓦岗农民起义军，后来投降李渊，侍奉李渊、李世民、李治三代皇帝，在很多战役中建有大功，深得太宗赏识。在他生病时，唐太宗亲自为他剪须和煎药。

李勣死后，唐太宗为其起冢。他的墓冢由3个高约6丈的锥形土堆组成，土堆下部合在一起，上部形成倒"品"字形的3个山头，象征阴山、铁山和乌德鞬山，其意是为表彰他生前破突厥之战功。墓前有一通石碑，高5.6米，碑座为1.2米巨龟形，碑首雕刻6条龙。碑文由唐高宗李治亲自撰书。武则天称帝时，李勣的孙子徐敬业起兵讨伐武则天。李勣不但被剥夺官爵，他的坟墓也被挖开，棺材被劈碎。武则天死后，唐中宗为李勣追复官爵，并重新安葬。现在我们看到的就是昭雪平反后重新修复的李勣墓。墓前有石人1对，左侧石羊、右侧石虎各3对。

除李勣墓外，昭陵博物馆内还有2个碑石陈列室和出土文物、雕刻绘画展厅。除展出近年来从昭陵的10多座陪葬墓中发掘出土的文物外，主要陈列昭陵范围出土的各式唐代碑石与墓志铭。因为这些碑石独有的巨大书法艺术价值，这座博物馆又被称为"昭陵碑林"。

唐代盛行立碑之风。昭陵陪葬墓群的级别之高、数量之大，独一无二，留下大量第一流的墓碑。唐太宗和唐高宗都酷爱书法，在他们的倡导下，书法艺术日臻精美，昭陵及其众多陪葬墓前的每块墓碑都堪称书法艺术精品。这些碑石多数都是原刻，绝无后人剔刻或伪造。当时刻碑的方法是先磨平碑石，然后用朱笔将碑文直接写在石上，叫作"书丹"（现在刻碑，是将碑文写在纸上，让石工勾勒上石），所以笔锋清晰，毫不走样。昭陵碑刻早就享有盛誉，就荟萃初唐书法艺术精华而言，昭陵碑林堪称中国之最。

据宋代金石学家著录，昭陵碑石原有80多通。当时有人成套出售拓本，叫《昭陵全拓》。可惜这些碑石在过去没有得到认真保护，到1949年只剩下22通。近50多年来，结合考古发掘和文物普查，又陆续发现和发掘出土了许多墓碑和墓志，形成了今日昭陵碑林的规模。

第一陈列室

这里展出的20通墓碑，是享誉已久的"昭陵全碑"的绝大部分。这些碑石形体高大，雕刻精细，均为初唐著名书法家书写的名人墓碑。初唐盛行楷书，最著名的书法家有欧阳询、褚遂良、虞世南和薛稷，号称"初唐四大家"。在这里可以看到他们的典范佳作。例如，褚遂良所书的《房玄龄碑》书法秀逸柔婉，笔力丰满；欧阳询所书的《温彦博碑》字体疏朗，笔力遒劲，是欧阳询传世的最后一件作品。

美中不足的是，这个陈列室的碑石均有破损。这批艺术瑰宝在20世纪20年代曾遭严重破坏。当时军阀混战，碑石无人过问，一些不法书商勾结地方官吏，将碑石拓片出售，价格高达银子2000两。为了进一步抬高价格，他们拓片后把碑上关键的字，如时间、人名、地名砸毁，让后人再拓不出完整碑文。后来的拓碑者也如法炮制，以致有的碑石甚至被砸成几段。

第二陈列室

这里陈列的是近50多年新发现或出土的碑石和墓志铭。这些碑石不仅是研究我国书法艺术的宝贵实物资料，也是研究唐代历史的稀有文字资料。因为这些碑石和墓志的内容除对死者歌功颂德外，对其官品职务、重要功绩及立功年代也有较详细的记载，这些都与当时的政治、经济和军事等重大事件有着密切的联系。

为了便于了解昭陵陪葬墓前石刻制度的完整性，昭陵博物馆特意保留了李勣墓碑及其周围石刻的原状与位置。李勣墓碑由高宗亲自撰文书丹。高宗崇尚王羲之的书法，他的书体深得王羲之秀逸洒脱风格的精髓。墓碑高5.65米，重约15吨（不含龟座），屹立于博物馆的中心。

近几十年来，考古工作者陆续发掘了10余座昭陵陪葬墓。虽然它们早年曾被盗掘，仍从中出土了大量文物，包括壁画、镇墓兽、金银器、铜镜、陶俑等。

"三梁进德冠"是迄今发现的唯一唐代冠帽，它与一柄宝剑均出土于李勣墓，估计是唐中宗为他平反昭雪后重新埋入的。

出土文物中数量最多的是陶俑。这是一批最早的唐俑，人物形象逼真，造型姿态多样，色彩明快鲜艳。这种彩绘釉陶俑的制作工艺也很独特：它以瓷土作胎，焙烧成型后，施以铅釉，然后再经烧制便成釉俑。昭陵出土的这种彩绘釉陶俑造型美观，姿态多样，神情生动。多种多样的发型和服饰反映了当时的物质文明和丰富多彩的文化生活，如站立于马背，戴一顶圆顶高帽的男立俑等。还有头戴翻沿帽、敞胸襟、满脸络腮胡、深目高鼻的陶俑。很明显，这些都是西域人的形象。携带水葫芦及野鸡、野兔的骆驼，则表现商旅们在"丝绸之路"上长途跋涉的情景。彩绘釉陶俑仅流行于初唐，是这一时期特有的，为我们研究这一时期的文化艺术提供了很有价值的实物资料。

The Zhaoling Museum

The Zhaoling Museum is built on the site of the tomb of Li Ji, a minister to three emperors in the Tang Dynasty.

Li Ji was named Xu Shiji originally, aliased Maogong. He joined the Wagang Peasant Insurrection Army at the age of 17. Later he capitulated to Li Yuan, assisting emperors Li Yuan, Li Shimin and Li Zhi, in governing the country. He was so appreciated by Tai Zong for the great feats he had performed in numerous battles that when he was ill, Emperor Tai Zong even served him personally.

After Li Ji's death, Emperor Tai Zong had Li Ji's tomb built into about three 20-meter-high hillocks representing mountains of Mount Yin, Mount Tie and Mount Wudejian, the bottoms of which were joined together. And the three peaks form the shape of an inverted Chinese character "品" (pin), which is in praise of his achievements in defeating Tujue (a nomadic tribe then). The tomb stone is 5.6 meters high with a 1.2-meter-long large stone tortoise as its base and six dragons carved on the top. The inscription on the tablet was composed by Li Zhi (Gao Zong) himself. When Wu Zetian came into power, Xu Jingye, the grandson of Li Ji, raised a rebellion. Not only was Li Ji deprived of his aristocratic title, but also his tomb was uncovered and his coffin was cut into pieces. After Wu Zetian died, Emperor Zhong Zong resumed Li Ji's title and rebuilt his tomb. Now here is the tomb rebuilt after Li Ji had been rehabilitated, with a couple of stone figures on the facade, three couples of stone sheep on the left and three couples of stone tigers on the right.

Besides Li Ji's tomb, there are also two exhibition halls for stone tablets and an exhibition hall for unearthed relics, carvings and paintings in this museum. The objects on display are not only works of art, but also many styles of stone tablets and epitaphs of the Tang Dynasty unearthed around this area in recent years. These stone tablets have great value in the art of calligraphy. Therefore this museum is also called "Forest of Stone Tablets of Zhaoling".

It was fashionable to install stone tablets in front of tombs in the Tang Dynasty. Since the satellite tombs of Zhaoling are unique in rank and quantity, large number of tombstones here are all first-class. Owing to the fact that both Tai Zong and Gao Zong, two emperors of the Tang Dynasty, were fond of calligraphy, the calligraphic art was becoming better and approaching perfection day by day. Every tombstone here is the superb work of calligraphy, for most of the stone were original and they were not copied or imitated by later generations. The way of inscribing the tablet called "Shu Dan" at that time is: grinding the stone flat first, then writing the article in red directly on the flat stone. (Now the way of inscribing is to write the article on the paper and sketch it by the stonemason on the stone.) So the strokes are very clear without losing shape at all. The stone tablets of Zhaoling are first class and have been well known ever since ancient times, for its assemblance of the cream of the calligraphy in the early Tang Dynasty.

It was recorded in the work of the epigrapher in the Song Dynasty that there were over 80 tablets around Zhaoling. A set of books of rubbings named *The Rubbings of Zhaoling* was for sale at that time. But it was a pity that the tablets did not get careful protection, so there were only 22 tablets left by 1949. Over the past 50 years, with the efforts of the archaeologists and the general survey of the antiques, many tomb stones and epitapgs have been found and unearthed, forming the present scale of the Forest of Stone Tablets of Zhaoling.

Exhibition Room I

Over 20 tablets on display here are the best part of the well-known Stone Tablets of Zhaoling. They are all large tombstones of the famous people with delicate engravings written by the famous calligraphers in the early Tang Dynasty. The regular script was fashionable at that time. The most famous calligraphers such as Ouyang Xun, Chu Suiliang, Yu Shinan and Xue Ji were called "the four master calligraphers in the early Tang Dynasty". Here we can appreciate their standard works of calligraphy. For instance, *The Tablet Inscriptions for Fang Xuanling* were written by Chu Suiliang with elegant and plump strokes. And *The Tablet for Wen Yanbo* was written by Ouyang Xun with vigorous strokes, which is also the last manuscript Ouyang Xun left for the world.

The blemish of this great work is that all the tablets in this hall were more or less damaged. These treasures of art suffered severe damages in the 1920s. The wars broke out among the warlords and nobody cared about the tablets at all. Some illegal booksellers, colluding with the local officials, sold the rubbings of these tablets at the price as high as 2,000 taels of silver. In order to get more profit from it, they even destroyed the key words after they got the rubbings, such as the time, the name of people or the places, which made it impossible to rub the complete articles any more. The criminals later followed suit so that some of the tablets were even broken into pieces.

Exhibition Room II

These tablets and epitaphs on display were newly unearthed in the recent 50 years. They are valuable textual materials for the further research of the system of the Tang Dynasty, because these inscriptions not only offered detailed records about the ranks, positions, important contributions of the buried and the years of their outstanding service, but also eulogized their virtues and achievements. These records were closely related to the significant events at the time, such as political, economic and military affairs.

In order to help people know about the intactness of the system of the stone carvings in front of the satellite tombs in Zhaoling, the Zhaoling Museum intentionally retains the original site and locations of Li Ji's tombstone and the stone carvings around it. Li Ji's tombstone was written by Emperor Gao Zong personally. Cao Zong appreciated Wang Xizhi's calligraphy very much, and his style was deeply affected by Wang's elegant, free and easy style. The tombstone, 5.65 meters in height and 15 tons in weight excluding the tortoise pedestal, stands in the centre of the museum.

Over the last scores of years, dozens of satellite tombs have been excavated one after another around the Zhaoling Mausoleum. Although some of them were robbed in early years, a large number of works of art were still unearthed from them, including murals, tomb guardians, gold and silver wares, bronze mirrors, pottery figures and so on.

"San Liang Jin De crown" was the only Tang crown discovered so far in China. Both this crown and a sword were unearthed from Li Ji's tomb. It is said that this was reburied after Emperor Zhong Zong redressed and rehabilitated him.

Among the unearthed works of art, pottery figures are the largest in quantity. These were the earliest of Tang figures, which look life-like with a variety of postures, bright and sprightly colored. And the way of manufacturing of these painted and glazed pottery figures is very special. In the process of making them, the first step is to make the molds out of porcelain clay. After the molds of the desired shapes are fired and glazed, they need to be fired with beautiful shapes and various postures again until they turn into glazed figures. The glazed pottery figures with beautiful shapes and various postures unearthed in Zhaoling look happy and gay. The different kinds of hair styles, dresses and adornments reflect the material civilization and the rich and colorful cultural life at that time, for instance, the standing male pottery figures on horsebacks, wearing a bowler hat, etc. Besides, there are also pottery figures with heavy beards, big noses, and sunken eyes. They wear bowler hats and unbuttoned clothes. Obviously, they are the images of the ethnic minorities in the western frontier. Yet the camels carrying water calabashes, pheasants and hares depict the scene of merchants trudging over a long distance on the Silk Road. The painted and glazed pottery figures were fashionable only in the early Tang, and were the peculiar products of this period as well. They offer valuable information for the study of the culture and art of this period.

乾陵博物馆

依永泰公主墓而建的乾陵博物馆内收藏着从乾陵陪葬墓内，主要是从永泰公主、章怀太子、懿德太子墓内出土的众多文物。这三座墓在五代至北宋时虽已被盗掘，但仍遗留大量陶瓷器皿、唐三彩、陶俑及墓志铭等随葬器物。

唐三彩是唐代一种带多种色彩釉的陶器，以驳杂斑斓的釉彩、鲜丽明亮的光泽、优美的造型为特点，有黄、绿、白、蓝、赭等多种基本釉色。"三彩"的意思是多彩，并不专指三种颜色，因在唐代风行一时而得名。它的制作过程是把高岭土经挑选、淘洗、沉淀、捏练等工艺后，捏制成型，经修饰、晒干后，放入窑内，经过1000℃左右焙烧，待冷却后，挂以配制好的彩料釉汁，再放入窑焙烧至900℃完成。

乾陵陪葬墓中出土的唐三彩，有各式三彩俑、三彩马、骆驼、三彩生活器皿等。三彩马中，形体最大的要数章怀太子墓出土的一匹马，高72厘米，长80厘米。各种三彩俑的姿势各不相同，造型十分生动。其中有几十个铠甲骑马俑，是文物中罕见的珍品。

懿德太子墓内出土的11片玉质哀册是乾陵博物馆内独有的珍品。哀册是帝王陵墓中放置的记述其生平功绩的祭颂文书。根据史书记载，隋代以前，陵墓均用竹册，唐代改用玉册。这11片玉质哀册是陵墓被盗后残存散落的。

博物馆内展出的还有各种陶俑、动物俑、玉器、金器、镇墓兽等，制作精美，造型生动，各具特色。

The Qianling Museum

The Qianling Museum, in the vicinity of the tomb of Princess Yong Tai, has a collection of numerous cultural relics unearthed from the satellite tombs at Qianling, mainly from the tomb of Princess Yong Tai, the tomb of Prince Zhang Huai and the tomb of Prince Yi De. Although the three tombs were once robbed from the Five dynasty to the Northern Song, lots of burial objects, such as porcelain vessels, tri-colored glazed pottery, pottery figures and epitaphs still remained inside.

Tri-colored glazed pottery of the Tang Dynasty is a kind of pottery with multi-color glaze characterized by the heterogeneous glaze, the sheen, and the delicate and exquisite designs. The main elementary glaze is yellow, green, white, blue and reddish brown, etc. "Tri-color" does not mean only three colors, but many colors instead. It was called "tri-colored glazed pottery of the Tang Dynasty", just because it was popularized during the Tang Dynasty. The manufacturing process of tri-colored glazed pottery involves the following steps: choosing china clay first, then pounding, washing, sedimenting and molding. After being made into different shapes, the molds then are decorated and dried in the sun. Next they are put in the kilns to be baked at a temperature of 1000℃. When they are cool, the ready-mixed colored glaze is applied. After all this is done, they are put again into the kilns to be fired at a temperature of 900℃.

The tri-colored glazed pottery of the Tang Dynasty, unearthed from the Qianling satellite tombs, contains all kinds of tri-colored figures, horses, camels and household utensils. Among the tri-colored horses, the biggest one, unearthed from the tomb of Prince Zhang Huai, is 72 centimeters high and 80 centimeters long. The various pottery figurines have different postures and look vivid and life-like. Some of the objects are rare antique treasures, such as dozens of armored pottery cavalrymen.

The 11 pieces of jade funeral documents, unearthed from the tomb of Prince Yi De, are unique treasures in the Qianling Museum. Funeral documents were accounts about the emperors' achievements. They were placed inside the tomb to praise the emperors. According to historical records before the Sui Dynasty, all the funeral documents were made of bamboo, then made of jade for a change in the Tang Dynasty. The 11 pieces of jade funeral documents were left after the tomb was robbed.

On exhibition in the museum are various kinds of pottery figures, pottery animals, jade and gold wares and tomb guardians. They are made with exquisite workmanship. Each looks vivid with its own features.

第四部分　古陵墓

黄帝陵

黄帝陵是中华民族始祖轩辕黄帝的陵园，位于黄陵县城北的桥山顶上。

黄帝是我国原始社会末期一位伟大的部落首领，是开创中华民族文明的祖先。他用玉作兵器，造舟车弓矢。其妻嫘祖能养蚕，其史官仓颉创造了文字，其臣大桡创造了干支历法，其乐官伶伦制作了乐器。我国后来能巍然屹立于世界四大文明古国之列，与黄帝的赫赫功勋是分不开的。

黄帝还以他惩罚邪恶、首次统一中华民族的伟绩而载入史册。原始社会末期，中华民族生活在以黄河流域为中心的广大地区：中部是炎帝领导的羌族居住区，东部是太皞领导的夷族居住区，南部是蚩尤领导的蛮族居住区，而西部和北部有羌族、狄族和戎族。黄帝族原先居住在西北方，后来在西北和中部一带游牧。蚩尤曾率领蛮族攻打炎帝，企图夺取中部地区，炎帝在一次与蚩尤的战争中失败，向黄帝求援，黄帝联合炎帝打败了蚩尤。后来，黄帝经过52次战争统一了中国。

据说黄帝活了118岁。有一次，在他出巡河南期间，突然晴天一声霹雳，一条黄龙自天而降。它对黄帝说："你的使命已经完成，请你和我一起归天吧。"黄帝自知天命难违，便跨上了龙背。当黄龙飞越陕西桥山时，黄帝请求下降安抚臣民。黎民百姓闻讯从四面八方赶来，个个痛哭流涕。在黄龙的再三催促下，黄帝又跨上了龙背，人们拽住黄帝的衣襟一再挽留。黄龙带走了黄帝，只剩下了黄帝的衣冠。人们把黄帝的衣冠葬于桥山，起冢为陵。这就是传说中的黄帝陵的由来。但是许多人说，黄帝死后就安葬在桥山。

黄帝陵区约四平方公里，山水环抱，林木葱郁。据统计，山上有千年古柏六万余株。山顶有一通石碑，上刻"文武百官到此下马"几个大字。据说，古代祭祀者都在此下马，步行到主陵前。陵前有一座祭亭，亭中央立一通高大石碑，碑上刻有郭沫若题的"黄帝陵"三个大字。祭亭后面又有一通石碑，上书"桥山龙驭"四字，再后面便是黄帝陵。

黄帝陵位于山顶正中，面向南，陵高约4米，周长约50米，陵前40米处有一个约20米的高台，旁边一石碑上书有"汉武仙台"四个大字。此台系公元前110年汉武帝刘彻巡游归来，祭奠黄帝，祈仙求神时所筑。从此，在清明节祭奠黄帝陵成为历朝大典，留下了许多朝代的御制祭文。建国前，国民党要员于右任、蒋鼎文、程潜等都祭扫过黄帝陵。中共中央在延安时期，也多次派代表祭奠黄帝陵。1937年清明节，毛泽东主席和朱德总司令派遣林伯渠赴黄陵主祭。

黄陵下的轩辕庙里面尚有一些建筑、古柏和石碑等文物。跨进庙门，左边有一颗巨大的柏树。树高19米，树干下围10米，中围6米，俗语称它"七搂八扎半，疙里疙瘩不上算"。一些外国学者称它为"世界柏树之父"。相传，这棵柏树为黄帝亲手所植，故称"黄帝手植柏"，距今已有4000多年的历史了。

庙门北边有一过厅和一碑亭，碑亭里陈放着47通石碑。最北边坐落着大殿，大殿前还有一株高大的古柏，叫"挂甲柏"。树皮斑痕密布，纵横成行，似乎有挂甲痕迹。树干上遍布洞孔，似乎有断钉在内；而柏液不断地从孔中溢出，实为群柏之奇。据传，这是汉武帝挂金甲时所留下的。

大殿雄伟壮丽，门额上悬挂有"人文初祖"四字大匾。大殿中间有富丽堂皇的黄帝牌位。

黄帝陵被国务院公布为全国重点文物保护单位。

PART FOUR ANCIENT TOMBS

The Mausoleum of Yellow Emperor

The mausoleum of Yellow Emperor, Xuanyuan, founder of the Chinese nation, stands at the top of Mount Qiao, north of Huangling County.

Yellow Emperor was a great tribal chief at the end of primitive time in China. He was honoured as the ancestor who had initiated Chinese civilization. He invented jade weapons, carts, boats, bows and arrows. Lei Zu, his wife, was good at raising silkworm; Cang Jie, his imperial historian, created the Chinese pictograph; Da Rao, one of his officials, worked out the first "Heavenly Stem and Earthly Branch Calendar";

Ling Lun, his official composer, developed musical instruments. All of these brilliant achievements put forth by Yellow Emperor are attributable to the later success of China as one of the world's four countries with an ancient civilization.

Yellow Emperor's exploits went down in history also because he had punished the evil and the wicked, and unified the Chinese nation for the first time. In that historical age, the Chinese people labored, lived and multiplied on the vast land around the Yellow River valley. Emperor Yan and his people of the Qiang tribe inhabited the middle; Tai Gao and his Yi tribe lived in the east; Chi You and his Man tribe lived in the south, and Qiang, Di and Rong tribes lived in the north and west. Yellow Emperor and his tribe led a nomadic life then, in the northwest. Later they migrated to the middle. In a battle launched by the Man tribe led by Chi You, whose aim was to seize the middle area, Emperor Yan was defeated and turned to Yellow Emperor for help. The combined forces defeated Chi You. At last, Yellow Emperor unified these tribes and became the first unifier of the Chinese nation after 52 battles.

Yellow Emperor was said to have lived to be 118. One day on an inspection tour to Henan, Yellow Emperor heard a sudden crack of thunder from the sky, and a yellow dragon descended in front of him. The dragon said to him: "You have accomplished your mission. Now, please return to Heaven with me." The emperor knew he was not in a position to run counter to Heaven's will and could do nothing but mount the dragon and go with it. When flying over Mount Qiaoshan of Shaanxi, the emperor asked the dragon to land so that he could appease his subjects. At the news, the people hurried over and wept bitterly. Having been urged by the yellow dragon, Yellow Emperor again mounted it. But the people got tight hold of his clothes, trying to make him stay. However, the yellow dragon took him away. All that had left was his hat and his clothes, which they buried on Mount Qiaoshan in a tomb. That is how the legend goes, yet many people believe that Mount Qiaoshan is exactly where the great man's final resting place.

The burial ground is about 4 square kilometers. It is surrounded by mountains and rivers, and is covered with lush forest. According to statistics, there are over 60,000 one-thousand-year-old cypresses there. Anyone who reaches the top will pass a stone tablet with the inscription: "Both civil officials and military officers must demount here." It is said that in the ancient times, those who came to pay homage would walk from this spot up to the tomb. In front of the tomb there is a memorial pavilion with a huge stone tablet, on which Guo Moruo's calligraphy was carved. It reads "Mausoleum of Yellow Emperor". Behind the pavilion, there is another tablet with four characters "Qiaoshan Long Yu" (Mount Qiaoshan Dragon Carriage).

A little farther up stands the Mausoleum of Yellow Emperor facing south, right in the middle of the mountain top, which is 4 meters high and 50 meters in circumference. About 40 meters in front of the tomb is a 20 meters high platform with a stone tablet on one side, which says "Han Wu Xian Tai" (Han Emperor Wu Di's Praying Platform). It is said to have been built in 110 BC for Emperor Wu Di of the Han Dynasty to pay homage to Yellow Emperor, and to pray for good luck on his way back from an inspection tour. Since then, it has been a state ceremony to pay homage to the Mausoleum on Qingming Festival of each year. Many eulogies to Yellow Emperor by emperors of later dynasties have been passed down through the ages. Before 1949, some famous senior statesmen of the Nationalist Party, such as Yu Youren, Jiang Dingwen and Cheng Qian visited here. The Chinese Communist Party Central Committee sent its representatives here to honor this great man when it was in Yan'an. On the Qingming Festival of 1937, Lin Boqu, entrusted by Mao Zedong and Zhu De, came to officiate at the ceremony.

At the foot of the mountain stands a temple known as the Xuanyuan Temple, where there are still some structures, ancient cypresses and stone tablets. The first thing that strikes one's eye upon entering the gate is a huge cypress, 19 meters tall, 10 meters in circumference at the bottom, and 6 meters in circumference in the middle. It would take more than seven people to encircle the tree with outstretched arms. Some foreign scholars call it "father of world cypress". Legend goes that it was planted by Yellow Emperor himself, and it could be over 4,000 years old.

To the north of the gate, there is a hall and a pavilion with 47 stone tablets on display. In front of the main hall of the temple stands another tall tree, known as the Cypress for Hanging Armor. It is covered with scars in regular patterns on its bark, seemingly, marked by armor. and holes can be found in the trunk, with broken nails inside. Cypress rosin flows out constantly from these holes, making this cypress unique among all the cypresses in the temple. According to legend, Emperor Wu Di left all these marks when hanging his armor on it.

Above the door of the magnificent main hall is a large plaque with four Chinese characters inscribed on it: "人文初祖" (Founder of the Human Civilization). Inside the hall is a gorgeous shrine for Yellow Emperor.

The Mausoleum of Yellow Emperor is now an important National Historical Monument in China.

秦始皇陵

秦始皇（公元前259年—公元前210年）姓嬴名政，13岁继承王位，22岁亲临朝政，公元前221年39岁时兼并六国，建立了中国历史上第一个封建王朝。

公元前221年，嬴政统一六国后，号称皇帝。他自称始皇帝，是希望他的子孙将依次称为"二世""三世"……以便秦王朝能世代相传。从此以后，中国历代统治者便都沿用"皇帝"这个称号。

秦始皇兼并六国后，即废除分封制，实行郡县制，并采取一系列措施统一了货币、度量衡、法律、车轨和文字。以前，每个国家都有自己的货币、度量衡、法律、车轨和文字等，相互间的交流和商业贸易十分不便。因此中国统一后，采取这些措施十分必要。为了抵御匈奴贵族的侵扰，秦始皇下令原有的七国长城应该连在一起，并在此基础上修筑了万里长城。所有这些措施对于消除分裂割据、巩固国家统一、促进经济和文化的发展都起了积极的作用，对2000多年的中国封建社会产生了重大影响。

为了加强对人民的思想控制，秦始皇下令，除了秦国史书、农业、卜算及医药等书籍外，所有诸子百家的书籍一律烧毁，他还下令一次坑杀了460个儒生，使中国的文化典籍遭到灭顶之灾。

中国统一后，秦始皇认为他功德无量，即使中国历史传说中的"三皇五帝"也无法与他相比，因此，他更加雄心勃勃。为了自己享乐，他征调了几十万刑徒修筑阿房宫，从秦都咸阳到骊山脚下，阿房宫绵延50公里。他住在阿房宫里寻欢作乐，通常除了几个侍从外谁也不知他的确切居处。秦末，阿房宫被一把火烧成灰烬，据说大火烧了三个月。可以想象，阿房宫有多么宏伟和壮观！

秦始皇继承皇位后，立即为自己修筑陵墓。公元前221年，他统一六国后，立即从全国各地征调70余万刑徒加紧修造陵墓，前后历时37年才告完工。

秦始皇陵位于骊山脚下，位于西安以东35公里处。陵园原来有内、外两重城墙。陵原高120米，由于2000多年的风雨剥蚀和人为破坏，现高46米。

据司马迁的《史记》记载：秦始皇棺木以铜铸成；始皇陵地宫里布满了宫

殿及楼台亭阁的模型，藏满了各种奇珍异宝；为了防止陵墓被盗，还安装了能自动发射的暗箭；工匠们还用水银做出能够流动的江河湖海如黄河、长江等以象征大地；墓顶用珍珠宝石制作出日月星辰以象征天体；用鲸鱼膏点的灯可以长明不灭。

秦始皇死后，秦二世继承皇位，下令凡是他父亲的没有生儿育女的妃子应该全部随他父亲而去。这些妃子被殉葬后，一个大臣建议，那些布置陵墓暗道机关的工匠知道太多秘密，于是，当秦始皇在墓室被安葬好，那些奇珍异宝被封好后，墓门立即被封闭，里面的工匠一个也没逃出。然后在陵墓封土上种植草木，以使它看起来像一座自然形成的小山。

司马迁这位伟大的历史学家对秦始皇陵的描述已经被考古发掘所证实，考古探测证明，秦始皇陵地宫基本完好。

秦始皇陵的文物极为丰富，除现已发掘出的兵马俑及彩绘铜车马外，陵墓周围到处堆积着秦砖、秦瓦，不但数量多，而且形式多样。1982年以来，经有关专家测定，发现秦始皇陵有强烈的汞活动，因而说明《史记》中"以水银为百川江河大海"的记载是正确的。《史记》关于秦始皇陵其他方面的记载也是可信的。同时，经考察发现，秦始皇陵地宫未曾被盗。随着科学技术的发展，特别是考古技术的进步，秦始皇陵地宫宝库必将重见天日。届时，一定会在世界考古界引起巨大的轰动。

The Mausoleum of the First Qin Emperor

The First Qin Emperor (259BC—210 BC), otherwise known as Emperor Ying Zheng, came to the throne of the Qin State at 13, and seized the helm of the state at 22. By 221 BC, when he was only 39 years old, he had annexed the six rival principalities and established the first feudal empire in Chinese history.

In the year 221 BC, after he unified the whole country, Ying Zheng styled himself the First Emperor, in the hope that the throne would be passed down to his descendants from one generation to another and that the hereditary system would be kept for ever. In fact, it was solely a myth. Each of the supreme rulers in later dynasties also called himself the Emperor.

After he annexed the other six principalities, the First Qin Emperor abolished the enfeoffment system, and adopted the prefecture and county system instead. Dramatic steps were taken by his order to standardize the coinage, weights and measures, the legal codes, the axle length of carts, and the written scripts. It was possibly because each of the seven states had a different system before the unification campaign, which would cause much inconvenience to the whole populace. In an endeavor to deal with the harassment by the Hun aristocrats, he ordered that the sections of the original defencing wall should be linked together, and on this basis, the Creat wall was built. All these measures played an important role in strengthening the unification of the whole country and promoting the cultural and economic development. They exerted an everlasting influence upon the 2,000-year-long feudal history of China.

In order to impose rigid stereotypes on the minds of his people, the First Qin Emperor ordered that all books of various schools should be burned except those on agriculture, divination, medicine and the Qin's history. Moreover, he also ordered that 460 Confucian scholars be buried alive. As a result, almost all of the classics were destroyed.

After the unification of China, the First Qin Emperor believed that his contributions to the State were beyond comparing, and he was even greater than the legendary Three Sovereigns and Five Emperors. Out of this belief, he became more arrogant and ambitious than ever. For the sake of his own pleasure, he had hundreds of thousands of conscripts built E'pang Palace, which extended 50 kilometers from Xianyang (the capital) to Mount Li. He confined himself to the palace and sought pleasure anywhere. Often, his whereabouts was unknown to all but a few of his attendants. Unfortunately, the palace was put on fire by the insurrection army at the end of the Qin Dynasty. The big fire lasted for three months. We can well imagine how grand and magnificent his palace must have been.

As soon as he ascended the throne, Ying Zheng ordered that a magnificent mausoleum should be built for him. After he seized the power of the Qin in 221 BC, more than 700,000 conscripts were gathered from all parts of the country to work on his mausoleum. In fact, it took 37 years to complete the project.

The Mausoleum of the First Qin Emperor is located at the foot of Mount Li, about 35 kilometers east of Xi'an. It used to be surrounded by an inner wall and an outer one. It was originally 120 meters tall. But over 2,000 years of erosion by wind and rain plus human destruction has reduced it to a height of 46 meters.

In *The Records of the Historian*, Sima Qian recorded, "The outer coffin was cast in molten copper, and the burial chamber was complete with palaces, halls and towers. Fine utensils, precious stones and other rarities were everywhere. Automatic crossbows were fixed to protect the tomb from robbery. The mercury lakes and waterways were built to represent the Huanghe River, the Changjiang River and even the vast ocean. The ceiling was decorated with pearls and gems to symbolize the celestial body, including the Sun and the Moon. The entire underground palace was presumably brightly lit by whale oil lamps for ever."

When he died, his son, the Second Qin Emperor, decreed that his father's concubines without children should follow him to the grave. After they were duly buried, there was a suggestion that the artisans responsible for the safety devices knew too much about the contents of the tomb. Therefore, once the coffin was placed in the burial chamber and the burial objects were all sealed up, the gate was closed to imprison all those who had worked inside the tomb. Later, trees and grass were planted all over the mausoleum so that it would look like a natural hill.

According to the archaeological excavation, Sima Qian's description is undoubtedly true, and the underground palace is still intact.

The Mausoleum of the First Qin Emperor is rich in cultural artifacts. Besides the terracotta army and the painted bronze chariots and horses, there are numerous Qin bricks and tiles of every description around the mausoleum. Experts have confirmed ever since 1982 that there is an intense mercury activity inside the mausoleum. We can therefore conclude that, what is described as "rivers and seas of mercury" in *The Records of the Historian* is reliable and true. According to the archaeological survey, the burial chamber has not been plundered or even broken into. With advances in technology, especially archaeological technology, all the treasures under ground will be exposed to the world. It will unarguably create a sensation in the field of archaeology all over the world.

汉阳陵

汉阳陵坐落于古咸阳塬之上，西临秦都旧址，东边是"泾渭分明"的自然景观，汉阳陵是西汉第四代皇帝汉景帝与王皇后的同茔异穴合葬墓。整个陵园南北对称，布局规整，以帝陵为中心四周由从葬坑、陪葬墓、刑徒墓地等环绕，彰显了汉代森严的等级观念以及皇家唯我独尊的观念。据考古发掘显示，汉阳陵所出土的文物达五万余件，件件都堪称世界级文物精品。

汉景帝刘启与其父文帝共同开创了中国历史上闻名于世的"文景之治",为汉武大帝独霸一方的局面奠定了坚实的基础。汉景帝在位期间,受其母窦太后的影响,坚持秉承"无为而治"的黄老哲学思想,与民休息、从谏如流、减轻赋税,以薄葬代替流行一时的厚葬之风,使得西汉政治稳定、经济繁荣,开创了汉代历史的辉煌。

经考古勘探证实,阳陵陵园内大小不一的外藏坑有190多个,其中81个为最高级别。位于汉阳陵帝陵外藏坑的展示厅建筑面积约为7800平方米,总投资为一亿元,通道由悬空型的玻璃所铺就,游客们置身其中便可真实地领略到脚下之地的神圣意义,想象两千多年前文景盛世的恢宏与豪迈。依据阳陵从葬坑的考古结果显示,事死如事生的观念在汉代已经根深蒂固,所发掘的文物有大量的人物陶俑、生活用具、粮仓、动物陶俑、兵器、车马列队等,反映了汉代帝王江山永固的思想,在来世继续实现其生前为国之君主的显赫地位。在这些制作精细、千人千面的男女陶俑中,有武士俑、侍女俑、宦官俑等,他们个个意气风发,象征着西汉王朝所推行的"九卿"制度。动物陶俑那栩栩如生的设计,包括猪、牛、羊、马、狗、鸡等,可谓六畜皆备,为宫室庆典之日所用,也象征着帝王在来世也能过上衣食无忧、锦衣玉食的帝王生活。此外,汉阳陵陪葬墓布局规整,排列有序,分为嫔妃墓冢和家族墓园,呈棋盘状分布,其中清理的古墓有300多座,出土文物可达5000多件,具有重要的研究价值。

在位于帝陵西北方向1500米处,有一处刑徒墓地,那里排列无序,葬式不一,死者或尸骨不全,或身首异处,除铁刑具外无任何随葬之物。从该墓地的发掘情况推断,汉景帝阳陵的修建与当时推行的刑徒制度密不可分,繁重的陵墓修建任务使得刑徒负重不堪,或被鞭打惩罚致死,或忍饥挨饿而死,刑徒们付出了鲜血和生命为当权者修建了一个通往天堂的"极乐世界"。

The Yangling Mausoleum in the Han Dynasty

The Yangling Mausoleum is located on the ancient Xianyang tableland, close to the former site of the capital of the Qin Dynasty in the west and adjacent to the natural landscape between Jinghe River and Weihe River in the east. It is a joint tomb of the fourth emperor of the Western Han Dynasty, Emperor Jing and Empress Wang, buried in the same grave but in different chambers. Its layout is regularly distributed and symmetrical formed on a south-north axis. It is centered round the mausoleum of and surrounded by burial pits, lesser tombs, and criminals' graves. Such a layout shows the rigid hierarchy and the royal concept of supremacy of monarchy. According to archaeological excavations, more than 50,000 pieces of relics have been unearthed in the Yangling Mausoleum, each of which is treasured as a world-class historic essence.

Emperor Jing named Liu Qi and Emperor Wen (Liu Qi's father) jointly initiated the world-famous golden era of Western Han Dynasty, known as "the Reign of Emperor Wen and Jing", which laid a solid foundation for Emperor Wu's succesful reign over China, especial the northwestern part. When he was on the throne, Emperor Jing, influenced by his mother Empress Dou, adhered to the Taoist philosophy of "natural governance" and created a peaceful and prosperous amenity atmosphere for the rank and file to live in. He realized this through following people's advice, reducing taxes and substituting the then popular lavish burial for the simple burial, thus achieving a political stability, economic prosperity and a historical glory in the Western Han Dynasty.

Archaeological prospection has proven that there are more than 190 external pits of various sizes in the Yangling Mausoleum, 81 of which are of highest class. Nowadays, the exhibition hall, located outside the Yangling Mausoleum, has a construction area of about 7800 square meters with a total investment of 100 million yuan. The passageway is so paved with suspended glass that tourists can truly appreciate the significance of the sacred place where they are treading on it, and recall the grandeur of the Western Han Dynasty 2,000 years ago. According to the archaeological findings in the burial pits, the concept of "one's afterlife must be the same as he lived when alive" is deeply rooted in the philosophy of the Western Han Dynasty. So there is a large number of unearthed relics such as pottery figurines, daily-life utensils, granaries, animal figurines, weaponry, chariots and horses etc., which reflect the thought of everlasting state power in the Western Han Dynasty and it was hoped that they will continue to inherit such a prominent position as the monarch of the country in the afterlife. All these exquisite pottery figures different from one another are vigorous and graceful, including warrior figures, maid figures and eunuch figures, all of which symbolize "the Nine-Rank system" implemented by the royal court. The lifelike design of the animal terracotta figures, including pigs, cattle, sheep, horses, dogs, chickens, known as six domestic animals, prepared for the celebration in the imperial court, symbolizes a luxurious royal life for the emperor to live in the afterlife without worries about food and clothing. In addition, the layout of the burial tombs is arranged in an orderly manner. The pits, divided into concubines' tombs and family cemeteries, are arranged in a checkerboard pattern. More than 300 tombs of them have been cleared with over 5,000 relics unearthed, which are of great research value.

Located about 1,500 meters northwest of the mausoleum, there is a graveyard specially built for guillotined, which is disorderly arranged in different burial manners. It is discovered that there are lots of corpses and skeletons either incomplete or beheaded lawbreakers, with nothing but some iron torturing tools as the burial objects. It can be inferred that the construction of the Yangling Mausoleum was closely linked to the enforcement of the criminal system at that time. The tedious construction work of the mausoleum exhausted and tormented these criminals, who worked like a beast of burden and suffered from either being whipped or being starved to death. It is those criminals who bled and sacrificed their lives for the sake of constructing a blissful world for the rulers—Sukhavati that leads to Heaven.

茂陵

汉武帝茂陵位于兴平市东南约9公里处，距西安40公里。西汉时，茂陵地属槐里县茂乡，故称汉武帝陵为茂陵。

汉武帝（公元前141—前87年）是西汉第五代皇帝。名刘彻，7岁时被立为太子，16岁继承帝位，在位54年，是我国历史上在位时间最长的皇帝之一。人们常常把秦皇汉武相提并论，这是因为，封建专制主义的中央集权制国家是由秦始皇建立的，然而真正完全巩固下来，是由汉武帝完成的。

为了把权力集中在封建朝廷，汉武帝利用种种借口剥夺各个诸侯国的爵位。如公元前112年，他以诸侯奉献祭祀祖宗的黄金成色或分量不足为借口，一次废除了106人的爵位。武帝以前，朝廷大臣为功臣及其子弟，一般官吏也多出于豪门权势之家。而汉武帝却不拘一格选拔人才，他设立了"太学"，以培养和选拔官吏，从而大大加强了封建专制主义的中央集权制度。

为了把财经大权集中在朝廷，汉武帝禁止民间以及地方政府铸钱，只准中央政府铸造的五铢钱通行；禁止民间冶铁煮盐，对盐铁实行官营专卖；同时对工商业者征收财产税，使朝廷收入大大增加。

中央集权的加强，封建经济的繁荣，使西汉王朝国力富足，空前强大。于是汉武帝发动了三次重大战役，打败了北部边境的强敌匈奴。他还多次派人打通西域，著名的"丝绸之路"便是在汉武帝时期开辟的。

汉武帝不仅是一位具有雄才大略的政治家和军事家，而且很喜欢诗歌和音乐。他设立了一个叫作"乐府"的机构，专门负责搜集民间诗歌和配乐谱曲，训练乐工。因此，汉代的许多民歌才得以保存到今天。乐府诗对后世影响极大，唐代大诗人李白、杜甫、白居易都曾模仿乐府诗歌，并加以继承和发扬。

为了巩固封建统治，进一步实行学术思想上的统一，汉武帝接受了儒家大师董仲舒的"罢黜百家，独尊儒术"的建议，从而结束了战国以来百家争鸣的局面。儒家思想逐步发展为我国封建社会的正统理论，且影响久远。

汉武帝的雄才大略使汉帝国达到了强盛的顶点，中国封建社会在政治、经济、军事、文化等方面都有了较大的发展，我国开始以一个高度文明和富强的国家而闻名于世。

汉武帝死后葬于茂陵，享年71岁。该陵全部用夯土筑成，形如覆斗，高46米，陵墓边长240米。陵园周围有夯筑城垣遗迹，平面呈方形，每边长400米，墙基宽5.8米。现在，东、西、北三面城垣仍有阙楼遗迹存在。

茂陵是西汉诸陵中规模最大、修建时间最长、随葬品最丰富的陵墓。汉武帝在位54年，仅茂陵就修了53年。到他寿终正寝时，陵上的树木已长得可合抱了。茂陵墓室里究竟藏了多少金银珠宝，谁也无从知道。但据史书记载，每年国家赋税的1/3都用于修筑茂陵和购置随葬品。据说，还在汉武帝生前，墓里的随葬品已经多得几乎装不下了。因此自东汉以后，茂陵就成了盗劫的对象。

一提到陵墓，不免使人有一种阴森恐怖的感觉。然而汉朝时的茂陵可不是这样。当时陵园周围建有许多达官贵人的住宅，陵园内有许多殿堂和房屋，住着众多的守陵人和宫女，光是在陵园内负责清扫工作和管理陵园树木的就有5000多人。陵园东南还专门修建了茂陵县城，居住有文武大臣、富豪名门计27万多人。那时，连京城长安的达官显贵，也把能搬到皇帝陵墓所在地附近去住看作是一件无比荣耀的事。

通过对茂陵陵园及茂陵县城遗址的考古调查，发现这里有大量的汉代建筑遗址，以及五角形水道、石子路面等城建设施。

茂陵四周有20多个贵戚功臣的陪葬墓。六战匈奴的青年军事家霍去病死后就葬在茂陵东侧1公里处。1978年在霍去病墓所在地建立了茂陵博物馆，展出在茂陵陵园出土的瓦当、汉砖、陶俑及其他珍贵文物和霍去病墓前的大型石刻。

The Maoling Mausoleum

The Maoling Mausoleum, tomb of Emperor Wu Di of the Western Han Dynasty, is located about 9 kilometers southeast of Xingping County and 45 kilometers from Xi'an. The mausoleum was in Maoxiang Town in Huaili County during the Western Han Dynasty, hence the name Maoling (the mausoleum at Maoxiang).

Emperor Wu Di (140 BC—87 BC), also called Liu Che, was the fifth emperor in the Western Han Dynasty. At the age of seven, he was made the crown prince. He came to the throne at 16 and was in power for 54 years. He was one of the emperors for the longest period in the history of China. The First Qin Emperor and Emperor Wu Di are usually regarded as equals, because the autocratic state of centralized power in the feudal society was established by the First Qin Emperor but consolidated by Emperor Wu Di.

In order to centralize the power under the feudal imperial court, Emperor Wu Di deprived every dependent state of their titles of nobility by means of various pretexts. For example, in 112 BC he revoked the titles of 106 princes with the excuse that the gold they offered as an oblation to their ancestors was not pure or underweighed. Before the reign of Emperor Wu Di, the ministers of the imperial court were mostly those who had rendered outstanding service, and their sons. Even ordinary officials mostly came from wealthy, powerful or noble families. However, Emperor Wu Di did not stick to the old rule. On the contrary, he was unconstrained and broad-minded in choosing talents. He even established the Imperial College from which to train and to choose qualified officials. These measures were adopted to strengthen further the system of centralization of the feudal autocracy.

To bring the financial and economic rights under the control of the imperial court, Emperor Wu Di announced that coin-minting was forbidden among the people and the local governments, and only the coins minted by central government could be in circulation. Metallurgy and salt processing were also forbidden among the people. The business run by the government enjoyed the exclusive right to sell salt and iron. Meanwhile the government levied a property tax on businessmen so the revenue of the court increased greatly.

The Western Han Dynasty became unprecedentedly rich and powerful, centralization strengthened and its feudal economy flourished. Emperor Wu Di launched three important battles, and defeated its formidable enemy, the Hun invaders on the northern border. He also sent men, more than once, to establish relations with the Western Regions. The well-known Silk Road was opened during his reign.

Emperor Wu Di was not only a statesman but also a strategist of great talents, and a lover of poetry and music as well. He set up an organization called "Yuefu", an official conservatory for collecting and composing folk songs and ballads and for training musicians. It was because of this that many folk songs in the Han Dynasty were preserved and passed down through the ages till today. Yuefu poems had a great influence on people of later periods. Poets like Li Bai, Du Fu and Bai Juyi in the Tang Dynasty, used to imitate and devolop the style of the Yuefu poems.

In order to consolidate feudal domination and to further achieve the unity of academic thought, Emperor Wu Di accepted, Dong Zhongshu's proposal of "rejecting the other schools of thought and respecting only Confucianism". Thus the period of "contention between a hundred schools of thought" came to an end. From then on, Confucian thought gradually developed into an orthodox philosophy and had far-reaching influence on the history of China.

Emperor Wu Di's great talent and bold strategy led the Han Empire to its prime. The feudal society of China made great developments in politics, economy, military affairs and culture. China began to make a name for itself in the world, as a highly civilized, wealthy and powerful nation.

At the age of 71, Emperor Wu Di died and was buried at the Maoling Mausoleum. His mausoleum was built of rammed earth in the shape of a four-sided dipper, 46 meters high and 240 meters long. Around the mausoleum there are vestiges of wall on the four sides, each of which was 400 meters long with a base of 5.8 meters wide. Today the vestiges of the eastern, western and northern watchtowers can still be clearly seen.

Among the tombs of the Western Han Dynasty, the Maoling Mausoleum was the largest in dimension, took the longest time to be built and had the richest funeral objects. Emperor Wu Di was in power for 54 years, yet the construction of Maoling Mausoleum took 53 years By the time he died, the trees at the mausoleum had grown so large that one could hardly get his/her arms around them. How much gold, silver, jewelry and other treasures were buried in the bomb? No one knows. But according to historical records, one third of the yearly taxes went into the construction of the mausoleum and the purchase of funeral objects. It was said that there was such a large number of funeral objects that the tomb could hardly hold them even before his death. So after the Eastern Han Dynasty, the Maoling Mausoleum became the target of grave diggers.

It is horrifying to mention graves, but Maoling does not give you that feeling. During the Western Han Dynasty, there were a lot of mansion built for high officials and noble lords around the Maoling cemetery. Inside the cemetery there were many palaces and houses inhabited by tomb keepers and palace maids. There were over 5,000 custodians responsible for the maintenance of the mausoleum. The town of Maoling County was purposely built to the southeast of the mausoleum. Generals, officials, noblemen and the rich lived in the town and numbered over 277,000. At that time, even high officials and noble lords felt great honor if they could move near to the emperor's tomb to live.

Through the archaeological research of both the Maoling cemetery and the remains of the town of Maoling County, many cultural relics have been discovered, including several remains of construction sites, pentagon sewer pipes, cobbled roads and other building installations from the Han Dynasty.

There are over 20 satellite tombs of high officials and noble relations around the Maoling Mausoleum. The famous young general Huo Qubing who, on six occasions, fought the Hun invaders bravely, was buried on the eastern side of the mausoleum 1 kilometer away. In 1978, the Maoling Museum was set up. Eave tiles, Han bricks, pottery figures and other valuable historical relics that have been excavated at the Maoling Mausoleum as well as the giant stone carvings that were originally placed in front of Huo Qubing's tomb, are now on display there.

霍去病墓

霍去病（公元前140—前117年）是今山西省临汾市人。他出身贫贱，父亲是一个衙役，母亲卫少儿是婢女。后来，霍去病的姨母卫子夫成为武帝的宠妃，舅父卫青被武帝拜为大将军，母亲卫少儿便经常出入皇宫。据说，霍去病生下不久，卫少儿抱着他入宫去探望妹妹。路过武帝殿前时，这个婴儿突然放声大哭。因伤风正卧床休息的武帝猛然间听到哇哇的哭声，惊得出了一身冷汗，伤风竟不治而愈了。武帝十分高兴，忙召卫少儿入内，并抱着孩子玩了一阵。当得知孩子还没有取名时，武帝就为他取了一个非同一般的名字"去病"。直到今天，霍去病墓上庙宇的香火仍常年不断，一些人指望他能"免灾去病"。

霍去病18岁时，因武艺超群被任命为侍中（负责保卫皇帝安全的官员）。他曾六次挂帅出征塞外，抗击匈奴，屡建战功，打通了河西走廊，保卫了西北边境的安全和"丝绸之路"的畅通无阻，被汉武帝拜为骠骑大将军。为了奖励他，武帝命人为他修了一所豪宅。霍去病却推辞说："匈奴未灭，何以家为！"这种为国忘家的精神为后世所称颂。然而这位杰出的青年军事家在战场上仅仅驰骋了六年，24岁时便不幸病死于祁连山。汉武帝悲痛万分，下令边界上五个郡的匈奴移民，穿上黑甲，护送霍去病的灵柩回长安。霍去病墓冢用土石叠成，象征祁连山，同时还雕刻各种巨型石人、石兽作为墓地装饰。

至今祁连山下仍流传着许多关于这位汉代名将的传说。在兰州五泉山，人们说，当年霍去病兵马途经这里，干渴难忍，于是霍去病以剑戳地，泉水涌出，留下了五个泉眼，以后此地便叫五泉山。在祁连山麓的酒泉，人们说，当年霍去病大败匈奴，攻占此地，汉武帝亲赐美酒犒劳霍大将军。霍去病没有一人独享，而是把御赐美酒倒入泉中，与三军将士共享，从此便有"酒泉"这个地名。

霍去病墓前现有石人、猛兽食羊、人与熊、小猪、跃马、伏虎、卧象、蛙、蟾、石鱼等形状的大型石刻16件，其中"马踏匈奴"雕刻最为有名。根据文献记载，这件石刻原来放在墓前，可能是该墓的主像。

西汉各代皇帝墓前都没有放置石刻，唯独在霍去病和出使西域的张骞墓前发现石刻，可能是霍去病在临终前向汉武帝提出请求才这样做的。汉族此前是没有在墓前放置石刻这一风俗的。最早的墓前石刻在霍去病和张骞墓前发现，可能是因为他们生前长期在西域战斗与生活，受西域少数民族文化影响，接受了西域风俗中陵前石刻可以"镇墓"这一观念。到东汉以后，这种观念被整个中原地区所接受，陵墓前放置石刻于是成为一种普遍现象。

霍去病墓于1961年被国务院列为全国重点文物保护单位。

Huo Qubing's Tomb

Huo Qubing (140 BC—117 BC) was born into a humble family in the present day Linfen City, Shanxi Province. His father was a messenger in a government office, and his mother, Wei Shao'er, was a slave girl. His aunt, Wei Tzufu (his mother's sister), became Emperor Wu Di's favourite concubine, and his uncle, Wei Qing (his mother's brother) was made a general by Emperor Wu Di. Thus, his mother had the privilege of being admitted to the imperial court. It was said that not long after the child's birth, Wei Shao'er took him in her arms to the court to see her sister. Passing the front gate of Emperor Wu Di's residence hall, the child accidentally let out a tremendous cry. The emperor, who was confined to bed with a cold, was startled by the loud outburst, and broke into cold sweat. As a result, his illness was miraculously cured without any treatment. The emperor was very happy about his recovery, and immediately invited

Shao'er into the court. He embraced the child and played with him for a while. When he learned that the child was not yet named, he offered the child the unusual name of "qubing", which meant "Curing Disease". Up to present day, joss sticks, candles and paper money have never ceased burning throughout the year in the temple at Huo Qubing's Tomb. Some people are doing so just with the hope that Huo Qubing would "help to avert disasters and cure their diseases".

At the age of 18, Huo Qubing was appointed as an imperial body-guard. Because of his bravery and unique fighting tactics he was put in charge of the Emperor's personal safety. As an outstanding general, he went to the border to fight against the Hun invaders six times. Each time he won a victory. He opened the Hexi corridor and guaranteed the security of the northwestern frontier and the Silk Road. Because of the many important contributions he made, he was respected as a valiant general by Emperor Wu Di. In order to reward him, the Emperor ordered a magnificent mansion built in his honor. But Huo Qubing didn't accept the offer. He graciously refused, by saying "I won't make a home for myself until the Hun invaders are wiped out." He has been always praised by later generations for his sacrifice for the nation. Unfortunately, this remarkable young general fought bravely for the country for only six years. When he was 24, he fell ill and died at Qilian Mountain. Emperor Wu Di was heart-breakingly sad at the hero's death. He then gave orders that all the Hun immigrants of the five prefectures along the border dress themselves in black, and escort Huo Qubing's coffin to his home in Chang'an, and bury him near Maoling. His tomb was constructed with earth and stone into the shape of a hill, which resembled Qilian Mountain. At the time of construction, gigantic statues of stone men and animals were engraved and placed as ornaments at the tomb site.

Up till now there are legends going around the Qilian Mountain about this Han-Dynasty general. It is said that once Huo Qubing and his men passed the Wuquan Mountain (the Five Springs Mountain) in Lanzhou. Being thirsty and exhausted, Huo Qubing pulled out his sword and stabbed the ground. The result was that spring water came gushing out profusely from the ground. Then there remained the five springs, after which the mountain was named. At Jiuquan (Wine Spring) in Qilian Mountain ranges, the legend goes that after Huo defeated the Hun invaders and took control of the area, Emperor Wu Di bestowed good wine to his general. Huo didn't enjoy it alone, but poured the wine into the spring, so that all his soldiers could enjoy the wine with him, thus the name Jiuquan came into being.

Today, in front of Huo Qubing's Tomb, there are large stone statues of men, fierce animals eating the sheep, a bull, a man with a bear, a piglet, a galloping horse, a crouching horse, a tiger lying in wait, a crouching elephant, a frog, a toad and two stone fish. The total number comes to 16 pieces, among which "The Hun Under Horse Hoofs" is the most famous carving. It is recorded in documents that this stone carving was originally placed in front of the tomb, and was most probably the main statue of the tomb.

Except the stone carvings in front of the tombs of General Huo Qubing and Zhang Qian who went on a diplomatic mission to the Western Regions, no stone carvings were available in front of any emperors' mausoleum in the Western Han Dynasty. Perhaps the stone carvings were placed in front of the tomb out of the request by Huo Qubing before his death. The Han people seldom lay stone carvings in front of tombs at that time. The earliest ones were found before the tombs of Huo's and Zhang's. This was probably because they had been fighting and living in the Western Regions for such a long time that they were influenced by the western cultures. Therefore, they accepted the customary idea that carved stones in front of tombs could keep the evil spirits away. From the Eastern Han Dynasty onward, the idea was accepted by the Han people in central China. Hence, erecting stone carvings in front of tombs became a common practice.

Huo Qubing's Tomb was designated by the State Council as an important National Historical Monument in China in 1961.

昭陵

昭陵是唐朝第二代皇帝太宗李世民的陵墓。公元626年高祖李渊禅位，李世民登上皇帝的宝座，他在位23年，创造了我国历史上盛极一时的"贞观之治"。公元636年，文德皇后长孙氏病故。太宗遵其"因山而葬""俭薄送终"的遗嘱，选择距长安城约80公里的九嵕山为陵址，定名昭陵。安葬了文德皇后，昭陵营建工程仍然没有停止。公元649年，太宗病故，与文德皇后合葬后封固陵墓，建陵工程至此竣工。昭陵位于陕西省礼泉县东北20公里处，是关中"唐十八陵"中规模最大、陪葬墓最多的一座。它开创了唐代帝王陵墓以山而筑的制度。因山为陵，就是选择自然山峰，从旁边凿洞为埏道，在山峰的底部修造地下宫殿。据有关资料记述，昭陵从埏道至墓室深约230米，前后安置5道石门。地宫宽敞富丽，几乎与长安城的宫殿差不多。埏道两侧设东西两厢，厢内放置石柜，柜内有装殉葬品的铁匣。陵山上还为护陵人员修建了游殿和房舍等。为了解决来往不便的困难，又沿山崖修了栈道。经过1000多年的沧桑巨变，昭陵的地面建筑早已荡然无存，现仅存几处废墟，如朱雀门、献殿、祭坛、司马门、皇城等。据记载，皇城建筑曾遭火焚，公元798年重修房屋378间。献殿遗址出土了一件陶鸱吻，高1.5米，重约150公斤。从这一屋顶装饰可推想当时宫殿建筑是多么高大宏伟。

昭陵陵园周长60公里，总面积2万公顷，共有陪葬墓167座。太宗李世民的灵寝位于陵园最北端，像皇宫在长安城北部一样，居高临下。陪葬墓中以魏征、李靖、李勣（徐懋功）的墓最与众不同。例如，李勣的墓冢形如三座山峰，象征阴山、铁山、乌德鞬山，以纪念他在这些地方所立的赫赫战功。墓前还依次排列着一对石人，左侧石羊、右侧石虎各三对。墓碑高5.6米，高宗李治亲自撰文书碑。这三座墓规模之大，足以说明墓主人的功勋和他们与唐王朝的特殊关系。陪葬墓中还有一些西北地区兄弟民族将领的墓，他们都在唐朝政权中担任过重要职务，有的还和唐皇室有联姻关系。

昭陵的营造工程是唐代著名美术家阎立德设计的，在规模和布局上都有独特的风格。驰名中外的"昭陵六骏"就是唐太宗在公元636年埋葬文德皇后长孙氏以后，诏令雕刻列置于昭陵北麓祭坛内的。"六骏"是六匹曾随李世民南征北战，为唐王朝的统一立过战功的骏马。石刻骏马姿态各异，但都矫健雄强，生气勃勃。

"昭陵六骏"石刻吸取了佛教艺术的浮雕法，以熟练的技巧、简洁的手法刻画真实的事物，具有极高的艺术价值。可惜这几件艺术珍品在20世纪20年代遭到破坏，其中有两件被盗运到国外，现存美国费城的宾夕法尼亚大学博物馆，其余四件在盗运时被发现，运回西安，今陈列在碑林石刻艺术博物馆内。在盗运过程中，这六件石刻都被打成数块，马身上原刻有射中的箭，现已模糊不清；太宗所题赞词和马的名称也都看不见了。所幸还有北宋游师雄立的昭陵六骏碑，以线刻手法记录了六骏浮雕的细部、名称、毛色特点、事迹及太宗赞颂这六马的诗文。

与六骏石刻一同列置在祭坛的还有14国君长石刻像。这些石像早年也被毁，现仅存4座像的题名像座。石像的形象没有具体记录，有些资料只说是"逾常形"，可知比普通真人的形体高大、魁伟。

唐代盛行在墓前立碑和在墓室内放置墓志石的风气。昭陵大部分墓前有碑，几乎每座墓内都有墓志石。大部分碑石现都保存在昭陵博物馆内。

唐朝是我国封建社会的鼎盛时期，唐太宗又是一个很有作为的皇帝，因此昭陵被誉为"天下名陵"。1961年，国务院公布昭陵为第一批全国重点文物保护单位，并修建了昭陵博物馆。

The Zhaoling Mausoleum

The Zhaoling Mausoleum is the mausoleum of Emperor Tai Zong (Li Shimin), the second emperor of the Tang Dynasty. He came to the throne in 626 AD when it was abdicated by Emperor Gao Zu (Li Yuan), his father. He was in power for 23 years. During his rule, there was a famous period known as the "Prosperous Zhen Guan Reign". In 636 AD, Empress Wende died of an illness. Her will read, "After I die, bury me in the mountain and hold a simple funeral for me". Emperor Tai Zong chose the Jiuzong Mountain, 80 kilometers from Xi'an, as the tomb site and named it "Zhaoling". The construction started soon afterwards. In 649 AD, Emperor Tai Zong died of an illness and was buried together with Empress Wende. The tomb was completely sealed and the construction came to an end.

The Zhaoling Mausoleum stands on the top of the Jiuzhong Mountain, 20 kilometers northeast of Liquan County in Shaanxi Province. It is the most sizable of the 18 imperial tombs of the Tang Dynasty on the Central Shaanxi Plain. These steps were involved in building a tomb in the mountain. First, choose a natural peak in the mountainous area. Next, chisel an opening from the cliff-side, and dig inward to form a straight passage. Finally, build an underground palace at the end of the passage just beneath the peak. According to historical records, there is a 230-meter passage from the opening to the coffin chamber inside Zhaoling Mausoleum. Five gates were installed along the passage. The underground palace, spacious and splendid, consists of two large halls. One is in the east and the other in the west. Inside these halls, there are several large stone boxes, each of which contains an iron casket with burial objects. Houses and verandas were built for the tomb keepers. A plank road was built along the cliffside to provide access to the mausoleum. With the passage of over 1,000 years, almost all its ground structures have disappeared, except for the remains of the Scarletbird Gate, the Sacrificial Hall, the Sacrificial Altar, the Gate Leading to the Secret Way and the Imperial City. According to historical records, the buildings in the Imperial City were burnt down. In 798 AD, about 378 rooms were rebuilt. An upturned crest was unearthed at the site of the Sacrificial Hall. It is 1.5 meters in height and 150 kilograms in weight. Such a crest shows the size and splendor of the building structures at the ground level.

Zhaoling Cemetery is 60 kilometers around. With its 167 satellite tombs, the cemetery covers an area of 20,000 hectares. Emperor Tai Zong's Mausoleum stands high up in the northernmost section of the cemetery. Just as the Imperial Palace overlooks all other palaces in the city of Chang'an, so this mausoleum looks over all other tombs from the peak. The tombs of Wei Zheng, Li Jing and Li Ji (Xu Maogong) are worth of note. Take Li Ji's tomb for example. It is shapd like three peaks. They represent Yinshan, Tieshan and Wudejian mountains, where he scored one victory after another. A pair of stone figures was placed in front of the tomb. On the left are three pairs of stone sheep and on the right are three pairs of stone tigers. The tomb stone, 5.6 meters tall, bears Emperor Gao Zong's inscription. These three tombs are extraordinary enough to show the contributions of the tomb occupants and their special relations with the imperial court. Among the tombs are those of the generals of the ethnic minority groups on the northwest region. They all held important positions in the Tang Dynasty. Several of them even had relation to the royal family by marriage.

Zhaoling Mausoleum was designed by Yan Lide, a famous artist of the Tang Dynasty. The design shows a great deal of originality. After Empress Wende was buried in 636 AD, Emperor Tai Zong gave orders that six stone horses be carved in bas-relif and placed within the Sacrificial Hall on the slope north of Zhaoling Mausoleum. In fact, the six galloping horse served him during his lifetime, and they had helped him win decisive victories and achieve his desired objectives. The stone horses are different in postures. They all look sturdy and vigorous.

The six stone horses reflect the bas-relief features of Buddhist art. They were carved with excellent skills and in a lively style. These stone carvings are of great artistic value. Unfortunately, all of them were damaged in the 1920s. Two of them were shipped abroad, and they are now kept in the Museum of the University of Pennsylvania, in Philadelphia, USA. The other four was discovered in the process of being stolen, then shipped back to Xi'an. They are now on display in the Forest of Stone Tablets Museum. In the course of being smuggled, the six stone horses were broken into pieces. As a result the patterns of arrows on the horse, Emperor Tai Zhong's words of praise, and the horses' names, cannot be clearly seen. Fortunately, the stone tablet which was erected by You Shixiong in the Northern Song Dynasty remains intact. The tablet bears a detailed introduction to the six horses, including their names, hair features and military deeds. It also records Emperor Tai Zong's words of praise for the horses.

Along with the stone horses, there are stone statues of 14 dukes. These statues were also damaged many years ago. Only four statues' pedestals remain intact. But their images are still unknown, since there are no detailed records about them. They are said to be unusual in size and are presumed to be stronger and taller than ordinary beings.

During the Tang Dynasty, it was a regular practice to install memorial tablets before tombs and to place epitaphs in coffin chambers. There are memorial tablets in front of most of the tombs in the Zhaoling Cemetery, and almost there is an epitaph in every burial chamber. Most of these artifacts are now preserved in Zhaoling Museum.

The Tang Dynasty was at the zenith of the feudal society in China. Emperor Tai Zong was considered the most capable and ableminded of all. The Zhaoling Mausoleum was authoritatively accepted as an important National Historical Monument in China in 1961. The Zhaoling Museum was set up in the same year.

乾陵

乾陵修建于公元684年，经过23年的时间，才基本竣工。乾陵以山为陵，坐落在海拔1047.5米高的梁山上。梁山有三座山峰，北峰最高，乾陵即建于此。南面两峰东西对峙，上面各有一座土阙，当地群众俗称"奶头山"。据史书记载，陵墓原有内外两重城墙，四个城门，还有献殿、阙楼等许多宏伟的建筑物。勘探表明：内城总面积240平方米，四面围有城墙，南有朱雀门，北有玄武门，东有青龙门，西有白虎门。陵前司马道两侧排列有雕刻精美、神态生动的石雕124件。从南往北有八陵柱形华表、翼马、朱雀各1对，石马5对，戴冠持剑的直阁将军石人10对。4个门外各有石狮1对，北门外有石马3对。另外，在南门外有为高宗皇帝和武则天歌功颂德的《述圣记碑》和《无字碑》两通，以及参加高宗葬礼的中国少数民族首领和友好国家使臣的石刻像61尊。在中国历史上，陵前石刻的数目、种类和安放位置是从乾陵开始才有固定制度的，一直延续到清代，历代大同小异。

"述圣记碑"

位于朱雀门外西侧的"述圣记碑"，全碑共七节，人称"七节碑"。据说，它由七节组成，取于"七曜"，与古人认为世界由日、月、金、木、水、土、火七种基本物质构成有关。七节碑高6.3米，重61.6吨。碑座上刻有各种碑纹。碑文8000余字，由武则天亲自撰文，唐中宗书写，颂扬了高宗的文治武功。碑刻成后，还在字画上填以金屑，现在仍可看到个别字的金饰。

"无字碑"

位于朱雀门外东侧的"无字碑"，高6.3米，重约98.8吨。碑侧线刻龙纹，碑头刻有八条螭身相交。所谓"无字碑"，就是说立碑时碑上没有刻一个字。为什么立一通"无字碑"呢？有人说，武则天是想让后世的人对她做出公允的评价；有人则说，武则天觉得自己功德无量，是无法用语言文字来表达的；也有人认为此碑可能是唐中宗所立，他不满武则天的独断专行，不愿违心地恭维她，但作为一个儿子，又不便对自己母亲提出非议，因此立无字碑让后人去评论。不管怎么说，在帝王陵前立无字碑在我国历史上确实是独一无二的。

宋、金以后，一些游人开始在碑上题字，于是"无字碑"就变成了"有字碑"。现在碑上共有13段文字。由于年代久远，风雨剥蚀，其中大部分字迹已无法辨认，唯有金代（公元1135年）用女真文字刻写，旁边用汉语翻译的"朗君行记"保存完整。女真文字现已绝迹，因此这通碑是研究女真文字和女真族历史文化的珍贵资料。

六十一尊王宾像

排列于内城东西阙楼两侧的61尊石人像，是武则天为了纪念参加高宗葬礼的少数民族首领和外国使臣而敕令刻制的。他们穿紧袖衣，腰束宽带，足蹬皮靴，显然没有唐代汉族服装的特点。这些石人双手前拱，表示祈祷。石人的头部绝大多数早已毁掉，现只有两尊有头、高鼻子、深眼睛，可能是来自西域的使臣。每个石人背后原来刻有国名、官职和姓名，因长期风化，多数字迹已无法辨认，仅有两尊石像背面字迹比较清晰。从字迹分析，一人来自如今的阿富汗，另一个来自伊朗。

乾陵不仅外观宏伟，而且内藏也十分丰富。据《述圣记碑》记载，唐高宗临终时曾遗言把他生前所喜爱的字画埋进墓内。武则天和唐高宗都处在唐朝的全盛时期，因此墓内陪葬品必定会应有尽有。

根据史书记载，除乾陵外，唐代帝王陵墓大部分在五代（公元907—960年）时被耀州节度使温韬所盗。据载，唯有在温韬盗挖乾陵时，因风雨太大，没有挖开。新中国成立后考古勘查也证明，乾陵墓道全部用石条填砌，层叠于墓道口直至墓门，共39层。各层石条均用铁拴板固定，并以铅液灌缝。在当时的历史条件下，要想挖开，确非易事。考古勘查还证明，陵墓四周没有盗洞，墓道的石条和夯土仍为原来合葬武则天时的样子。因此，我们估计，乾陵可能还未被盗掘过。

乾陵范围很广，方圆约40公里，周围还有王公贵族陪葬墓17座。

The Qianling Mausoleum

The Qianling Mausoleum was built in 684 AD, and brought into completion 23 years later. It is located on Liangshan Hill, 1,047.5 meters above sea level. Of the three peaks of Liangshan Hill, the north peak, where Qianling is located, is the highest. The two peaks in the south face each other, east to west. On each of the two peaks stands the remains of a watch tower. The folk call the two peaks "Nipple Hills". According to historical records, there used to be two city walls that formed an inner city and an outer city. There were four gates and many splendid buildings, such as the dedicatory hall, and gate towers. It has been proven through exploration that the total area of the inner city was about 240 square meters. There was a gate on each side of the inner city: namely the Scarlet Bird Gate in the south; the Tortoise Gate in the north; the Blue Dragon Gate in the east and the White Tiger Gate in the west. On both sides of the sacred way in front of the tomb, 124 exquisite and lively stone statues are lined up from north to south. They include a pair of octagonal cloud pillars, a pair of winged horses, a pair of scarlet birds, five pairs of stone horses, and ten pairs of guarding generals with helmets on their heads and swords in their hands. There is a pair of stone lions in front of each city gate. There are three pairs of stone horses in front of the north gate. In addition, outside the south gate there are two tall tablets: the "Tablet to the Holy Deeds of Emperor Gao Zong" and the "Wordless Tablet to Wu Zetian". There are also 61 stone statues, representing the heads of the ethnic minority groups and the envoys from friendly countries. They came to attend Emperor Gao Zong's funeral. With reference to the number, variety and arrangement of stone carvings, the Qianling Mausoleum set a good example for other similar constructions till the early

Qing Dynasty. The arrangement of stone carvings was largely identical in successive dynasties.

The Tablet to the Holy Deeds of Emperor Gao Zong

The "Tablet to the Holy Deeds of Emperor Gao Zong", located west of the Scarlet Bird Gate, consists of seven joints. It is also called the "Seven-joint Tablet." It is said that the seven joints symbolize the Seven Elements in the universe, that is, the Sun, the Moon, Metal, Wood, Water, Earth and Fire. The ancient Chinese believed that the universe was composed of these seven elements. The tablet measures 6.3 meters high, and weighs 61.6 tons. The pedestal for the tablet was carved with various figures of beasts. The inscription on the tablet was composed by Wu Zetian and written by Emperor Zhong Zong. It contains over 8,000 characters, singing the praises of Emperor Gao Zong's political achievements and military exploits. When the tablet was carved, the strokes of characters were coated with gold fillings, so even today the remains of gold fillings on some characters are still discernible.

The Non-inscribed Tablet

The Non-inscribed Tablet, or "the Wordless Tablet", located to the east of the Scarlet Bird Gate is 6.3 meters high, and weighs 98.8 tons. The sides of the tablet were carved with figures of dragons. The top part of the tablet was carved with eight oysters intersecting each other. Why was the "Wordless Tablet" set up for Empress Wu Zetian? Some say that she wanted people of later generations to give her a just and fair appraisal. Others say she thought that her merits and virtues were so immeasurable that they were beyond words. Still some others think that it was probably set up by Emperor Zhong Zong, who was dissatisfied with her arbitrary decisions and peremptory actions on the one hand and unwilling to flatter her against his conscience on the other. But as her son, it was inappropriate for him to reproach her. So he set up the "Wordless Tablet" to let people of later generations appraise her. Anyway, such a tablet has not been found before any other imperial mausoleums in the country.

Ever since the Song and the Jin dynasties, 13 paragraphs have been inscribed. Now, the "Wordless Tablet" has become a tablet with words. Owing to the passage of time and the ravages of wind and rain, most of the inscription on the tablet is not clear. Only "Lang Jun's Travelogue", which was carved in Nüzhen script in the Jin Dynasty

(1135 AD), remains intact with its Chinese translation. Nüzhen script, the language of an ethnic minority group, has disappeared. Therefore, this tablet is of great value for the study of the language, the history and culture of Nüzhen nationality.

The 61 Stone Statues

The towers east and west of the inner city are flanked with 61 stone statues. In order to commemorate the heads of the Chinese minorities and the envoys from foreign countries that attended Emperor Gao Zong's funeral, Wu Zetian ordered these stone statues to be carved. They wore close-sleeved clothes, wide belts around the waistline and long boots—signs that show they were minorities or envoys from other countries. They were saying prayers with their hands cupped before their chests. Their heads were mostly damaged long ago. Now only two statues are completed with heads, high noses and deep-set eyes. Most probably, they were envoys from the Western Regions and Central and Western Asia. Their nationality, official positions and names can be found on the backs of the stone statues. Having been exposed to the weather over the years, most of the characters are already undecipherable. Only the stone statues of the envoys who allegedly came from Iran and Afghanistan bear clear inscriptions.

The Qianling Mausoleum is not only magnificent in style, but rich in burial objects. According to the *Records of Emperor Gao Zong's Holy Deeds*, Emperor Gao Zong asked, in his last words, to have his favorite calligraphic works and paintings buried with him in his mausoleum. Besides, as Emperor Gao Zong and his consort Wu Zetian were living at the peak of the Tang Dynasty, the mausoleum must have had just about everything you would expect to find there.

Most imperial tombs of the Tang Dynasty were robbed by Wen Tao, governor of Yaozhou, during the Five dynasties. Historical records say it was a rainy day when Wen Tao was digging into the Qianling Mausoleum. The stone of the mausoleum was so hard that he couldn't break open. The results of the archaeological survey conducted ever since 1949 show that the tomb passage, from the entrance to the gate of the burial chamber, was built of rectangular stone blocks piled layer upon layer, 39 layers in all. Each layer of stone blocks was fastened together with iron bolts. All the crevices between the layers were filled with molten lead. It was far from easy to break into the tomb at that time. It has been verified that there were no holes around the tomb, and the stone blocks and rammed earth along the tomb passage remain the same as when

Emperor Gao Zong and his consort were buried. Therefore, it is believed that the tomb has not been robbed.

The Qianling Mausoleum has a circumference of 40 kilometers, with 17 satellite tombs around it.

杨贵妃墓

杨贵妃墓位于兴平市城西12.5公里的马嵬坡。

杨贵妃,名玉环,今山西永济人,被称为我国古代的一大"美人",原为唐玄宗李隆基第十八子寿王李瑁的妃子。唐玄宗见杨玉环不但美丽,而且通晓音律,能歌善舞,便授意杨玉环自请出家做道士,住在太真宫,号杨太真。玄宗不久将她召回,宠爱无比,册封为贵妃,礼遇与皇后无异。其兄杨国忠被封为宰相,把持朝政。

公元755年,节度使安禄山造反,迅速攻破东都洛阳,向长安逼近。唐玄宗带领一班朝臣仓皇出逃,西行至马嵬坡,随行将士杀死杨国忠,又逼唐玄宗赐死杨贵妃。玄宗无奈,只得忍痛割爱,命人将杨贵妃勒死,杨贵妃当年才38岁。

杨贵妃墓占地约0.16亩,高3米左右,封土四周砌以青砖。关中地区帝王将相、皇亲国戚陵墓数百座,为什么唯独杨贵妃墓砌砖呢?据传,妇女用杨贵妃墓上的土搽脸,不但可以除去脸上的黑斑,而且会使皮肤变得细腻白嫩,因此贵妃墓上的土被称为"贵妃粉",远近的妇女竞相来此取土搽脸,连外地游人也要带一包墓土回去。这样墓堆越来越小,守墓人不断给墓添土,然而不久还是被取光了。为了保护坟墓,后来只好用青砖把它包起来,这样人们就无法再从墓上取土了。

贵妃墓周围有三面回廊,上面嵌着历代很多名人到此游历后的题咏石刻。多数题咏都指责朝廷政治腐败,为杨贵妃鸣不平,认为贵族争权夺利,使地方割据势力扩大,从而造成了安禄山之乱;让杨贵妃一个弱女子负罪,实在冤枉。有的题咏指责李隆基无情无义,感叹一个女子嫁给这样的帝王还不如嫁给一个普通老百姓。

据文献记载,公元757年,官军收复长安。李隆基自成都回来,曾密令迁葬杨贵妃。所以,此墓是原来的墓,还是迁葬后的新墓,或只是杨贵妃的衣冠冢,都无法确证。杨贵妃墓现为陕西省重点文物保护单位。

Lady Yang's Tomb

The tomb of Lady Yang is located at Maweipo, 12.5 kilometers west of Xingping County.

Yang Yuhuan, also known as Lady Yang, was born in Yongji, Shanxi Province, and was considered one of the "beauties" in ancient China. She was originally the lady of Li Mao, who was the prince and eighteenth son of Li Longji (Emperor Xuan Zong). The emperor found that Yang Yuhuan was not only a beautiful girl, but also a wonderful singer and dancer. So he incited her to leave home to become a Taoist nun. She lived in Taizhen Temple and adopted the Taoist name Yang Taizhen. Emperor Xuan Zong loved her so much that he soon made her his favorite lady, and treated her like an empress. Lady Yang's brother, Yang Guozhong, was made chancellor, who manipulated the imperial court and managed all royal affairs.

In 755 AD, a military officer, An Lushan, rose up in rebellion. After a short time, the eastern capital Luoyang was taken over, and Chang'an, his next prize, was in great danger. Emperor Xuan Zong took his courtiers and fled west in a great hurry. When they reached Maweipo, the generals and soldiers that had fought all the way with him killed Yang Guozhong, the chancellor. Then they forced the Emperor to order Lady Yang to commit suicide. Helpless and despaired, Xuan Zong had to part reluctantly with his favorite lady. Finally, she was hanged at his order. She was only 38 years old then.

The tomb occupies an area of 0.16 acre. It is 3 meters high and is covered with bricks. In central Shaanxi, there are hundreds of tombs that belong to emperors, generals, chancellors, royal family members and their relatives. Why is Lady Yang's Tomb alone covered with bricks? It is said that the women at that time used the earth from the tomb to make up their faces. In doing so, their facial blemishes were removed, and their skin became delicate and smooth. Therefore, the earth of her tomb was called "Lady Yang's Powder". So women living far and near, came in large numbers to try the magic earth on their faces with the intention of becoming pretty. Even tourists from other places would take some home when they visited the tomb. Gradually, the size of her tomb decreased. Though the caretaker never stopped adding new earth to the tomb, it was still gone before long. Later, bricks were used to cover the whole tomb so that its earth could not be taken away.

There is a winding corridor along each of the three sides of the tomb, where the stone inscriptions of eminent people can be seen. Most of the inscriptions criticize the imperial court for its political corruption and incompetence, and complain of Lady Yang's ill-treatment. They also attribute An Lushan's rebellion to the power struggle among the noblemen and rampant growth of the local forces. Lady Yang, a weak woman, was unfairly the victim of their struggle. Some of the inscriptions blame Li Longji for his mercilessness and heartlessness. There is a suggestion that to be an emperor's wife was no better than to marry an ordinary man.

According to the historical records, the armed forces of the Tang government took over Chang'an in 757 AD. After coming back from Chengdu, Li Longji secretly gave orders that Lady Yang's tomb be moved. Is the present tomb the original one or is it relocated? Or is it the tomb which only contains the personal effects of Lady Yang? It has never been certified. Lady Yang's Tomb is now an important historic monument in Shaanxi Province.

章怀太子墓

章怀太子墓位于乾陵东南约 3 公里处，是乾陵 17 座陪葬墓之一。

章怀太子名李贤，是唐高宗与武则天的第二个儿子，也是高宗子女中比较有才华的一个，深为高宗所喜爱，曾被立为太子。他曾召集全国的著名学者注释过《后汉书》。书中谈到汉高祖刘邦死后，其妻吕后大量起用吕家的人，排挤朝廷大臣，篡夺汉室刘姓天下的史实。武则天认为这是在含沙射影地将她比作吕后，忌恨在心，于是千方百计地加害李贤。为了保护自己，李贤不得已在他居住的东宫马坊里暗藏武器，以防不测。武则天发现后便以私藏武器，图谋不轨为借口，将李贤废为庶人，流放到巴州（今四川巴中市）。公元 684 年，李贤在巴州神秘地死去，年仅 31 岁。对于李贤之死，众说纷纭，但多数人认为是武则天怕李贤东山再起而派人害死的。唐中宗复位后，于公元 706 年，即武则天死后的第二年，将李贤遗骨迁到乾陵陪葬。公元 711 年，唐睿宗追封李贤为"章怀太子"。

1971 年 7 月至 1972 年 2 月国家对章怀太子墓进行了发掘。考古发掘结果证实：章怀太子墓的地面形制和内部结构与永泰公主墓基本相同，只是规模小一些。墓由长斜坡形墓道、4 个天井、4 个过洞、6 个便房、砖砌甬道和前后墓室组成。墓道全长71米，宽3.3米，深7米。该墓虽然被盗，但仍出土各种陶俑、三彩俑、生活用具等陪葬品600多件。尤其是出土的高达1米以上的文臣俑、武士俑和彩绘镇墓兽，造型极为生动。墓中壁画共50多幅，计400平方米，保存基本完好。其中《迎宾图》《狩猎出行图》《打马球图》和《观鸟捕蝉图》等壁画中的人物，比例匀称、和谐、准确，造型逼真，技巧圆熟，显示了唐代绘画艺术的高度水平。

墓道西壁的《打马球图》，画有骑马人物20多个，前面五人手执球杖，正在驱马抢球。其中一人作反身击球状，姿态矫健，得心应手。这幅壁画形象地再现了唐代马球比赛紧张惊险的夺球场面。唐代马球从波斯（今伊朗）传入中国，风行于宫廷。当时宫廷中上至皇帝，下至文武百官，甚至妇女都爱打马球。唐代的宫城和禁苑里多半筑有马球场，有的贵族官僚还有自己的马球场。唐代以后，马球运动开始流行全国，直到明朝末年才开始逐渐失传。

墓道中部东壁的《迎宾图》形象地再现了唐代官员接待外国使臣的场面。前面两个是热情的唐朝官员，后面三个是外国使臣。经考证，外国使臣中的一个是东罗马帝国人，第二个是朝鲜人，第三个是我国古代少数民族的突厥人。这幅壁画反映了唐王朝活跃的外交及唐王朝与我国其他少数民族友好往来的实况。

前墓室西壁的《观鸟捕蝉图》描绘了宫女们的宫廷生活。画面上三个宫女，年长的似乎饱受了宫廷生活的煎熬，正若有所思，望天长叹；另外两个则以观鸟和捕蝉来排除心中的烦闷。

The Tomb of Crown Prince Zhang Huai

The tomb of Crown Prince Zhang Huai is one of the 17 satellite tombs. It lies 3 kilometers southeast of the Qianling Mausoleum.

Crown Prince Zhang Huai was called Li Xian and was the second son of Emperor Gao Zong and Empress Wu Zetian. He was comparatively talented among Gao Zong's children. Gao Zong was fond of him and made him the crown prince. Li Xian once summoned famous scholars from all over the country to annotate *The Historical Records of the Later Han Dynasty*. The book referred to the historical fact that Lü Hou, wife of Emperor Gao Zu, founder of the Han Dynasty, put many people from her family in important positions. She pushed out many courtiers and usurped the supreme power of the country which was held by the Liu Family after her husband's death. Wu Zetian thought that she was attacked by insinuation and compared to Lü Hou. She felt angry about this. So she tried every means to bring harm to Li Xian. To protect himself, Li Xian hid some weapons in the stable at the Eastern Palace where he lived. When Wu Zetian discovered this, she deprived him of the title of crown prince and made him a commoner. She exiled him to Bazhou, (present-day Bazhong County, in Sichuan Province) on the pretext that he had hidden weapons secretly and was plotting an armed rebellion. In 684 AD, Li Xian died mysteriously in Bazhou. He was only 31 years old then. There are various sayings as to the cause of his death. But most people believed that Wu Zetian was afraid that he would stage a comeback, so she had him murdered. After Emperor Zhong Zong returned to the throne, he had Li Xiann's remains buried near Qianling in 706 AD, following Wu Zetian's death. Emperor Rui Zong posthumously awarded him the title of Crown Prince Zhang Huai in 711 AD

The excavation of the tomb of Crown Prince Zhang Huai was carried out from July 1971 to February 1972. The ground and the interior structure of the tomb are basically the same as those of Princess Yong Tai, but only a bit smaller in scale. The tomb consists of a long, sloping tomb passage, four skylights, four passages, six niches, a brick corridor, an ante-chamber and a burial chamber. The tomb passage is 71 meters long, 3.3 meters wide and 7 meters deep. Although the tomb was once robbed, over 600 articles were unearthed. They include various ceramic figurines, tri-colored ceramic figurines, articles for daily use and other burial objects. The figures of civil officials and warriors are vivid and life-like. They are over 1 meter tall. Together with guardians, they are worth special attention. There are more than 50 murals in the tomb, which occupy 400 square meters, and remain basically intact. Of these paintings, *Courtiers and Foreign Envoys*, *Hunting Procession*, *Polo Game* and *Watching Birds Catching Cicadas* are all true to life and skillfully drawn. These murals demonstrate the superb artistic skill of the Tang Dynasty.

On the western wall of the tomb passage there is a fresco entitled "Polo Game", which depicts 20 figures on horse back. With mallets in hand, the five at the head are trying to chase the ball. One of them hit the ball dexterously behind his back. He looks strong and vigorous. This painting conjures up a thrilling spectacle of players trying to chase the ball at a polo match in the Tang Dynasty. Polo was introduced to China from Persia (present-day Iran) during the Tang Dynasty. It was very popular at the royal court. All the people of the court, from the emperor to civil and military officials and even women, liked playing polo. There were polo grounds in most of the imperial palaces and hunting reserves. Some noblemen had their own polo grounds. After the Tang Dynasty, polo became popular throughout the country. It gradually diminished towards the end of the Ming Dynasty.

The painting entitled "Courtiers and Foreign Envoys" was found on the eastern wall in the middle of the tomb passage. It vividly reproduces the scene of Tang officials greeting foreign envoys. In the front are two enthusiastic Tang officials, and behind them are three foreign envoys. Research confirms that the first envoy came from Eastern Roman Empire, the second from Korea, the third from the Tujue tribe, an ethnic minority tribe in ancient China. This mural reflects the active exchanges of friendly and diplomatic visits between China and foreign countries during the Tang Dynasty.

Watching Birds Catching Cicadas on the western wall of the antechamber depicts the life of the maids in the imperial palace. There are three maids in the painting. The older one seems to have suffered a lot in life in the palace. She looks as if she was thinking of something. She gazes at the sky and complains of its infinity. The other two are trying to get rid of their worries by watching birds and catching cicadas.

懿德太子墓

懿德太子墓位于乾陵东南方。

懿德太子李重润是唐中宗李显的长子，因不满武则天的专制，于公元701年在洛阳被处死，时年19岁。公元705年，李显复位后，追封其为懿德太子，公元706年其墓由洛阳迁来陪葬乾陵。

1971年7月至1972年5月国家对该墓进行了发掘。其墓有封土堆和围墙，围墙南有石狮1对，石人2对（1对只残留底座）、石华表1对（已残，倒塌后埋入地下）。墓由墓道、3个过洞、7个天井、8个小龛、前后甬道、前后墓室等8个部分组成，全长100.8米。

此墓规模宏大，随葬品十分丰富。墓内壁画比较完整，有40幅，分别绘在墓道、过洞、天井、前后甬道和前后墓室墙壁上。题材有仪仗队、青龙、白虎、城墙、阙楼、乐伎、男仆、宫女等，显示出李重润的显赫地位和特殊身份。如仪仗队中，永泰公主有12戟，章怀太子有14戟，而李重润则有48戟，属帝王一级。仪仗队有196人，由步队、骑队和车队3个部分组成，阵容庞大，气势不凡。还有《架鹰图》《侍女图》《列戟图》等。《侍女图》在墓前室,南北对称,各有宫女7人。这些壁画色彩绚丽,画中人物姿态各异,真实地反映了唐代宫廷的日常生活。这批壁画琳琅满目,技巧娴熟,犹如一个唐代地下绘画展览,是陕西唐墓壁画的一次重要发现。

石椁内外的线刻画很细致,具有唐代线刻画线条流畅、刚劲、明快的特点。

懿德太子墓出土的文物有1000多件,有陶俑、三彩俑、陶器和金、铜、铁器等。

The Tomb of Crown Prince Yi De

The Tomb of Crown Prince Yi De lies to the southeast of the Qianling Mausoleum. Prince Yi De, called Li Chongrun, was the first son of Li Xian, the fourth emperor of the Tang Dynasty. He was killed in Luoyang in 701 AD for his anger with Wu Zetian's dictatorship. He was only 19 years old then. In 705, when Li Xian returned to the throne, he was awarded posthumously the title of Crown Prince Yi De. In the year of 706, his body was moved from Luoyang to the Qianling Mausoleum area and was buried in a satellite tomb.

The excavation of the Tomb of Crown Prince Yi De was carried out from July 1971 to May 1972. There were a mound and enclosure walls. To the south of the wall were a pair of stone lions, two pairs of stone figures (one was destroyed and only the pedestal remains), and a pair of obelisks (destroyed and buried in the earth). The tomb consists of a tomb passage, three doors, seven skylights, eight niches, front and back tunnels as well as front and back tomb chambers. It is 100.8 meters long.

The tomb is large in scale and abundant with burial articles. There are 40 well-preserved mural paintings on the wall of the tomb passage, doorways, skylights, front and back tunnels as well as front and back chambers. In the paintings are guards of honor, the Blue Dragon, the White Tiger, city walls, watch towers, musicians, butlers and maids of honor, which show Li Chongrun's special identity and extraordinary status. Take the mural guards of honor for example. In the Tomb of Princess Yong Tai, twelve halberds were painted on the wall; in the Tomb of Pince Zhang Huai, 14 halberds were painted; yet in this tomb, 48 halberds were painted just as in an imperial mausoleum. The mural painting depicts 196 guards of honor in three parts: infantrymen, cavalrymen and chariots. They look strong and powerful. There are also mural paintings entitled "Out for Hunting" "Maids of Honor" "Display of Halberds" and so forth. The two mural paintings entitled "Maids of Honor" are found symmetrical against the south and north walls of the front chamber, each consisting of seven maids. Rich in color and different in carriage, the "Maids of Honor" truly represents the daily court life in the Tang Dynasty. These mural paintings in the Tomb of Prince Yi De are reflection of high artistic attainments and a feast for the eye. They constitute an underground exhibition of the Tang mural paintings. The excavation of the tomb has brought about an important discovery of the Tang Dynasty mural paintings in Shaanxi.

The carved sketches on both sides of the stone outer coffin are fine and smooth, and they give a good expression to the features of the Tang-style carved sketches: smooth, clear and powerful.

More than 1000 pieces of historical artifacts have been unearthed from the Tomb of Crown Prince Yi De, including pottery figures, tri-colored glazed figures, earthen ware as well as gold, bronze and iron ware.

永泰公主墓

永泰公主墓是乾陵17座陪葬墓之一。

永泰公主名李仙蕙，是唐中宗李显的第七个女儿，唐高宗和武则天的孙女。公元701年，永泰公主死于洛阳，年仅17岁。根据墓志铭记载，李仙蕙因难产而死。而据史书记载，她因议论武则天与张易之、张昌宗的丑事而被武则天"杖杀"（也有赐白绫死的说法）。中宗即皇位后，追封惨死的女儿为"永泰公主"，并于公元705年将永泰公主与其丈夫合葬于乾陵东南。

永泰公主墓前排列有石狮1对，石人2对，华表1对。1960年至1962年，国家对永泰公主墓进行了发掘清理。这是新中国成立以来发掘唐墓中最大的一座。墓冢为覆斗形，墓道全长87.5米，宽3.9米，墓室深16.7米。全墓由墓道、5个过洞、6个天井、甬道、8个便房、前后墓室组成，象征着永泰公主生前居住的多宅院落。墓道两侧画有巨大的青龙、白虎和由身穿战袍、腰佩贴金宝剑的武士组成的仪仗队。天井两侧的8个便房内放着各种三彩俑群和陶瓷器皿等随葬品。发掘时在第六天井附近发现了一个盗洞，盗洞口有一副骨架，骨架旁边有一把铁斧，四周还散落有金、玉饰品。估计是一伙盗贼为了能多分得赃物，就毫不留情地把仍在洞内的最后一个同伙砍死。永泰公主墓被盗的时间大概在五代或宋初。

永泰公主墓虽然被盗，但仍出土了壁画、陶俑、木俑、三彩俑、金、玉、铜器等珍贵文物计1000余件。特别是三彩俑，造型精致，色彩鲜艳，纹饰奇特，反映了唐代高度发展的陶瓷工艺水平。墓内壁画丰富多彩，墓道、过洞、甬道和墓室顶部都有壁画。前墓室象征客厅，壁画以着华丽服装的侍女为主。这些手中拿着各种生活用品的侍女体态丰盈，神态各异，有的似乎在悄声细语，有的似乎在点头赞许，有的则在环顾四周，她们仿佛正行进在路上，准备去侍奉主人。后墓室墓顶画有天象图：东边是象征太阳的三足金鸟；西边是象征月亮的玉兔；中间是银河，漫天星斗，颗颗在天体中都有固定的位置。这充分反映了当时高度发达的天文学。由于千余年来雨水带着泥沙顺盗洞而下，许多精美的壁画都遭到了破坏。然而，幸存的壁画却不失为唐代绘画的精品。

后墓室停放着永泰公主与其丈夫合葬的庑殿式石椁，石椁内外均刻有线刻画，十分精美。石椁内的木棺因长期浸泡在淤泥中，早已腐烂。

The Tomb of Princess Yong Tai

The tomb of Princess Yong Tai is one of the 17 satellite tombs of the Qianling Mausoleum.

The name of Princess Yong Tai was Li Xianhui. She was the seventh daughter of Tang Emperor Zhong Zong (Li Xian) and the grand daughter of Tang Emperor Gao Zong and his wife Empress Wu Zetian. In 701 AD, Princess Yong Tai died in Luoyang, Henan Province. She was only 17 years old then. According to the epitaph, Li Xianhui died during childbirth. The historical records, though, say that she was beaten to death, because she talked about the scandalous affairs between Wu Zetian and her catamites Zhang Yizhi and Zhang Zongchang. After rising to the throne, Emperor Zhong Zong posthumously conferred the title of Princess Yong Tai upon his daughter, who had died a tragic death. And in 705 AD, he ordered the remains of his daughter and her husband to be buried together in the southeast of the Qianling Tomb.

The path to Princess Yong Tai's tomb is lined with a pair of stone lions, two pairs of stone figures, and a pair of obelisks (ornamental stone columns). The excavation of the tomb was carried out between 1960 and 1962. It is the largest of the Tang tombs excavated since 1949. The tomb is pyramid-shaped, 87.5 meters long and 3.9 meters wide. The burial chamber is 16.7 meters deep. The tomb consists of a main passage, five doorways, six skylights, a corridor, eight small niches, an antechamber and a burial chamber. The burial chamber represents the house where she lived before her death. The walls on both sides of the tomb passage are covered with murals of the Blue Dragon, the White Tiger, and warriors in uniforms, with gilded swords in their belts. In the eight small niches on both sides of the skylights there are a multitude of tri-colored glazed pottery figurines, pottery and porcelain wares, and some other burial objects. In the course of the excavation, a hole once dug by grave robbers was discovered near the sixth skylight. Near the opening, a skeleton was found, with an iron axe and gold and jade ornaments. A handful of grave robbers once entered the tomb, and passed gold, jade and other treasures out of the hole. In order to have a greater share of the stolen goods, those who had already come out of the tomb ruthlessly knifed the last man while he was still in the tomb. It might have happened during the Five dynasties or early in the Song Dynasty.

Although once robbed, the tomb of Princess Yong Tai still held more than 1000 valuable cultural artifacts. These treasures were murals, pottery and wooden figurines, tri-colored glazed pottery figurines, gold vessels, jade articles, and copper wares. The tri-colored glazed pottery figurines, which are beautifully shaped and have peculiar decorative design in many bright colors, demonstrate the high artistic level of the Tang ceramic industry. Inside the tomb, the walls are covered with rich and varied murals. The tomb passage, the doorways, the paved path leading to the tomb, the two chambers and their ceilings, are all decorated with murals. The antechamber represents the drawing-room. The murals mainly depict elegantly-dressed ladies in waiting. They carry themselves with grace and wear different expressions from one another. Some seem to be speaking in whisper, some nodding approvingly and others looking around. They look as if they are on the way to serve Princess Yong Tai. On the ceiling of the burial chamber there are painted firmaments and celestial bodies. In the east, there is the rooster with three legs, symbolizing the sun. In the west, there is the Jade Hare representing the moon. In between runs the Milky Way, dotted with stars, each of which has its set position in the celestial body. This mural greatly reflects the highly developed astronomy at that time. Because the muddy rain waters flew time and again through the hole into the tomb over the years, many of the exquisite murals were mutilated. However, those that have survived can yet be regarded as masterpieces of painting of the Tang Dynasty.

In the rear chamber lay the outer stone coffin of Princess Yong Tai and her husband. The middle of the coffin was carved with exquisite pictures on both sides. The inner wooden coffin has completely rotted away due to its saturation in silt over a long period of time.

第五部分　西安地标性建筑

西安钟楼与鼓楼

在西安繁华的东、西、南、北四条大街交汇处，巍然屹立着一座雕梁画栋、气势雄伟的古典建筑，它古时用来在清晨敲钟报时，所以叫钟楼。从建成之日起，钟楼就一直被看作是古城西安的象征，现为陕西省重点文物保护单位。

钟楼始建于1384年，最初位于西大街的迎祥观。当时，那里是西安城的中心。1582年扩建时，钟楼位置偏到城西侧，于是将原来的钟楼拆掉，在扩大了的西安城正中，即现在的位置，重新修建钟楼。

关于钟楼，民间流传着种种神奇的传说。明朝，关中几次发生地震，死伤几万人。于是就有人说，西安城中心有一条大川流过，川中有条蛟龙在兴风作浪，因此引起了地震。西安知府对此话深信不疑，即命全城铁匠赶制了一条百余丈长的铁链，将蛟龙锁住，沉入川底。后又征用5000能工巧匠，在蛟龙被锁住的市中心夜以继日地赶修钟楼，以便将蛟龙牢牢地锁住压在川底，使它再无法兴风作浪。说也奇怪，自从修了这座钟楼，西安也就没再发生过地震。

这个传说听起来十分荒诞，然而并不是一点缘由也没有。明太祖朱元璋出身贫苦，父母早逝后，只好给别人放羊，后又出家当了和尚。古代皇帝被称为"真龙天子"，朱元璋当皇帝后，怕全国各地出现真龙天子和他争位，于是就下令各地广修钟楼镇压龙气。秦中自古帝王都，龙气尤盛，朱元璋当然更为害怕。因而西安的钟楼不但修的早，而且也修得高大雄伟。

钟楼基座是正方形，占地1377.4平方米，高8.6米，宽35.5米，全部用青砖砌成。楼为砖木结构，高36米。外部重檐三层，但内部仅上下两层。楼檐四角攒顶，檐下饰有彩绘斗拱。"斗拱"是我国古代木结构建筑的特点之一，在世界建筑史上也是独一无二的。它不但能使建筑更加牢固，而且更加美观。斗拱在商代就已出现，在我国青铜器的花纹上，可以看到较完整的斗拱图案。

新中国成立后，市人民政府对钟楼进行了三次大规模的修葺，使这座古建筑又放出了昔日的光彩。现在，沿钟楼内楼梯盘旋而上，古城风貌尽收眼底，在晴朗的日子里，还可以看见远处的终南山呢！

在钟楼西北方500米处，可以看到又一座宏伟的古建筑——鼓楼，和钟楼遥遥相对。它创建于公元1380年，比钟楼早四年。以前楼上悬架一面大鼓，傍晚击鼓报时，与钟楼上的钟形成"晨钟""暮鼓"，古称作鼓楼。后来鼓楼不再用来报时，只是在战争时才擂鼓报警。

鼓楼楼基面积为1924平方米，楼基高34米，基座用青砖砌成。楼体呈长方形。外部为重檐三滴水的歇山顶式，外部楼檐均饰有斗拱，内部上下两层。四周有回廊，内外贴金彩绘，金碧辉煌。它充分显示了我国古代劳动人民在建筑方面的高超技术。

鼓楼现在是陕西省重点文物保护单位。人民政府曾经对它进行了两次大规模的整修，使这座古建筑恢复了昔日宏伟壮丽的风貌。钟楼和鼓楼交相辉映，使古城西安更加美丽壮观。

PART FIVE   LANDMARKS IN XI'AN

The Bell Tower and the Drum Tower in Xi'an

The Bell Tower is a classical building with carved beams and painted rafters. It stands in the center of the downtown area where the North Street, the South Street, the East Street and the West Street meet. It houses a huge bell which was originally used to strike time every morning in ancient times. Ever since its establishment, it has become the symbol of Xi'an. Now, it is an important historical monument in Shaanxi Province.

The Bell Tower was first built in the Yingxiang Temple in 1384, which used to mark the center of the city. It was moved to its present site in 1582 as a result of the city's expansion program. There have been various legendary tales about the Bell Tower. In the Ming Dynasty, tens of thousands of people were killed in several earthquakes on the Central Shaanxi Plain. So there was a story that the quakes were caused by a huge dragon in the undercurrent that flowed beneath the city. Interestingly, the local governor heard the story and accepted it as true. Then he ordered all the smiths in the city to make a 300-meter chain to keep the dragon under control. He also ordered 5,000 craftsmen to build the tower at the site under which the dragon was chained. As a result, the dragon was weighed down to the bottom of the undercurrent, and stopped its evil spells.

The tale may sound absurd, however, it is not without reason. The first emperor Zhu Yuanzhang of the Ming Dynasty was born into a poor family. His parents died when he was young. He had to work for rich landowners as a shepherd. Later, he went to a temple and became a monk. In ancient China, the emperor was often referred to as a "dragon emperor". When he ascended the throne, he was afraid of being replaced by someone as a "real dragon". Therefore bell towers were often constructed all over the country to repress the "spirit of dragons". Xi'an was established as the site of imperial capital ever since ancient times. Naturally the so-called "spirit of dragons" was indomitable. No wonder Emperor Zhu Yuanzhang was in panic. The Bell Tower in Xi'an was not only built earlier, but also taller than any other in the country.

The base of the tower is 1,337.4 square meters in size, 8.6 meters high and 35.5 meters wide. It was laid with blue bricks all over. The whole building, 36 meters above ground, is a brick-and-wood structure. Three storeys of eaves can be seen from the exterior of the building, but there are only two storeys inside. The eaves are supported by colored dou gong, a traditional structural system in which brackets are joined with columns and crossbeams. The use of dou gong, made the whole building firm and beautiful. In fact, the dou gong, structure has its origin in the Shang Dynasty. The design of dou gong appears on bronze wares dating back to the Warring States Period.

Since 1949, Xi'an Municipal Government has launched three repair programs on the tower. As a result, the tower now looks as great and magnificent as it was hundreds of years ago. Today, if you climb the tower by way of its wooden stairs, you will have an extensive view of the city. If you are lucky to get on it on a fine day, you might see as far as Zhongnan Mountain on the southern outskirts of the city.

About 500 meters northwest of the Bell Tower stands another magnificent building, the Drum Tower. It was built in 1380, four years earlier than the Bell Tower. There used to be a huge drum in the tower which told the time at dusk, hence, its name the Drum Tower. The bell in the Bell Tower and the drum in the Drum Tower have been referred to as "the Morning Bell" and "the Dusk Drum". Later, the drum was no longer used to tell time but only to give warnings in times of war.

The base of the Drum Tower is 1,924 square meters in size, and 34 meters in height. It was also built with blue bricks. The building takes a rectangular shape and shows tiers of eaves. It has only two storeys inside. There are corridors around the tower on each tier. The outer eaves are decorated with networks of wood arches. The elegance and grandeur of its structure reveals much of the superb workmanship of the Chinese people.

The Drum Tower is now a historical monument in Shaanxi Province. After two large-scale renovations, the tower has been restored to its former beauty. With the two towers rivaling each other, the ancient city of Xi'an is even more beautiful and spectacular than ever before.

城墙

早在明王朝建立前,当朱元璋攻克徽州后,一个名叫朱升的隐士便告诉他应该"高筑墙,广积粮,缓称王"。朱元璋采纳了这些意见。当全国统一后,他便命令各县普遍筑城。而朱元璋以为"天下山川,唯秦中号为险固"。西安古城垣就是在这个建城的热潮中,在唐皇城旧城基础上扩建起来的。

明代1370年扩建后的西安城墙高12米,顶宽12至14米,底宽15至18米,周长约13.7公里。

城墙每隔120米修敌台一座,突出在城墙之外,顶与城墙面平,这是专为射杀爬城的敌人设置的。敌台之间距离的一半,恰好在弓箭的有效射程之内,便于从侧面射杀攻城的敌人。城墙上共有敌台98座,上面都建有驻兵的敌楼。

古代武器落后,城门又是唯一的出入通道,因而这里是封建统治者苦心经营的防御重点。西安城东、西、南、北四座城门,都分别有正楼、箭楼、闸楼三重城门。闸楼在最外面,其作用是升降吊桥。箭楼在中,正面和两侧设有方形窗口,供射箭用。正楼在最里面,是城的正门。箭楼与正楼之间用围墙连接,叫瓮城,是屯兵的地方。瓮城中还有通向城头的马道,缓坡无台阶,便于战马上下。全城垣共建有马道11处。

城墙四角都有突出城外的角台。角台除西南角是圆形的——可能是为了保持唐皇城转角原状外,其他都是方形的。角台上修有较敌楼更为高大的角楼,表明了这里在战争中的重要地位。

城墙上外侧筑雉堞，又称垛墙，共 5984 个，上有垛口，可以射箭和瞭望。内侧矮墙为女墙，无垛口，以防兵士来往行走时跌下。

最初的西安城墙完全用黄土分层夯打而成。城墙最底层用土、石灰和糯米汁混合夯打，异常坚硬，后来又将整个城墙内外壁及顶部砌上青砖。城墙顶部每隔 40 至 60 米有一道用青砖砌成的水槽，用于排水，对西安古城墙的长期保护起了非常重要的作用。

城四周环绕着又宽又深的护城河，正对城门处设有可以随时起落的吊桥，吊桥一升起，进出城的通路便被截断。

明代西安城垣曾是一个庞大而精密的军事防御体系，也为我国现存最完整的一座古城堡。西安古城墙显示了我国古代劳动人民的聪明才智，也为我们研究明代历史、军事和建筑等提供了不可多得的实物资料。

如今，西安古城垣经过重修，面貌焕然一新。城垣四周的环城公园内依壁垒高耸的古城墙，外临沟阔壕深、碧波荡漾的护城河。公园内花木繁茂，假山扑朔迷离，具有我国民族特色的各种古典建筑物错落有致。别具风格的环城公园与雄伟壮观的古城垣交相辉映，把古城西安点缀得更加美丽多姿。

The City Wall

At the time when Zhu Yuanzhang conquered Huizhou, long before the establishment of the Ming Dynasty, he was admonished by a hermit named Zhu Sheng, who told him to "build high walls, store abundant provisions and take your time in proclaiming yourself emperor". Zhu Yuanzhang followed his advice. Once the whole country was unified, he sent orders to the local governments to build city walls. Zhu assumed that "out of all the mountains and rivers in the world, the central Qin is the most strongly fortified and strategically impregnable". The city wall of Xi'an is an extension of the old Tang Dynasty's royal city, as a result of this wall building campaign.

The city wall, after its extension in 1370 in the Ming Dynasty, stands 12 meters high. It is 12-14 meters wide across the top, 15-18 meters thick at the bottom and 13.7 kilometers in length.

There is a rampart every 120 meters apart, that extends out from the main wall. The top of the rampart is at the same level as the top of the wall. The ramparts were built to allow soldiers to see those enemies who would try to climb the wall. The distance between every two ramparts is just within the range of arrow shot from either side.

This allowed soldiers to protect the entire wall without exposing themselves to the enemies. There are altogether 98 of them on the walls; each has a sentry building on top of it.

The weapons in ancient times were primitive. The gates of the city wall were the only way to go into and out of town. Therefore, these gates were important strategic points. The feudal rulers racked their brains to defend them. In Xi'an, each of the east, west, south and north gates consists of three gate towers: zhenglou, zhalou, jianlou. Zhalou tower stands away from the wall. It is used to lift and lower the suspension bridge. Jianlou tower is in the center of the others. There are square windows in the front and on the two sides to shoot arrows from. The zhenglou tower is the inner one and is also the main entrance to the city. Jianlou and zhenglou are connected by walls and the encircled area is called wongcheng in which soldiers could be stationed. From wongcheng, there are also horse passages leading to the top of the wall. These are gradually ascending slopes that make it easy for war horses to ascend and descend. There are altogether 11 horse passages around the city.

A watch tower is located on each of the four corners of the wall. The one at the southwestern corner is round, probably after the model of the imperial city wall of the Tang Dynasty, but the other three are square, higher and larger than the sentry building on the ramparts. This shows the strategic importance of the corners of the city wall in war times.

Along the outer crest of the city wall, there are 5,984 crenellations or battlements. Under each crenel there is a square hole, from which arrows were shot and watch was kept. The lower inner wall on the top of the city wall is called parapets. They have no crenels. They were designed to prevent soldiers from falling off the wall when traveling back and forth on top of the wall.

The city wall of Xi'an was first built of earth, rammed layer upon layer. The base layer was made of earth, quicklime, and glutinous rice extract, tempered together. It made the wall extremely strong and firm. Later, the wall was totally coated with bricks. On top of the wall, there is a brick water passage trough every 40-60 meters. They are used for drainage. They have played a very important role in the long-term protection of the city wall of Xi'an.

A moat, wide and deep, runs around the city. Over the moat, there used to be a huge suspension bridge which cut off the way in and out of the city, once lifted.

Thus, the Ming Dynasty city wall formed a complex and well-organized system of defense. It is also the most complete city wall that has survived through China's long history. The city wall itself is a true display of the ability and wisdom of the working people in ancient times. It provides invaluable and substantial material for the study of the history, military science, and architecture of the Ming Dynasty.

Today, after the repairs that have been made on the wall by the local government, the city wall has taken on a new look. A circular park has been built in between the high wall and the deep moat, all around the city. The thriving trees and flowers, the rockeries in the park, and the buildings of classical Chinese architecture, together with the city wall, make Xi'an all the more beautiful.

大雁塔

大雁塔位于西安南郊大慈恩寺内，距市中心约 4 公里，是我国佛教名塔之一。

大慈恩寺创建于公元 589 年，初名无漏寺。到公元 648 年高宗李治做太子时，因生母文德皇后早逝，为补报慈母大恩，重修此寺，取名大慈恩寺。据传高宗当年每日早晚从含元殿遥望慈恩寺礼拜。唐代的慈恩寺规模极大，共有 13 个院落，总计房屋 1897 间，云阁禅院，重楼复殿，异常豪华。唐王朝灭亡后，大慈恩寺也渐渐颓废毁坏。现存的寺院建筑大部分是明代时重修的。唐王朝为了请当时名闻遐迩的玄奘法师担任大慈恩寺的住持，特令在寺内修了翻经院。

玄奘

玄奘是中国杰出的翻译家和伟大的旅行家。公元 628 年，28 岁的他独自从长安出发到印度去学佛经，先后在印度各地从事佛教研究达 17 年之久，于公元 645 年带着 657 部经卷返回长安。他往返跋涉 5 万公里，历尽千辛万苦。玄奘根据自己的旅途见闻写的《大唐西域记》，记述了他亲历的 128 个国家和地区的地理位置和风土人情，是研究这些地区历史、地理的珍贵资料。明朝小说家吴承恩以玄奘取经为背景，写出了我国妇孺皆知的四大名著之一《西游记》。玄奘还把我国的古代经典《老子》译成梵文，传入印度。他对古代中印文化的交流，特别是佛教文化的沟通，做出了卓越的贡献。

在请玄奘移居大慈恩寺时，朝廷举行了空前隆重的仪式，出动了 1500 乘锦彩轩车。长安城里所有僧侣都手持香炉和鲜花，随行诵经。朝廷文武百官和皇帝的卫士列队护送。太宗皇帝亲自率领太子、王子和后宫嫔妃登上城楼，焚香目送，数十万人夹道观看。太宗还从全国挑选了著名学者和名僧数百人协助玄奘译经。玄奘在大慈恩寺译经达 12 年之久，共译出佛经 75 部，1335 卷。太宗和太子李治分别为他译的佛经写了《大唐三藏圣教序》和《述三藏圣教序记》，称颂他献身佛教事业的精神。这两篇文章由唐代大书法家褚遂良书写后刻成碑文，至今仍镶嵌在大雁塔底层南门两侧。

大雁塔

公元 652 年，玄奘上表，请求在慈恩寺内建塔以保存从印度带回的佛经和佛像。高宗欣然同意，并用死亡宫女的遗物资助玄奘建塔。玄奘十分高兴，他不但亲自设计图样，还参加搬运砖石的建塔劳动。

大慈恩寺门前有一对威武的石狮，这是明代雕琢的，象征守护寺院的卫士。

寺内的大雁塔创建于公元 652 年，初为 5 层，高 60 米。因土心砖表渐渐颓坏，公元 701 年至 704 年重建时增至 10 层。后遭战乱破坏，于公元 930 年至 933 年再次修葺时改为 7 层。现在的大雁塔大体保持着这次修葺时的面貌：高 64 米，共 7 层。

大雁塔是楼阁式砖塔，采用磨砖对缝（意思是将砖的 6 个面磨光，用石灰、三合土、米浆粘连）的砌垒技术。大雁塔的特点是：砖结构体现出木结构的斗拱风格；砖墙上显出"棱柱"来，可以明显分出墙壁开间。这些都是中国特有的传统建筑艺术形式。大雁塔塔身高大，结构坚固，外观庄严、朴实、大方，充分体现了我国古代劳动人民的智慧和才能。

塔底层四周门楣上雕刻有天王及佛像等线刻画，这些画刻工高超，形象生动，线条流畅，是研究唐代绘画及雕刻的重要资料，其中尤以西门楣的线刻画最为珍贵，是研究唐代建筑的珍贵艺术品。

大雁塔的得名还有一段有趣的故事呢！传说玄奘在印度取经时曾住在一座大乘佛寺内。印度佛教分大乘、小乘两派。大乘吃素，小乘吃荤。玄奘住的这座寺院附近有一座小乘寺。一天该寺的僧人因吃不到肉而发愁，那天正好是菩萨布施日。一个和尚仰天叹道："大慈大悲的菩萨一定不会忘记今天是什么日子！"他正说着，一群大雁飞来，头雁坠地而死。僧侣们个个惊愕万分，以为菩萨显灵，送来大雁以解疾苦。从此，全寺和尚不再吃肉并改信大乘佛教。他们还在大雁落地处修建了一座塔，取名"雁塔"。大雁塔就是玄奘依照印度那座"雁塔"的形式设计建造的。为了颂扬佛教，纪念玄奘，后来人们就称慈恩寺塔为"雁塔"。半个世纪后，荐福寺塔修成了。两塔遥遥相对，风采各异。因荐福寺塔比雁塔小，人们就将这座塔叫大雁塔，而将荐福寺塔改叫小雁塔了。

钟楼与鼓楼

寺院内有两座小楼：东边的小楼叫钟楼，里面悬挂有明代1543年铸的一口铁钟，重15吨；西边的小楼叫鼓楼，楼里存有一面大鼓。钟、鼓用于为僧众报时。

大雄宝殿

寺内第一座殿堂叫大雄宝殿，中间的三座塑像是释迦牟尼三身像。中间的叫法身佛，西边的叫报身佛，东边的叫应身佛。释迦牟尼为佛教始祖。他原是古印度迦毗多国的王子，生于公元前565年，死于公元前486年，大约与中国的孔子处于同时代。他29岁出家修行，35岁成道，成道以后在印度各地传播佛教。三身佛东侧有释迦牟尼的十大弟子之一迦叶；西侧立有释迦牟尼的堂弟阿难，他侍从释迦牟尼25年，也是他的十大弟子之一。再两侧是十八罗汉，都是释迦牟尼的弟子。罗汉是小乘佛教理想的最高果位。

法堂

第二座殿堂叫法堂，供奉的是阿弥陀佛。阿弥陀佛主持西方极乐世界，只要念佛人一心称念"阿弥陀佛"，他就能接引念佛人死后到西方"净土"，故又称其为"接引佛"。东面墙上三张拓片中间的那张叫"玄奘负笈图"。玄奘背着沉重的佛经，脚穿草鞋，背篓上还悬挂着一盏油灯，可以想象他当时不畏艰险，日夜兼程，想早日返回长安的情景。两边是玄奘的弟子圆测和窥基的拓片。圆测是新罗（今朝鲜）人，窥基是唐初名将尉迟恭的侄子。由此可见玄奘在当时不凡的名声地位。

雁塔题名

唐代新考中的进士都要登大雁塔留诗题名，象征从此步步高升，青云直上。著名诗人白居易就留有"慈恩塔下题名处，十七人中最少年"的佳句，表达了他少年得志的喜悦心情。明代时，陕西的乡试举人追慕唐代进士们雁塔题名的韵事，也相携到塔下题诗留名。这些字迹仍保留在塔门门楣和石框上，给古城西安留下了历史的余晖。现在，我们也不妨仿效那些金榜题名的唐代新贵们，登高望远，尽情领略古城西安的风光。遗憾的是，我们却不能在雁塔上题诗留名了。

Dayan Pagoda

Situated in the Da Ci'en Temple, about 4 kilometers from the urban center, Dayan Pagoda (also called Da Ci'en Temple Pagoda) is one of the famous Buddhist pagodas in China.

Originally built in 589 AD in the Sui Dynasty, the temple was named the Wulou Temple. In 648 AD, Emperor Li Zhi, then still a crown prince, sponsored a repair project on the temple in memory of his mother, Empress Wende. It then assumed the present name the Da Ci'en Temple (the Temple of Thanksgiving). The emperor was said to pay homage to the temple twice a day (in the morning and at dusk) by looking in its direction from the Hanyuan Palace. The temple consisted of 1,879 magnificent rooms and was a place of grand extent in the Tang Dynasty. However, it went into gradual decay after the downfall of the Tang Dynasty. The halls and rooms that have survived the ages were actually built in the Ming Dynasty. The Tang Regime gave orders to build a chamber for the translation of Buddhist scriptures and appointed the widely renowned Master Xuan Zang (Monk Tripitaka) the head of the temple.

Xuan Zang

Xuan Zang was both a great translator and traveler. At the age of 28 in 628 AD, he went to study Buddhism in India. He spent 17 years doing research into Buddhism in various places. Later in spite of many hardships, he covered a distance of 50,000 kilometers and returned to Chang'an in 645 AD with 657 sets of Buddhist scriptures. His *Travels in the Western Regions* was based on what he had witnessed in about 128 countries and regions. He recorded their geographic locations and customs. His works provide an important source of information for the study of the history and geography of these regions. Wu Cheng'en, a famous novelist of the Ming Dynasty, wrote a novel — *Journey to the West* against Xuan Zang's experience in his search of the Buddhist truth. The book is one of the four most famous novels in the history of Chinese literature. Xuan Zang translated one of the Chinese Classic *Lao Tzu* into Sanskrit and introduced it to India. He was indeed a great contributor to the Buddist cultural exchanges between India and China in ancient times.

On the day when he moved into the temple, the imperial court held a ceremony of unprecedented grandeur for him. The procession consisted of 1,500 decorated chariots. On the same day, all the monks from the capital followed the procession, holding bunches of flowers and incense burners in their hands, and reciting passages from Buddhist scriptures. Civil and military officials and the Emperor's bodyguards also followed the master into the procession. Even the Emperor and his whole royal family stood on the city gate tower, burnt incense sticks and respectfully watched the procession. Later, the Emperor selected hundreds of renowned scholars and Buddhist monks to help Xuan Zang in his endeavor to translate the Buddhist scriptures that he had brought back from India. Xuan Zang stayed in the temple for 12 years and translated 75 sets, a total of 1,335 volumes of Buddhist scriptures. In praise of the Master's dedication to Buddhism, Emperor Tai Zong wrote *Preface to the Holy Religion*, followed by Crown Prince Li Zhi's *Notes on the Preface to the Holy Religion*. Chu Suiliang, a famous calligrapher of the Tang Dynasty, inscribed the two texts on the stone tablets on both sides of the south gate to the ground floor of the pagoda.

Dayan Pagoda

In 652 AD, Xuan Zang proposed to the court that a pagoda should be built inside the temple to store the scriptures and statues that he had brought back from India. The Emperor readily agreed with him, and raised funds by selling the things left behind by deceased court maids. Master Xuan Zang was so pleased that he designed the pagoda and moved stones and bricks to the construction site.

The two fierce-looking stone lions before the front gate of the temple stand there as if they were two sentinels guarding the place.

The five-story pagoda, 60 meters high, was brought into completion in 652 AD. Owing to the decay of its rammed earth and bricks, the pagoda increased to ten storeys when it was under reconstruction from 701 to 704. However, the winds of war in the years to come brought the pagoda almost to ruins, which in turn resulted in the construction of a seven-storey structure with a height of 64 meters.

This storied pagoda is an architectural marvel. It was built with layers of bricks but without any cement in between. The dou gong (bracket) style in traditional Chinese architecture features the construction of the pagoda. The seams between each layer of bricks and the so-called "prisms" on each side are clearly visible. The pagoda is characterized by its towering height, structural compactness, imposing appearance and unaffected style. It is indeed a good reflection of people's wisdom and talent in ancient China.

The Heavenly King and the Buddha in line drawings appear on the door frames and horizontal bars on the four sides of the pagoda's base. They are vividly portrayed in smooth lines and show a high level of workmanship. They serve as an important source of the study of paintings and sculptures of the Tang Dynasty. Out of these artistic works, the one on the horizontal bar of the west door is the most precious. It is a rare piece of art for the study of the Tang architecture.

There is an interesting story about the name of the pagoda. It is said that Master Xuan Zang once stayed in a Mahayana temple in India. In fact, there are two major sects of Buddhism in India, the Mahayana and the Hinayana. The Mahayana believers are vegetarians while those of the Hinayana are non-vegetarians. Near the temple where he stayed, there was a Hinayana temple. One day, a monk was just worried about the shortage of meat in the temple. But it happened to be the General Alms Day of the Buddha, another monk looked up at the sky and sighed: "Our beloved Buddha, the Great and Merciful, will not forget what day it is today!" At these words, a flock of wild geese flew over the temple. The head goose dropped dead to the ground. The monks were all puzzled by this, and they concluded that this must be the result of the Buddha's spirit at work: to provide them with the wild goose. Ever since then, the monks of the temple became vegetarians and began to believe in Mahayana Buddhism. They also set up a pagoda where the wild goose dropped dead, and called it the Wild Goose Pagoda or Dayan Pagoda today. The Pagoda that greets us today was actually modeled after its Indian prototype. It was given the same name in memory of Xuan Zang and in praise of Buddhism. After about half a century, the pagoda at the Jianfu Temple was built. The two pagodas face each other over a distance, but assume different styles. Since the one in the Jianfu Temple is smaller than the Dayan Pagoda, it is often called the Xiaoyan Pagoda.

The Bell Tower and the Drum Tower

Inside the temple where the pagoda is situated, there are two small buildings. The one on the east side houses a bell, and the one on the west side houses a drum. The bell, cast with iron in the Ming Dynasty, weighs 15 tons. Together with the drum, the bell was used to strike time for the monks in the temple.

The Great Hall of the Buddha

Inside the Great Hall of the Buddha in the temple, there are three incarnations of Sakyamuni. The one in the middle is called Fashen Buddha. The one in the west side is called Baoshen Buddha and the one on the opposite side is called Yingshen Buddha. Sakyamuni, the founder of Buddhism, was prince of the Kingdom of Dapila in India. He was born in 565 BC, and died in 486 BC. He was an approximated contemporary of Confucius in China. Sakyamuni left home in search of monkhood when he was 29 and achieved his purpose at 35. He then spent the rest of his life travelling in India and preaching his principles. The figure on the east side, beside the three incarnations of the Buddha is Jia Ye, one of the ten great disciples under Sakyamuni. The one on the other side is Ahnan, Sakyamuni's cousin. He served Sakyamuni for 25 years as one of his ten great disciples. Along both sides are the 18 arhats, who were also Sakyamuni's disciples. Arhats are the highest ideal position in Hinayana Buddhism.

The Doctrine Chamber

This is the Doctrine Chamber where the Amitabha Buddha is worshiped. He is in charge of the Western Paradise. At the word of the Amitabha Buddha, one will be led to the Paradise upon his death. Therefore, the Amitabha Buddha is also called the Buddha of Guidance. On the wall at the east side of the chamber, there are three rubbings. The one in the middle is called "Xuan Zang on his Way Back to Chang'an". With rolls of scriptures on his back, a pair of straw sandals on his feet and an oil lamp on top of the rolls, Xuan Zang is making his way back to the capital. Beside the portrait of Xuan Zang, there are pictures of Yuan Ce and Kui Ji, two of his disciples. Yuan Ce was from Xinluo (present-day Korea), Kui Ji was the nephew of the famous general Yuchi Gong of the early Tang Dynasty. Judging from the social status and background of the disciples who followed him, Xuan Zang was proved to be a renowned figure during his day.

Inscription on Dayan Pagoda

In the Tang Dynasty, every successful candidate who passed the imperial examination would climb up the pagoda and write poems and inscriptions to indicate that he would have a soaring career in the future. The famous poet Bai Juyi once wrote, "Here under the Ci'en Pagoda, I inscribe my name as the youngest of the seventeen candidates". He revealed his pride and happiness when he became successful at a young age. The fashion of writing poems and leaving inscriptions on the horizontal bars over different doors and their stone frames by the successful candidates went on as far as the Ming Dynasty. These poems and inscriptions have survived till this day as a fine mirror of the city's past. Now let us do what those successful candidates did: climb the pagoda and enjoy the sight of the old capital. But the pity is that we cannot inscribe our names and our poems on the pagoda as those successful people did long ago!

大雁塔北广场

大雁塔北广场以大雁塔、大慈恩寺为核心，北起雁塔路南端，南接大慈恩寺北外墙，东西两侧以广场东西路为界，整体工程占地41.5英亩，建筑面积约11万平方米，总投资约5亿元，于2003年底正式建成并对外开放。

大雁塔北广场由水景喷泉、文化广场、园林景观、文化长廊和旅游商贸设施等组成。整体设计风格大气恢宏，其矩阵喷泉广场、水景广场均刷新了亚洲纪录，也成为亚洲雕塑规模最大的广场。该广场以大雁塔为中心轴，由北向南中轴线上分布有北入口景区、中央大型水景喷泉广场和南端的"大唐盛世"浮雕景区。北广场南北高差9米，分成九级，每个踏步为五级，意为"九五之尊"，由北向南逐级而望，体现了对大雁塔的膜拜之意。

北入口景区

北入口处以"大唐盛世"书卷铜铸雕塑为开篇，上面镌刻着唐代的"贞观之治""开元盛世"字样，图文并茂地向世人展现了一代大唐盛世风貌，以书卷的形式去呈现，不禁让人们感受到古都长安所彰显的深厚历史文化底蕴。两个万佛灯塔与八个6米高的大唐文化列柱是进入北广场的标志。灯塔的设计借鉴了敦煌莫高窟的表现形式凸显佛教文化题材，反映了大唐佛教的盛行，其密檐式的设计风格与大雁塔的外形结构相映成趣、相得益彰，这种统一的设计理念符合中国传统的审美情趣。两侧的大唐文化列柱运用莲花宝座、佛寺塔顶多种佛教传统文化符号无不体现大唐佛文化的繁盛。

中央水景喷泉广场及水道两侧主景区

中央水景区的音乐喷泉和水舞表演成为大雁塔北广场一道独具特色的靓丽风景,为古都西安增添了几分时尚与优雅的魅力,成为西安的"城市会客厅""城市新名片"。主水道喷泉位于广场中轴线上,随不同的音乐节奏形成独特的矩阵和叠水景观,样式多变,水柱形态各异。每当华灯初上之时,在千年古塔的映衬下,变幻万千的水柱随音乐律动,婀娜多姿,景象宏伟壮观,美不胜收,实现了声、光、水、色的完美交融,体现了水与塔的动静和谐之美。

大雁塔北广场主水景区两侧为禅修林区,这里栽种了许多体现佛教文化的树木,包括银杏、白皮松树和菩提树,象征着佛教的三种境界。此外,大唐精英人物雕像,有李白、杜甫、陆羽、王维、韩愈、怀素、僧一行、孙思邈等八大精英人物,反映了大唐盛世在诗歌、书法、茶道、医药、天文学领域所取得的骄人成就。唐诗园林区使唐诗文化与园林景观融为一体,彰显其多元的文化内涵。漫步于北广场,步行道两侧的灯柱上别出心裁地点缀着脍炙人口的唐代著名诗句,使游客们在悠闲漫步之余欣赏并吟咏唐诗经典,感受着中国传统文化的魅力。主水景区的南端向游客呈现了一组组展现大唐盛世的浮雕作品,气势壮观,场景宏大,用浪漫主义手法勾勒了大唐盛世的现实景象,每一个主题都体现着一段大唐传奇,每一幕都向世人陈说着一段令人记忆犹新的大唐故事。

大雁塔北广场处处彰显着盛唐文化与佛文化相结合的设计理念,成为西安乃至中国唯一的盛唐文化广场,是市民休闲、观光、旅游的好去处,成为今天西安国际大都市的新名片。

The North Square of the Dayan Pagoda

The North Square of Dayan Pagoda is centered on Dayan Pagoda and the Da Ci'en Temple. It starts at the southern end of Dayan Pagoda Road in the north and connects to the outer wall of the Da Ci'en Temple in the south. The east and west sides of the square are bound by the eastern and western roads of the square. The whole project covers an area of 41.5 acres and has a construction area of about 110000 square meters with a total investment of 500 million yuan. The North Square was officially completed a, opened to the public at the end of 2003.

The North Square of Dayan Pagoda consists of waterscape fountains, a cultural square, garden landscape, a cultural corridor, the other tourist and commercial facilities. The overall design style is magnificent. Its Matrix Fountain Square and Waterscape Square have both set Asian records. It is also the largest square with most sculptures in Asia. The square has the Dayan Pagoda as its central axis. From north to south, the central axis is distributed with the north entrance scenic area, the central large waterscape fountain square and the relief scenic area of "Golden Era of Grand Tang Dynasty" at the southern end. The height difference between the northern end and the southern end is 9 meters. There are nine sections in total, with each section consisting of five steps. In traditional Chinese culture, when the figure 9 and 5 are used together, it connotes "the supremacy of monarchy". Looking from the north to the south step by step, tourists may express their reverence and worship towards the Dayan Pagoda.

Scenic Area at the Northern Entrance

The northern entrance begins with a bronze sculpture of a scroll called "The Golden Era of Grand Tang Dynasty". The inscription reads "Reign of Zhen Guan" and "Prosperity of Kai YFuan" in the Tang Dynasty. The Sculpture shows the gorgeous achievements and splendid culture of Tang Dynasty with illustrations and pictures. The bronze sculpture is presented in the form of a scroll in order to make people feel the profound historical and cultural significance of the ancient capital— Chang'an. Two Wanfo lighthouses and eight 6-meter-high grand Tang cultural columns are placed at the entrance of the North Square. The design of the lighthouses draws some enlightenment from the design of Dunhuang Mogao Grottoes to highlight Buddhist culture, reflecting the prevalence of Buddhism in the Tang Dynasty. The design of dense eaves and the outer structure of the Dayan Pagoda are perfectly matched, adding charm to each other. This unified design concept conforms to the traditional aesthetic taste of China. On both sides of the Datang cultural column, various traditional Buddhist cultural symbols on the lotus throne and the top of the Buddhist temple all reflect the prosperity of Buddhist culture in Tang Dynasty.

Central Waterscape Fountain Square and Main Scenic Spots on Both Sides of Waterway

The musical fountain and water dance performance in the central water scenic area has become a unique and beautiful scene in the north square of the Dayan Pagoda. Such scenery adds fashion and elegance to the ancient city, so it is known as "the Reception Hall" and a "new city card" of Xi'an. Located along the central axis of the square, the large fountain displays a unique matrix and overlapping landscape with different rhythms of music, with varied and changing styles of water columns. Whenever the lights are on, the ever-changing water column is dancing with the music with the-thousand-year-old Pagoda in the background, displaying a magnificent and gorgeous scene. It is the perfect blend of sound, light, water and color, reflecting harmony between dynamic water and the tranquil pagoda.

On both sides of the main water scenic area is the Zone for Meditation, where many trees embodying Buddhist culture were planted, including ginkgo, white-bark pine and bodhi trees, symblizing the three realms of Buddhism. The statues of Tang Dynasty elites, including Li Bai, Du Fu, Lu Yu, Wang Wei, Han Yu, Huai Su, Sengyihang and Sun Simiao, reflect the remarkable achievements of Tang Dynasty on poetry, calligraphy, tea ceremony, medicine and astronomy. Tang poetry Gardens integrate Tang poetry culture with garden landscape and highlight its diverse cultural connotation. Walking along the North Square, lampposts on both sides of the walkway are decorated with famous poems of the Tang Dynasty, where tourists can enjoy and chant Tang poetry classics while walking leisurely, feeling the charm of Chinese traditional culture. At the southern end of the main water scenic spot, groups of emboss works showing the Golden Era of Tang Dynasty are presented to tourists. These grand and magnificent emboss works are vividly presented in a romantic manner to reveal the glamour of the Tang Dynasty, each theme indicating a legend at time, each scene presenting a memorable story of the Tang Dynasty.

The North Square of the Dayan Pagoda manifests the integration the Tang culture and Buddhism and it is a unique and the only cultural plaza in Xi'an and in China as well. It has gained popularity among citizens: a "sanctuary" where people can enjoy themselves—strolling leisurely, seeing around and going sightseeing. It has now become a show card of Xi'an—an international metropolis.

大唐不夜城

大唐不夜城位于西安市曲江新区，以盛唐文化为背景，以大雁塔为依托，以唐风元素为主线，以体验消费为特征，分为六个唐风街坊，一条亚洲最大的景观大道，三大主题文化广场，四大文化艺术场馆，八大文化旅游商贸工程，总投资50亿元，着力打造集购物、餐饮、娱乐、休闲、旅游、商务为一体的一站式消费天堂。

大唐不夜城作为西安城市的新名片，由玄奘文化广场、贞观文化广场、开元庆典广场等三大主题广场由北向南依次贯穿分布，其中贞观文化广场是其核心部分，总投资逾十亿元，由西安大剧院、西安音乐厅、曲江美术馆和曲江电影城四组文化艺术性建筑组成，游客可体验中外文化艺术、不同地域风情的艺术精品。因而此地成为西部乃至全国文化艺术的集散地和发源地。

大唐不夜城的中轴景观大道是一条1500米长的大唐不夜城横贯南北的中央雕塑景观步行街，整体雕塑群由九组富于文化内涵的雕塑景观组成，与现代化的水景系统、灯光系统、立体交通系统完美结合，相得益彰，将历史古韵的雕塑与现代时尚元素巧妙融合，再现大唐文化盛景。

开元盛世雕塑气势雄伟恢宏，尽显大唐之国泰民安、繁荣昌盛的盛世风貌；载舟覆舟群雕体现了大唐时期推行的仁政、关注民生、以人为本的治国理念；大唐精英谱群雕，展现了中国作为当时世界上第一个人口超过百万的国际化大都市，在诗歌、书法、绘画、科技等领域取得的显赫地位；万国来朝雕塑体现了历经贞观之治、开元盛世的大唐王朝是当时世界上最为强盛的文明国家，是世界各国人们普遍向往的东方乐土，都城长安更是众望所归的圣地，云集着数量惊人的西域胡人。唐朝文化远播东西，中华文明影响世界。万国来朝雕塑表现的就是大唐王朝万国来朝的盛世景象。武后行从雕塑展现了作为中国历史上唯一的一位女皇武则天的丰功伟绩。该组雕塑以唐代仕女画家张萱的《皇后行从图》为蓝图，连接在贞观广场和开元广场之间，上承贞观之兴，下启开元之盛，完整地展示大唐盛世气象。

贞观纪念碑是不夜城的地标性雕塑，雕塑中间为唐太宗李世民，他威武地端坐于高头大马之上，意气风发，勒马前行，四周由号手、缰绳旗手、鼓手组成的仪仗队及文臣武将紧密相随。碑体正面雕刻"贞观之治"四字，背面为贞观政要名录数百字。该纪念碑将大唐时期的雕塑元素和西方纪念碑式雕塑创作手法相结合，反映大唐帝国的繁荣盛况和李世民的文治武功。

The Grand Tang Sleepless Plaza

Grand Tang Sleepless Plaza is located in the Newly – developed Qujiang Zone of Xi'an. Focusing on the prosperous culture of the Tang Dynasty, based on the Dayan Pagoda, featured with the Tang ethos and characterized by experiential consumption.

The Grand Tang Sleepless Plaza is divided into six Tang-style blocks, the largest landscape avenue in Asia, three theme cultural squares, four cultural and artistic galleries, and eight culture-tourism-trade projects. 5 billion yuan is invested in it with the purpose of one-stop consumer paradise such as shopping, catering, entertainment, leisure, tourism and business affairs.

As a show card of Xi'an, Grand Tang Sleepless Plaza runs through the north to the south, covering Xuan Zang Square, Zhen Guan Square and Kai Yuan Celebration Square, of which Zhen Guan Square is the kernel part. More than one billion yuan is invested in four cultural and artistic complexes, including Xi'an Grand Theatre, Xi'an Concert Hall, Qujiang Art Gallery and Qujiang Movie Theatre. Domestic and overseas tourists can experience different cultures and appreciate competitive artistic works of different countries and regions. So Xi'an is becoming the hub and origin of West China's culture and art.

The landscape avenue along its central axis is a 1500-meter-long pedestrian mall dotted with sculptures form south to north. The overall sculpture group consists of nine sculpture landscapes enriched with cultural connotation, perfectly combined with the modern hydro-scape system, lighting system and 3D traffic system, presenting an ingenious integration of ancient historical charm and modern elements so as to bring forth the splendid cultural scenery of the Tang Dynasty.

The Sculpture describing the Kai Yuan Golden Era, majestic and magnificent, shows peace and prosperity of Tang Dynasty; the Sculpture denoting the idea of "Water can carry a boat, but it can also overturn it" reflects the concept of benevolent governance, the concern for people's livelihood, and people-oriented governance of the Tang Dynasty; The Sculpture of Tang elites shows China, as the world's first international metropolis with a population of more than one million, had a prominent position in poetry, calligraphy, painting, science and technology. The Sculpture of pilgrims to China shows that the Tang Dynasty was then the most powerful and civilized country in the world after undergoing the two golden eras known as the Reign of Zhen Guan and the Reign of Kai Yuan. It was the oriental paradise that people all over the world yearned to visit. Chang'an, the capital city, was also a popular holy place, with a startling number of foreigners from the Western Regions. The culture of the Tang Dynasty was spread far and wide and Chinese civilization had great impact on the world. Such a sculpture can best depict the prosperity of the Tang Dynasty, with its glorious achievements attracting people from different countries to China. The Sculpture of Empress Wu's Journey shows her glorious achievements during the reign of Wu Zetian, the only empress in Chinese history. This group of sculptures is based on the blueprint of a famous painting done by Zhang Xuan, a well-known woman painter, good at drawing traditional beauties. Such a sculpture linking the Zhen Guan Square with Kai Yuan Square, perfectly reveals the prosperity of Tang Dynasty during different eras.

The Zhen Guan Monument is a landmark sculpture of the Grand Tang Sleepless Plaza. In the middle of the sculpture is Li Shimin, Emperor Tai Zong of the Tang Dynasty. Riding on the horse and in a high spirit, he reined his horse and galloped forward with the guard of honor composed of trumpeters, flag bearers and drummers, officials and officers following him. "Reign of Zhen Guan" was inscribed in the front age of the tablet and the name lists of politicians on the back. The sculpture of the Tang Dynasty and the creation techniques of the west are well combined in this monument sculpture, thus reflecting the prosperity of the Tang Empire and Emperor Li Shimin's political and military achievements.

小雁塔

在西安城南1公里处的荐福寺内，有一座典型的密檐式佛塔叫作小雁塔，它和大雁塔交相辉映。

雁塔晨钟
小雁塔内有一口金代（公元1192年）铸成的大铁钟，钟声清脆悦耳，5公里之外都听得清清楚楚，人称"神钟"。这口钟高4.5米，口沿周长7.4米，重10吨，钟上面刻有"皇帝万岁，臣佐千秋，国泰民安，法轮常转"十六字吉祥语。据说如果有人思念远方的亲人，只要把亲人的名字和去处写在一张黄笺上，钟声就会把思念之情传到千里之外的亲人耳中。因此，"雁塔晨钟"曾被誉为关中八景之一。

荐福寺
荐福寺创建于公元684年，是唐高宗李治死后百日，臣民为其献福而建的，所以最初起名叫献福寺。公元698年改名荐福寺。荐福寺是我国另一位伟大的翻译家义净法师的译经处。他于公元671年由海路到印度求法，历时20多年，游历30余国，于公元695年带梵文经卷400部归国。途中曾在印度尼西亚的苏门答腊岛长期居住和考察。他在荐福寺译经共56部，并著有《大唐西域求法高僧传》一书。此书堪称是玄奘《大唐西域记》的姐妹篇，对后世研究中国和印尼之间的文化交流史提供了宝贵的资料。

小雁塔

小雁塔建于公元707年，共15级，约45米高。相传，当年义净法师为了保存从印度带回的佛经，上表请求朝廷出资修建荐福寺塔。皇帝李显极其懦弱，凡事都要皇后拿主意。皇后得知此事后，即令后宫嫔妃及宫娥彩女都捐钱修塔。宫女们争先恐后，慷慨解囊，捐的钱建了这座塔还未用完。

雁塔"神合"

在漫长的岁月中，小雁塔还有一段"神合"的历史呢！公元1487年，陕西发生了六级大地震，把小雁塔从上到下震裂了一条一尺多宽的缝子。然而时隔34年，在1521年又一次大地震中，裂缝在一夜之间又合拢了。人们百思不得其解，便把小雁塔的合拢叫"神合"。1555年9月，一位名叫王鹤的小京官回乡途中夜宿小雁塔，听了目睹过这次"神合"的堪广和尚讲的这一段奇事后，惊异万分，便把这段史料刻在小雁塔塔身北门楣上。新中国成立后修复小雁塔时，才发现它不是"神合"，而是"人合"。原来古代工匠根据西安地质情况特地将塔基用夯土筑成一个半圆球体，受震后压力均匀分散，这样小雁塔就像一个"不倒翁"一样，虽历经70余次地震，仍巍然屹立。这不能不令人叹服我国古代能工巧匠建筑技艺的高超！

1555年，陕西华县发生大地震，小雁塔顶两级被震毁，所以，现在只剩13级。1965年，本着对古建筑"整旧如旧"的原则，国家对小雁塔进行了彻底修复。塔身用五道钢筋混凝土腰箍加固，塔壁一砖一石都经过检查，重建了塔内旋梯，安装了照明和避雷设备。

大雄宝殿

寺内的大雄宝殿是明代重建的。奇怪的是大殿上瓦的颜色却不一样。原来这里还有一段感人的故事呢！明英宗时，西域番僧勺思吉就任荐福寺住持。那时的荐福寺除了小雁塔外，其余建筑早在唐末就被毁坏了。勺思吉不忍看到寺院这幅破败景象，便竭尽自己的积蓄，且广为募化，筹资修葺荐福寺。然而资金仍不够。于是他带头从唐代以来的殿址瓦砾堆中挖能用的砖瓦，用在新修的殿堂上。竣工后，他修了本章，绘成图样，呈礼部转奏英宗，请求皇帝为修复一新的寺院命名。英宗一看图上的殿堂顶用了绿琉璃瓦，勃然大怒，不但下令斩杀勺思吉和满寺僧众，还要把荐福寺夷为平地。原来明代规定只有皇宫才能用绿琉璃瓦盖顶，别处用了就犯"欺君之罪"。后经大臣们劝谏，英宗才降旨礼部查清事由。经调查方知这寺内大殿上用的绿琉璃瓦全是勺思吉带领众僧一片一片从数百年废墟中挖出来的。英宗这才赦免了勺思吉等众僧的死罪，荐福寺与小雁塔遂得以幸存。这大殿上的绿琉璃瓦大概就是当年的犯禁之物吧。

The Xiaoyan Pagoda

Xiaoyan Pagoda is located in the Jianfu Temple, 1 kilometer south from the downtown area.

Morning Bell Chimes

Inside the temple, there is a huge iron bell which dates back to the Jin Dynasty (1192 AD). The sound of the bell is crisp and pleasant, and can be heard as far as 5 kilometers away. The local natives often call it the "Magic Bell". It is 4.5 meters in height, 7.4 meters in cercumference along the rim, and 10 tons in weight. The bell is carved with Chinese auspicious words, which means in English "Long live the Emperor" "The vassals will help him for ever" "May the state be stable and the people live in peace" and "May the Buddhist spirits prevail for ever". It is said that if one missed his beloved relations far away from him, the only thing he could do was to write their names and addresses on a piece of yellow paper, and the sound of the bell would pass the message to them. The Xiaoyan Pagoda is well known for its "Morning Bell Chimes", which used to be one of the Eight Famous Scenic Attractions in central Shaanxi.

The Jianfu Temple

The Jianfu Temple was built in memory of Emperor Li Zhi on the the 100th day anniversary of his death in 684 AD. Therefore, it was originally named the Xianfu Temple (Temple of Sacrificial Offerings). The present name didn't come into being until 698 AD. The temple is also the place where the great translator Monk Yi Jing translated Buddhist scriptures. Yi Jing set out by sea for India in search of Buddhist principles in 671 AD. Having traveled across over 30 countries of more than 20 years, he came back to Chang'an with some 400 sets of holy Sanskrit scriptures in 695 AD. On his way back, he stayed on the island of Sumatra in Indonesia and made some field trips there. Yi Jing translated 56 sets of scriptures in the Jianfu Temple and wrote the book *A Biography of Eminent Tang Monks in Search of Buddhist Truth in India*. The book can be regarded as companion to *Pilgrimage to India* by Xuan Zang. It is of great help to the study of Chinese and Indian history, and the history of the cultural exchanges between China and Indonesia.

The Xiaoyan Pagoda

The Xiaoyan Pagoda was set up in 707 AD. It has 15 storeys and is about 45 meters above ground. The story goes that when Yi Jing appealed to the imperial court for funds to build a pagoda, so as to preserve the holy Buddhist scriptures, the cowardly Emperor Li Xian asked the Empress for advice as he often did. When she heard of this, she ordered all the imperial concubines and court maids to donate money for the construction of the pagoda. The ladies were so generous in their donation that there was still money left over even after the project was completed.

The "Magical Healing" of the Pagoda

There is a story about "Magical Healing" of the pagoda. In 1487 AD, Shaanxi Province was attacked by an earthquake of six points on the Richter scale. As a result, the pagoda was left with a one-foot crack from the top to the bottom. 34 years after the quake, there came another one! Amazingly, the crack healed overnight. The process was later called the "magical healing". In September 1555, Wang He, an official from the capital, put up for the night in the temple on his way home. After he heard about the "magical healing" from Kan Guang, a monk who had witnessed the incident, he was very surprised and engraved this story on the lintel of the north gate to the pagoda. However, when repair work started after 1949, it was found that the healing was not "magical", but "human". The foundation of the pagoda took the shape of a hemisphere. Therefore, it evenly divided the stress and impact of the earthquakes. The pagoda has survived 70 quakes, and it still stands as firm as ever. The marvelous workmanship of the ancient builder is undoubtedly admirable.

In 1555, there was another earthquake in Huaxian County of Shann Xi province.

As a result, the top two storeys of the pagoda were destroyed. The present structure has only 13 storeys. In the spirit of "restoring the old to the original", the local government embarked on a repair program on the pagoda in 1965. Its main framework was reinforced with steel and concrete. Every brick and stone was checked. The staircase was also rebuilt. Lighting was provided inside, and a lightning rod was fixed on the top.

The Great Hall of the Buddha

The Great Hall of the Buddha in the temple was built in the Ming Dynasty. The roof tiles come out in surprisingly different colors. Actually, there is a moving story about this. When Emperor Ying Zong of the Ming Dynasty was in power, Monk Shao Siji, who was from a tribe in the Western Regions of China, served the Jianfu Temple as the abbot. Except for the pagoda, almost all of the buildings inside the temple were destroyed at the end of the Tang Dynasty. Monk Shao Siji couldn't bear the sight of the ruined temple. He collected all his savings and went out for donations for the repair and maintenance of the temple. However, he still did not have enough money. Thus, with Shao Siji in the lead, the monks went around picking up tiles still usable from the ruins of the Tang Dynasty, and used them on the Great Hall of the Buddha under repair. When the repair work was finished, he wrote a report and handed it to the emperor for a new name through the Ministry of Rites, together with a sketch of the temple. However, when Emperor Ying Zong saw from the sketch that the temple had green glazed tiles on the roof, he burst into a rage. He ordered that Monk Shao Siji and other monks be sentenced to death, and the whole Jianfu Temple be leveled ground. The reason for his anger was that only the court itself could use green tiles. Using green tiles on other structures was considered an act of infidelity to His Majesty! At the earnest request of some vassals, the Emperor changed his mind, but ordered the Ministry of Rites to find the cause of the matter. Later, it was made clear that the glazed green tiles were from the ruins of the past dynasties. The Emperor withdrew the death sentence on the monks. As a result, the Jianfu Temple and its pagoda survived despite the royal restrictions on the use of green tiles in the Ming Dynasty.

第六部分　古寺庙

法门寺

　　法门寺位于扶风县城北10公里的法门镇，距西安以西120公里。它是我国古代安置释迦牟尼佛骨舍利的著名寺院。

　　法门，意为修行者必入之门。法门寺始建于东汉，寺因塔而建。法门寺塔，又名"真身宝塔"，因葬有释迦牟尼的一节手指骨而得名。公元前485年，释迦牟尼灭度，印度摩揭陀国孔雀王朝阿育王（公元前268—前232年在位）皈依佛教。为了使佛光远大，他将佛祖骨分成84000份，分葬于世界各地，并建成84000座塔。我国有19座佛祖舍利塔，法门寺塔就是其中之一。因此，法门寺塔和寺有"关中塔庙之祖"的称誉。

　　塔初建时名阿育王塔，唐贞观年间改建成四级木塔。木塔在保存了近2000年后，于公元1569年遭地震倒塌。1579年，扶风县佛教徒募化钱财，开始重建真身宝塔，历时30年，将原来木塔改建为13层八棱砖塔，高47米。该塔建造得极为壮观。但由于重量过大，地下又建有舍利地宫，造成上重下轻，所以砖塔建成54年后，在地震中法门寺塔身向西南歪斜。1976年，扶风县阴雨连绵，又遭四川松潘大地震的影响，该塔更加严重地向西南倾倒。1981年，这座"斜塔"的西半侧终于在一个阴雨绵绵的季节里垮塌，仅留半个塔面危立在残台破砖之上。

　　1985年，陕西省政府决定仿照明代的砖塔重建新塔。在清理塔基时，意外发现了地宫。同时在地宫中发现了深藏千年之久的释迦牟尼指骨舍利和供养舍利的大批珍贵文物。

　　根据这次在地宫里发现的碑文记载，佛指舍利一直藏在法门寺塔基内。从公元5世纪的北魏到唐代的400多年间，皇帝们由于迷信迎请佛骨可以保佑国泰民安，曾几次打开地宫，将佛骨请出供奉。这种活动在唐末愈演愈烈，最铺张的要数唐懿宗咸通十四年，即公元872年的一次迎奉活动。这也是历史上最后一次迎请佛骨。这次迎请活动事先准备了两年，当时从京城长安到法门寺100多公里间，车马昼夜不绝，茶水饮食摆满路旁，供香客随便享用。佛骨由万人组成的仪仗队，刀杖齐全的皇家御林军导引。长安城内张灯结彩，文武百官沿街迎候。

然而，迎佛骨三个月后唐懿宗便归了西天。他的儿子僖宗将佛骨送还法门寺并封闭了地宫。此后，各代再也没有进行过迎佛骨活动。

法门寺地宫总长21.2米，面积31.84平方米，是迄今国内发现的规模最大的寺塔地宫。地宫所发现的四枚佛指骨，最令人瞩目。第一枚舍利藏在后室的八重宝函之中，长40.3毫米，上下俱通，竖置在金塔基银柱上；第二枚藏在中室汉白玉双檐灵帐之中，形状与第一枚相似；第三枚藏在后室秘龛五重宝函的白玉棺之中，管状，长37毫米，白中泛黄；第四枚舍利藏在前室彩绘菩萨阿育王塔内，色泽、形状与第一、二枚相似。经中国佛教协会会长赵朴初和副会长周绍良先生鉴定，其中第三枚是灵骨，即佛祖的真身指骨，其余三枚为"影骨"，即唐朝皇帝为保护真骨而命人仿制的。但在佛教徒眼中，"影骨"也是圣骨，与真身舍利具有同等意义。

法门寺发现的佛指骨是目前世界仅存的佛指骨真身舍利。地宫内出土的其他众多文物，也堪称国宝。

唐代织金锦工艺之精湛令人吃惊。织锦所用的金丝，最细的直径仅为0.1毫米，比头发还细。以丝线为芯，以金丝一圈圈缠绕，1米长的金丝要绕3000多圈。武则天供奉的绣裙就是用这种织品制成的。

秘色瓷为青瓷的一种，工艺复杂难度高，由于配方秘而不宣，故称秘色瓷。法门寺发现的秘色瓷是迄今为止首次发现，为鉴定这种瓷的时代和特点提供了标准器。

法门寺发现的金银器是等级极高的珍品。四面十二环鎏金禅杖无论质料、形体、工艺，都堪称世界佛事法器之最。法门寺地宫珍宝的数量之多、品种之繁、质量之优、保存之完好、等级之高，在考古发掘中前所未有，对研究唐代的政治、经济、文化、宗教、科技、艺术、中外交流等具有极重要的学术价值，而且为宗教旅游和考古提供了不可多得的条件。

法门寺院内碑刻很多，皆属珍贵史料。其他如明成化八年（公元1472年）铸造的铁钟，重3600斤，音盖数里，称"法门晓钟"，为扶风八景之一；隋文帝所送的卧虎石，泼水虎形即现，堪称一绝；《法门寺》戏中人宋巧娇告状的跪石，给无数游人留下遐思。

现在法门寺塔院已按明代的记载规划重修。法门寺塔按明塔原样重建，保留了地宫并增修了参观通道。塔院右侧按唐代建筑式样修建了法门寺珍宝馆，供游人参观。法门镇也按旅游的需要进行了整体规划建设，气象焕然一新。

PART SIX Ancient Temples

The Famen Temple

The Famen Temple is located in Famen Town, 10 kilometers north of Fufeng County, 120 kilometers west of Xi'an. It is a famous temple in China. It was built in ancient times to house the fingerbones of Sakyamuni, the founder of Buddhism.

"Famen" means the initial approach to become a Buddhist believer. The Famen Temple was constructed in the Eastern Han Dynasty because of the stupa there. The Famen Temple stupa, also known as "the Real Spirit Pagoda", is famous for the fact that it houses a finger bone of Sakyamuni. In 485 BC, after Sakyamuni's nirvana, the Buddhist King Asoka (268 BC—232 BC) of ancient India decreed that in order to spread Buddhism he would divide Sakyamuni's relics into 84,000 bits and send them to places all over the world. 84,000 stupas were constructed to house them. There are 19 such stupas in China. The Famen Temple Stupa is one of them. Thus the Famen Temple and its stupa enjoyed the reputation of being the "forefather of pagodas and temples in Central Shaanxi".

The Famen Temple Pagoda was originally called Asoka Stupa. During the years of Zhen Guan (627 AD—649 AD) in the Tang Dynasty, it was reconstructed into a four-storey wooden structure. After nearly 2,000 years of existence, the wooden stupa fell down in 1569 due to an earthquake. In 1579, Buddhists in Fufeng County collected alms and donations to rebuild the stupa into an exquisite and splendid brick octagonal pagoda of 13 storeys, 47 meters high. It took 30 years to complete the whole project. Because of the massive weight of the stupa and the relatively small underground palace, 54 years after its completion, the stupa began to tilt toward the southwest. In 1976, because of constant rain in Fufeng County and the impact of Songpan earthquake that occurred in Sichuan, the tilt of the stupa increased toward the southwest. In 1981, the western side of this tilted stupa collapsed after incessant rains. Most of the body of the stupa collapsed shortly thereafter. Only part of the body remained on an incomplete platform of broken bricks.

In 1985, the Shaanxi Provincial Government decided to rebuild the stupa in the style of the Ming Dynasty. While clearing the stupa foundation, the underground palace was accidentally discovered. For more than 1,000 years, the palace had housed the remains of the finger bones of Sakyamuni and other valuable relics that enshrined these precious bones.

According to the tablet inscriptions discovered in the underground palace, the finger bone had always been kept inside the Famen Stupa. During the 400 years from the Northern Wei period to the Tang Dynasty, emperors of different periods believed that the worship of the finger bone could bless the security of the nation and bring a stable life to the people. So the emperors opened the palace several times, and worshiped the enshrined finger bone. This type of worship became more and more frequent. The most extravagant ceremony took place during the 14th year of the reign of Tang Yi Zong in 872 AD. This was also the last time of the imperial worship. It took two years to make preparations for the ceremony. At that time when the ceremony was about to take place, many activities were seen along the road for over 100 kilometers, from the capital city, Chang'an, to the Famen Temple. Horses and carts never ceased moving to and from and people set up food stalls along both sides of the road, so the pilgrims could enjoy whatever they liked. Buddha's finger bones were guarded by the royal guards armed with swords and staffs. The Guard of Honor was composed of over 10,000 people. The capital city was brightly lit and beautifully decorated for such an occasion. All the court officers and officials were part of the ceremony.

However, three months after the greeting ceremony for Buddha's finger bone, Tang Yi Zong passed away. Emperor Xi Zong, his son, returned the finger bone to the Famen Temple and closed the underground palace. Since then there has never been another greeting ceremony for Buddha's finger bone.

The underground palace at the Famen Temple, 21.2 meters long, covers an area of 31.84 square meters. It is the largest palace among all the temples and stupas discovered so far in China. The four finger bones discovered there are most riveting. The first one was kept in an eight-layer chest in the back room. The finger bone, 40.3 millimeters long and hollow all through, hung vertically on a silver bar on a gold stupa base. The second, which is like the first in shape, was kept in a double-eave miniature jade coffin in the central room of the palace. The third one was kept in a five-layer miniature jade coffin, which was retained in a secret niche in the back room. This finger bone is tube-like, 37 millimeters long and is slightly yellow. The fourth one was kept in a colored King Asoka stupa in the front room. Its color and shape are very much like that of the first and second finger bone. Zhao Puchu, Chairman of the All-China Buddhism Association and Zhou Shaoliang, Vice Chairman of the Buddhism Association, determined that the third finger bone is the original, which means it is the only real finger bone of the Buddha. The other three were "shadow bone", imitations which the Tang emperor had made in order to protect the real one. But in the eyes of Buddhist believers, even the "shadow bones" were so sacred that they enjoyed the same significance and importance as the real one.

The finger bone discovered at the Famen Temple is the only real finger bone of the Buddha that has been discovered and maintained in the world. Many other relics were also unearthed from the underground palace. They are considered to be national treasures.

The technique of gold brocade weaving developed in the Tang Dynasty was surprisingly exquisite. The gold thread used in weaving was only 0.1 millimeter thick, finer than a hair. Silk thread was taken as the cord around which the gold thread coiled. One meter of the thread could make 3000 circles. The embroidered skirts that Emperess Wu Zetian consecrated were made out of this material.

The secret celadon is a kind of Chinese green porcelain. The techniques used to make the celadon are very intricate. The court kept all of this information a secret, which is indicated by its name, "secret celadon". The secret celadon unearthed at the Famen Temple was a breakthrough for the study of the history of Chinese porcelain. It provides much information for the determination of the age and characteristics of this type of porcelain.

The gold and silver ware unearthed at the Famen Temple is of high quality and great value. The four-face, twelve-ring gilded monk's cane is the most precious Buddhist staff in terms of style, technology and material. The discovery of the underground treasures in the Famen Temple is unprecedented in all the archaeological findings of the Tang Dynasty, as far as the variety, quality and the state of preservation of the treasures are concerned. These valuable relics provide us with important data for the study of social, technological and artistic exchanges between China and other parts of the world. So many cultural relies also provide rare resources for religions tourism and archaeology.

There are many inscribed stone tablets in the temple. They contain valuable historical data. An iron bell cast in 1472 (the 8th year of Chenghua reign of the Ming Dynasty), weighs 3,600 kilograms. It can be heard several miles away when struck. "The tolling of the Famen morning bell" was one of Fufeng County's famous eight attractions. The lying stone tiger which was presented by the Sui Emperor, Wen Di, is really a superb piece. The stone reveals a tiger's image when it is splashed with water. The story, which is said to be the one in the traditional opera *The Famen Temple* where Song Qiaojiao kneels to bring a lawsuit, is often thought-provoking to the tourists.

Both the Famen Temple and the Famen Temple Stupa have been rebuilt based on the model from the Ming Dynasty. The underground palace remains intact, and a passage into it for visitors has been constructed. On the west side of the Famen Temple a museum housing the excavated treasures was built according to the architectural style of the Tang Dynasty. Famen Town has been reconstructed as well for the sake of tourism in the area.

化觉巷清真寺

化觉巷清真寺是西安七万多穆斯林进行宗教活动的主要场所，也是全国重点文物保护单位。这座清真寺没有阿拉伯伊斯兰教清真寺那种金碧辉煌的大圆顶、高耸入云的宣礼塔，色彩缤纷的镶嵌图案和令人目不暇接的阿拉伯花纹。相反，这里处处是亭台楼阁、雕梁画栋，从设计施工到艺术造型，既有中华民族的传统风格，又有伊斯兰教清真寺的格调和特点。

提起清真寺，就不能不谈谈伊斯兰教是如何传入中国的。

伊斯兰教创立于公元7世纪初，于7世纪中叶传入中国。当时，一些阿拉伯商人和旅行者经波斯和阿富汗到达中国的西北地区，和中国建立了外交、贸易和军事联系。同时，另一些阿拉伯人从阿拉伯海出发，经孟加拉湾和马六甲海峡到达中国的广州、泉州、杭州和扬州等城市。他们中间很多人在中国定居下来并和汉族妇女结了婚，他们的后裔遂成为中国的穆斯林。而大批穆斯林移居中国则是在13世纪初，时值成吉思汗"西征"，占领了今西亚地区直到欧洲东部和今伊朗北部的广大地区。这些地区的许多穆斯林被迫从军，后来定居中国。他们中间多数人是士兵，也有一些是工匠和官吏，在元史中被统称为"回民"。这些回民以后又跟随忽必烈南下，统一了中国，建立了元朝。伊斯兰教于是流行全国，中国很多地方也都修建了清真寺。许多穆斯林还在各级政府及军队中任职。

14世纪初，不少穆斯林参加了朱元璋的农民起义。起义军中的穆斯林首领英勇善战，为明朝的建立立下了赫赫战功，因此，明初历代皇帝都曾下令要保护伊斯兰教，并在各地建造清真寺以表彰他们的功绩。16世纪初，伊斯兰教在新疆确立了统治地位。甘肃、宁夏、青海一带的少数民族也接受了伊斯兰教，其中包括回、维吾尔、哈萨克、柯尔克孜、塔吉克、塔塔尔、乌孜别克、东乡、撒拉、保安等十个民族。西安的穆斯林主要是回族。现在我国的穆斯林人口共有1700万。

化觉巷清真寺是西安最大的清真寺，也是我国建筑最早、规模较大、保存较完善的清真寺之一。据《创建清真寺碑记》载，该寺建于公元742年，但从寺内建筑风格来看，可能建于明代。全寺共有4个院落，占地12000多平方米，建筑面积近4000平方米。

前院木牌坊建于17世纪初，高约9米，琉璃瓦顶，异角正檐，距今300余年，仍保存完好。

第二进院落中心有一座石牌坊，它的两侧各立一通冲天雕龙碑，记载历代重修情况。碑阴分别刻有宋代大书法家米芾"道法参天地"和明代书法家董其昌"敕赐礼拜寺"手书，是中国书法艺术中斗方大字的珍品。

第三进院落入口处的敕修殿里藏有推算伊历的阿拉伯文"月碑"，碑文是清初寺内一个叫小西宁的掌教编著的。院落中心有一座三层八角形木质结构的"省心楼"，它和阿拉伯伊斯兰教清真寺的宣礼塔作用相同，是呼唤教徒们来礼拜的塔楼。省心楼南北两厢，分别建有布局雅致的客厅和经堂。西南方向的五间厢房叫"水房"，是教徒礼拜前沐浴的地方。

第四进院落中央有一座"凤凰亭"，是教徒们等候礼拜的地方。主亭为六角形，两个侧亭为三角形，三亭连在一起，形如凤凰展翅，故名"凤凰亭"。亭后有一海棠形鱼池，绕过鱼池，是占地约700平方米的月台，月台顶端就是面积近1300平方米的礼拜殿，一次可容纳1000多人礼拜。殿内天棚藻井达600多幅。大殿的墙壁、门及藻井上的图案，均为蔓草花纹和阿拉伯文字组成的彩绘图案。大殿两端的"神坛"是阿訇带领教徒们面向麦加，高诵《古兰经》，虔诚礼拜的地方。

中国的伊斯兰教徒和世界各地的伊斯兰教徒有着同样的风俗习惯。他们每天礼拜五次，分别是在黎明、中午、下午、黄昏和夜晚等五个时间举行。

根据我国宪法规定，中国公民有宗教信仰的自由，各民族有保持和改革风俗习惯的自由。伊斯兰教教徒和中国其他各族人民一样，享受平等的权利。他们的风俗习惯也普遍地受到尊重。

The Mosque in Huajue Lane

The Mosque is the major spot for the religious activities of over 70000 Moslems in Xi'an. It is also an important National Historical Monument in China. Unlike Arabian mosques with splendid domes, skyward minarets, and dazzling patterns, this mosque possesses much Chinese tradition in both design and artistic outlook. It assumes the striking features of Chinese pavilions, with painted beams and engraved ridgepoles.

However, it would be useless to talk about the Mosque without knowing how Islam was introduced into China.

Islam, as a religious order, was founded in the early 7th century and was introduced to China in the mid-7th century. At that time, some Arabian merchants and travelers came to the northwestern region by way of Persia and Afghanistan to establish diplomatic, trade and military contacts with China. Others started their voyage from the Arabian Sea, crossed the Bangladesh Bay and the Strait of Malacca, finally arrived at Guangzhou, Quanzhou, Hangzhou, Yangzhou and other Chinese cities. Later, many of them settled down and married the local women. Their children became the first generation of Chinese Moslems. However, massive immigration of Moslems to China did not take place until, as late as, the early period of the 13th century. As a result of his Western Expedition, Genghis Khan conquered vast expanses of land from Central Asia to East Europe, including the northern part of Iran. Many of the Moslems in these conquered areas were forced to enlist in the army. Later, they made China their permanent home. Many of them were soldiers and some were smiths and officials. They were called the Hui people in the history books of the Yuan Dynasty. The Hui people later followed Kublai Khan down to the South, helping him unify China and establish the Yuan Dynasty. In the wake of this conquest, Islam spread all over China and mosques began to appear everywhere. Many Moslems held positions both in the military and civil services in the Yuan Dynasty.

A lot of Moslems took part in Zhu Yuanzhang's uprising in the early 14th century and made great contributions to the founding of the Ming Dynasty. Therefore, all the emperors of the Ming Dynasty issued mandates to protect Islam and to set up mosques in honor of the Moslems for their great contributions. In the early 16th century, Islam dominated Xinjiang and spread its influence to Gansu, Ningxia and Qinghai. The religion also deeply influenced so many minority ethnic groups as the Hui, the Uygur, the Kazak, the Kirgiz, the Tajik, the Tartar, the Uzbek, the Dongxiang, the Salar, the Bonan in the three provinces. The Moslems in Xi'an are mainly the Hui people. There are approximately 17 million Moslems in China.

The Mosque is the most sizable of its kind in the city of Xi'an, and also one of the oldest and best-preserved mosques in China. *The Stone Tablet on the Building of the Mosque* says that it was built in the Tang Dynasty. However, judging from its architectural style, it was probablly built in the Ming Dynasty. Its four courtyards cover an area of more than 12000 square meters, with a building area of 4000 square meters.

The still intact wooden memorial arch in the front yard was built at the turn of the 17th century. With glazed tiles, spectacular corners, and upturned eaves, it stands about 9 meters high, and has a history of more than 300 years.

The stone memorial gateway in the center of the second courtyard is flanked by two tall tablets, with dragons carved on each. They record the details of the repair work ever conducted since the building of the mosque. One tablet bears the characters by Mi Fu, the master calligrapher in the Song Dynasty: "May Islam Fill the Universe." The other bears the characters by Dong Qichang, the Ming Dynasty master calligrapher: "Royally Bestowed." These characters are typical examples of traditional Chinese calligraphy.

At the entrance of the third courtyard is a hall built by the order of the Royal Court, where a "Crescent Tablet", showing the calculation of the Islamic Calendar is stored. The calendar was compiled by Xiao Xining, who was in charge of the mosque in the early period of the Qing Dynasty. A three-storey octagonal wooden structure called the Retrospection Tower stands in the center of the courtyard. It functions the same as the minaret in an average Arabian mosque. Orders are often sent from the tower to call the Moslems to come to worship. Respectively on the south and north wings of the tower are the Reception Chamber and the Scripture Chamber. Both of them are elegantly laid out. The five wooden houses, called "water houses" in the southwest section of the mosque are where the believers bathe themselves before they attend their services.

Inside the fourth courtyard, there is a structure called the Phoenix Pavilion, a place where worshipers wait for services. The pavilion, in fact, is a complex of three small buildings. The six-gable structure in the central part is adjoined by two three-gable buildings on each side which make it look like a flying phoenix, hence its name. Just at the back of the pavilion there is a fish pond, and beyond it is a platform with an area of 700 square meters. Across the platform stands the 1,300-square-meter prayer hall. It can holds over 1,000 worshipers at a time. The ceiling is decorated with over 600 panels. The walls of the hall, as well as the panels, are decorated with patterns of trailing plants and Arabic letters. The shrine at the western end of the hall is where the imam and worshipers chant *The Koran* and pay homage while facing in the direction of Mecca.

The Moslems in China share much the same customs with their brothers and sisters elsewhere in the world. They worship five times a day: at dawn, at noon, in the afternoon, at dusk, and at night.

The Constitution of China acknowledges that each citizen has the freedom of religion, and that each ethnic group has the freedom to preserve or reform its own customs. Of course, the Moslems in China enjoy equal rights with other ethnic groups, and their religious beliefs and customs are respected everywhere in the country.

兴教寺

兴教寺是我国唐代著名翻译家、旅行家玄奘法师长眠之地，位于西安城南约20公里处。

玄奘从印度取经回来后，倾注全部心血译经19年，不幸积劳成疾，于公元664年圆寂于玉华宫（在今陕西铜川市）。玄奘去世后，遗体运回长安，安葬在东郊白鹿原上。白鹿原地势很高，在皇宫内的含元殿就能看到。高宗十分敬重玄奘，当听到玄奘逝世的噩耗，曾罢朝致哀，连连哀叹："朕失国宝矣。"每当看到白鹿原上玄奘的茔墓，高宗都禁不住伤心泪下。他想长期这样下去必然有损自己的身体健康，于是于公元669年诏令将玄奘的遗骨迁葬到远离长安城的少陵原上，同时修建了寺院。唐肃宗为玄奘的舍利塔亲自题写了塔额"兴教"二字，意思是要继承玄奘的事业，大兴佛教。从此，这个寺院就叫兴教寺。

唐末，兴教寺因战乱被烧毁，唯一幸存的是玄奘和他两位弟子的舍利塔。现在的兴教寺是1922年和1939年重修的。新中国成立后，人民政府又多次拨款整修这座唐代名刹。兴教寺现在是全国重点文物保护单位。

大雄宝殿内的铜佛像是明代遗物，玉佛像是缅甸赠送的。佛像前经常摆放有点心、炸食，这些都是当地群众来寺院上香时献的供品。我国宪法明文规定，公民有信仰宗教的自由，因而兴教寺香火四季不断。

东边的藏经楼内珍藏有历代经卷数千册。

西边的三座楼阁式仿木结构砖塔就是幸存下来的玄奘及其两个上座弟子的舍利塔。中间是玄奘的舍利塔，共5层，23米，塔底的拱形券洞里有玄奘法师的泥塑像。塔背镶有《唐三藏大遍觉法师法铭》，碑文记叙了玄奘的生平事迹。东边是玄奘上座弟子圆测的舍利塔，西边是玄奘另一位上座弟子窥基的舍利塔。玄奘弟子有上千人，怎么唯独这两人能享有如此殊荣，被陪葬在玄奘左右呢？这里还有一段有趣的故事呢！

传说玄奘从印度回来后，就在慈恩寺内潜心译经。尽管他不分昼夜地伏案工作，然而单靠他一人何年何月才能译完那600多部经卷呢？且随着年龄的增长，他身体又日渐不支。于是玄奘决心物色几个有志于佛学研究的人，教会他们梵文，一则帮助自己译经，二则在自己百年之后，能将自己的事业继承下去。一天，玄奘在曲江岸上散步，偶然遇到了一位气度不凡的少年，经询问，得知他是唐开国元勋尉迟恭之侄，叫尉迟洪道。玄奘决心收他为徒。太宗得知后，赐尉迟洪道法名窥基。窥基聪慧好学，刻苦钻研佛教经论，很快学会了梵文。他不但成为玄奘译经的得力助手，还撰写了多部佛学著作。他17岁出家拜玄奘为师，把毕生的精力都奉献给了佛教事业，直到50岁时，死在译经院的书案旁。人们为了表彰他译经不辍的精神，特地将他陪葬在玄奘法师的舍利塔旁。

比起窥基来，圆测成为玄奘的弟子就颇费一番周折。圆测是新罗（今朝鲜）王的孙子，乘遣唐使船来到长安。他很想拜玄奘为师，却又怕玄奘不肯收他为徒，就设法买通了大慈恩寺的守门僧人，每天晚上在窗外偷听玄奘给窥基传授唯识论。一天晚上，圆测正在窗外偷听，却不料被窥基发现，当即被"捉拿归案"。圆测长跪在地，恳求玄奘收他为徒。圆测不但精通梵文，而且熟悉汉语，在长安佛教界颇有名气。窥基害怕他夺走自己上座弟子的位置，就故意刁难。他让圆测讲解唯识论，如有讲错的地方，玄奘就不会收他为徒了。圆测将计就计，趁势将偷听到的唯识论滔滔不绝地讲了一遍。玄奘十分满意，当即收他为徒。后来，圆测成为唯识宗的继承人之一。他临死前，嘱咐弟子将自己陪葬在师傅的舍利塔旁。

The Xingjiao Temple

About 20 kilometers to the south of Xi'an lies the Xingjiao Temple. The temple is the burial ground for the remains of Xuan Zang, a famous translator and traveler of the Tang Dynasty.

After he returned from India with Buddhist scriptures, Xuan Zang spent 19 years in translating the Buddhist scriptures into Chinese. The constant overwork first caused his illness, and then his death. He died in 664 AD at the Yuhua Palace (in today's Tongchuan City, Shaanxi). His remains were then carried to Chang'an, and buried on Bailu Plateau, which has a high elevation and can be clearly seen from Hanyuan Imperial Palace. When he was alive, Xuan Zang was deeply respected by Emperor Gao Zong. His death therefore caused the emperor great sorrow. The moment he heard the bad news, the emperor stopped all the imperial affairs to pay tribute to the master. He said repeatedly with a sigh, "I have lost a national treasure". The emperor wept each time he saw Xuan Zang's tomb on the distant plateau. This continuous deep sorrow would surely have done harm to his health. Thus, Xuan Zang's remains were removed to Shaoling Plateau in 699 AD, which was far from his imperial palace. At the same time, a temple was built in memory of him. Emperor Su Zong wrote the two characters "Xing Jiao" on the stupa in memory of Xuan Zang, which means what Xuan Zang had started should continue and that Buddhism should flourish, hence the name of the present temple.

The war-ridden years at the end of the Tang Dynasty destroyed almost the entire temple except for the stupas of Xuan Zang and two of his disciples. The present temple was actually built between 1922 and 1939. After 1949, the People's Government sponsored a series of repairs on the temple. It is now an important National Historical Monument in China.

The bronze Buddha in the main hall dates back to the Ming Dynasty, and the jade Buddha is the present from Burma. Pastry and fried cakes are tokens of homage offered by the local worshipers. It is stipulated in the Constitution that Chinese citizens enjoy freedom of religious belief. Many Chinese Buddhists enjoy such freedom, as is evidenced by the joss sticks and candles in the temple all year round.

The building on the east side of the temple is the depositary of Buddhist scriptures, which contains thousands of copies of Buddhist scriptures.

The three pavilion-style stupas, modeled after wooden structures, are the only survivors of the temple. The one in the middle is Xuan Zang's stupa. It is a five-storey structure, 23 meters high. There is a clay sculpture of Xuan Zang inside the arch cave at the base of the stupa. Inlaid on its backside is a tablet with the "Epigraph of Master Dabianjue of the Tripitaka", which tells the life story of Xuan Zang. The stupa on the east side is for Yuan Ce, and the one on the west is for Kui Ji. Both of them were Xuan Zang's senior disciples. You may wonder why these two disciples were so honored as to be buried alongside their master. There is, however, an interesting story about it.

The legend goes that Xuan Zang buried himself in the translation of Buddhist scriptures in the temple immediately after he returned from India. He diligently worked around the clock. The translation of over 600 scriptures was indeed an impossible task for a single man, considering the fact that he was getting old and his health was failing. Therefore, Xuan Zang decided to find some people who were willing to dedicate themselves to the study of Buddhism. He would teach them Sanskrit, and they could not only assist him in the translation, but also carry on his work after his death. One day, as he was taking a stroll on the bank of the Qujiang River, Xuan Zang came across a young man with a remarkable character. On inquiry, he learned that the youth was Yuchi Hongdao, a nephew of one of the founders of the Tang Dynasty, Yuchi Gong. Xuan Zang wanted the young man to be his disciple. Later, Emperor Tai Zong gave the youth the Buddhist name, Kui Ji. An intelligent and hardworking young man, Kui Ji soon obtained a good command of Sanskrit, and devoted himself to the study of Buddhist scriptures and theories. He was a capable assistant to Xuan Zang, and wrote many books on Buddhism as well. He died at the age of 50 at a desk in the translation chamber, and was buried alongside his master in memory of his devotion to Buddhism.

Compared with Kui Ji, Yuan Ce had a hard time in becoming Xuan Zang's disciple. He was the grandson of the emperor of Xinluo (now Korea). He came to Chang'an on an envoy mission. He was eager to have Xuan Zang as his master, but was afraid of being declined. He bribed the door-keeper at Da Ci'en Temple so that he could be allowed to listen to Xuan Zang's teaching Kui Ji by eaves-dropping at night. He was, however, caught red-handed one night by Kui Ji. He then knelt down and pled to be accepted as a disciple. Yuan Ce was versed in both Chinese and Sanskrit, and gained much fame in the Buddhist circles in Chang'an. Kui Ji was afraid that Yuan

Ce could outdo him. He tried to make things difficult for Yuan Ce by making him interpret the Buddhist classics to Xuan Zang. Kui Ji thought, if Yuan Ce made a mistake, Xuan Zang would not accept him as a disciple. Yuan Ce was pleased to have the chance and poured out what he had learned by eaves-dropping. His eloquence greatly impressed Xuan Zang, who immediately made him his disciple. Later, Yuan Ce became one of the successors of Weishi Sect. During the last minutes of his life, he requested that he should be buried beside his master.

青龙寺

青龙寺位于西安城东南的铁炉庙村村北高地上，距城约3公里。

青龙寺原来是隋代的"灵感寺"，建于公元582年。公元711年改名"青龙寺"。青龙寺是日本佛教密宗的祖庭。9世纪初至中叶，日本曾派遣大批僧人到唐朝求法，著名的"入唐八家"中有六人曾在青龙寺受法，空海和尚是其中之一。

空海，号弘法大师，公元774年生于日本赞岐园（今香川县）。公元804年随日本遣唐使藤原葛野橘入唐求法，在青龙寺拜惠果为师，学习密宗。惠果为其灌顶并赠法号"遍照金刚"。空海遂成为真言密宗的第八代座主。惠果还请人为空海缮写新译佛经，临摹密宗历代教祖像，铸造密宗法器。空海学习刻苦，不到两年便完成学业回国。

空海回国后，在高野山建造金刚寺，创立真言宗。他不但精通法典，且精于书法。相传唐皇宫墙上王羲之的墨迹因年久而残缺不全，德宗皇帝命空海补写。空海挥毫而就，和王羲之的真迹一般无二，德宗皇帝叹为观止。空海楷、草、行、隶、篆等五种书体都极出色，因此被誉为"五笔和尚"。他同嵯峨天皇、橘逸势被称为"日本三笔"。他的《风信贴》被后人视为书法典范，真迹已成国宝。他一生写了许多专著，影响深远。《文镜秘府论》是研究唐诗的杰作；《篆录万象名义》是日本第一部汉语辞书；《执笔法》是日本研究中国书法的最早著作。他参照汉字草书，创造了日语字母"平假名"，沿用至今。他依照唐朝学制，在京都创办"综艺神智院"，吸收平民子弟入学。空海回国时，带回许多经论和王羲之真迹。他还把中国的灌溉技术、毛笔制作方法传到日本，促进了中日之间经济和文化的交流。日本当代知名作家司马太郎写的长篇小说《空海的环境》，就是以空海入唐求法的事迹讴歌中日人民的友好情谊的。

空海纪念碑已于 1982 年在青龙寺建成,寺内其他殿堂也已相继重建完毕,供广大游人参观。

The Qinglong Temple

The Qinglong Temple is located on the tableland north of Tielumiao Village, about 3 kilometers southeast from the downtown area of Xi'an.

The temple, set up in 582 AD, used to be called "Linggan Si" (Temple of Inspiration) in the Sui Dynasty. The present name didn't appear until 711 AD. The Qinglong Temple was the place of origin of the Japanese Mi Sect of Buddhism. From the early to the middle period of the 9th century, many Japanese monks were sent to China to study Buddhism. Six of the eight famous Japanese who came to China in the Tang Dynasty studied at the Qinglong Temple. Kukai, a famous monk was one of them.

Kukai, with a given Buddhist name Master Hongfa, was born at Sanudinokuni (present-day Dagawaken County) in Japan in 774 AD. In 804 AD, he came to China with the Japanese envoy HuTzuwara Kuzunomaro to study Buddhism. It was in Qinglong Temple that he acknowledged Hui Guo as an Esoteric Sect master. Master Hui Guo poured holy water on the Japanese youth's head as a sign of acceptance, and gave him the Buddhist title Bian Zhao Jin Gang (Buddha's full-time warrior attendant). Kukai thus became the eighth master of Mi Zong or Esoteric Sct / Dctrine (Shingon in Japanese) Hui Guo also ordered people to have the newly translated Buddhist scriptures and pictures of Esoteric Sect masters copied for Kukai. He also had special religious instruments of the Esoteric Sect made for him. Being an extremely studious monk, Kukai finished his studies in less than two years and then went back to Japan.

After his return, Kukai built the Buddhist Warrior Attendant Temple at Koyasan and founded the Zhenyan Sect (the True Word Sect). Kukai was not only versed in the Buddhist teachings, but also a great calligrapher. It is said that when part of Wang Xizhi's writing on the walls of the royal palace faded with the passage of time, Emperor De Zong asked Kukai to mend them. Kukai accomplished the task in one breath and the rewritten characters looked exactly the same as those of the former renowned calligrapher. On seeing this, the Emperor couldn't help admiring his superb skill of calligraphy. Having possessed remarkable talents in all the five forms of Chinese calligraphy (regular script, cursive script, running script, clerical script and seal script), Kukai was thus called the "five-styled monk". Together with Emperor Sagatenno and Tatibananchayanri, he was praised as one of the "Three Brushes of Japan". His work *Fushinho* has been regarded as a calligraphic model, and the original is considered a national treasure. Apart from this, he also wrote many other influential books on specific subjects. His *Bundyohifuron* is a masterpiece for the study of the Tang poetry. His *Tenreibansyomeigi* was the first Chinese dictionary in Japan. His *Siipituhos* was the earliest works on Chinese calligraphy. Referring to the Chinese cursive script, Kukai invented the system for the Japanese language—Hiragana, which is still in use today. He also established an institution of Sogeishinchiin in Kyoto after the Tang educational system which drew students from ordinary families. When he went back to Japan, he took with him many volumes of Buddhist scriptures and original works of Wang Xizhi's calligraphy. He also introduced the Chinese techniques of irrigation and brush-making to Japan and helped to advance the economic and cultural exchanges between the two countries. The novel *Kukainofukei* written by the contemporary Japanese writer Shibaryotar is based on Kukai's life in China. It was written to praise the friendship between the two peoples.

A monument in memory of Kukai was set up in 1982 at the Qinglong Temple. The halls have been restored so that tourists may come for a visit.

香积寺

香积寺在西安城南约17.5公里的长安区郭杜乡香积寺村。该寺建于公元706年，是净土宗二世祖善导法师的衣钵弟子怀恽为祭祀善导圆寂而修建的。香积寺建成后成为净土宗的活动中心，因此该寺被视为净土宗发源地。

善导是我国佛教净土宗的主要创始人之一。他生于公元613年，俗姓朱，泗州（安徽北部）人。幼年从密州（今山东境内）明胜出家。他在公元641年去并州石壁山玄中寺（今山西交城县境内）拜访高僧道绰，归为其门下，深谙《观经》奥义。公元645年，道绰和尚圆寂，善导又来到唐都城长安，开始时住终南山悟真寺，后又经常在长安城中的光明寺广传教义。他于公元681年病故，终年69岁。他的弟子怀恽等人，将善导的遗骨安葬在长安终南山麓的神禾原上，并建立砖塔以示纪念。后来他的弟子在塔周围建立了香积寺。

净土宗于东晋时期从印度传入中国，兴盛于北魏。净土宗提倡专念"阿弥陀佛"的名号，就可以抵达"西方净土"的极乐世界。"阿弥陀佛"是梵语，意为无量光明，无量寿命，无量品德智慧等。唐代净土宗得到长足的发展，中唐以后，广泛流行于社会各阶层。

传说"天竺有众香之国，佛名香积"。该寺取名香积寺，意思是把善导法师比作香积佛。香积寺位于潏、滈两河交汇的神禾原西端。唐代诗人王维曾游过此寺，留有《过香积寺》五言律诗："不知香积寺，数里入云峰。古木无人径，深山何处钟。泉声咽危石，日色冷青松。薄暮空潭曲，安禅制毒龙。"这首诗描绘了寺院环境的幽静宜人。

寺内的善导塔是公元680年修建的。塔由青砖砌成，平面正方形，为仿木结构。塔原为13级，因年久残毁，现存11级，高约33米。塔身周围保存有鞍形的12尊半裸石佛像，雕刻精巧，实为珍品。塔基层四面有门，南门楣额上嵌有砖刻的"涅槃盛事"横额，是公元1768年修补时所做。塔身四面有用楷书刻写的《金刚经》，字迹雅秀，笔力遒劲，十分引人注目。

香积寺在唐代曾盛极一时。怀恽召集四方僧众多次在寺内举行隆重祭祀。唐高宗李治曾赠佛金利千余粒，还有百宝幡花，令其供养。武则天和唐中宗母子多次亲临膜拜。

唐代的善导塔现已做了整修，塔内有木梯直通塔顶。新修大殿内安放着日本友人赠送的善导大师像、供桌、铜磬、木鱼等。殿前安置着他们赠送的石灯。大雄宝殿前十棵苍劲的柏树，象征着中日两国人民间的友谊像松柏一样万古长青。

The Xiangji Temple

The Xiangji Temple is located in Xiangji Si Village of Chang'an County, which is 17.5 kilometers south of the City of Xi'an. The temple was built in 706 AD by Monk Huai Yun, in commemoration of the death of his master, Shan Dao, the heir to the founder of Jingtu (Pure Land) Sect of Buddhism. It later became the center of Jingtu sect and was considered to be the birth place of the sect.

Born in 613 AD in Sizhou (in the north of Anhui Province) from a family named Zhu, Shan Dao was one of the chief founders of the Jingtu Sect in China. When still a boy, he left home and became a monk in Mizhou (present-day Shandong Province). In the year 641 AD, he became a disciple of Master Dao Chuo at the Xuanzhong Temple on the Shibi Mountain in Bingzhou (now Jiaocheng County of Shanxi Province). There he later became remarkably versed in *Guanjing*, a Buddhist classic. Upon the death of Dao Chuo in 645 AD, Shan Dao came to the capital, Chang'an, where he spread his beliefs at the Guangming Temple, though he at first took residence in the Wuzhen Temple at Mount Zhongnan. He died of illness at the age of 69 in 681 AD. The location of the present Xiangji Temple was the place where upon his death his disciple Huai Yun and others buried his remains and set up a brick pagoda in memory of him.

Jingtu Sect of Buddhism was first introduced to China from India in the Eastern Jin Dynasty, and flourished in the Northern Wei Dynasty. Believers of this sect think that if they keep saying "Amitabha", they would enter the Western Paradise after their worldly journey was finished. The Sanskrit term "Amitabha" means infinite brightness, life, wisdom and virtue. The Tang Dynasty saw rapid development of the Jingtu Sect. It enjoyed great popularity among the people during the latter part of the Tang Dynasty.

According to the legend, India was a place of incense. The temple was therefore named Xiangji, meaning the Temple of Incense, and Master Shan Dao was likened to the Buddha of Incense. Situated at the western end of the Shenhe Plateau where the Ju and Hao rivers converge, the temple offers tranquility and elegance and was highly praised in a verse by Wang Wei, a famous Tang poet, who once passed by the temple:

Whereabouts of the Temple you query,

High into the clouds there it emerges.

With shadowed paths un-trodden,

The bells ring in the deep valley.

While the spring waters tinkle,

The sun bathes the pine trees.

And when the tambourine sounds over the dusk pool,

Dhyan kills the evil dragon.

Shan Dao Pagoda in the temple dates back to 680 AD in the Tang Dynasty. Built of blue bricks, this square pagoda is modeled after the wooden structure. The vicissitudes of time have reduced the once 13 storeyed pagoda to 11. Now it is about 33 meters high. Around the pagoda are 12 saddle-shaped, half-naked stone buddhas, which show marvelous workmanship in sculpture and have proven themselves to be rare treasures. There are doors on the four sides of the base of the pagoda. On the lintel of the southern door are four Chinese characters — "涅槃盛事", meaning "The Heyday of Nirvana". These characters date back to 1768. On the four sides of the pagoda are the

"Diamond Sutra" in regular script. The calligraphy has much elegance and vigour in its strokes, and is very appealing to the visitors.

The temple saw its heyday during the Tang Dynasty. There Huai Yun often summonted the monks and believers from various parts of the country to offer sacrifices to Buddha. Emperor Li Zhi once bestowed about 1000 Buddhist relics and embroidered streamers to the temple to be enshrined there. Emperor Li Xian and Empress Wu Zetian often came to the temple to pay homage to Buddha.

Shan Dao Pagoda has been repaired. A wooden flight of stairs was built to reach the top. In the newly-built Great Hall of the Buddha of the temple stand is a statue of Shan Dao, a sacrificial table, a pair of brass Buddhist percussion bells, and a wooden fish (also a percussion instrument). They were the presents from Japanese friends. In front of the temple stands stone lamps. They are also gifts from the Japanese friends. The ten towering cypresses in front of the Great Hall of the Buddha symbolize the ever lasting friendship between the Chinese and the Japanese people.

草堂寺

草堂寺位于西安市西南25公里的圭峰北麓，今鄠邑区草堂营村。

草堂寺是后秦时（公元401年）御苑逍遥园内的一小部分，是高僧鸠摩罗什当年翻译佛教经典的圣地。鸠摩罗什祖籍印度，出生于中国龟兹（今新疆库车）。他生来聪明异常，人称"圣童"。鸠摩罗什七岁随母出家，博通经典，精通经藏、律藏、论藏，被尊为"三藏法师"。公元401年，鸠摩罗什几经周折被后秦王姚兴迎请到长安，姚兴待以国师之礼。鸠摩罗什居住在逍遥园内，和"沙门"3000余人翻译梵文经典97部，427卷。这是中国第一次用中国文字大量翻译外国经书。由于他既通梵语，又精汉文，所以所译的经书受到八方称赞，被称为中国佛教三大翻译家之一。当年的译经场地是一座构造简单的堂屋，以草苫盖顶，所以起名"草堂寺"。

鸠摩罗什在草堂寺译出中论、百论、十二门论。这三论在当时十分盛行，后称"三论宗"，鸠摩罗什则是这一宗的开山鼻祖。他在这里还曾译成实论，当时也普遍弘扬，后称"成实宗"。鸠摩罗什所译的经论涉及中国佛教十宗说的八宗，所以对佛教在中国的传播和中外文化交流贡献很大。三论宗在唐时又传入日本，因此鸠摩罗什在日本佛教界也享有盛名。

鸠摩罗什于公元413年圆寂后葬于草堂寺。今寺内西侧有建于唐代的"姚秦三藏法师鸠摩罗什舍利塔",石色灿烂,玉润夺目。据史书记载,塔石为西域所贡。塔高2.34米,8面12层,用8种不同颜色的玉石雕刻而成,故称"八宝玉石塔"。整个塔身工艺技巧精妙绝伦,堪称稀世之珍。

寺内还有一口奇特的烟雾井。《户县县志》记载:"井中腰有石一块,相传昔时每见一蛇卧石上,辄有白气一股由井上腾,缭绕于省城西南,所谓草堂烟雾者此也。"这股缭绕于省城西南的烟雾,借助西风的力量,向帝都长安飘去,并与其相连,形成关中八景之一的"草堂烟雾"。真正的烟雾可能是由地热引起的。这股升腾上来的热气,再与周围的山岚水气以及草堂寺上空缭绕的香烟混为一体。井上现修建了一座古朴的敞亭,上有赵朴初题的"烟雾井"三个字。

今日草堂寺内柏竹交翠,名花香叶,环境幽雅,空气清新,实为理想的旅游胜地之一。

The Caotang Temple

The Caotang Temple (also known as the Straw-thathched Temple) is located at the northern foot of Guifeng Mountain in the Caotangying Village, Huyi district, 25 kilometers southwest of the city of Xi'an.

Once part of Xiaoyao Garden in the period of Late Qin (401 AD), the Caotang Temple later became a sacred place where the Buddhist master Kumarajiva translated Buddhist scriptures. Of Indian blood and born in Qiuci (now Kuche County of Xinjiang Uygur Autonomous Regin), Kumarajiva possessed extraordinary talents and thus was called a prodigy when he was small. At seven, he left home together with his mother, and became a monk. He was already versed in three Buddhist classics: namely Sutrapitaka (Jing Zang), Vinayapitaka (Lü Zang), and Abhidha Crmapitaka (Lun Zang). Thus he gained the name, Master Tripitaka (Master of Three Buddhist Classics). After miscellaneous ups and downs, Kumarajiva was invited to Chang'an in 401 AD by Yao Xing, King of Late Qin, and was treated as the national master. He stayed with 3,000 other monks in the imperial garden, where 97 sets, 427 volumes of Buddhist scriptures were translated from Sanskrit into Chinese, the greastest effort ever undertaken till that day in Chinese history. Because of his versatility in both Sanskrit and Chinese, Kumarajiva's translation was widely appreciated. He has been referred to as one of the three greatest translators of Buddhist scriptures in China. The translation office of that day was a simple thatch-roofed house, hence the name the Caotang Temple.

At this temple, Kumarajiva translated Madhyawikasastra (Zhong Lun), Satasastra (Bai Lun) and the Twelve Sastras (Twelve Men Lun), all of which were very popular Buddhist classics at that time. Kumarajiva was thus the originator of the Three Classics Sect. He also translated Satyasiddhi Satra (Shi Lun) which was also very popular. He was thus regarded as the founder of the Cheng Shi Sect. Kumarajiva's translation of Buddhist scriptures, covered eight out of ten main Buddhist sects in China, making great contributions to the cultural exchanges between China and foreign countries. The Three Classics Sect was introduced into Japan in the Tang Dynasty, gaining still more fame for Kumarajiva among Buddhist circles there.

Kumarajiva died in 413 AD and was buried in this temple. A stone dagoba of unique brilliance was set up at the western side of the temple during the Tang Dynasty. The inscriptions on the monument read "In Memory of the Yao Qin Master Kumarajiva". According to historical records, the stones for the dagoba were contributed by the Western Regions then. The eight-side, twelve-storey dagoba is 2.34 meters high and is engraved with jade of eight different colors, hence the name "Dagoba of Eight Treasure Stones". It is a dagoba of such exquisite workmanship that the whole structure is truly a rarity.

A well inside the temple possesses quite a unique character. It emits gusts of mist now and then. The *Annals of Huxian County* reads: "There is a piece of stone on one side, halfway down the well. The legend goes that whenever there is a snake lying on the stone, the mist would come out, clouding over the southwestern part of Chang'an." The mist traveling as far as the ancient imperial capital of Chang'an under favorable winds, represented one of the Eight Famous Scenic Attractions in central Shaanxi—The Mist of the Caotang Temple. The real cause of the mist, however, might be geothermal vapor, which, once out of the well, gets mixed with the smoke of incense over the temple. An elegant and antique-looking pavilion has been built over the well. It has the inscriptions by the famous calligrapher and Buddhist Zhao Puchu, "The Misty Well".

The temple is richly planted with lush cypresses and bamboos, and fragrant flowers. The quiet environment and fresh air make it an ideal place for tourists.

楼观台

楼观台是我国著名的道教圣地，有"天下第一福地"之称。它位于周至县东南15公里处的终南山麓，距西安70公里。

楼观台得名于公元前11世纪的西周。相传周代大夫函谷关令尹喜在这里结草为楼，夜观天象，所以最初名为"草观楼"。有一天，尹喜看见从东面飘来一股紫气，预知将有真人从这里经过。后来果然老子西游路过此地，他便将老子迎到草楼，恳请老子为其著书。于是老子在草楼写下了千古不朽的《道德经》，共5000余字，并在楼南高岗筑台讲经，叫作"说经台"。楼观台由此得名。

老子姓李，名耳，字聃，是我国春秋时期著名的思想家，道家创始人，被道教奉为教主。据《史记·老子列传》记载，老子曾任东周守藏室的官吏（掌握图书的史官），博学多才，孔子曾经向他请教过问题。后来因周王室内乱，老子弃官，周游天下。老子开创的道家哲学思想流派包含极为深刻的哲学原理，至今受到人们的重视。他著的《道德经》被译为多国文字，在海外广为流传。

楼观台南依秦岭，北临渭河，竹林茂密，古树成荫，素有"洞天福地"之称，是一个风景秀丽的游览之地。

相传周穆王曾到此游历，建造宫室，名"楼观宫"。秦始皇在楼南建宫，亲来求神拜仙。汉武帝在楼北也曾立宫。晋惠帝在这里植树千万余株，迁来居民300多户，进行维修保护工作。隋文帝初年，又进行了大规模的修葺。

唐代，楼观台达到极盛时期，唐高祖李渊在太原起兵抗隋，他的女儿平阳公主在户县聚众响应，得到楼观台掌教道长在人力、物力上的大力支持。李渊一度在军事上处于困境，于是亲自到楼观台卜问吉凶。掌教道长竭力鼓励说："陛下盛德感天，圣祖垂佑，何寇之不可诛也。"由于这些原因，李渊灭隋建唐后，决定奉老子为祖宗，并亲到楼观台拜谒老子祠，将楼观台改名为宗圣宫。还下诏将道教尊奉为国教，排在儒教和佛教之前。唐玄宗对道教更是推崇备至，以夜梦老子为名，又把宗圣宫改为宗圣观，从此楼观台为道教圣地。

楼观台在宋、元、明、清各代都进行过维修。唐代的欧阳询、王维、李白，宋代的米芾，元代的赵孟頫等文人学士都曾来过这里，咏诗题写，刻石留念。

楼观台遗留到今日的主要胜迹有说经台、炼丹炉、吕公洞、化女泉、楼观塔、老子墓，以及宗圣宫、会灵观、玉华观、延生观等遗址。

宗圣宫遗址

宗圣宫是楼观台的主体建筑之一，明、清以后逐渐衰败。现在遗址范围内仍存留建筑基础、石狮、石牛、石碑碣、银杏树和九株石柏。其中一株枝杈藤结，顶端似三只雄鹰蹲踞，名曰"三鹰柏"。另一株名为"系牛柏"，传闻老子当年所骑青牛就拴在这棵古柏上。树下有一石牛恬然静卧，安详自若。院内还有一株直径约五六米，高大挺拔的银杏树，据说此树有2000余年树龄，是亚洲第二大古银杏树。

说经台

说经台是楼观台现存最大的一组古建筑，现已成为楼观台的中心。整个建筑群建在海拔560米左右的峰顶上，这里竹林茂密，古树成荫。

进入山门，一个八角形水池映入眼帘。该水池名叫"上善池"，取"上善若水"之意。老子曾说"天下莫柔弱于水，而攻坚强者莫之能胜"。意思是说，水是天下最柔弱的，但它可以冲决一切坚硬的东西，体现了道家"柔弱胜刚强"的思想。

山门两侧是说经台的碑厅，保存历代碑刻70余件，较有名的是唐欧阳询隶书《大唐圣观记》碑和唐苏灵芝行书《唐老君显见》碑。出碑厅沿蜿蜒山道盘旋而上，道旁崖壁间镶嵌着许多古代名人的墨迹和诗词刻石，以宋代米芾题的"第一山"和苏东坡游楼观台题诗最为珍贵。

老子祠

穿过说经台山门，沿着蜿蜒曲折的盘道登上说经台顶，就可以见到老子祠。这里是传说中老子讲经的地方。大殿正中有老子塑像，老子塑像前有一立一跪两尊塑像，跪者是老子的弟子徐甲，站者是位美女。传说老子为了考验徐甲学道是否心诚，将拐杖插在地上，用七香草化作一个美女，徐甲一见，动了凡心。老子于是收杖显出真身，徐甲惊恐万状，急忙跪下认罪。泥塑反映的就是这个故事。传说当年老子插杖的地方变成一眼清泉，叫作"化女泉"，位于说经台西面1公里处的地方。

大殿后是收藏各种版本的《道德经》及历代研究《道德经》等文献典籍的"藏经阁"。阁前两棵古柏下，放置着一台奇异的八角形石碾盘。相传这是老子从女娲那里"借"得的一块可以发出声响的灵石，用来碾长生不老药。轻叩该盘，立刻会听到嗡嗡的金属撞击声，其回声传入山谷，悠扬动听，久久不散。

炼丹炉

炼丹炉位于一座荆棘丛生的山峦上,距山下约 2.5 公里,与说经台所在山峰遥相呼应。炼丹炉是一座青砖砌成的方形石室,长 3.6 米,宽 2.7 米,高约 2 米。室顶呈八棱形,象征八卦。室内有残损青石雕像一尊。从炼丹炉沿东南扶栏盘旋而上,可领略"仰天池"风光。相传"仰天池"是老子当年冶炼长生不老丹蘸火的池子。

老子墓

老子墓位于化女泉以西 3 公里处。墓冢呈圆形,高 4 米,墓前竖有清代毕沅书"老子墓"碑石一通。

The Louguantai Temple

The Louguantai Temple is a famous Taoist shrine in China, and it is revered as "the first land of the blessed under heaven". The temple is situated on the hillside north of the Zhongnan Mountains, 15 kilometers southeast of Zhouzhi County and 70 kilometers from Xi'an City.

The Louguantai Temple assumed its name as far as the 11th century BC. According to legend, Yin Xi, magistrate of Hangu Pass or an official of the Zhou Dynasty, built a thatched tower for nocturnal observations of the heavenly bodies, therefore, the temple was initially called the Thatched Observatory. One day, he noticed a violet current of air drifting westwards, and accordingly, predicted that an immortal would pass by. Quite to his expectations Lao Tzu arrived on his journey west. He welcomed Lao Tzu on to the tower and earnestly requested him to write him a book. Lao Tzu agreed and thereafter, completed a 5,000 character classic of immortal value entitled *The Classic of the Way*. Besides, he built a high platform south of the tower for teaching the classic. It is known as the Preaching Platform today. This is the evolutional process of the Louguantai Temple.

Lao Tzu, alias Li Er, otherwise known as Lao Dan, established himself as a famous philosopher in the Spring and Autumn Period of China. He has been revered as the founder of Taoism. According to *A Biography of Lao Tzu in the Records of the Historian* by Sima Qian (a famous historian in 200 BC), Lao Tzu, was once a historiographer and a file clerk in charge of the imperial archive. He was erudite and well-in-formed, and even Confucius consulted him. But owing to the strife in the imperial court, Lao Tzu abandoned his post, and began to roam far and wide. The school of Taoist thoughts created by him represents profound philosophic theories, and it has been highly thought of. His *Classic of the Way* has come out in multiple languages and enjoyed a wide circulation overseas.

The Louguantai Temple is situated south of the Qinling Mountain Range and north of the Weihe River. Bamboo trees spread like a green blanket over the hillside and give deep shade. It enjoys the name of "an abode of immortals", and establishes itself as a scenically beautiful resort.

According to legend, King Mu of the Zhou Dynasty once traveled here and had a palatial mansion built, with the Louguantai Palace as its name. The First Qin Emperor had a temple built south of the tower and prayed to the gods or consulted celestial beings in person. The Han Emperor Wu Di had a temple built north of the tower. During Emperor Hui's reign of the Jin Dynasty, tens of thousands of trees were planted, and more than 300 households were relocated for the maintenance and protection of the grounds. Again, large-scale repair work on the temple was carried on in the early years during Emperor Wen's reign of the Sui Dynasty.

The Louguantai Temple came to its prime in the Tang Dynasty. When Li Yuan, the first emperor of the Tang Dynasty placed himself at the head of the uprising against the Sui empire in the city of Taiyuan, his daughter, Princess Pingyang, obtained full support both in material and manpower from the high priest of the Louguantai Temple in her effort to respond to her father's revolt in the area of Huxian County. Li Yuan used to face an unfavourable military situation at one time and he went in person for divination. The high priest told him encouragingly: "The Heaven has been moved by Your Majesty's great character. The Celestial Ruler will bless you. What enemy can't you wipe out?" Just for this reason, Li Yuan revered Lao Tzu as his ancestor and went in person to pray at Lao Tzu's Temple and renamed the Louguantai Temple as Holy Ancestor's Palace, after the founding of the Tang Dynasty. Later, he also gave an imperial edict to establish Taoism as state religion, thus placing Taoism above Confucianism and Buddhism. Emperor Xuan Zong was all the more faithful to Taoism when he succeeded the throne. For the reason that he dreamed of Lao Tzu, he changed Holy Ancestor's Palace into Holy Ancestor's Temple. Since then, the Louguantai Temple has become a Taoist shrine.

Maintenance of the temple was undertaken respectively in the dynasties of the Song, the Yuan, the Ming and the Qing. Men of letters composed poems and inscribed their imperssions on stones when they paid a visit to the shrine. Among them the famous ones are Ouyang Xun, Wang Wei and Li Bai of the Tang Dynasty, Mi Fu of the Song Dynasty and Zhao Mengfu of the Yuan Dynasty.

Some historical sites have survived the ages, including the Preaching Platform, the Immortality-pill Furnace, Lü Dongbin's Cave, the Goddess Spring, the Louguantai Pagoda, Lao Tzu's Tomb, the Holy Ancestor's Palace, the Huiling Temple, the Yuhua Temple and the Yansheng Temple.

The Remains of the Holy Ancestor's Palace

The Holy Ancestor's Palace, one of the mainframe structures in the Louguantai Temple, was on the way to collapse after the Ming and Qing dynasties. Still available on the site are the foundation base, stone lions, stone tablets, gingko trees and nine cypresses. One of the cypresses is overgrown, with twigs and branches, layer upon layer. It looks as if three hawks were resting on its crest. Figuratively, it is "cypress of three hawks". Another is called "an ox tying cypress". According to legend, it is the very tree to which Lao Tzu tied his black ox. Under the tree lies a stone ox, with great composure. In the courtyard there is also a tall gingko tree, five to six meters in diameter. They say the tree has grown for more than 2,000 years, and it is the second biggest of its kind in Asia.

The Preaching Platform

The Preaching Platform is the most sizeable structure available in the temple premise. As the centre of the Louguantai Temple, it is situated on a peak with an altitude of 560 meters. Bamboo groves spread like blanket over the peak, and old trees give deep shade.

Upon your entrance into the mountain, you will see a pond in the shape of an octagon. It is called Acme-of-Perfection Pond. The connotation of this name is "The highest efficacy is like water". Lao Tzu once said: "Water is the weakest of all under heaven, but attacks the strongest beyond compare." Bluntly speaking, the weakest of all the elements as it is, water is powerful enough to destroy whatever is solid. The quotation actually represents the Taoist notion: "the weak can defeat the strong."

The halls flanking the entrance to the Preaching Platform house more than 70 carved stone tablets that have survived the ages. For example, *A Monument to the Taoist Shrine of the Tang Empire* by Ouyang Xun in official script and *A Monument to the Presence of Lao Tzu's Soul* by Su Lingzhi in running script. Out of the hall and up the twisting path nearby, you will see the cliff with inscriptions of calligraphy and poems by ancient men of distinction. The most valuable of these inscriptions are Mi Fu's "First Mountain" and Su Dongpo's poem on his visit to the Louguantai Temple.

Lao Tzu's Shrine

Go through the entrance to the mountain and follow the twining path to the Preaching Rostrum, you will find yourself in front of Lao Tzu's Shrine. According to the legend, it marks the place where Lao Tzu taught his disciples *The Classic of the Way*. The shrine houses a remoulded statue of Lao Tzu, with two other statues in front of his, one on its feet, the other in squatting posture. They say the standing statue is a beauty and the squatting one is Xu Jia, one of Lao Tzu's disciples. In order to test Xu Jia's loyalty to his cultivation, Lao Tzu touched a blade of sweet grass on the ground with his walking stick, and magically it turned into a beauty. At the sight of the lady, Xu Jia was sexually aroused. When he noticed it, Lao Tzu withdrew his walking stick and revealed his real self. Xu Jia, seized with panic, did not hesitate to kneel down and to confess his sin before his master. This is a legendary story about the three clay statues. Again according to the legend, a spring emerged later on the spot where Lao Tzu had plunged his walking stick. It is called the Beauty Spring. It is located 1 kilometer west of the Preaching Platform.

Behind the main hall is the Taoist Scriptures Chamber. It houses various editions of *The Classic of the Way* as well as the ancient literature and books on the Classic that have survived the ages. Under the two old cypress trees growing in front of the chamber, there is an octagonal millstone previously used for grinding elixir. According to the legend, Lao Tzu "borrowed" this resonant magic millstone from Nü Wa, a legendary ancestress of Chinese people. When you knock at it gently, it produces loud clinking sounds. The sounds then spread out and echo in the deep valley.

The Elixir-making Furnace

The Immortality-pill Furnace stands on the lofty hill overgrown with brambles and far apart from the Preaching Platform. The Furnace is 2.5 kilometers from the foot of the hill. It is a blue-bricked structure in the shape of an octagon. It's 3.6 meters long, 2.7 meters wide and 2 meters upwards. The octagonal shape represents the Eight Diagrams. There is also a spoilt marble statue within. The twisting and twining path southeast of the Immortality-pill Furnace leads to the Heavenward Pool. Legend goes that it is the very pool where Lao Tzu used to give cold treatment to his elixir.

Lao Tzu's Tomb

Lao Tzu's Tomb is located 3 kilometers west of the Beauty Spring. It's 4 meters high, and shapes like an ellipse. In front of the tomb stands a memorial tablet inscribed with the three characters "老子墓", meaning "Lao Tzu's Tomb", which were written by Bi Yuan, a calligrapher of the Qing Dynasty.

第七部分　宫苑园林与国家森林公园

华清池

华清池位于西安城东约 30 公里处。据史书记载，西周曾在这里建过"骊宫"。秦始皇时砌石筑池，取名"骊山汤"。汉代扩建为"离宫"。唐太宗李世民曾在这里修建"温泉宫"。公元 747 年，唐玄宗命环山筑宫，宫周建城，改名为"华清宫"。因宫建在汤池上，又名"华清池"。

华清池坐落于骊山脚下。骊山是秦岭的一条支脉，海拔 1256 米，满山松柏青翠欲滴，远远望去，犹如一匹黑色骏马。古代称黑马为骊，故名"骊山"。

唐代的华清池毁于安史之乱。现在的华清池只是当时华清宫的一小部分。今天我们看到的华清池，是在清代重建的基础上不断整修扩建而成的，占地面积 85560 平方米。

走进华清池的西门，迎面可以看到九龙池、莲花汤和飞霜殿等，都是 1959 年按唐代建筑风格重建的。

飞霜殿

飞霜殿在唐代是玄宗皇帝和杨贵妃的寝殿。当时殿前汤池之中，整日雾气升腾。每当冬季大雪纷飞，宫内玉龙飞舞、银装素裹时，唯独飞霜殿前，雪化为白霜，因此得名。

九龙池

飞霜殿前的汤池叫九龙池。相传在很古老的时候，关中大旱，玉帝命老龙率八条小龙降雨。当旱象刚刚消除，众龙麻痹松懈时，旱情再度加剧。玉帝一怒之下，便将众小龙压在玉堤之下，并在堤两头各压晨旭亭和晚霞亭，命众小龙终日口吐清流为民灌田；又将老龙压在玉堤上端的龙吟榭下，使其尽职尽责监视众小龙。九龙池由此得名。

石舫

九龙池西侧的九曲回廊直通如同龙船般浮于水面的石舫。石舫上有当年玄宗皇帝的御汤"九龙汤"。唐时每年10月，玄宗李隆基都要率后宫嫔妃及百官来华清宫避寒，年底才返回长安。九龙汤当时用晶莹的白玉砌成，石面上隐约可见鱼龙花鸟之状。池中有一双用白玉石雕成的才出水际的并蒂莲花。泉水自瓮口涌出，喷注到白莲上，所以御汤也叫"莲花汤"。

温泉水源

华清池内的骊山温泉水源及"西安事变"旧址五间厅都位于华清池东部。骊山温泉共有四个泉眼，每小时流量达112吨，水温为43摄氏度。泉水含有石灰、碳酸钠和硫酸钠等多种矿物质，适于沐浴疗养，对皮肤病、风湿病、关节炎、肌肉疼痛等多种疾病有一定的疗效。夕佳楼处的水源发现于3000多年前的西周时期，每小时流量达25吨。

西安事变

沿着温泉水源东侧的台阶拾级而上，就来到蒋介石在"西安事变"时的住处——五间厅。

"西安事变"发生在1936年12月12日，因此又名"双十二事变"。1936年，蒋介石亲自来到西安布置"剿共"，驻守西安的国民党东北军将领张学良和西北军将领杨虎城发动了震惊中外的西安事变。

1936年12月12日清晨5时，张学良和杨虎城两位将军派东北军卫队一个连包围了华清池。蒋介石听到枪声后，只披了件睡衣，从后窗跳出，跌跌撞撞地爬到骊山半山腰，在一块名叫虎斑石的石隙中躲藏起来。东北军战士立即搜山，终于在上午8时左右找到了蒋介石，并把他押送到西安。

为了避免内战，联合抗日，中共中央主张和平解决西安事变，并应张、杨电请，派周恩来率中共代表团前往西安。周恩来等在西安做了大量工作，终于迫使蒋介石接受了张学良和杨虎城两位将军"联共抗日"的主张。12月25日张学良护送蒋介石回南京，西安事变得到了和平解决。

西安事变的和平解决结束了国共十年内战的局面，促进了抗日民族统一战线的形成和发展，开始了国共合作的新时期。西安事变成为中国现代历史的伟大转折点。

兵谏亭

1946年，国民党政府在蒋介石藏身的虎斑石处修了"民族复兴亭"，也叫"正气亭"，现称"兵谏亭"。亭子东侧石隙中，安有铁链、铁环，游人可以攀缘而上，观看游览。

烽火台

骊山的西绣岭上，西周烽火台遗址仍依稀可辨。烽火台是古代的报警设施，多筑于山头上，有专人看管。一旦敌人来犯，烽火台立即传递信号报警。据说西周时每个山头都筑有烽火台，无论什么时候敌人进犯，士兵都点燃狼粪，以狼烟为信号向其他诸侯国求援。为什么用狼粪呢？据说狼粪燃烧时，其烟笔直冲天，人们在很远的地方也能看见。

周幽王曾在华清池建行宫，在骊山上筑烽火台。他有一名宠妃叫褒姒。她虽然貌似天仙，却总是阴沉着脸，从来不笑。周幽王不遗余力想逗她高兴，但都无济于事，十分发愁。一天，一位大臣献计举烽火，戏诸侯，以博得褒姒一笑。这个计策十分成功。当看到各诸侯国的将士汗流浃背，气喘吁吁地赶来，只不过是空忙一场时，褒姒不禁冷笑一声。幽王大喜，赏了那个大臣黄金千两。幽王以后又多次烽火戏诸侯。一天，敌人真的进犯，幽王急令举烽火，但各诸侯国都以为幽王故伎重演，因此没有前去救援。结果，幽王被杀，西周灭亡。中国著名的"一笑千金"和"烽火戏诸侯"的典故即由此而来。

华清宫御汤博物馆

1982年4月，人们在基建施工时偶然发现了唐华清宫御汤建筑遗址。经考古专家发掘清理，在4200平方米面积内发现了五个汤池遗址，并确认它们分别是历史上记载的星辰汤、莲花汤、海棠汤、太子汤和尚食汤。在这些遗址上建成的唐华清宫御汤博物馆于1990年10月正式开放。"海棠汤"是当年唐玄宗为其宠妃杨玉环专门修建的浴池，因此也叫贵妃池。浴池为台式，上下两层，长3.6米，宽2.9米，用8块青石砌成，整个池面形状犹如一朵盛开的海棠花。

除了五个汤池外，博物馆还展出在考古发掘过程中发现的陶水管、各种瓦当和铺地砖等盛唐时期的建筑材料。

大型山水情景剧《长恨歌》

"在天愿做比翼鸟,在地愿为连理枝。天长地久有时尽,此恨绵绵无绝期。"传颂千年的唐诗名句和恢宏博大的盛唐气象,莫不让人心驰神往。在历史中,华清池是唐玄宗与杨贵妃爱情故事的见证者。时隔千年,它又一次担当了这个历史使命。以唐华清宫遗址为背景,以盛唐文化为主题,以白居易诗作中脍炙人口的名篇《长恨歌》改编而成的中国首部大型山水情景舞剧《长恨歌》,在华清宫轮番上演。

《长恨歌》情景舞剧斥资5000万元,具有亚洲唯一的全天候折叠式全色真彩LED软屏、国内首创水中机械组合多变式立体活动舞台和户外演出设施全隐蔽式设计,成为中国最大的水上舞台,并请来了国内一流的音乐、舞美、灯光、音响、服装、道具大师和阵容庞大的专业演出团体,演职人员218人,剧长60分钟,通过《奉诏温泉宫》《贵妃出浴》《贵妃醉酒》等13个场景,生动再现唐玄宗和杨贵妃的悲欢离合、生死离别的爱情故事,诠释历史长诗《长恨歌》的深刻内涵。

梨园

中华梨园历史悠久,梨园艺术不仅是中华民族文化的国粹,更是联系海内外华人情感的精神纽带。承古续今,华清池的梨园文化与温泉沐浴文化两大品牌受到海内外专家学者的热切关注。白居易的《长恨歌》问世以来,华清池作为唐明皇李隆基与杨贵妃传奇爱情故事的发生地而家喻户晓。唐玄宗李隆基与杨贵妃及随驾梨园弟子在唐华清宫中开创了梨园艺术先河,后世梨园弟子将唐明皇奉为梨园鼻祖。1995年考古工作者在唐华清宫遗址区域内获得重大考古发现,并在此基础上将唐玄宗与杨贵妃教习梨园弟子演练歌舞的场所唐华清宫梨园恢复和建立起来,这是目前全国仅存的三座梨园遗址中唯一展出的一座。华清宫不仅是唐代梨园弟子活动的重要场所,也堪称是中国戏曲的发源地。

PART SEVEN   GARDENS AND NATIONAL FOREST PARKS

The Huaqing Pool

The Huaqing Pool is located about 30 kilometers east of the city of Xi'an. Historically, during the Western Zhou Dynasty, a stone pool was built and was given the name Lishan Tang (Lishan Hot Spring). The site was enlarged into a bigger palace during the Han Dynasty, and was renamed the Li Palace (the Resort Palace). During the Tang Dynasty, Li Shimin (Emperor Tai Zong) ordered the construction of the Hot Springs Palace, and Emperor Xuan Zong had a walled palace built around the Lishan Mountain in the year 747. It was known as the Huaqing Palace. It also had the name of the "Huaqing Pool" because of its location over the hot springs.

The Huaqing Pool is located at the foot of the Lishan Hill, a branch of the Qinling mountain range. It stands 1,256 meters above the sea level. It is covered with pines and cypresses and looks very much like a black dark green galloping horse from a long distance. In classical Chinese, a black horse was called "Li", and this is how it got its name, Lishan.

The Huaqing Pool was destroyed during An Lushan and Shi Siming's Rebellion at the end of the Tang Dynasty. The present-day site is only a small part of the orginal of the Huaqing Palace. Huaqing Pool which we see today was rebuilt on the site of the Qing Dynasty structure. The palace covers an area of 85,560 square meters.

Entering the West Gate of the Huaqing Pool, you will see the Nine-dragon Pool, the Lotus Flower Pool, the Frost Drifting Hall, etc. All these structures were rebuilt in 1959 according to the Tang Dynasty architectual style.

The Frost Drifting Hall

The Tang Emperor, Xuan Zong and his favorite lady, (Lady Yang Yuhuan), used to make their home in the Frost Drifting Hall. There is always mist and vapor in the air over the pool in front of the Hall. In winter, snowflakes fly in the air, and everything in sight becomes white. However, the snowflakes thaw immediately in front of the Hall. This owes a great deal to the lukewarm vapor that rises out of the hot spring, hence the name "the Frost Drifting Hall" that we see today.

The Nine-dragon Pool

In the vicinity of the Frost Drifting Hall lies the Nine-dragon Pool. According to legend, the Central Shaanxi Plain was once stricken by a sever drought a long time ago. By the order of Jade Emperor (the Supreme Deity of Heaven), an old dragon came with eight young ones, and made rain there. Yet when the disaster was just abating, the dragons lowered their guard and relaxed vigilance, and the drought became serious again. In a fit of anger, Jade Emperor kept the young dragons under the Jade Causeway, with the Morning Glow Pavilion and the Sunset Pavilion built on the east and west sides of it to make the young dragons spout clear water all day long to meet the needs of local irrigation. He had the old dragon confined to the bottom of the Roaring Dragon Waterside Pavilion which was situated at the upper end of the Jade Causeway. The old dragon was obliged to exercise control over the young ones. And this is how it got its name, the Nine-dragon Pool.

The Marble Boat

The Nine-bend Corridor, which lies to the west of the Nine-dragon Pool, leads directly to the Marble Boat. This boat resembles a dragon boat, floating on the pool. In the Marble Boat lies the Nine-dragon Hot Spring Pool where Emperor Xuan Zong would take his baths. Every October he would take his court ladies and hundreds of his officials to the Huaqing Palace and spend his winter days here, return to Chang'an at the end of the year. The Nine-dragon Hot Spring Pool was originally built with crystal jade. Its surface was decorated with carvings of fish, dragons, birds and flowers. In the pool, twin lotus flowers carved out of white jade could be seen as well. The spring water wells up from a mouth of a spring, and spouts up to the lotus flowers. Hence the name the Lotus Flower Pool (the Lotus Flower Hot Springs).

The Source of the Hot Springs

The sources of the hot springs that flows into Huaqing Pool and the Five-room Hall, the historical site of the Xi'an Incident, are all situated to the east of the Huaqing Pool. In this area there are four hot springs. They have a flow of 112 tons an hour with a constant temperature of 43℃. The spring water contains lime, sodium carbonate, sodium sulphate and other minerals, which makes it suitable for bathing and the treatment of quite a few diseases such as dermatosis, rheumatism, arthritis and muscular pain. The source of the spring water at "the Fine Sunset-bathed Pavilion" was discovered about 3,000 years ago, roughly in the Western Zhou Dynasty. Its water flows averages 25 tons per hour.

The Xi'an Incident

Climb the steps east of the source of the hot springs, and you will gradually see the Five-room Hall where Chiang Kaishek stayed temporarily during the "Xi'an Incident".

In 1936, Chiang Ksishek flew to Xi'an to scheme "the suppression of the Communist Party". Two leaders of Northeast and Northwest Armies, Zhang Xueliang and Yang Hucheng launched the famous "Xi'an Incident" which shocked the world.

Early in the morning of December 12, 1936, their plan began. Zhang Xueliang, together with Yang Hucheng, ordered a squad of body guards to surround the Huaqing Pool. Chiang Kaishek heard the gunshots and he was so terrified that he crept out of a window in his nightgown and slippers. He staggered up the Mount Li, and hid himself, halfway up, behind a stone in a crevice. Those soldiers began to search the hill immediately. At 8:00 in the morning they found Chiang, and escorted him to Xi'an.

In order to avoid a civil war and try to establish a united national front for the resistance against Japan, the Chinese Communist Party Central Committee, stood for a peaceful settlement of the incident. Therefore, a delegation headed by Zhou Enlai was sent to Xi'an at the invitation of Mr. Zhang and Mr. Yang. Zhou Enlai and his delegates did a lot of work there. Ultimately Chiang Kaishek was forced to accept the proposal made by his two generals. On December 25, Zhang Xueliang escorted Chiang kaishek back to Nanjing. Consequently "Xi'an Incident" was settled peacefully.

The peaceful settlement of "Xi'an Incident" put an end to the civil war which had lasted for ten years, and accelerated the formation and development of the National United Front for the Resistance against Japan. Moreover, it is a new page of the cooperation between the Communist Party and the Nationalist Party and marked a great turning point in modern Chinese history.

The Remonstration Pavilion

In the year of 1946 the Nationalist Government had the "National Rejuvenation Pavilion" built near the crevice where Chiang Kaishek had hidden himself during the Incident. It was then called "Justice Pavilion" or "Rejuvination Pavilion". Now it has the name of "Remonstration Pavilion". Iron chains and rings are available all the way up to the crevice east of the pavilion by which visitors can climb up to take a look at Chiang Kaishek's shelter.

The Beacon Tower

Located on the Xixiu Ridge (The West Embroidery Ridge) of Lishan Hill, the remains of the Beacon Tower of the Western Zhou Dynasty is easily identified.

The beacon tower was built at the top of the mountain to give alarm of border attacks in ancient times. It was constantly manned by special guards. Once the enemy pressed the border, the signal from the beacon tower would be sent. It is said that in the Western Zhou Dynasty, on the peak of every mountain a beacon tower was built. Whenever the enemy came, the soldiers would send signals by burning wolf's droppings to seek help from other dukes. Why were wolf's droppings used? It is said that when wolf's droppings were burnt, their smoke went straight up to the sky, and people could see it from a far distance.

King You of the Western Zhou Dynasty had a palace built in the Huaqing Pool, and a beacon tower on top of Lishan Hill. The King had a favorite concubine named Bao Si. Though she was ravishingly beautiful, she always wore a sad face and never smiled. King You left no stone unturned to make her happy, but in vain. So the King became very much worried. One day, one of his ministers suggested that the beacon be lit to make fun of other duke states to make Bao Si smile. Sure enough the trick worked very well. At the sight of the signal, the soldiers of other duke states hurried to the foot of Lishan Hill. They were wet through with sweat and out of breath, but only to find themselves deceived. Dismay in the wake fell upon everyone. Bao Si was amused to see them mortified and gave a cold smile. The King was delighted and awarded 1,000 pieces of gold to the minister, who put forward the idea. Later the joke was repeated several times. One day when a real danger threatened him, King You had the beacon fire lit again, but the dukes thought that the King was playing the same trick again to please his concubine. No one came to his rescue, therefore, the Western Zhou Dynasty was overthrown and the King was killed. Hence the Chinese saying "A single smile costs 1,000 pieces of gold" and "The sovereign rulers are fooled by the beacon fire".

The Museum of the Imperial Pools of the Huaqing Palace

In April, 1982, on a construction site that was well under way, the ruins of the imperial pools in the Tang-Dynasty Huaqing Palace were discovered. After excavation and sorting out the information at hand, archaeologists found the ruins of the five pools in an area of 4,200 square meters. They proved them to be the Star Pool, the Lotus Flower Pool, the Crabapple Pool, the Crown Prince Pool and the Shangshi Pool, all of which were recorded in history. The Museum of the Imperial Pools in the Tang-Dynasty Huaqing Palace was built on their ruins and was opened to public in October 1990. "The Chinese Flower Crabapple Pool" was specially built by the order of the Tang Emperor, Xuan Zong, for his favorite lady Yang Yuhuan to bathe in. Therefore, it was also called Lady Yang's Pool. The pool was like a platform with two layers, 3.6 meters long, 2.9 meters wide. It was built of 8 pieces of stone. The overall view of the pool resembles a Chinese crabapple in full blossom.

Beside the five pools on display in the museum, there are also pottery sewer pipes, and various types of tiles and bricks that were unearthed during the excavation. These were building materials during the prosperous Tang Dynasty.

A Magnifit Melodrama— "The Everlasting Regret"

"In Air, we'd be two lovebirds flying wing to wing. On Earth, we'd be two trees twining from spring to spring. Away may the boundless sky and vast earth die, but this vow unfulfilled will be regretted for aye." The famous widely read verse sounds like the Tang Dynasty in its prime in Chinese history and certainly arouses great emotions and feelings in the readers. In history, the Huaqing Pool witnessed the romance between Xuan Zong, the Tang Emperor and Lady Yang, the Concubine. 1,000 years later, the same theme is represented on the stage as if it was revivified. Against the background of the remains of the Huaqing Palace, with a theme of the prosperous Tang-Dynasty culture, *The Everlasting Regret*, the first sweeping melodrama in China was put on stage in the Huaqing Palace for many times. It was based on and adapted from the universally acknowledged stanza in Bai Jüyi's poem.

The convertible water stage with an investment of 50 million yuan is considered to be the largest one in China, with invisible outdoor facilities and a solid and movable arena. Besides, the stage is equipped with foldaway full-color LED panel, which is exclusive in Asia. With a cast of 218 working staff, the dramaturgic group consists of professional performers, high-ranking masters in music, dance, spotlight, sound effect, costume, and props. The running time of the Melodrama is 60 minutes, compmosed of 13 scenes, such as *Summoned to the Hot Spring Palace*, *Lady Yang coming out of Bath*, *Lady Yang Intoxicated*. It vividly recaptures the tragic romance between the Tang Emperor and his beloved concubine Lady Yang and interprets the annotation of the epic poem *The Everlasting Regret*.

The Theatric Garden

The theatric garden boasts a long history in China and its artistry is not only the quintessence of the Chinese culture, but also a psychological countersign among the Chinese both at home and abroad. Since ancient times, experts and scholars alike have shown growing concern for the two cultures at the Huaqing Pool: one concerning the Theatric Garden, the other concerning the Hot Spring. Ever since the publication of *The Everlasting Regret* by Bai Juyi, a famous poet in the Tang Dynasty, the Huaqing Pool has been widely known as the place where the love story between Emperor Li Nongji and Lady Yang Guifei (his concubine) happened. In the Theatric Garden, the Emperor and Lady Yang, the Beauty taught theatric disciples how to perform, how to play musical instruments and how to sing songs, thus initiating the theatric garden art. Therefore, Emperor Xuan Zong was worshiped as the forerunner of the theatric garden. In 1995, archeologists made great discoveries in the remains of the Huaqing Pool and rebuilt the Theatric Garden in its original place. Of the three existing theatric gardens in China, this is the only one open to the public. The Huaqing Palace serves not only as the rehearsal theatre for theatric disciples, but also as the birth place of Chinese operas in various forms.

大明宫

大明宫作为大唐帝国的大朝正殿，是唐代的政治中心和国家象征，它位于唐京师长安（今西安）北侧的龙首原之上，这里地势高凸，且恰逢一条绵延六十里象征着龙脉的山原自长安西南部的樊川北走，故被称为龙首，人称龙首原。其地面积为3.2平方千米，是明清北京紫禁城的4.5倍，堪称全世界最辉煌壮丽的宫殿群，被誉为千宫之宫、丝绸之路的东方圣殿。整座宫殿规模宏大，建筑雄伟，王维诗句"九天阊阖开宫殿，万国衣冠拜冕旒"描绘了当时的盛景。

大明宫始建于唐太宗贞观八年（634年），原名永安宫，是唐太宗为其父李渊修建的夏宫。李渊去世后，改称为大明宫，是唐长安城三座主要宫殿中规模最大的一座（其余两座为太极宫和兴庆宫）。自唐高宗起，大明宫成为国家的统治中心，先后有17位唐朝皇帝在此处理朝政，历时达200余年。唐朝末年，整座宫殿毁于战火，其遗址位于今陕西省西安市城区的北郊。1961年，大明宫遗址被中华人民共和国国务院公布为第一批全国重点文物保护单位之一。

整个宫城呈中轴对称结构，沿正门丹凤门进入大明宫，正对含元殿，两者之间为长600余米的御道，向北依次为含元殿、宣政殿、紫宸殿等组成的南北中轴线，后部以太液池为中心组成内庭，分布着麟德殿、三清殿、大福殿、清思殿等数十座殿宇楼阁。大明宫宫城共有城门九座，南面正中为正门丹凤门，北面正中为玄武门。作为唐大明宫中轴线上的正南门，丹凤门有五个门道，其余各门均为三个门道，在大明宫诸门中规格最高，体现其千般尊严、万般气象的皇家气派。自建成之日起，丹凤门就成为唐朝皇帝出入宫城的主要通道。丹凤门上有高大的门楼，是唐朝皇帝举行登基、宣布大赦等外朝大典的重要场所。它的规制之高、规模之大均创都城门阙之最，对研究唐长安城和中国都城考古均有重要价值，被文物考古界誉为"盛唐第一门"。

含元殿、宣政殿、紫宸殿是大明宫三大殿，正殿含元殿，是大明宫中轴线上南起第一座殿宇，规制宏伟，与北京故宫太和殿地位相当，是当时唐长安城内最宏伟的建筑，在建造之时充分利用了龙首原高地的特点，视野开阔，可俯瞰整座长安城，是举行重大国家庆典和朝会之所，发挥着国家礼仪的功用。含元殿正北是宣政殿，为皇帝临朝听政之所。宣政殿作为常朝的殿堂，是大明宫中轴线上三座主要朝廷主殿的核心，大唐许多重大历史事件和诏令，都是从这里策划和发出的。紫宸殿位于宣政殿以北，为大明宫的第三大殿，称为"内朝"，群臣在此朝见皇帝。皇帝在紫宸殿听政，而百官在宣政殿外候旨，听候传唤。皇帝日常的一般议事，多在此殿，故也称天子便殿。含元、宣政、紫宸组成的外朝、中朝、内朝格局多为后世的宫殿所效仿，北京紫禁城的太和殿、中和殿、保和殿三殿便是这种格局的体现。

太液池是大唐王朝最重要的皇家园林，池内造有蓬莱、方丈、瀛洲三座仙山。如今的太液池也是遗址公园内最柔美的区域，在此游人仿佛能够看到盛唐皇家园林的景象。麟德殿位于大明宫的西北部，是宫内规模最大的别殿，也是唐代建筑中形体组合最复杂的大建筑群，是唐朝皇帝举行宫廷宴会、观看乐舞、娱乐表演、会见来使的主要场所，史载麟德殿大宴之时，殿前廊下可坐人数可达3000，并表演百戏，还可在殿前击马球。当时，唐代的官员以能出席麟德殿宴会为荣。如今在这里每天都轮番上映着再现大明宫往日辉煌的演出，让游客们产生一种梦回大唐之感。

此外，极富道教色彩的建筑物在大明宫中也随处可见，反映了道教在唐代宫廷中的极盛。李唐王朝以老子后裔自居，对道教的祭祀活动甚至超过了祭祖、祭天等，道教建筑的等级极高，内部装潢极为豪华，如三清殿为大明宫宫苑区最重要的道教建筑，其出土的建筑材料及装潢构件之华丽，被考古学者认为是绝无仅有的一处。然而，这些庙宇主要位于大明宫的后庭北部和东部的边缘地带，尽管等级很高，仍与以前朝三大殿为首的主要建筑群之间形成了明显的统属和拱卫关系，这表现出唐代皇权的强大，对宗教文化的绝对统领地位。

千年前龙首原上的大明宫，曾占据人类文明的制高点，是我国古代宫殿建筑的杰作，充分展示了包容开放、奋发进取的盛唐精神和中华民族璀璨夺目的文化成果。如今大明宫遗址作为人类文化遗产的重要组成部分，具有极高的历史、科学和艺术价值，是中华民族乃至世界的共同财富。

The Daming Palace

As the main hall of the Tang Dynasty, the Daming Palace is the political center and national symbol of the Tang Dynasty. It is located on Longshou tableland, a high terrain, to the north of Chang'an, the capital of Tang Dynasty (Xi'an today). As there happens to be a 60-mile-long mountain winding passage like a dragon from Fanchuan, southwest of Chang'an, to the north, the name of Longshou means "the Head of Dragon", so it is called Longshou Tableland. It covers an area of 3.2 square kilometers, which is 4.5 times that of the Forbidden City constructed in the Ming and Qing dynasties in Beijing. It is often referred to as the most magnificent palace complex in the world and known as "The Palace of all Palaces" and "the Oriental Holy Palace along the Silk Road". The whole palace is magnificently constructed, lofty and grand on a large scale, just as it is depicted in Wang Wei's poem, "When the gate of the palace opens, emissaries from various countries stream to pay homage to the emperor", which vividly describes the magnificent scene at the time.

The Palace was built in 634 AD, the eighth year of Zhen GFuan during the reign of Tai Zong. It was originally constructed as a summer resort for Li Yuan, Tai Zong's father and was formerly known as the Yong'an Palace (Ever-lasting Peace Palace). After Li Yuan died, it was renamed the Daming Palace, which is the largest of the three main palaces in Chang'an in the Tang Dynasty (the other two being the Tai Chi Palace and the Xingqing Palace). Since the reign of Gao Zong, the Daming Palace had become the governing center of the country. 17 successive emperors in the Tang Dynasty were enthroned in this palace ruling the country for over 200 years. At the end of the Tang Dynasty, the entire palace was destroyed during the war. The site is located today in the northern suburbs of Xi'an, Shaanxi Province. In 1961, the Daming Palace site was listed by the State Council as one of the important National Historical Monuments in China.

The Palace has a symmetrical structure with a central axis. When entering the Palace from the Danfeng Gate (the South Main Gate) you face the Hanyuan Hall, there is a 600-meter-long royal passage. Along the axis proceeding northwards are the Hanyuan Hall, Xuanzheng Hall, Tzuchen Hall; the inner royal court surrounding the Taiye Pool is composed of a dozen of halls and pavilions such as the Linde Hall, the Sanqing Hall, the Dafu Hall and the Qingsi Hall. There are nine gateways in the Daming Palace, with Danfeng Gateway directly to the south and the Xuanwu Gateway to the south. As the main gateway on the axis, the Danfeng Gateway has five doorways, the other gateways has three doorways. This gateway has the highest class, which shows the royal momentum and its supremacy. Upon its completion the Danfeng Gateway became the main passageway for emperors to go into and come out of the Imperial Palace. On top of the Danfeng Gateway, there is a lofty gate-tower where many grand ceremonies such as enthronement, amnesty and so on were once held. It is ranked No. 1 among all the gate-towers with regard to its design and scale. It is of significant value for archaeological research of the ancient cities both in Chang'an and China. The Danfeng Gateway has been regarded as "No. 1 Gate of the Tang Dynasty" in the archaeological field.

The Daming Palace is composed of three grand halls, the Hanyuan Hall, the Xuanzheng Hall and the Tzuchen Hall respectively. The Hanyuan Hall, the main hall, is the first one located along the central axis starting from the south of the Daming Palace. It is a magnificent structure, equivalent to the Hall of Supreme Harmony of the Forbidden City in terms of historical significance. Before construction, its high terrain on the Longshou Tableland was carefully taken into consideration. It was so constructed that emperors could enjoy a panoramic view of the whole city of Chang'an. It was also a place for holding major national celebrations and court gatherings of ministers. The Hanyuan Hall played a pivotal role in the national etiquette. To its north is the Xuanzheng Hall, where emperors held court meetings and handled administrative affairs. As the core of the three main halls, it was once used as the imperial court where many significant decrees were issued. To the north of the Xuanzheng Hall is the Tzuchen

Hall, the third important hall often referred to as the "inner court", where ministers paid homage to emperors, who listened to their subjects' suggestions and dealt with state affairs, while hundreds of government officials would wait outside to be summoned. Generally speaking, emperors conducted their routine administrative work in the Tzucheng Hall, so it is often called "Regent Hall". The layout of this imperative hall (the outer court, the middle court and the inner court of the Huanyuan Hall, the Xuanzheng Hall and the Tzuchen Hall respectively) was often imitated by later-generation palaces. A good case in point is the construction of the Triple Hall of the Forbidden City in Beijing.

The Taiye Pool is the most important royal garden of the Tang Dynasty. There were three fairy rockeries such as Penglai, Fangzhang and Yingzhou. Today's Taiye Pool is also the most picturesque area in the park, where visitors can experience and see the scene of the prosperous Tang Dynasty. The Linde Hall is located in the northwest corner of the Palace, the largest minor hall in it. It is also the most sophisticated architectural complex in the Tang Dynasty where Tang emperors would hold court banquets, appreciate musical dancing performances and meet envoys. It is recorded that the veranda in front of the hall was large enough to house 3000 people, who could enjoy performances and play polo. At that time it was a great honor for court ministers in the Tang Dynasty to attend such a banquet. Today, various performances that reproduce the brilliance and glory of the Daming Palace are put on in turn and that brings people back to the grand Tang Dynasty.

In addition, the Taoist architectural structures can be seen everywhere in the Daming Palace, which shows that Taoism was extremely popular in the court of the Tang Dynasty. Emperors of the Tang Dynasty regarded themselves as descendants of Li'er (Lao Tzu), for they share the same family name—Li. The Taoist sacrificial activities were more popular than other religious rites such as ancestor worship and heaven sacrifice. The Taoist buildings are of the highest class with luxurious interior decorations. For example, the Sanqing Hall is the most important Taoist building in the Daming Palace. The building materials and decoration components unearthed here are simply gorgeous, which have been considered as "one and the only one". However, these temples are located in the northern part of the back yard and in the east marginal zone. Despite its classiness in degree, its subordinate position could be clearly seen, compared with the three main Halls in the frontal complex along the axis. This evidently shows the supremacy of the royal power of emperors, who absolutely dominated the religious culture in the Tang Dynasty.

Located on the Longshou tableland a thousand years ago, the Daming Palace played an overwhelmingly important role in human civilization. It is a masterpiece in all the ancient Chinese palace architectures. It has fully demonstrated the open, tolerant and enterprising spirit of the Tang Dynasty and the dazzling cultural achievements of the Chinese nation. As an important element of cultural heritage today, the Daming Palace Site has a historical, scientific and artistic value. It has become a great wealth shared by both China and the whole world.

大唐芙蓉园

大唐芙蓉园位于陕西省西安市城南的曲江开发区，原唐代芙蓉园遗址以北，仿照唐代皇家园林精心建造，是中国第一个全方位展示盛唐风貌的大型皇家文化主题公园。大唐芙蓉园占地面积165英亩，其中水域面积49英亩，建筑面积近十万平方米，总投资13亿元，自2002年动工至2005年正式对外开放，历时三年，由中国工程院院士张锦秋女士担纲总体规划与建筑设计，彰显大唐文化内涵，体现古典皇家园林气派，借曲江山水演绎盛唐名园，被称为"盛唐主题天下第一园"。2005年4月11日，大唐芙蓉园开园之日，联合国特派代表以及来自巴西、伊朗、土耳其、奥地利、日本等国的使节和代表，文化艺术名人以及企业界知名人士以及市民群众约一万人出席了开园盛典，使得海内外宾客再次领略了盛唐文化，重温了唐代诗人杜甫描述的"三月三日天气新，长安水边多丽人"的踏青民俗风情。

大唐芙蓉园分为帝王文化区、水秀表演区、歌舞文化区、茶文化区、诗歌文化区等14个景观文化区，集中展示了唐王朝璀璨多姿、无与伦比的文化艺术。园内主要景点有紫云楼、凤鸣九天剧院、唐市、仕女馆、陆羽茶社、杏园、诗魂、曲江流饮等。这些景点主要倚芙蓉湖而建，分布在芙蓉湖四周，紫云楼为整个景区的中心，是帝王文化区的标志性建筑，体现了唐代的帝王风范。历史上的紫云楼，据载建于唐开元十四年，每逢曲江大会，唐明皇必登临此楼，欣赏歌舞、赐宴群臣、与民同乐。依史料重建的紫云楼位于现园区中心位置，也是全园最主要的仿唐建筑群之一，主楼共计四层，每层都以不同的角度、不同的载体共同展示了盛唐帝王文化。一层由反映贞观之治的雕塑、壁画和大型唐长安城复原模型、国家一级唐文物展等组成。二层为唐明皇赐宴群臣、八方来朝、万邦来拜大型彩塑群雕。紫云楼是园区内一个重要的景点表演区,三层的多功能表演厅上演宫廷演出"教坊乐舞"。四层设有如意铜塔投掷游戏。

水秀表演区位于紫云楼观澜台前的湖面,是大唐芙蓉园集水幕电影、音乐喷泉、激光火焰、水雷水雾为一体的世界级大型现代化水体景观。全球最大的电影水幕,宽120米,高20米,以激光辅助突出水幕上水的流动质感,利用激光表演组成了音乐、喷泉、激光三者相结合的水上效果,火焰、水雷、水雾各种变化多端的感官刺激性效果设计,使游人们从视觉、听觉、触觉上感受到这一集声光电水火为一体的绝无仅有的水秀表演。

歌舞文化区位于紫云楼南的凤鸣九天剧院,是歌舞文化区内一个富有盛唐风韵的现代化皇家剧院。剧院装修豪华,体现皇家风范。剧院的主打节目"梦回大唐"以现代艺术手法,配以全新视听效果,展现了盛世大唐的精神风貌。

位于园区茶文化区内的以唐代"茶圣"陆羽命名的"陆羽茶社",彰显唐代茶文化主题,是一个由帝王茶艺、文人茶艺、世俗茶艺、茶艺表演组成的综合性高档茶艺会所。在这里游客不仅可以品尝到香茗,还可以欣赏到茶艺表演。

唐诗是我国古典诗歌的瑰宝,也是世界文化遗产的明珠。以诗魂及唐诗峡为代表组成的诗歌文化区,用雕塑的形式展示了唐代诗歌文化,让游客在观赏雕塑艺术的同时,领略唐代诗人的旷世风采,唐诗的内在精髓;同时,游客还可以观赏运用中国园林造景、中国雕塑、中国书法、中国印章刻字、图形纹样等多种传统艺术手法塑造出的大型景观艺术雕塑。

大唐芙蓉园创造了众多第一:中国首个五感(视觉、听觉、嗅觉、触觉、味觉)主题公园;拥有全球最大户外香化工程;拥有中国最大规模的仿唐建筑群;拥有中国最大的展现唐代诗歌文化的雕塑群,拥有中国单体规模最大的仿唐建筑紫云楼,园内仿唐建筑涵盖了盛唐时期所有建筑形式;拥有全球最大的水幕电影,堪称中华历史之园、精神之园、自然之园、人文之园和艺术之园。

The Grand Tang Paradise

The Grand Tang Paradise, also known as the Furong (Cotton-rose Hibiscus) Garden, is located in the Qujiang Development Zone, south of Xi'an City, and to the northern part of the original site of the Cotton-rose Hibiscus Garden in the Tang Dynasty. It is constructed after the imperial garden in the Tang Dynasty and considered the most sizable cultural theme park in the Northwest Region of China. It has roughly an area of 165 acres surrounding a willow-lined lake of about 49 acres, and a total sum of

1.3 billion RMB has been invested in the project, which fully demonstrates the charm and grandeur of the Tang Dynasty. The whole setting is inviting and captivating and it looks and feels very much like a classical Chinese landscape painting. Its construction began in 2002 and was completed in 2005. It was officially opened to the general public on April 11,2005. The royal garden is designed by Zhang Jinqiu, a member of the prestigious Chinese Academy of Engineering and the director of the China Northwest Building Design Research Institute. It is typical of the elegant and grand architecture style in the Tang Dynasty, and it is spoken of highly as "the First Park in the Theme of Tang Dynasty". On the opening day, there were about 10,000 visitors in the garden, including representatives of the United Nations, celebrities from art, culture and business fields, the locals in Xi'an as well as envoys and representatives from countries like Brazil, Iran, Turkey, Austria, Japan and many other countries. All those guests at home and abroad once again immerged in the cultural atmosphere and reviewed the mores of outing expressed by Du Fu in his poem: "March third is refreshing and sunny, along the stream are ladies gay and happy."

There are altogether 14 landscapes including the imperial culture, the water performance, the music and dance culture, the tea culture, the poetry culture and so on. The Grand Tang Paradise displays the splendid and incomparable culture and art glamor of ancient China, highlighting the great Tang Dynasty in different aspects. The main scenery in the park includes the Ziyun Building, the Phoenix Theatre, the Ancient Market, the Maids of Honor Gallery, the Lu Yu Tea House, the Apricot Garden, the Poetry Society, the Drinking Feast at Qujiang. These views are mainly built around the Lotus Lake. The Ziyun Building, the landmark of the imperial cultural area, is the center of the whole scenic area, symbolizing the imperial architecture style of the Tang Dynasty. It is recorded that the original Ziyun Building was built in the 14th year of Kai Yuan Rein in the Tang Dynasty. Whenever ceremonies came around in Qujiang, Emperor of the Tang Dynasty would ascend the building to enjoy banquets and appreciate music and dances with civilians. The Ziyun Building is a four-storied structure, imitating the original Tang style. These stories show the imperial culture from different perspectives. On the first floor there are sculptures, murals and a large-scale restoration model of Chang'an City in the Tang Dynasty, and the exhibition of A-class Tang archeological items. On the second floor, there are painted sculptures of Emperor of the Tang Dynasty holding banquets in honor of his ministers and pilgrimages paid by envoys from other nations. The multi-functional performance hall on the third floor is the place for music and dance performances. On the fourth floor one can play a game of throwing coins into an auspicious copper tower.

The hydro-performance is shown on the lake surface in front of the Billow-watching Platform of the Ziyun Building. It is a world-class and modern hydro-landscape integrated with water-screen films, music fountains, laser flames and water sprays. The king-size film water-screen alone in the world is 120 meters high and 20 meters wide, assisted by laser to highlight the texture of water flowing on the screen. Thus the hydro-effect is achieved through varied sensory stimulations of music, fountains and laser. Flames, lightening and water-spray are designed to make tourists feel in vision, audition and tactility, the unique power of this spectacular show of hydro-performance through sound, light, electricity, water and fire.

Music and dance performances are shown in Phoenix Hall (a royal theatre with the charm of prosperous Tang Dynasty) to the south of Ziyun Building. The primary show is Dream of Great Tang presented with modern artistic techniques and stunning audio-visual effects to reveal the spirit and the features of the prosperous Tang society.

There is a tea house in the garden, which is named after Lu Yu (the great master of tea in the Tang Dynasty). It is a comprehensive and topnotch tea club where the imperial tea art, literati tea art and secular tea art are shown forth. Tourists here can not only enjoy sipping tea, but also appreciate artistic performances relevant to tea culture.

The Tang poems are the gems of Chinese classical poetry and a bright pearl of the world cultural heritage. The Poetry Culture Section is manifested through lofty poets and great poems in the Tang Dynasty. This section shows not only the poetic culture in the Tang Dynasty in the form of life-like sculptures while visitors appreciate these sculptures, feel the graceful bearing of the Tang poets and become steeped in the Tang poems; but they can also appreciate the large-scale artistic landscape sculptures constructed in the traditional art form, such as Chinese classical gardens, sculptures, calligraphy, seal cutting and various graphic patterns.

There are many "firsts" created in the Paradise: the first theme park of five senses (of vision, audition, smell, touch and taste); the first outdoor beautification project; the first largest-scale Tang-style building complex; the first largest-scale groups of sculptures and the first largest hydro-film screen, all of which show that they are "the Garden of Chinese History" "the Garden of Spirit" "the Garden of Nature" "the Garden of Human Culture" and "the Garden of Art".

曲江池遗址公园

曲江池遗址公园，北临大唐芙蓉园，南至秦二世陵遗址，占地面积247英亩，由著名建筑大师张锦秋院士设计规划，于2008年7月1日在原曲江池基础上建成。曲江遗址公园以曲江池水为中心，依托周边丰富的旅游文化资源和人文传统，恢复再造曲江南湖、曲江流饮、汉武泉、黄渠桥等历史文化景观，再现曲江池历史上的山水人文格局。

曲江池不仅是中国古代风景园林的典范，而且具有千年的悠久历史。它兴于秦汉，盛于隋唐。从秦汉离宫"宜春院"的修建到隋唐宫苑"芙蓉园""曲江池"的大规模营建，曲江池成为著名的游览胜地。盛唐时期，这里宫殿连绵，楼阁起伏，达官贵人、文人墨客、仕女侍从，集会宴饮于曲江。进士及第后，也来曲江大摆筵席，饮酒作乐，所谓"曲江流饮"，被称为"关中八景"之一。此外，一系列诸如雁塔题名、寒窑故事等传说典故赋予了曲江池更加丰富的文化内涵进而使其闻名遐迩。如今曲江池的修建和开放让游人领略到丰富的盛唐文化魅力。

曲江池遗址公园，与周边的曲江寒窑遗址公园、秦二世陵遗址公园、唐城墙遗址公园等，形成一个城市生态景观带，共同构成人文西安的新标志，成为西安实现城市现代化和历史文化遗产保护和谐共生的成功典范，为西安市民提供一个自然、休闲、和谐的城市活动区。

The Qujiang Pool Site Park

Built on the original site of the Qujiang Pool, the Site Park covers an area of 247 acres, is bounded by the Tang Paradise in the north and the Mausoleum of Qin the Second in the south. It is artistically designed by Zhang Jinqiu, a famous architect and an academician. It was completed on July 1st, 2008. Propped by the rich cultural resources of tourism in the surrounding areas, the park takes the Pool as its center, with the South Lake, the Drinking Feast at Qujiang, the Hanwu Spring and the Huangqu Bridge around. It is constructed with an effort to restore the historical and cultural landscape, such as reproducing the landscape and cultural pattern in the history of the Qujiang Pool.

The Qujiang Pool is not only a model of ancient Chinese landscape garden, but also boasts a history of 1,000 years. It developed in the Qin and Han dynasties and flourished in the Sui and Tang dynasties. From the construction of "Yichun Garden" in the Qin and Han dynasties to the large-scale construction of "Furong Garden" and "Qujiang Pool" in the Sui and Tang dynasties, the Qujiang Pool has become a famous tourist attraction. During the prosperous Tang Dynasty, numerous palaces and pavilions were constructed one after another. High-ranking officials, scholars, court maids and attendants gathered and feasted at the Qujiang Pool. It was a trend for candidates who passed the imperial examination to hold grand ceremonies, banqueting friends and relatives at the Qujiang Pool. It is historically known as "The Drinking Feast at Qujiang", which is one of "The Eight Famous Scenic Attractions in Central Shaanxi". In addition, a series of legends and allusions, such as inscriptions on the Dayan Pagoda and the tragic love story in the Shabby Kiln, endow the Qujiang Pool with richer cultural connotations and nationwide fame. Today, the reconstruction and opening of the Qujiang Pool help tourists to appreciate the rich cultural charm of the prosperous Tang Dynasty.

The Qujiang Pool Site Park, together with the surrounding parks like the Shabby Kiln Site Park, the Mausoleum Site Park of Qin the Second and Tang City Wall Site Park, forms an urban ecological landscape zone and jointly symbolizes Xi'an in a new meaning. It has now become a successful model in urbanization and the protection of historical and cultural heritages harmoniously, thus providing urbanites with a natural, leisurely and ideal area for amusements.

兴庆宫公园

兴庆宫公园位于西安古城东侧，是在唐兴庆宫遗址上修建的。

这里原是唐长安隆庆坊的一部分，也是唐玄宗李隆基做太子时的藩邸所在地。李隆基即位后，于公元714年改建旧邸为宫，为避其名讳将隆庆改为兴庆。后经几度扩充，将附近的永嘉、道政、兴安、胜业诸坊的一部分划入宫内。公元728年，唐玄宗开始在兴庆宫理政，这里遂成为唐代封建统治的中心。公元753年，又修筑了宫城，从而形成一组完整的建筑，与太极宫、大明宫一起被称为"三内"。

唐开元、天宝年间，国势兴盛，兴庆宫建筑更加豪华，园林布局也更为讲究。据史书记载，玄宗李隆基曾在宫内兴庆殿接见过波斯景教教士和日本友人。"安史之乱"以后，兴庆宫失去政治上的重要地位，成为安置退位的太上皇的处所。唐玄宗退位后，就住在这里。经过唐末战乱，兴庆宫殿宇楼台几乎全部毁灭，到清初，这里已经成为一片废墟。

1957年，为了满足广大群众文化活动的需要，西安市政府决定在兴庆宫遗址修建兴庆公园。现在全园占地面积50公顷。园内碧波荡漾，树木葱郁，草坪如茵，百花似锦，风景优美宜人。沉香亭、花萼相辉楼、南薰殿、缚龙堂和长庆轩等，均为仿唐建筑，沿用旧名称，大体在原址方位上建成，造型古朴秀丽，别具风格。为了增进中日友谊，纪念日本友人阿倍仲麻吕（晁衡），园内还修了一座纪念碑。

兴庆湖

兴庆湖是兴庆公园的第一景，位于公园中央，占地10公顷，约是全园面积的五分之一。兴庆湖是在唐兴庆宫龙池原址上修筑的。据史籍记载，唐玄宗与其嫔妃大臣经常在这里泛舟游乐。

沉香亭

据说，当时兴庆宫的沉香亭是用沉香木建成，所以称"沉香亭"。亭周围栽植着各色牡丹、芍药。玄宗李隆基和杨贵妃一年一度在此赏花，还在此召见过著名诗人李白，命他作诗咏牡丹花开。

勤政务本楼

勤政务本楼位于兴庆宫的西南角，唐玄宗将此楼取名为"勤政务本楼"，意思是他要勤于政事，关心人民疾苦。唐玄宗是我国历史上最有作为的帝王之一。执政初期，他励精图治，奋发有为，开创了"开元盛世"局面，使我国封建社会走向巅峰。最初，勤政务本楼是皇帝处理朝政、主持科举考试的地方，后来成为玄宗举行歌舞宴会的场所。尤其是每年八月五日玄宗生日，百官献寿，宫内除了各种歌舞演出外，还有大象、犀牛、舞马等表演。因为勤政务本楼西、南两面均临大街，所以常常引来老百姓观看，时常堵塞交通。

花萼相辉楼

花萼相辉楼是兴庆宫的主要建筑之一。玄宗是以宫廷政变方式获取皇位的。

为了防止其兄弟以同样方式谋取皇位，玄宗特在兴庆宫建造这座宫殿，取名"花萼相辉楼"，比喻兄弟之间应当亲如手足，相互扶助，如同花萼相辉一样。玄宗常在这里与他的几个兄弟宴饮游乐，有时玩到深夜，便留他们在花萼相辉楼过夜，兄弟几人同床共枕，以笼络他们。

The Xingqing Palace Park

The Xingqing Palace Park is situated on the eastern outskirts of the ancient city of Xi'an. It was built on the former site of the Xingqing Palace of the Tang Dynasty.

The site proper, initially formed one part of the Longqing Fang (Fang refers to the living quarters) in the city of Chang'an. It also served as the official residence of Li Longji when he was made the crown prince. Later he became the Tang-Dynasty Emperor Xuan Zong. His former residence was reconstructed into a palace named the Longqing Palace after he succeeded to the throne in 714 AD. Before long, the Longqing Palace was renamed the Xingqing Palace, to avoid using the same character "Long" as in the Emperor's name. Expansion on the palace was undertaken once again in later years. As a result, parts of the neighbouring Fang, such as Yongjia, Daozheng, Xing'an and Shengye were successively absorbed by the palace. Emperor Xuan Zong began to administer state affairs here in 728 AD, and the palace consequently became the centre of feudal dominations in the Tang Dynasty. In the year 753 AD, it was completed with its surrounding walls. The Xingqing Palace, the Taiji Palace and the Daming Palace were then known as the "three interior palaces".

During the reign Tianbao in the Tang Dynasty, the state became prosperous. The palace was rebuilt, all the more luxurious, and the gardens were tastefully planned. According to of historical records, Emperor Xuan Zong once granted an interview to Persian Nestorian priests and Japanese friends at the Xingqing Palace. After An-Shi Rebellion, the Xingqing Palace lost its importance in politics and became a palace where Emperor Xuan Zong lived after his abdication. The halls and buildings in the Xingqing Palace were almost totally destroyed through the chaos caused by war in the late Tang Dynasty and remained in ruins up to the beginning of the Ming Dynasty.

In 1957, in order to meet the recreation needs of the broad masses, the Municipal Government of Xi'an decided to build the Xingqing Park on the site of the Xingqing Palace of the Tang Dynasty. The park now covers a total area of 50 hectares. The dark blue water ripples in the lake, the ground is tastefully decorated with verdant trees, blooming flowers and carpets of green lawns. The scenery in the park looks quite elegant and delightful. All the buildings such as the Chenxiang Pavilion, the Flower Shedding Brilliance Gallery, the Nanxun Hall, the Dragon-tying Hall and the Changqing Hall were reconstructed on their original sites in the architectural style of the Tang Dynasty, and their old names are still used. In order to promote the Sino-Japanese friendship, a monument, in memory of a Japanese friend, Chao Heng (his chinese name), was erected several years ago.

The Xingqing Lake

The Xingqing Lake, the primary scenery in the park, is located in the centre of the park, and covers an area of 10 hectares. It was equal to nearly 1/5 of the total area of the park. It was laid out on the site of the original Dragon Pool of the Xingqing Palace in the Tang Dynasty. According to historical records, Emperor Xuan Zong used to go boating, sightseeing and feasting together with his concubines and officials here on the lake.

The Chenxiang Pavilion

It is said that the Chenxiang Pavilion was built with agolloth eagle-woods, hence its name. Around the pavilion, there are varieties of precious flowers, such as tree peony and herbaceous peonies. Emperor Xuan Zong, together with his favourite concubine Lady Yang, used to share the pleasure of appreciating flowers in bloom every year. He once met the famous poet Li Bai here and asked him to improvise a poem about the peony blossom.

The Administration Building

The Government Administration Building is situated in the southwest corner of the Xingqing Palace. Emperor Xuan Zong named it "the Government Administration Building" just to indicate that he would be industrious in state affairs, and be concerned about the joys and sorrows of the people. He was one of the emperors who made the greatest achievements in Chinese history. During his early years in power, he roused himself, and vigorously acted to make the Tang Dynasty the most prosperous Dynasty of all. The feudal society of China was thus led to its peak. At the very beginning, the Administration Building was the place where imperial affairs were dealt with and imperial examinations were held. Later it became the place for Emperor Xuan Zong to hold parties and to give banquets. Especially, on the fifth day of the eighth lunar month, the Emperor's birthday, the palace would then be a bustling place, with all the officials offering birthday presents and the halls filled with various kinds of shows to make Emperor happy. Furthermore, there were also performances of elephants, rhinoceros and dancing horses. With the building facing the streets both to the south and to the west, common people came in large numbers to watch as well. As a result, the traffic was always heavy.

The Flower Shedding Brilliance Gallery

The Flower Shedding Brilliance Gallery was one of the main buildings of the Xingqing Palace. Emperor Xuan Zong gained his imperial crown by staging a palace coup. To keep his brothers from doing the same thing, he had this building built in the Xingqing Palace. He gave it the name "the Flower Shedding Brilliance Gallery", so it would serve as a metaphor to indicate that brothers ought to be dear to each other, and help each other, like the shedding of brilliance between flowers and calyxes. He often feasted and strolled about with his brothers here. Sometimes when it was far into night, he would put them up for the night here and spent the night together with them, so as to win them over.

西岳华山

西岳华山坐落在陕西省华阴市城南，海拔 2200 米，距西安以东 120 公里。它北瞰黄河，南依秦岭，素以奇险著称于世。

华山共有五大峰，即东峰朝阳、西峰莲花、中峰玉女、南峰落雁、北峰云台。五峰耸立于群山之中，远处望去，恰似一朵盛开的莲花，因此得名华山。因为在中国古代，"花"与"华"两个字通用。

"华山自古一条路"，由北向南，贯穿北峰、中峰、东峰、南峰、西峰，计程约20公里。一路行去必经千尺幢、百尺峡、老君犁沟、上天梯、苍龙岭等绝险要道，饱尝华山之险。此外，山上还有长空栈道、鹞子翻身等一般人闻所未闻的险景。若游者亲临其境，奇峰峭壁，险径危石，鬼斧神工，必定不胜惊骇，长叹而行止。山上还有众多的古建筑，庙宇亭阁点缀于山巅峰谷，每当云雾缥缈之时，游人常有身临仙境之感。

玉泉院

玉泉院位于华山北麓谷口，总扼入山之颈，是攀登华山的起点。玉泉院内有清泉一眼，据说与山顶镇岳宫玉井潜通，泉水清澈甘美，玉泉院因此得名。今院内古松成荫，回廊曲折，多亭台楼阁。相传为五代（公元907—960年）隐士陈抟老祖所造，清乾隆年间重修。现在，玉泉院经多次整修，面貌已焕然一新。院内碑石上刻有珍贵的书法文字。

青柯坪

从玉泉院至青柯坪为进山道路，约10公里。道路两旁高峰平峙，小路曲折迂回，上下不定，使人未登华山，已备尝登山之艰苦。至青柯坪，谷道忽尽，豁然开朗，山路转为突上。青柯坪有东道院、通仙观等庙宇。游人至此，可稍事歇息。

北峰

北峰，又名云台峰。自青柯坪向东，经回心石，来到千尺㠉。千尺㠉凿在几乎笔直的石壁上，石级仅容足尖，必须扶着铁索才能攀登。石级尽处如同洞口，一块大铁板便可堵死上山之路，真可谓一夫当关，万夫莫开。攀上百尺峡，来到修在悬崖上给人以突兀凌空之感的老君犁沟。这条沟自上而下约500级，相传道家始祖老子驱其乘牛，一夜犁成此道，故有此名。沟头尚有老君挂犁处。走过此处，便来到总辖四峰的北峰。北峰只有一岭南通，三面悬绝，十分险要。峰顶有庙宇。

苍龙岭

苍龙岭，古称搦岭或夹岭，是一条南北长达1500米，宽仅1米，陡上陡下的石级通道。其中间突起，形同鲫鱼背。两旁山谷深不可测。若在此遥望青松白云，耳旁风声大作，令人目眩心惊，不敢侧视。岭尽处有怡神岩，岩上刻有"韩愈投书处"五字。相传唐代大文学家韩愈至此，不由得惊恐万状，自认为难以生还，就写了遗书投下岭去，后来终于得助脱险。攀登苍龙岭，险峻地擦耳岩和上天梯亦是必经之处。

中峰

中峰，又叫玉女峰。相传春秋时秦穆公之女弄玉被隐士萧史优美的箫声打动，不愿再过骄奢淫逸的宫廷生活，而随萧史乘龙、凤到此隐居。现在峰上有玉女洞、玉女洗头盆、玉女梳妆台和玉女驾凤亭等遗迹。

东峰

东峰峰顶的朝阳台是观看日出的最佳处，故又称朝阳峰。此峰突兀而立，上下皆难。站在峰顶南望秦岭，只见岗峦起伏，似万顷波涛滚滚而来；下视原野，黄河渭水交汇成汪洋一片。清晨，火红的太阳在阵阵的松涛声中从东方冉冉升起。宇宙苍穹，山川大地，无比宏伟壮阔，令人目不暇接。东峰下有一悬崖，其绝壁的赤色石与苍岩交织成一只天然巨掌，"关中八景"之首的"华岳仙掌"指的就是这个地方。相传在远古时，华山与首阳山原是一脉相连，阻挡着黄河水的去路。巨灵神以手劈山，让滔滔河水东流，于是在华山上印下了这只掌痕。此外，东峰有甘露池、青虚洞等景观。下棋亭和鹞子翻身两处，更是险陡异常。

南峰

南峰又称落雁峰，海拔2200多米，是华山最高峰。四周都是松林，而峰顶却犹如一块巨石，草木无存，风势猛烈，需爬行才能到达。峰顶上有历代文人骚客的题字留咏。南峰上的建筑，名为金天宫，也称白帝祠。峰顶有老君洞，相传道家始祖老子曾隐居于此。洞北有太上泉，泉水碧绿，冬夏不竭，俗称仰天池。由峰东下，可至长空栈道。此处以铁栈插壁，承以青石板，宽不到8寸，即使是胆大过人的人，也要扶着铁索面壁屏气，缓步而行；胆小者则只能望而却步。南峰上还有老子峰、炼丹炉、八卦池等胜迹。

西峰

西峰峰顶翠云宫前有一巨石，状如莲花，故又称莲花峰。西峰奇拔峻峭，最能代表华山的风格。"西岳峥嵘何壮哉！黄河如丝天际来……白帝金精运元气，石作莲花云作台……"李白曾以这样壮丽的诗句来赞颂华山。峰顶有一座翠云宫，据传，神话故事《宝莲灯》中三圣母之子小沉香劈山救母之处就在这里。翠云宫旁边有一块巨石，巨石中间的裂缝形如斧劈过，名斧劈石。石旁树立一柄铁铸长把大斧，据传为当年沉香所用。峰顶有突出的摘星石。峰的西北面，笔立如削，空绝万仞，人称舍身崖。崖畔有苍鹰盘旋。峰顶云雾缭绕。极目远眺，秦川茫茫，若隐若现，令人心旷神怡。

由于各处安全保护措施的加强和华山索道的修建，奇险无比的华山，正在变为中外游人的"坦途"。

西岳庙

历史上的华山被人们称为神山，位于华山以北7公里的西岳庙是历代帝王祭祀华山神的场所，1988年被国务院公布为全国重点文物保护单位。因此，游览华山，不可不去西岳庙。

我国古代修庙祭山的制度开始于汉武帝时期。西岳神是历代王朝共同尊奉的神灵，所以，西岳庙自公元前134年创建开始，就被定为祭祀华山神的地方，历代王朝对其都进行过整修，到清代1779年才形成今日的格局及规模。历经2000多年的发展与扩建，西岳庙现在占地面积约119880平方米，四周城墙高8米，周长1825米，是五岳庙中最为宏伟壮观的城墙。西岳庙建筑规格极高，形似北京故宫，素有"小故宫"之称。

西岳庙坐北朝南，是五岳庙中唯一正对主峰的祭庙。西岳庙的整体布局前窄后宽，建筑布局前低后高，至高点在庙后的万寿殿上。站在这里，南望华山主峰，与庙内的主要建筑西凤楼、大殿、御书房，恰成一条直线。这也正是整个庙宇的中轴线，并且一直延伸到华山主峰。站在这条中轴线上的任何地方，都可以看见华山五峰。

由于西岳庙在历史上主要是皇家及达官显贵的祭祀场所，又是皇帝外出巡视的必到之地，在选址上可谓匠心独运：它位于开阔的平原上，一面面对华山主峰，另一面背靠渭河、黄河、洛河三水交汇之处，一旦有意外情况发生，水、陆两路都能进能退。

Mount Hua

With the Yellow River to the north and the Qinling Mountain Range at the back to the south, Mount Hua stands in the south of Huayin County, 120 kilometers east of Xi'an, with an altitude of 2,200 meters. It is always known for its precipitousness.

There are five peaks of Mount Hua: the Morning Sun Peak, the Lotus Flower Peak, the Jade Lady Peak, the Wild Goose-resting Peak and the Cloudy Terrace Peak. From a distance, these five peaks look like a lotus flower among the mountains, hence the name of Mount Hua (Hua means flower in Chinese).

As the saying goes "There has been only one path up Mount Hua since ancient times", this road runs for some 20 kilometers, around five prominent peaks. This trail passes a number of perilous places: the Thousand-foot Precipice, the Hundred-foot Crevice, Laojun's Furrow (Laojun, the patriarch of Taoism.), the Heavenward Ladder and the Blue Dragon Ridge. The Cliffside Path and the Sparrow Hawk's Cliff are a lot more dangerous. Upon reaching the top, visitors can enjoy the awesome grandeur of these peaks. The peaks are peculiar, the cliffs are steep, and the path is difficult and dangerous. All are so extraordinary as if they were created by spirits. The sights and situations make climbers tremble with fear, but gasp in admiration, too. The ancient buildings are one of the main attractions. The peaks and valleys are dotted with temples and pavilions, which are constantly clad in mist. Climbers feel as if they were making a tour of fairyland.

The Jade Spring Garden (Yuquan Garden)

The Yuquan Garden (Jade Spring Garden) is located at the entrance of the valley on the hillside north of Mount Hua. It is the starting point to go to the top. Inside the garden there is a cool, sweet spring, hence its name "Jade Spring Garden". The spring is said to come from an underground flow that runs from the Jade Well in the Zhenyue Temple. The old pines border the winding paths, and give deep shade. Legend has it that Chen Tuan, a hermit in the Five dynasty Period (907 AD—960 AD), built the gardens, terraces, towers and pavilions. Restoration was carried out during Emperor Qian Long's reign in the Qing Dynasty, which makes the whole garden look nice and beautiful today. The stone tablets are inscribed with valuable calligraphy.

The Qingke Terrace (Qingke Ping)

The path, from the Jade Spring Garden to Qingke Terrace, is about 10 kilometers in length. This path is flanked by steep cliffs and paved with stone slabs. Halfway up this winding path, you will feel exhausted and want to turn back before the actual climb begins. When you arrive at the Qingke Terrace, the ravine path comes to an end and a beautiful view suddenly makes it all worthwhile. Here you can take a short break and look around Dongdao and Tongxian temples. Another steep climb from the Qingke Terrace is ahead of you.

The North Peak

The North Peak is also called the Cloudy Terrace Peak. As you continue your way from Qingke Terrace, you will soon pass a huge rock named "Turn Back", and you will find yourself at the bottom of the Thousand-foot Precipice. This precipice is cut into the face of a nearly perpendicular cliff. The steps there are only toeholds, and you will have to grasp iron chains for support. The upper part of the precipice is shaped like an opening to a cave. A large sheet of iron could well block your way completely, if it were placed there. To put it vividly, if one man were guarding the pass at this point, thousands of people would be unable to get through. After the Hundred-foot Crevice, you ascend to Laojun's Furrow. It is also cut into the cliff. You will feel that the furrow must be ascending right up into the sky. Nearly 500 steps are hewn up from the bottom part of the furrow. Legend has it that Lao Tzu, the founder of Taoism, once drove his ox to this place and ploughed the furrow in only one night. At the end of the furrow, he is said to have hung his plough. By and by you will finally reach the North Peak. It is the only access to the other four peaks. The North Peak has only one hill that leads to the south with three sides disconnected with anywhere, and it is fairly steep. Here again, you can see a few lonely temples.

The Canglong Ridge (Canglong Ling)

The Canglong (Blue Dragon) Ridge was also known as Ni Ridge or Jia Ridge in ancient times. It is 1,500 meters long and only one meter wide. This ridge winds up and down irregularly with its central part protruding into the air rather like the backbone of a carp. On either side of the ridge, cliffs fall off into deep valleys. Looking across into the distance, you will get a misty view of green pines and floating clouds. You will hear the sound of the wind roaring into your ears. You may be so filled with apprehension and dizziness that you may fear to look at the view on either side. At the other end of the ridge is the Yishen Cliff, which is inscribed with five Chinese characters: "Han Yu Threw Down His Will." The story goes that Han Yu, a Tang Dynasty poet, once reached this spot. He was in such fear that he concluded that his end was at hand and threw down his last will on that very spot. Fortunately, he was rescued. If you are determined to ascend to the Canglong Ridge, you cannot avoid either the Ear-touching Cliff or the Heavenward Ladder on your way up.

The Central Peak

The Central Peak is called the Jade Lady Peak. Legend has it that Nong Yu, the daughter of King Mu of the Spring and Autumn Period, was so moved by the music which Xiao Shi, a hermit, played on a vertical bamboo flute, that she gave up a happy and luxurious palace life, and together with Xiao Shi, flew here on the backs of a dragon and a phoenix and lived in seclusion. The Jade Lady's Cave, the Wash Basin, the Stone Dressing Table and the Phoenix Pavilion are what we can see here today.

The East Peak

The East Peak is also called the Morning Sun Peak. It is the best place to see the sunrise. The peak shoots dramatically up into the sky. Therefore, both the ascent and the descent are difficult and dangerous. You can stand on the peak, look far to the south, and you will see faint waves of mountains of the Qinling Mountain Range. As you look down, you will also get a misty view of the vast fields and the blending waters of the Yellow River and Weihe River. Every morning the fiery red sun rises gradually over the roaring might of these two rivers. At this moment, the view is splendid: the vast sky, the wavy mountain and the deep valleys. On the side at one cliff there is the impression of a huge hand colored in a mixture of blue and brown. Yellow The story goes like this: Mount Hua was originally linked to the Shouyang Mount. Together they blocked the flow of the Yellow River. With his hand, Juling God split the mountain into two, and made a way for the river to pass, consequently leaving the print of his hand on the cliff. It is known as "God's Hand Print on Mount Hua". (The place It is the first among the Eight Famous Scenic Attractions in Central Shaanxi.) Besides, there is more scenery around here, such as the Sweet Dew Pool and the Qingxu Cave. The Chess Pavilion and the Sparrow Hawk's Cliff, which are close to the peak, are so dangerously situated that only those with enough courage are able to reach them.

The South Peak

The South Peak (Wild Goose-resting Peak) is situated at an elevation of 2,200 meters. It towers over all other peaks on the mountain. It is covered by pines and cypresses that provide deep shade, and extend for several miles. The top of the peak is a bare rock. Here there is no grass, and the wind is always strong. It can be reached only through crawling. When you ascend to its summit, and look down, you can only feel that "there is only the vast sky overhead, and no other peaks anywhere that can reach the same height". This huge rock carries inscriptions carved by men of letters of various periods of time. The building on the South Peak is named the Golden Heaven Temple (also known as the White Emperor's Temple). According to the legend, Laojun's Cave at the top is the very place where Lao Tzu once lived as a hermit. To the north of the cave is the Taishang Spring. Its water is dark blue, and never runs dry at any time of the year. The spring is also known as "Heavenward Pond". Descending eastward, you will notice the Cliffside Path. This path juts out from the cliff and is as narrow as 8 inches. Iron bars have been fixed into the cliff to support the marble slabs which make this path. So even those with much courage have to grasp the iron chains firmly, hold their breath and try to walk along steadily. The remnants of Lao Tzu's Summit, the Immortality-pill-making Furnace and the Eight Diagrams Pit can also be seen at the top.

The West Peak

Because of a huge lotus-shaped rock in front of the Cuiyun Temple (Jade Green Cloudy Terrace Temple) at the top, the West Peak is known as Lotus Flower Peak. Its sheer steepness best exemplifies the characteristics of Mount Hua. Li Bai, a Tang-Dynasty poet, once wrote a few lines to eulogize the mountain:

Oh, what a mountain, so lofty and steep!

The Huanghe River, like a silk thread,

Flows hither from the horizon.

Full of vitality is the mountain,

Above a terrace of clouds, as though,

The White Emperor's spirit descended.

In accordance with the fairy tale *Lotus Lantern*, the West Peak is the place where little Chen Xiang, son of Holy Mother, split the mountain to rescue his mother. Close to Cuiyun Temple lies a huge rock which seems to have been split into two with an axe, hence its name "Split Rock with an Axe". Not far off stands a long-handled axe which is said to have been used by this filial son. At the top of the peak lies another prominent rock. It is called the Star-picking Rock. The northern side of the peak is characterized by perpendicular cliffs of great height. It is known as Life-abandoning Cliff.

Hawks soar here and there, clouds and mist drift above the peak. Looking far into the distance, you can get a misty view of the Central Shaanxi Plain, and suddenly you will feel completely relaxed and happy.

Thanks to the safety and protection measures already taken, Mount Hua is now becoming more accessible to visitors both local and foreign, with the aid of cable cars.

The Temple at Mount Hua (Xiyue Miao)

In the past, Mount Hua was regarded as mountain of divinity and the temple, which lies 7 kilometers north of it, served as a place for the emperors of different dynasties to hold sacrificial ceremonies for the God of Mount Hua. In 1988, this temple was categorized as an important National Historical Monument in China. Since then, it has become a favourable tourist attraction.

The custom of building temples for the sacrifice to a mountain initiated in the times of Emperor Wu Di of the Western Han Dynasty. Mount Hua used to be regarded as god by all the dynasties. Therefore, the temple of Mount Hua became the place for the sacrifice to the God of Mount Hua after it was built in 134 BC. With the restoration of the temple by each dynasty, the present setup took shape in 1779 of the Qing Dynasty. Through over 2,000 years' development and expansion, the Temple of Mount Hua covers an area of about 119,880 square meters now. The walls, 1,825 meters long and 8 meters high, are the most magnificent walls among the temples of the Five Mountains. The standards of the construction of the temple are so high that it looks like the Imperial Palace of Beijing, hence the name "Small Imperial Palace".

The Temple of Mount Hua is the only sacrificial temple among the temples of the Five Mountains and it faces south and the highest peak of the mountain. As far as the overall layout is concerned, the front is narrow and the back wide. The complex looks low in the front and high at the back with the Wanshou Palace at the highest spot. Standing here, you will see the highest peak of Mount Hua in the south, which is on the same axial line with the main constructions, such as Phoenix Tower, the Main Hall and the Imperial Study. This line is exactly the axis of the temple which extends to the highest peak of Mount Hua. Standing anywhere on the axis, you can see the five peaks of Mount Hua.

Since the Temple of Mount Hua used to be the sacrificial temple for the imperial families and a necessary stop for the inspection tours of emperors, the location of this temple was carefully chosen. It is located on a vast plain with the highest peak of Mount Hua in front and Weihe River, the Yellow River and the Luohe River merged together at back. If anything unexpected happens, it is safe to retreat through either the land or the rivers.

太白山国家森林公园

太白山国家森林公园位于秦岭主峰太白山北坡的眉县境内，总面积2949公顷，分为8个景区，有各种景点137个。

太白山国家森林公园海拔在620—3500米之间，是我国现有森林公园中海拔最高的。由于高差大，气候、土壤、植物等均表现出明显的垂直分布规律：自下而上分为暖温带、温带、寒温带、严寒带等；与之相对应，呈现出不同的森林景观，自下而上有六个垂直分布的景观林带，具有典型的生物群落。植物种类繁多，有高等植物1550余种，苔藓植物300余种。此外还有大量的蕨类、地衣和菌类。有野生鸟兽260余种，属国家一、二类保护的野生动物有金丝猴、羚牛、云豹、红腹角雉、大鲵等。

太白山国家森林公园有多种景观奇特、壮丽的自然地貌。园内有低山、中山、高山三个地貌类型，景观各具特色。黄土覆盖的石质低山区在海拔1300米以下，兼有黄土地貌与石质山地地貌特点，分布有许多石洞。奇峰林立的中山区在海拔1300米之间，山势陡峭，险峰对峙，沟谷狭窄，怪石嶙峋，飞瀑深潭，景观多变。冰川刨掘的高山区在海拔2600米以上，山势平坦开阔，第四纪冰川遗迹清晰可见。角峰巨石，千姿百态，妙趣横生。强烈的冻融风化，大量块砾形成"石河"景观。太白国家森林公园地质构造保存完整，岩石种类较多，被誉为"天然地质博物馆"。

太白山国家森林公园温泉资源得天独厚。处于森林公园入口处的眉县汤峪温泉由11个泉眼、3口井组成，水质优良，含有20多种对人体有益的矿物质和微量元素。

The National Forest Park at Mount Taibai

This National Forest Park is situated in Meixian County on the northern hillside of Mount Taibai, the highest peak of the Qinling Mountain Range. It occupies an area of 2,949 hectares, with 137 scenic attractions of every description distributed in 8 large scenic zones.

The park stands 620 to 3,500 meters above sea level, the highest of its kind in China. The vast difference in altitude results in a distinctive vertical distribution of climate, soil and vegetation. The park experiences four different temperature zones in ascending order: warm temperate, luke-warm temperature, frigid temperature and severe-cold temperature. Accordingly, there are six different forest landscape zones vertically. They are representative of unique bio-communities. The park has a variegated mass of plants, including 1,550 higher plants and 300 moss plants. Besides, lichen, fern and artemisia are also large components of its vegetation. It has more than 260 species of wild birds and animals, and those within first and second categories under state protection are the golden-haired monkey, the takin, the clouded leopard, the red-bellied tragopan and the giant salamander.

Grotesque and splendid landforms scatter over the park. There are three types of hills: low, medium-sized and high. These landscape zones assume distinctive features. The loess-covered stony low hills below an altitude of 1,300 meters are characterized by loess and stony hilly landforms, and there are many stone caves in them. Landscape varies from place to place in the medium hilly area. Available here are steep hills, symmetrical peaks, narrow vales and gullies, jagged and oddly-shaped rocks, deep water pools and gushing waterfalls. The glaciated high hilly area lies smooth and outstretched, and shows signs of the quaternary glacier everywhere. Angular peaks and gigantic stones come in thousands of shapes, and present a lively sight. The landscape of "stone rivers" has grown out of boulders as a result of severe erosion by the melting ice and wind. The park is famed as "a natural geology museum" for its intact geo-tectonics and varied rocks.

The park is endowed with rich hot spring resources. The Tangyu Hot Spring Sanitarium in Meixian County, situated at the entrance of the park, gets its water source from 11 spas and 3 wells. The spring water is top-quality and contains more than 20 kinds of healthy minerals and trace elements.

楼观台国家森林公园

楼观台国家森林公园位于周至县城东南15公里的终南山北麓，因这里有我国道教史上称为"天下第一福地"的楼观台而得名。

楼观台不但因历史古迹闻名,而且以森林景观秀丽而见长。它依山傍水,林茂竹秀,山清水碧,植被为终南山之冠。这里峰峦沟谷纵横相间,地质构造复杂,生物种类繁多。主要森林树种有120多种,有珍贵动物大熊猫、金丝猴等30多种。1982年国务院决定在这里投资建立森林公园。

公园内峰奇谷幽,古木参天,青竹万杆,浓荫罩地。最高峰天池海拔1350米。森林分布层次鲜明:海拔1000米处有油松、刺柏;1000米以下分布着大片栎类、刺槐、核桃、橡树林、灌木林和竹林。

园内辟有秦岭树木园,有华山松、杨树等用材树,漆、柞、橡等经济树,板栗、核桃等果树,杜仲等药材,稀有珍贵的七叶树、冷杉以及灌木林等。园内竹类品种有近百种,居全国第二,除本地的淡竹外,还有四川的寿竹,福建、湖南的毛竹等用材竹,以及墨竹、斑竹等观赏竹。另外,园内还拟建秦岭濒危珍稀树木园、观赏树木园、秦岭野生动物园等。现在楼观台国家森林公园已经成为陕西省一处独具特色,融自然、人文景观为一体的旅游胜地。

The National Forest Park at the Louguantai Temple

This National Forest Park is situated on the northern hillside of the Zhongnan Mountain, 15 kilometers southeast of the seat of Zhouzhi County. It is well-known to the outside world as the location of the Louguantai Temple or as that of "the first land of the blessed under heaven" in China's history of Taoism.

The Louguantai Temple is famous not only for its historical remains, but also for its beautiful forest landscape. It is surrounded by green hills and blue waters. Bamboo trees are verdant and luxuriant. It ranks first in the area of the Zhongnan Mountain for vegetation vigor. It is characterized by crisscross vales and hills, complicated tectonics and variegated organisms. It boasts more than 120 varieties and 30 rare animal species such as pandas and golden haired monkeys. The park began to take shape in 1982.

In the park there are grotesque peaks, deep and secluded vales, towering old trees, and shady bamboo trees. The highest peak of Mount Tianchi is 1,350 meters above the sea level. Vertical distribution is the distinctive feature of its forest: At an altitude of 1,000 meters, there are Chinese pines and Taiwan junipers; Below this vegetation zone are large patches of quercus citrina, locust, walnut and oak trees as well as groves and thicket bamboo.

The park has an arboretum for trees growing on the Qinling Mountain Range.

These trees fall into several categories: timber, cash, fruit and official. Within these categories are Mount Hua pines, poplars, lacquer trees, toothed, oaks, Chinese chestnuts, walnuts, Tu-chung (Eucommia ulmoidas), Chinese buckeyes, firs, firewood trees and thickets. The variety of bamboo trees ranks second in the entire country. Nearly one hundred varieties of bamboo are available in the park, including henon bamboo, native to the area, longevity bamboo from Sichuan Province, moso bamboo (timber), black bamboo and mottled bamboo (ornamental) respectively introduced from Fujian and Hunan provinces. The park plans to build an arboretum, an ornamental plantation and a Qinling-Mountain wild life zoo. Up to this day, it has developed into a unique tourist attraction with both natural and artificial features in Shaanxi Province, taking both natural and human elements as an integral whole.

秦岭北麓风景名胜区

西安秦岭自然风景区生态旅游资源丰富,适合休闲度假。该区内有王顺山、楼观台、朱雀、太白、太平等国家森林公园和六个省级森林公园,三处国家级自然保护区,一处国家级地质公园以及骊山国家级风景名胜区。动植物种类繁多,数量巨大,环境优良,景观多样,是疗养健身、休闲度假、观光游览胜地。另外,该区人文景观丰富、品位高,有以宗教文化为特色的寺庙道观,如宗圣宫、悟真寺、重阳宫、兴教寺等,涵盖了佛教、道教、伊斯兰教、基督教等教派。有反映不同王朝兴衰的宫殿御苑遗址与帝王陵墓;有反映古代经济、社会、政治的石刻艺术、典籍与各种艺术珍品;有反映人类发展进化历史的遗址、化石和器物。这些资源都凝聚着深厚的文化积淀,而且许多在国内外都是独一无二的,享有很高的声誉。

The Scenic Resort at Qinling Mountains

The northern foot of the Qinling Mountains is a natural scenic resort with many natural resources for holiday-makers. Within the range of the scenery, there are one national geo-park, three national nature reserves, six forest parks up to the provincial level and some well-known national forest parks, such as the Zhuque Park, the Taibai Park and the Taiping Park. What is more, the National Park of Mount Li is also located here. With numerous wild plants and animals, amiable environment and various landscapes, the place has become a drawcard to tourists either for the purpose of sightseeing or recreation. In addition, this resort is rich in artificial tourist attractions of good taste. There are many religious buildings, such as the Zongsheng House, the Wuzhen Temple, the Chongyang Palace and the Xingjiao Temple, which cover almost all the religions sects, ranging from Buddhism, Taoism, Islamism and Christianity. It is right here that one can witness and experience the remains of imperial palaces and mausoleums, which display the ups and downs of dynasties; carved stones, books and art treasures, which reflect the ancient politics, society and economy; and historic ruins, fossils and utensils, which mirror the evolution of mankind. With a long history and profound cultural heritage, many of them gain a high reputation for being unique in China and beyond.

第八部分 红色旅游

八路军西安办事处纪念馆

八路军西安办事处纪念馆位于西安城内西五路北新街七贤庄,于1959年正式建成开放。

八路军驻西安办事处是中共中央和八路军自1937年至1946年驻西安的公开合法机构。

1936年12月西安事变和平解决后,第二次国共合作形成,中国共产党在西安市七贤庄一号设立了公开机构"红军联络处"。1937年7月,抗日战争全面爆发,为了争取国民党共同抗日,红军改编为国民革命军第八路军。"红军联络处"也于同年9月改为"八路军驻西安办事处"。工作人员由原来的数十名增加到200多名。

办事处的主要任务是宣传党的抗战主张,扩大抗日民族统一战线,输送爱国进步青年去延安,壮大革命力量,为陕甘宁边区和前方领取、采购、转送抗战物资,支援抗战。

在办事处开展工作期间,国民党千方百计进行破坏,想方设法进行监视。当时西安人口不到50万,而国民党在西安的职业特务就有5000多人。他们在办事处周围设立了20多处监视点,还装扮成小商贩、人力车夫、补鞋匠等监视和跟踪往来办事处的进步人士,甚至对办事处的人员绑架、暗杀等。

在险恶的环境中,办事处的全体人员坚持了党中央和毛主席提出的"发展进步势力,争取中间势力,孤立顽固势力"的方针,在对反共顽固派的斗争中,实行了"有理、有利、有节"的原则,粉碎了敌人的阴谋破坏活动,扩大和巩固了抗日民族统一战线,为抗日战争的胜利做出了贡献。抗日战争胜利后,国民党反动势力发动了全面内战,办事处被迫于1946年9月撤回延安。

中国共产党老一辈无产阶级革命家刘少奇、周恩来、朱德、林伯渠、董必武、叶剑英、邓小平和彭德怀等同志都曾先后到办事处指导工作。国际友人白求恩、史沫特莱等也曾来过办事处。

八路军驻西安办事处旧址包括七贤庄一、三、四、七号院。为了向人民群众进行革命传统教育，1959年，一号院恢复了原貌并成立了"八路军西安办事处纪念馆"。纪念馆陈列了大量的文件、手稿、书刊、图片及证章、电话等革命文物，生动而具体地显示了办事处成立的经过、历史任务、办事处同志工作学习和与敌人英勇智斗的情景。刘少奇、周恩来、朱德、叶剑英、邓小平及其他领导同志住过的房间都按原样布置陈列。

PART EIGHT REVOLUTIONARY MEMORIALS

The Memorial of the Eighth-Route Army—Xi'an Liaison Office

The Memorial Museum of the Eighth-Route Army—Xi'an Liaison Office lies in Qixian Village on Beixin Street, along Fifth West Boulevard. It is the site of the former Eighth-Route Army—Xi'an Office. It was officially opened to public in 1959.

The Eighth-Route Army—Xi'an Office was an open, legal organization of the Central Committee of the Communist Part of China and the Eighth-Route Army between 1937 and 1946.

After the peaceful solution of the Xi'an Incident in December, 1936, the second cooperation between the Nationalist Party and the Communist Party was formed and the Red Army Liaison Office—the Chinese Communist Party's open organization in Xi'an, was set up in Courtyard No. 1 of Qixian Village. In July, 1937, the nationwide War of Resistance against Japan began. In order to persuade the Nationalists to fight against Japan jointly, the Red Army was reorganized as the Eighth-Route Army of the National Revolutionary Army and the Red Army Liaison Office was renamed as the Eighth-Route Army-Xi'an Office in September, 1937. The number of the staff went up from several dozens to over 200.

The main tasks of the office were to publicize the Party's advocacy of resistance against Japan and to expand the National United Front. It helped escort patriotic progressive youths to Yan'an to enhance the revolutionary forces. It received, purchased and transported logistic supplies to the Shaanxi-Gansu-Ningxia border regions and to the rear areas to support the War of Resistance.

While the Liaison Office was at work, the Nationalists tried every possible means to sabotage it. There were then fewer than 500,000 residents in the city of Xi'an, but there were more than 5,000 professional Nationalist spies in plain clothes. They set up over 20 checkpoints around the office. They disguised themselves as peddlers, rickshaw men and shoe repairmen. They either followed or kept a close watch on the progressive personages who were in contact with the office. They even threatened the staff of the office by kidnapping and murdering them.

Even under such perilous circumstances, the whole staff of the office adhered to the policy proposed by Mao Zedong and the Central Party Committee: "Expand the progressive forces, win over the middle ones, and isolate the die-hards." In the struggle against the die-hard bigots against communism, the staff stuck to the philosophy of "fighting on just grounds" "to our advantage" and "with restraint". They crushed the conspiracy of the enemy's sabotage, and consolidated the Anti-Japanese National United Front. They also made contributions to the victory in the War of Resistance against Japan. After the war, the Nationalist reactionary forces launched an all-out civil war. The Xi'an Office had to withdraw to Yan'an in September, 1946.

The proletarian revolutionaries of the old generation of the Chinese Communist Party, such as Liu Shaoqi, Zhou Enlai, Zhu De, Lin Boqu, Dong Biwu, Ye Jianying, Deng Xiaoping, Peng Dehuai and many other leading figures had been to this office on an inspection tour. Dr. Norman Bethune, Smedly and some other foreign friends had also visited the office.

The site of the former Xi'an Office includes court-yards No. 1, No. 3, No. 4, and No. 7 at Qixian Village. In order to educate the masses about the revolutionary tradition, Courtyard No. 1 was restored to its original state in 1959 and the Memorial Museum of the Eighth-Route Army—Xi'an Office was set up there. Exhibited in the Memorial Museum are revolutionary relics, such as documents, manuscripts, books, magazines, pictures, badges and radio transmitters. These artifacts show vividly how the office was set up, what its historical tasks were, how the office functioned, and how staff worked, studied and fought against the enemies bravely and resourcefully. The rooms are now laid out in their original state where those above-mentioned leading figures once lived.

延安革命纪念地

延安市位于陕西省北部,东临黄河,与山西省相邻。延安历史悠久,一直是陕北地区政治、经济、文化和军事的中心,留下了大量珍贵的历史文化遗产。中华民族始祖黄帝的陵墓就位于延安黄陵县,黄河壶口瀑布也位于延安境内。

延安之所以驰名中外,更是因为它在中国现代史上的特殊地位。1935年10月,中央红军在突破国民党军队的围追堵截后,胜利完成了举世闻名的万里长征,抵达陕北吴起县。1937年10月,中共中央进驻延安城,从此,延安成为中国人民革命斗争的指导中心和总后方,全国人民向往的革命圣地。党中央和毛主席曾在延安生活和工作了13个春秋,在这里领导全党、全军和全国人民取得了抗日战争和解放战争的胜利,建立了新中国,为延安留下了最为可贵的精神财富——延安精神。

延安市区有100多处革命旧址,有"革命博物馆城"的美称。1961年3月4日,国务院把延安革命旧址列入第一批全国重点文物保护单位。1982年,延安市被列为全国24座历史文化名城之一。现在恢复开放的革命旧址有凤凰山麓、杨家岭、枣园、王家坪和南泥湾等五处。

凤凰山麓

凤凰山麓绵延于延安城西南方向。延安城区从北到南沿凤凰山麓而建。位于延安城内凤凰山的凤凰村是中共中央机关抵达延安后的第一个驻地,当时,中共中央是以租用的名义向当地群众借住的,共有窑洞15孔,房屋50间。毛泽东、朱德、周恩来等中央领导都曾居住于此,同时,红军参谋部也设在这里。

毛泽东在凤凰山麓居住期间,写下了大量文章及著作,仅收入《毛泽东选集》的就有16篇。奠定了毛泽东哲学基础的著名哲学论著《实践论》和《矛盾论》就是毛泽东在凤凰山麓居住期间完成的。另外,他还在此写下了著名的军事著作《论持久战》。

毛主席在凤凰山麓接见了国际共产主义战士、加拿大人白求恩医生。白求恩医生以身殉职后,毛主席在此写下了《纪念白求恩》这篇著名文章,号召全党向白求恩医生学习,做"毫不利己,专门利人"的模范。

美国记者史沫特莱女士在凤凰山麓采访了朱德总司令,并根据他的传奇人生写下了《伟大的道路》。

中共中央在凤凰山麓期间召开了一系列会议，做出了我党历史上很多重要决议，如清算了张国焘分裂红军、另立"中央"的错误路线，解决了怎样坚持独立自主原则，处理国共两党关系等问题。同时，中共中央在毛主席领导下兴办了许多干部学校，有力地提高了我党干部的素质，从政治上和组织上为全面抗战做了充分准备。

1938年11月20日，十多架日本飞机突然轰炸延安城，中央机关连夜搬迁到位于延安城西北的杨家岭。

杨家岭

杨家岭位于延安城西北约3公里处。抗日战争时期，这里是一个仅有十几户人家的小山村。1938年11月20日，由于日本飞机轰炸延安城，中共中央机关由城内凤凰山麓迁到这里。从那时起至1947年3月，党中央一直在此居住。在此期间，党中央领导解放区军民开展了轰轰烈烈的大生产运动，召开了具有伟大历史意义的中国共产党第七次全国代表大会和著名的延安文艺座谈会，为我党奠定了争取更大胜利的基础。

杨家岭革命旧址内的主要建筑有中央大礼堂，中央办公厅大楼以及毛泽东、朱德、周恩来、刘少奇等中央领导人的旧居。

中央大礼堂建成于1942年，是由中央机关工作人员协助民工就地取材，用砖石修成的。礼堂由正厅、舞厅和休息室三部分组成。1945年4月23日至6月11日，中共第七次代表大会在这里隆重召开。毛主席分别为大会写下了开幕词和闭幕词，即《两个中国之命运》和《愚公移山》。刘少奇在《关于修改党章的报告》中，首次提出了"毛泽东思想"的概念，并进行了深刻的阐述。

中央办公厅大楼建成于1941年，因造型像飞机，又称"飞机楼"。1942年5月2日到5月23日，中共中央宣传部在此召开了延安文艺座谈会，毛主席在座谈会上发表了著名的《在延安文艺座谈会上的讲话》。

毛泽东在杨家岭居住期间正是抗日战争最艰苦的时期。为了克服困难，指导中国革命，毛泽东在这里完成了大量的理论著作，仅收入《毛泽东选集》的就有40篇。1946年8月，毛泽东与美国记者安娜·路易斯·斯特朗在杨家岭的第十四孔窑洞前的树下进行了一次长谈，做出了"一切反动派都是纸老虎"的论断。从此处往下看，可以清楚地看到毛主席当年承包的小菜园。当年，毛主席就是在杨家岭向全党、全军发出了"大生产运动"的动员令。

1944年11月初，周恩来离开杨家岭，再次前往重庆与国民党政府进行谈判。

王家坪

王家坪革命旧址位于延安市西北方向的王家坪村，隔延河与延安城相望。据说王家坪最初叫牡丹坪，因当地老百姓多种植牡丹花而得名。后来一位王姓人家将多数地方买去，改名为王家坪。

毛泽东、周恩来、叶剑英、彭德怀等中央领导都曾在这里居住过。1937年1月至1947年3月，这里是中央军委的所在地。西安事变后，王家坪成了八路军的总司令部，后来改为中国人民解放军总部。

王家坪革命旧址分为南北两院，南院为政治部所在地，北院为司令部所在地。主要建筑有军委礼堂、毛泽东会客室旧居以及朱德、周恩来、彭德怀、叶剑英等领导人的旧居。中共中央军事委员会会议室及礼堂是王家坪最醒目的建筑。当年，军委与司令部的大型会议和晚会都在这里举行。

中央军委与中国人民解放军总部在这里领导全国军民取得了抗日战争的伟大胜利。毛泽东在这里写下了著名的《和美国记者安娜·路易斯·斯特朗的谈话》等著作，制定了在解放战争时期的作战方针和各项军事原则。1946年1月，毛泽东曾在这里与刚从国外学习归来的大儿子毛岸英谈话，鼓励他去农村这所"劳动大学"，在实际劳动中学习和锻炼。

朱德在王家坪居住期间，直接领导八路军359旅，克服重重困难，把荒无人烟的南泥湾建成了"陕北江南"。

1947年，彭德怀在王家坪居住期间指挥了著名的保卫延安的战斗。

1947年3月，国民队军队占领延安后，王家坪的部分建筑物遭到破坏。新中国成立后，依照原样进行了修复。

枣园

枣园位于延安城西北，距城区约8公里。这里原来是陕北军阀高双成的庄园，因园内种有大量枣树，故名"枣园"。

党中央抵达延安后，中央社会部等部门于1939年初住进枣园，并将枣园易名为"延园"。1944年至1947年3月，这里又成为中共中央书记处的所在地，毛泽东、朱德、周恩来、刘少奇、任弼时等中央领导人都在此居住过。

园内的中央书记处小礼堂是1942年建成的。礼堂内的墙壁上挂有毛主席的亲笔题词"为人民服务"。

1943年至1946年初，毛主席在此居住，并由这里亲赴重庆和国民党谈判。

1944年9月8日，中央机关为中央警卫团战士张思德同志举行追悼大会。

追悼大会上毛主席发表了著名的《为人民服务》的演讲。后来，这五个大字成了中国共产党的座右铭。如今在延安枣园墙外的西北角山下，仍留有当年毛主席演讲的讲台。

大生产运动期间，周恩来和任弼时都被评为"纺线英雄"。当年，周总理被评为"纺线英雄"后，谦虚地说："群众是真正的英雄，只要群众发动组织起来，深入开展劳动竞赛，劳动互助，就能克服一切困难。"

园内有一条长5公里的水渠，是1939年10月到1940年4月由当地群众和中央机关人员共同修成的，老百姓亲切地称此渠为"幸福渠"。1945年春节，老百姓到枣园为一心为天下百姓着想的共产党送上了一幅锦旗，上面写着"为民谋利"四个大字。

The Revolutionary Memorial Sites in Yan'an

Yan'an is situated in the northern part of Shaanxi Province, bordering Shanxi Province to its east across the Yellow River and next to Gansu Province to its west. It has served as the political, economic, cultural and military center of Northern Shaanxi for a long time. So one can find a lot of time-honored historic sites here, among which are the Mausoleum of the Yellow Emperor, and the renowned Hukou Waterfall.

Yan'an is famous for a greater part due to its significance in the Chinese modern history. In October 1935, the Chinese Red Army broke through the Nationalist Army's round-up and blockade, and reached Wuqi County in Northern Shaanxi, marking the end of the world-famous Long March. Ever since October in 1937 when the Central Committee of the Communist Party of China was stationed in Yan'an, the city had become the headquarters for the Chinese people's revolutionary war and a sacred place appealing to most Chinese people. During his 13 years' work in Northern Shaanxi, the late Chairman Mao Zedong led the Chinese people to the success of the Anti-Japanese War and the War of Liberation. Such success not only led to the founding of a new China in 1949, but also yielded a most precious spiritual inheritance—the Yan'an spirit.

With over 100 historic sites, Yan'an was honored as "a City of Revolutionary Museum". On March 4, 1961, Yan'an was listed by the State Council among the first group of the important National Historical Monuments in China. Then in 1982, it was listed as one of the 24 National Historic and Cultural Cities. Up to date, five of the historic sites in Yan'an have opened to the public. They are the Phoenix Hill, the

Yangjia Ridge, the Date-tree Garden, the Wangjia Terrace and the Nanni Sinus.

The Phoenix Hill (Fenghuang Shanlu)

The city of Yan'an was built along The Phoenix Hill, which runs on the southwest of the city. At the foot of the hill was the site where the Central Committee of the Communist Party of China was first stationed after they arrived in Yan'an. The village including 15 cave-dwellings and 50 rooms was rented from the local farmers then. During that period, high-ranking party officials such as Mao Zedong, Zhu De, Zhou Enlai lived in the village, and the Consultative Department of the Chinese Red Army was also stationed there.

It was right here in this village that the late Chairman Mao wrote a lot of articles, 16 of which were put into *Anthology of Mao Zedong*. "On Practice" and "On Contradictions" were two philosophical articles that laid a solid foundation for Mao Zedong Thought. "On Protracted War" was a famous military essay.

It was also at this place that Chairman Mao met with the Canadian doctor Norman Bethune, a famous international communist. After Bethune died at his post, Chairman Mao wrote the famous article "In Memory of Bethune" in which Chairman Mao called on all the party members to learn from Bethune and try to "always think of others rather than of themselves".

An American woman journalist Ms. Smedley interviewed Zhu De, the Commander in Chief of the Eighth Route Army, and composed her book *A Great Way* on the basis of Zhu's life story.

During the period when the Central Committee of the Communist Party of China was stationed there, a series of conferences were held and a lot of important resolutions were made. For example, Zhang Guotao's mistakes of splitting the Red Army to establish "a new central committee" were exposed and corrected. The problems of how to stick to the rules of independence and self-reliance as well as how to maintain a harmonious relation between the Communist Party and the Nationalist Party were also solved. Apart from this, a lot of schools for training party officials were set up, which greatly enhanced the quality of the staff and made a sufficient preparation for the Anti-Japanese War.

On November 20, 1938, Yan'an City was bombed by over ten Japanese fighter planes. The work place of the Communist Party Central Committee was then moved to the Yangjia Ridge, northwest of Yan'an City, on that very night.

The Yangjia Ridge (Yangjia Ling)

The Yangjia Ridge Revolutionary Site lies about 3 kilometers northwest of Yan'an City. During the Anti-Japanese War, it was merely a small village resided by fewer than twenty households. On November 20, 1938, after Yan'an City was bombed by Japanese fighter planes, the functional department of Central Committee of the Communist Party of China was moved here from the Phoenix Hill, and stayed here until March 1947. During this period, the Central Committee initiated the Great Production Campaign among the army soldiers and the masses in the liberated area, held the significant Seventh Congress of the Communist Party of China and the famous Yan'an Forum of Literature and Art. All this had laid a solid foundation for greater success for the Communist Party in the coming years.

The main buildings inside this revolutionary site consist of the great assembly hall, the office building and the former residence of Mao Zedong, Zhu De, Zhou Enlai and Liu Shaoqi.

With the help of the Central Committee staff, the local people built the assembly hall in 1942 with such materials as bricks and stones they found nearby. The building is separated into three parts: the main hall, the ballroom and the lounge. From April 23, 1945 to June 11, the Seventh Congress of the Communist Party was held here. Chairman Mao addressed for both the opening and closing ceremonies: "Two Destinies for China" and "The Foolish Old Man Who Removed the Mountains". Liu Shaoqi initiated the phrase Mao Zedong Thought in his "Report on Revising the Party Constitution" and explained it intensively.

The office building was built in 1941. It was nicknamed "airplane building" for it appears in the shape of an airplane. From 2 may to 23 may in 1942, the Yan'an Forum of Literature and Art was held here and Mao delivered his famous speech "the Talk at the Yan'an Forum of Literature and Art".

It was the toughest period of the Anti-Japanese War when Mao lived at the Yangjia Ridge. In order to overcome difficulties and guide Chinese revolution, he composed a lot of theoretical works, among which 40 articles were put into *Anthology of Mao Zedong*. In August 1946, Mao conversed for a long time with the American journalist Anna Louise Strong under the trees in front of the fourteenth cave dwelling, and concluded, "All the reactionaries are paper tigers". From here one can have a clear view of the small vegetable plot which Mao once tilled. It was at the Yangjia Ridge that Mao aired his mobilization of the Great Production Campaign.

In early November 1944, Zhou Enlai left the Yangjia Ridge for Chongqing for another negotiation with the Nationalist Party.

The Wangjia Terrace (Wangjia Ping)

This revolutionary site is situated in the Wangjia Terrace Village to the northwest of Yan'an across the Yanhe River. The place was once called Peony Land due to the widely grown peony flowers at the place. Later, most of the land was bought over by the Wangs, a wealthy family, so the place acquired its new name "the Wangjia Terrace" (The Wangs' land).

Mao Zedong, Zhou Enlai, Ye Jianying, Peng Dehuai, and many other party leaders once lived at Wangjia Ping. During the ten years between January 1937 and March 1947, the Central Military Commission was stationed here. Then after Xi'an Incident, The Wangjia Terrace became the Commander-in-chief's Headquarters of the Eighth Route Army. Later it was converted into the Headquarters of the Chinese People's Liberation Army.

The Wangjia Terrace Revolutionary Site consists of two courtyards. The southern one was the political headquarters and the northern one the commander's headquarters. The main buildings include the auditorium of the Military Commission, Chairman Mao's former sitting room, and the former residence of Zhu De, Zhou Enlai, Peng Dehuai and Ye Jianying. Among them the meeting room and the auditorium are the most eye-catching. In those days, most of the large-scale meetings and parties were held there.

It was at the Wangjia Terrace that the Military Commission and the Headquarters of People's Liberation Army led Chinese people to the success of the Anti-Japanese War. It was also here that Chairman Mao wrote such famous articles as "A Talk with American Journalist Anna Louise Strong", and worked out the fighting strategies and military principles for the War of Liberation. It was again at this place that in January 1946, Chairman Mao held a talk with his eldest son Mao Anying, who just returned from his study abroad, and encouraged him to work in the countryside to gain some first-hand experience through physical labor.

During his stay at the Wangjia Terrace, Zhu De was in charge of the 359th Brigade of the Eighth-Route Army. Through the soldiers' hard work, the desolated Nanni Sinus was transformed into the "Land of Plenty in Northern Shaanxi".

In 1947, Peng Dehuai commanded the war of defending Yan'an.

In March 1947, Yan'an was occupied by the Nationalist military forces. Some buildings at the Wangjia Terrace were destroyed. Nevertheless, they were renovated after the founding of People's Republic of China.

The Date-tree Garden (Zao Yuan)

The Date-tree Garden Sacred Site is located 8 kilometers northwest of Yan'an City. It was once a manor owned by a Northern Shaanxi warlord named Gao Shuangcheng. It gained the name the Date-tree Garden (a yard of date trees) simply due to the widely planted date trees.

After the Central Committee of the Communist Party of China arrived in Yan'an, it stationed its social department and other sectors at the Date-tree Garden, and changed its name to Yanyuan. It was also where the Secretariat of the Central Committee of the Communist Party of China sat between 1944 and 1947. Party leaders such as Mao Zedong, Zhou Enlai, Zhu De, Liu Shaoqi and Ren Bishi also lived here for this brief period of time.

The small assembly hall was constructed in 1942. On its walls inside there hangs Mao's autograph meaning "Serve the People".

Mao lived at the Date-tree Garden between 1943 and 1946. It was here that he left for Chongqing to hold negotiations with the Nationalist Party.

On September 8, 1944, Mao Zedong delivered the well-known speech entitled "Serve the People" at the memorial service held for Zhang Side, a security regiment soldier of the Party Central Committee. Later the title of this speech became the maxim for the Chinese Communist Party. Today you can still find the platform where Mao delivered his speech to the northwest of the yard.

During the Great Production Campaign, Zhou Enlai and Ren Bishi were conferred the title "Spinning Hero". On receiving the reward, Zhou said humbly: "The masses are real heroes. As long as the masses can be mobilized to conduct labor emulation and help each other, there will be no unconquerable difficulties."

A five-kilometer irrigation ditch running through the yard was dug between October

1939 and April 1940 with the joint efforts of the local people and staff of the Party Central Committee. Therefore, it was called "Happiness Ditch". On the New Year's Day of 1945, the local people paid a visit to the Date-tree Garden bringing to the selfless Communist Party a silk banner on which inscribed were "Seek Interests for the People".

第九部分　陕西非物质文化遗产

秦腔

秦腔是我国现存最古老的剧种。秦腔俗名"乱弹",不仅是陕西地方戏,而且也流行于甘、宁、青、晋南、豫西、内蒙古、川北等地区,为群众所喜闻乐见。秦腔在其漫长的发展过程中积累了4000多个剧目,居各剧种之首。

秦腔艺术源远流长。起源有秦汉、唐、金元、明清诸说,其中以唐代说为多。相传唐玄宗李隆基曾设专门培养演员的梨园,教人演唱宫廷乐曲和民歌。梨园的乐师李龟年原是陕西民间乐人,所作《秦王破阵乐》被称为"秦王腔",简称"秦腔"。其后,秦腔受宋词的影响,从内容到形式日臻完美。清乾隆时,秦腔名旦魏长生自蜀入京,他精湛的演技轰动京城,观者如潮。梅兰芳说:"秦腔跟京剧有密切的关系。有人说过,京剧的主要曲调'西皮'就受秦腔的影响很大,此外,在剧本和表演方面,都有相似的地方……秦腔的历史比京剧要远得多。"秦腔可分为东西两路,西路入川为梆子;东路在山西为晋剧,在河南为豫剧,在河北为河北梆子。秦腔可以称为"百戏之祖"。

秦腔唱腔的突出特点是高亢激越,要求用真嗓音演唱,一般不用假音,保持了原始和豪放的特点。"唱戏吼起来"为陕西十大怪之一。

近年来,陕西电视台的《秦之声》演播的秦腔在农村收视率很高。每到夏季傍晚,西安城墙根下群众自发组织"自乐班",自拉自唱,引来不少观众,成为一种大众喜闻乐见的娱乐形式,也成为一道景观。由各界组织的不同形式的秦腔演唱比赛也接连不断,丰富了群众精神生活,促进了秦腔不断向前发展。

PART NINE The Intangible Cultural Heritage of Shaanxi Province

Shaanxi Opera

Shaanxi Opera is the oldest of all the Chinese operas that are still in existence today. It is not only popular in Shaanxi, but also in Gansu, Ningxia, Qinghai, Southern Shanxi, Western Henan, Inner Mongolia and Northern Sichuan. During its long history, more than 4,000 traditional programs have been accumulated, which outnumbers those of any other local operas.

Different versions reveal that Shaanxi Opera possibly originated in the Qin, the Han, the Tang, the Jin, the Ming or the Qing dynasties, but the Tang Dynasty seems most likely to be the answer. It is said that Emperor Xuan Zong, Li Longji, once set up an institute called "Li Yuan". "Li Yuan", or The Theatric Garden, is a place for performer training where royal music and folk songs were taught. Once, Li Guinian, a musician composed a program *The First Qin Emperor Breaks through Round-ups*. The program was later called "Emperor Qin's Opera", or "the Qin Opera" (the Shaanxi Opera). Poems in the Song Dynasty also posed their influence on the Shaanxi Opera, and bettered both its content and style. During the Qianlong reign in the Qing Dynasty, a famous actor of the Shaanxi Opera called Wei Changsheng went to Beijing and his superb performances were well received. Mei Lanfang, the famous actor of the Beijing Opera once said: "the Beijing Opera is closely linked with the Shaanxi Opera. The major tone 'Xi Pi' in the Beijing Opera was said to be created with the influence of the Shaanxi Opera. Besides, they are similar in scripts and performances... The history of Shaanxi Opera is much longer than that of the Beijing opera." The Shaanxi Opera can be divided into the western style and the eastern style. Sichuan BangTzu belongs to the western, while the Shanxi Opera, the Henan Opera, and the Hebei BangTzu belong to the eastern. As a matter of fact, the Shaanxi Opera is well worthy of the name "ancestor of all Chinese local operas".

Sonorous and exciting singing is the typical feature of the Shaanxi Opera. Since falsetto is not practiced, the singing is always real and unsophisticated. "Shouting when performing" is one of the ten local peculiarities.

In recent years, the Shaanxi Opera in the program *Voice of Shaanxi* over Shaanxi TV appeals particularly to the countryfolks. On summer evenings, local people form their own troupes and carry out their own performances which always attract large audience. Contests organized by amateur performers from all walks of life not only entertain people, but also help promote the development of the opera.

陕西锣鼓

锣鼓在中国文化史上占有重要的地位,陕西又是中国锣鼓的胜地。从工程开工、竣工、开业、喜庆,到逢年过节都是锣鼓震天。锣鼓已成为陕西人民一种娱乐和社交的工具。

陕西锣鼓具有节奏明快、形式多变、气势宏大的独特风格。既能在野外表演,又适合于舞台演出。表演气氛热烈,深受群众喜爱。

陕西锣鼓种类较多,安塞腰鼓以其悠久的历史,鲜明的地方特色,独特的表演风格被誉为"中国第一鼓"。

安塞位于陕北,地势险要,历代为兵家必争之地。相传古时,戍边守塞士卒在战斗时用腰鼓来助威,鼓舞士气;战斗胜利后,用它来欢庆。随着岁月流逝和时代的变迁,腰鼓渐渐成为一种纯粹娱乐的工具,特别是每年春节,当地人民用打腰鼓的形式来欢庆丰收,增添节日欢乐气氛。

安塞腰鼓参加者一般为男性,分为两种表演形式:一种是路鼓,即行进中边走边打;另一种是场地鼓,即在广场、舞台或指定地点表演。

安塞腰鼓从1951年在天安门广场表演后,先后在国内和国外参加了多次比赛和表演,取得了优异的成绩。1986年正月,由800名安塞农民组成的腰鼓队参加了中日合拍的大型电视系列片《黄河》的拍摄。安塞腰鼓现已成为大型民间艺术活动的保留节目。

另外,咸阳牛拉鼓、洛川踏鼓、宜川胸鼓等都各具特色,深受当地人民喜爱。

The Drum and Gong Performance

The drum and gong performance which has occupied a prominent position in Chinese cultural history is mostly found in Shaanxi. It always accompanies the beginning and ending of projects, opening ceremonies, and celebrations of special occasions.

Throughout history, gongs and drums have become important assistance in entertainment and social life of the local people.

The performance is characterized by such features as brisk rhythm, variability and magnificence. It is suitable for both open-air entertainment and stage performance. The excitement in the performance never fails to arouse the audience's interest.

The performance consists of different types. The time-honored Ansai waist-drum performance that bears a distinctive and unique style is esteemed as "No. 1 Chinese drum performance".

Ansai is located at a place of strategic significance in Northern Shaanxi. It is said that during battles beating waist-drum could boost the morale of the soldiers. When success was achieved, Waist-drums were beaten for celebration. Today, they have become tools for entertainment. On every Spring Festival, the local people will beat waist-drums to celebrate the harvest of the year. It always makes the occasion enjoyable all the more.

In most cases, only men are involved in the waist-drum performance. One type of its kind is beating the drums during the course of procession and another is playing in squares, on stages or at other designated places.

In 1951, a waist drum performance was carried out at Tian'anmen Square. After that such a performance was found at many different contests and shows, and satisfactory results were always achieved. In the first lunar month of 1986, a team consisting of 800 Ansai farmers took part in a Sino-Japanese TV series *The Yellow River*. Today such a performance is known to be one of the traditional programs in some large-scale folk artistic activities.

Besides, the Xianyang bull-drawn drum performance, the Luochuan performance and the Yichuan chest-drum performance are all distinctive drum performances that enjoy a great popularity among the local people.

唐乐舞

唐乐舞是西安旅游最受欢迎的文化娱乐项目之一。它以历史记载和民间传说为创作源泉,通过乐器演奏和舞蹈表演向观众展示了1300多年前的唐朝宫廷生活及社会习俗。唐乐舞艺术团的表演不仅受到国内人民的热烈欢迎,而且也广泛地受到关注中国文化的国际友人的喜爱。

在整场表演的乐器演奏部分,主要呈现的是中国特有的乐器琵琶和排箫,代表曲目有《游春图》和《春莺啭》。舞蹈部分更加异彩纷呈。《秦王破阵乐》表现出李世民所带军队的慷慨士气。《霓裳羽衣舞》相传由杨贵妃所创,据说有一次唐玄宗梦见自己神游月宫,遇见仙女身着霓裳翩然起舞。能歌善舞的杨玉环便根据他的描述编成了这支著名的舞蹈。《踏歌》再现了当时流行于宫廷与民间的一项庆祝活动。每年中秋,皇室成员便会来到骊山脚下的华清池附近,加入庆祝的人群,向人们表达美好的祝愿。

通常情况下,观众可以一边欣赏唐乐舞,一边享用唐宫宴。这样的活动不但可以使他们体会到当年唐朝宫廷的豪华生活以及丰富的社会习俗,更重要的是,可以向他们展示中国音乐和舞蹈艺术的悠久历史及绚丽多姿的色彩,从而使他们更深刻地理解中国几千年文化的深厚底蕴。

Music and Dance Performances in Tang Style

The Performance of the Tang Dynasty Music and Dance is one of the most attractive entertainment activities for tourists to Xi'an. It takes roots from the historical records and folk legends about the Tang Dynasty and shows to the audience the court life and social costumes of more than 1,300 years ago through such performances as instruments playing and dancing. The Tang Dynasty Music and Dance Troupe has won warm acclaim in China as well as warm welcome among foreigners who take a profound interest in Chinese culture.

In the segment of instrumental playing, the performers mainly present to the audience pipa, a hand-plucked traditional instrument, and paixiao, a blowing instrument. Two of the most representative music articles are: *Happy Spring Outing* and *Spring Orioles Song*. The dance segment boasts even greater charm. *The First Qin Emperor Breaks through Round-ups*, which was about Li Shimin, vividly shows the morale of his powerful commanding troops. *The Feather Dress Dance* was created by Lady Yang, the favorite imperial concubine of Emperor Xuan Zong. According to the legend, once Xuan Zong had a dream in which he traveled to the palace of the moon. In the palace he met some celestial women, dressed in feathers and rosy clouds dancing in the sky. After the emperor awoke, Lady Yang created and performed this dance according to the emperor's recollection. *The Tage* shows the style of dance that was popular in the palace and among the common people as welles of the Tang period. It represents the Tang people celebrating the Mid-Autumn Festival each year in a beautiful area near the Huaqing Pool at the foot of the Lishan Mountain. The royal family joined the happy crowd and gave blessings to the subjects in his empire.

The Tang Palace Dinner is usually served together with the performance. With such enjoyment the audience can gain not only an experience of the Tang court life and the social customs, but more importantly, a thorough understanding of the history of the traditional Chinese music and dances. All this are expected to make the audience be much better acquainted with the age-old Chinese culture.

民间剪纸

陕西民间剪纸，常被群众用作刺绣的花样，但最普遍的还是作为窗花。每当过年过节，关中平原一间间灰白瓦房和陕北高原一孔孔土窑洞的窗户上，人们在白生生的窗纸上贴上鲜红色的各种窗花，表达了美好的愿望，给节日增添了许多喜庆的气氛。

陕西窗花题材多样：人物、鸟兽、花草、鱼虫，无所不有。陕西剪纸总的特点是粗犷、豪放、简练、夸张。不同的地域又赋予剪纸以不同的风格：陕北剪纸显得古朴、淳厚、刚健、豪迈；关中剪纸则于简练中见精巧，豪放中见秀丽。

陕西剪纸历史悠久，由于它产生于中国古代文化的重要发祥地，又长期保留在人民中间，因此，它似乎在给我们娓娓动听地讲述着中华民族悠久的历史和古老的传说，强烈地拨动着人们的心弦。

The Paper-cuts

The paper-cuts, though often used as patterns for embroidery, serve as window decorations. When the Spring Festival comes, the windows of the grey houses on the Central Shaanxi Plain and of the cave houses on the Northern Shaanxi Plateau are decorated with paper-cuts. With bright red paper-cuts of all kinds on snow-white window paper, the atmosphere appears a lot more festive. At the same time, the paper-cuts contain people's good wishes.

The subject matter of Shaanxi paper-cuts varies greatly. They can be human figures, birds and animals, flowers and plants, fish and insects. Shaanxi paper-cuts are considered to be both bold and unconstrained, brief and exaggerated works of art. Different parts of the province have different styles. The Northern Shaanxi's paper-cuts look comparatively simple, vigorous and generous while the Central Shaanxi Plain's paper-cuts are of simplicity mingled with exquisiteness, and have a boldness mingled with beauty.

Shaanxi paper-cuts have a long history. Originating in the cradle of ancient Chinese culture, they have been handed down from generation to generation among people. They seem to tell us vividly of the ancient stories of the Chinese nation which are always touching.

皮影戏

皮影是中国民间广为流传的道具戏之一。它是借助灯光把雕刻精巧的皮影人映照在屏幕上，由艺人们在幕后操动皮影人，伴以音乐和歌唱，演出一幕幕妙趣横生的皮影戏。

皮影戏历史悠久，相传萌芽于汉，发展于唐，至宋已十分兴盛。陕西皮影分东、西两路，不仅唱腔种类繁多，表演技术高超，而且皮影人的雕镂技艺达到了很高的水平。

陕西皮影制皮考究，造型生动，刀法细腻，刻工精巧，色彩鲜明，纹饰优美，装饰性极强。其风格古朴高雅，自成一格，不仅可用来表演，还可作为艺术品欣赏。

The Shadow Play

The Shadow Play is one of the most popular plays in China. With the aid of lamp light, the silhouettes of finely-cut leather figures are casted upon a screen. The figures, manipulated by actors from behind the screen and accompanied with music and singing, give many vivid and interesting shadow performances.

The play has a long history. According to the legend, it came into being in Han Dynasty, was developed further in the Tang Dynasty and flourished in the Song Dynasty. The Shaanxi shadow play may be divided into eastern and western schools. They vary not only in the accompanying music and the skill of acting, but also in the superb skill of the artistic carving of the leather figures.

The figures of the Shaanxi shadow play are vividly shaped and elegantly carved, due to the particular way leather is made. The bright colors and beautiful features of the figures also make them very good decorations. Being simple and elegant, the leather figures of the Shaanxi shadow play have a style of its own. They are not only good for shadow play, but also regarded as interesting articles of art.

户县农民画

陕西省西安市鄠邑区（户县）是全国闻名的农民画乡。全区有业余美术作者数千人。该区农民历来就有剪纸、绘画、编织等传统艺术和工艺技术。县里从10岁左右的孩子到60多岁的老人，不少人都能挥笔作画。户县农民画诞生于1958年。到现在，他们已用黑板报、壁画、水粉画、剪纸、木刻、幻灯等形式创造了几十万幅作品。

陕西农民画源于民间，过去多用于画炕围、锅台、箱柜等，所画内容多取材于人物、动物、花鸟等，讲究装饰性，以反映丰富多彩的农家生活而形成独特的艺术风格。农民画采用白描的形式，想象大胆丰富，色彩反差强烈，深受国内外游客和专家的好评。

户县农民画的特点之一在于"写意"，作者凭借着对农家生活丰富的体验和饱满的热情，大胆的想象力，以及在长期的民族艺术活动中形成的民间审美情趣，创造出了属于自己的独特艺术风格。如《大枣丰收》中，红枣比人头还大，《磨豆腐》中驴耳朵比身子还长。

另外，户县农民画的艺术风格新颖，种类又非常多，在农民艺术家的长期创作活动中，形成了壁画、年画、宣传画、水墨画、装饰画、连环画、版画、剪纸及其他艺术形式。

The Huxian Peasant Paintings

Huyi Borough (used to be called Huxian County) of Xi'an in Shaanxi province is well-known for its peasant paintings. With several thousands amateur artists this county boasts a long history of traditional arts and crafts, such as paper cutting, painting, embroidery and knitting. Among the peasants ranging from 10 to 60 years old, many can draw well. The Huxian peasant paintings originated in 1958. Since then, peasants in Huxian have created hundreds of thousands of artistic paintings. They paint with a distinctive style, by means of blackboard, newspapers, murals, gouaches, paper-cuts, wood-cuts and slides.

The artistic style originated from the local people's life. In the past, the paintings appeared on the walls of kangs (heated beds), on the plane of kitchen range and on wooden chests and wardrobes. Persons, plants, animals and birds are common subject matters of these paintings. Inspired by some bold and unconstrained imagination, the peasant painters draw a clear and plain sketch and then paint with colors of strong contrast. Such unique artistic works are always well received by tourists and experts alike.

One of the characters of the Huxian peasant paintings is "freehand brushwork". The painters form their own unique artistic style through their rich experiences of rural life, their great zest, their full imagination and their folk aesthetic temperament. The most representative works are *Harvest of Dates*, in which dates are painted bigger than people's heads, and *Making Beancurd*, in which the ears of a donkey are even longer than its body.

The Huxian peasant paintings can also be divided into many different categories. Through years of practice, the painters have created a large variety of artistic styles such as murals, New Year's paintings, posters, gouaches, ink and wash, decorations, picture-stories, engraved pictures and paper-cuts.

第十部分　地方小吃

樊记腊汁肉夹馍

腊汁肉是一种陕西传统风味名吃，即用白吉馍夹腊汁肉。而在陕西，人们俗称这种吃法为"肉夹馍"，如果有人称它为"馍夹肉"，反而会被人笑话。

我国加工腊汁肉的历史悠久，在《周礼》一书中提到的"周代八珍"中的"渍"，据考证就是腊汁肉。"樊记"腊汁肉是西安的老字号。

相传唐朝长安城有位姓樊的官宦人家，有一年陕南发大水，许多灾民逃到长安，樊家开仓放粮，并资助一青年葬母安业。十年后，这位青年靠经营腊汁肉成为富户。为报恩，他借樊老爷八十大寿之机，用百株花椒木做了一口上等棺木，又从10头生猪身上剔下500斤精肉，烹制成上等腊汁肉放进棺内，密封后送进樊府。樊老爷因客人甚多没有在意，棺木由家人抬入后院柴房，一放就是几年。后来，樊老爷被削职为民，一病离开了人世。没过几年，家产变卖一空，生活艰难。这时，家人禀告柴房内有一棺木，可变卖度日。樊夫人叫人打开察看时，却见满满一棺木腊汁肉，香气四溢，色泽鲜嫩。她让家人拿一些上街去卖，一会儿就卖完了。消息不胫而走，登门买肉的人越来越多。眼看棺木中的腊汁肉即将卖完，樊夫人又买来鲜肉，用棺木中的肉汁煮成新腊汁肉，味道仍很鲜美。于是，樊家开起肉铺，经营起腊汁肉来，名气也越来越大。到清光绪年间（1904年），祖籍"烹饪之乡"陕西蓝田的樊炳仁和樊凤祥父子在西安经营起腊汁肉。他继承唐代传统技法并加以改进，在诸多腊汁肉铺中独树一帜，名噪古城。

1989年，樊记腊汁肉荣获国家商业部"金鼎奖"。

PART TEN   THE LOCAL SNACKS

The Fan's Cured Pork in Pancakes

The Fan's cured pork in pancakes (a sort of sandwich) is one of the traditional Shaanxi delicacies. In fact, they are pancakes made of high-quality wheat flour stuffed with cured pork. The popular name among the local people is "pancakes in cured meat". If you call them "pancakes with cured pork", the native would consider it awkward and laughable.

Cured pork bears a long history in China. Researches prove that "Tzu" out of the "Eight Treasures of the Zhou Dynasty" recorded in *The Rites of the Zhou Dynasty* refers exactly to cured pork. Fan's cured pork appeared in Xi'an a long time ago, and there is a story about it.

In the Tang Dynasty, an official called "Fan" lived in Chang'an. Once he helped those flood-stricken refugees from Southern Shaanxi with his grain storage, and financed a young man when his mother died. Ten years later, this young man became wealthy through his cured pork business. To show his gratitude, he went to Fan's eightieth birthday party with an intricately built coffin made of Chinese prickly ash wood. In the coffin there hid cured pork made of 250 kilograms of lean pork. Since there were many guests on the day, Fan did not take any notice of the coffin. The coffin was put in the storage house. Several years later, Fan was deprived of his official post and died of illness. The family had no means of making a living but to sell property. At last, they found the coffin in the storage. When the family opened it, there was the aromatic and freshly looking curd pork. Mrs. Fan sent some of it for sale in the market, and it was well received. The news spread quickly. More people rushed to the family for the pork. Mrs. Fan put some fresh pork into the juice. The newly cooked cured pork was just as delicious. Then the Fans ran a store to sell cured pork and its fame went apace. Later, during the reign of Emperor Guang Xu in the Qing Dynasty (in 1904), Fan Bingren, the father, and Fan Fengxiang, the son, both descendants of the Fans, came from Lantian to Xi'an and opened their cured pork store. After some improvement was made upon the traditional techniques, their store surpassed all the others in the same trade.

In the year 1989, Fan's cured pork in pancakes won the "Gold Tripod Prize" awarded by National Business Ministry.

牛羊肉泡馍

牛羊肉泡馍是陕西著名清真小吃,号称"陕西一绝"。它是在古代牛羊羹的基础上发展起来的。早在公元前 11 世纪的西周时就将其列为王室和诸侯的"礼馔"。《史记》中就有关于牛羊羹的诗句。宋元时,随着回民大量移居西安,牛羊肉泡馍更是倍受欢迎。

牛羊肉泡馍的吃法,相传与宋太祖赵匡胤有关。赵匡胤早年贫困潦倒,流落于长安街头。一日饥寒交迫,求牛羊肉铺施舍一勺汤泡馍,吃后饥寒全消。十年后,赵匡胤已是宋朝的开国皇帝。一次,他出巡长安,又来到这家牛羊肉铺,命店主做一碗羊肉汤泡馍。店主连忙让妻子将烙饼掰碎,精心配好调料,浇上汤又煮了煮,还放上几大片羊肉端上。没想到皇帝吃后大加赞赏,当即给店主赏银百两。此事很快传遍长安,来吃这种羊肉汤泡馍的人越来越多。由于生意兴隆,店小二来不及给客人掰馍,于是改为客人自己掰馍,此法一直流传至今。

1644 年,西安专营羊肉泡馍的"老马家"在桥梓口开业,食客盈门,誉满古城。1900 年,八国联军占领北京,慈禧太后携光绪避居西安,特地来此店品尝,倍加赞赏,并写下"天赐楼"三个大字。从此,"天赐楼"名声大振。

The Shredded Pancakes in Mutton or Beef Broth

This snack is a local Moslem delicacy honored as "a superb dish in Shaanxi". It is originated from mutton and beef custard in ancient times that was listed as royal food in the Western Zhou Dynasty. Poems about it can also be found in Sima Qian's *Historical Annals*. Then in the Song and Yuan dynasties, this delicacy gained even greater popularity because of an increase in the Moslem population in Xi'an.

There is a legend that connects the table manner for this delicacy with Emperor Tai Zu, Zhao Kuangyin, the first emperor of the Song Dynasty. Zhao was poverty-stricken and reduced to be homeless at an early age. One day when he was wandering in the street, he begged in a meat store for some hot mutton broth. After eating his shredded pancakes mixed in the hot broth, he felt much warmer and energetic. Ten years later, Zhao came to his throne. Once when he was on an inspection tour in Chang'an he came to the store where he had begged for broth and asked for a dish of shredded pancakes in hot broth. The owner asked his wife to bake some pancakes, broke them into small pieces, cooked for a few seconds with seasoning and broth and at last added several mutton slices. To his surprise, when the dish was served, Zhao enjoyed it immensely and awarded the owner with 100 taels of silver. With the spread of the story, more people came to the store to try this delicacy. Since the helpers in the store were fully occupied, the diners had to break the pancakes by themselves. This is still practiced today.

In 1644, a restaurant named "Lao Ma's" opened at QiaoTzukou specialized in selling this delicacy. Everyday the restaurant was crowded with diners and thus its business boomed by leaps and bounds. Later, after the Eight-Power Allied Forces occupied Beijing in 1900, Empress Dowager Ci Xi and Emperor Guang Xu fled to Xi'an. Ci Xi thought highly of the dish after she tasted it and wrote down three Chinese characters for the restaurant "Tian Ci Lou" (restaurant conferred by the royal family). Ever since then, the restaurant grew much more famous.

老童家腊羊肉

西安老童家腊羊肉，色泽红润，肉质酥松。

相传1900年八国联军攻打北京，慈禧太后携光绪皇帝仓皇逃到西安。有一次，她乘坐御辇途经西大街桥梓口，车子正在上坡，慈禧闻到一股浓郁的香味，就问什么东西这么香。当时陕西巡抚回答说，是一家卖牛羊肉的正在煮肉，主人姓童，叫老童家。太后闻听，馋涎欲滴，干脆喝令停车，派人购买，尝后大加称赞。王公大臣们为了博取慈禧的欢心，遂由兵部尚书赵福桥的老师邢庭维手书"辇止坡"金字招牌一面，悬挂于老童家门口。从此，"辇止坡老童家腊羊肉"名噪古城，此牌现仍挂在门口。

The Tong's Cured Mutton

The Tong's cured mutton in Xi'an is known for its freshly red color, special taste and softness.

Legend has it that in 1900 when the Eight-Power Allied Forces invaded Beijing, Empress Dowager Ci Xi fled to Xi'an with Emperor Guang Xu. One day Ci Xi passed the West Street in her imperial carriage. While going up the slope, she caught a strong aromatic smell and asked where the delicious smell came from. The provincial governor told her that it came from a restaurant selling mutton and beef. It was called the Tong's after the name of the owner. Ci Xi felt so salivating that she stopped to have a try. After tasting she sang high praise of the meat. The official then sent for Xing Tingwei, tutor of Zhao Fuqiao, Minister of Military Department, and had him write on a wooden board "Nian Zhipo", which means the slope was where the imperial carriage once stopped. The board still bears to the eyes today the golden inscription. Ever since then the great fame of the restaurant spread all over this ancient city.

葫芦头泡馍

葫芦头是西安特有的一种传统风味。它的基本原料是煮熟的大小猪肠。吃时顾客先把烙饼，掰成碎块儿，厨师再把猪肠、鸡肉、海参、鱿鱼等放在碎饼上，用煮沸的骨头原汤泡三四次，然后加熟猪油和青菜等。吃时佐以糖蒜、辣酱等，鲜香滑嫩，肥而不腻。

相传，唐代著名医学家孙思邈将烹制猪肠的方法传授给长安一家饮食店店主，并将一个药葫芦赠给店主调味。店主按照孙思邈的指点改进制作方法，长安"葫芦头"从此有名，千年流传。

Shredded Pancakes and Chitterlings in Broth

Hulutou or chitterlings in broth is a local delicacy in Xi'an. The raw materials are cooked intestines, big or small. Before it is serving, customers need to break the pancakes or flapjacks into small pieces, then the chef soaks them in the boiling bone soup three or four times with cooked intestines, chicken, sea cucumber and squid on top. Afterwards, lard and greens are added to it. It is often served with cloves of preserved sugared / sweet garlic and chili sauce, tender and savory, not at all fattening.

Tradition has it that this culinary art was passed down from Sun Simiao, the famous doctor in the Tang Dynasty, to a restaurant owner in Chang'an with a gourd-shaped bottle of herbal medicine to enrich the flavoring and seasoning. After the restaurant owner improved the delicacy with Sun Simiao's instruction, it became known as shredded pancakes and chitterlings in broth for thousands of years.

荞面饸饹

荞面饸饹由荞面经轧制而成,一般凉食,也可以热吃。凉吃时,放入盐、醋、芥末、蒜和辣椒即可。热吃时,把饸饹放入热汤中烫热捞出,然后配上青菜,浇上臊子就可食用。

饸饹味微苦,清香利口,有通气利肠、清热解毒等作用,是四季皆益的食品。

Buckwheat Noodles

The buckwheat noodles are made by pressing the buckwheat flour doughs through a special device with holes. They can be served either hot or cold. If it is served cold, flavor it with salt, vinegar, mustard, garlic sauce and hot chili. If it is served hot, warm it up in the hot soup and scoop it up and top it with cooked vegetables and sauces.

Buckwheat noodles taste a little bitter but delicious and they are beneficial all the year round for its antipyretic nature.

甑糕

甑糕是陕西关中地区的传统早点食品,是以糯米和红枣制成的一种甜糕。它是由最古老的炊具"甑"演变而成的甑锅蒸制而成的,所以叫作甑糕。大枣具有益气、补血、养肾、安神等功效。甑糕枣香浓郁,绵软粘甜,是一种滋补养身的食品。

Rice-date Paste in a Steamer

The rice-date paste in a steamer (Zeng Gao) is a traditional snack for breakfast in Central Shaanxi. It is made from glutinous rice and dates in a steamer which is developed from an ancient cooking vessel Zeng, hence the name Zeng Gao. Dates have a lot of medicinal functions such as enriching the blood and calming the nerves and Zeng Gao has a strong flavor of dates and is soft, sticky and tasty.

凉皮

凉皮是陕西关中及陕南地区的传统小吃。关中地区凉皮一般用麦面蒸制，而陕南地区一般用米面蒸制。

凉皮吃时放入面筋、豆芽、黄瓜丝等，然后泼上辣子油、酱油、醋、蒜汁等各种调料，拌匀即可食用。

凉皮一般凉拌着吃，也可以炒着吃。热炒时可以加入肉丝、火腿肠、青菜等。

Cold Rice-flour Noodles

The cold noodles are a local dish in Southern Shaanxi and Central Shaanxi. The cold noodles in Central Shaanxi are generally made from quality wheat flour through steaming while those popular in Southern Shaanxi are made from the rice flour through the same process.

The cold noodles are served after they are mixed with gluten, bean sprouts, sliced cucumber, chili oil, soy sauce, vinegar, and garlic sauce.

The cold noodles are usually served as cold snacks. Sometimes, they can be served as hot snacks after they are stir-fried with sliced meat, sausage and greens.

岐山臊子面

岐山臊子面历史悠久，早在清代就已经闻名。做臊子面的面条必须要用上等面粉手工擀成。臊子用猪肉、黄花菜、鸡蛋、木耳、豆腐等原料和多种调味品制成。吃时先将面条煮熟捞入碗内，然后浇汤，再放入臊子。岐山臊子面汤多面少，味酸辣，因发源于陕西岐山县而得名。

The Qishan Wheat-flour Noodles

The Qishan noodles have a long history and became well-known as early as the

Qing Dynasty. The noodles must be hand-made of good wheat flour. The saules include pork shreds, citron day lily, egg, wood fungus, and bean curd which are flavored with a variety of spices. Before they are served, the noodles are first scooped and then mixed with ingredients. The Qishan noodles originated in Qishan County, hence the name The Qishan Noodles. When they are served, there is more soup, which tastes sour and hot, than noodles in the bowl.

乾县锅盔

锅盔是乾县著名小吃。乾县锅盔大似锅盖，边薄中厚，表面有轮辐状花纹，硬实筋道，酥香可口，是馈赠亲友的佳品。锅盔制作时掺少量水，用文火干烙而成，因为成品含水量少，极耐储存，便于携带，素为陕西人出门远行随身携带的食品。"乾县锅盔像锅盖"被列为关中十大怪之一。

Pancakes Baked in Wok

Pancakes baked in wok (Guo Kui), a well-known snack in Qianxian County, is thick in the middle and thin on the verge with designs of the wheel on the surface. It is crisp and tasty and is always a good present for friends and relatives. In the process of making it, the wheat flour is mixed with a limited amount of water to make a paste and then baked over soft fire so that it is easy to be stored and handy to be carried because it contains almost no moisture. That is why it is often the custom of the local people of Shaanxi to travel with it as their food. Guo Kui is one of "the Ten peculiarities" in Central Shaanxi and it is often described as big as a manhole cover.

第十一部分 地方土特产

富平柿饼

富平柿饼,属陕西省富平县特产,中国国家地理标志产品,具有甜、软、糯、无核四个特点。早在明清两代,富平柿饼曾充当贡品。新中国成立后,富平柿饼多次参加全国地方名产展览。富平柿饼以当地生产的传统名优柿子品种富平尖柿为原料,经过清洗削皮、日晒压捏、捏晒整形、定型、捂霜等多道工序精细制作而成,柿饼肉多霜厚,入口即化,甜美入心。富平尖柿营养丰富,富含蛋白质、脂肪、无机盐、维生素等14种营养物质和微量元素,居国内同类产品之冠,具有止咳、化痰、除口疮等疗效,是冬春时令食品,更是馈赠亲朋好友之上佳礼品。

PART ELEVEN   THE LOCAL PRODUCES

Persimmon Cakes in Fuping County

The persimmon cake is a kind of special local produce of Fuping County, Shaanxi Province. It is China's national geographical indication product featuring four characteristics: sweet, soft, glutinous and coreless. As early as the Ming and Qing dynasties, the Fuping persimmon cakes had been items of tribute to the royalty. Since the founding of the People's Republic of China, the Fuping Persimmon cakes have been on display many times as one of the national famous local products. The bottom-pointed persimmons are of high quality and therefore are often used as raw materials, out of which traditional persimmon cakes are made. They go through a multi-process such as cleansing, peeling, sun-drying, pinching, reshaping finalizing, and riming. They are pulpy, frosty, sweet and tasty. Besides, they are also rich in 14 various nutrients like protein, fat, mineral salt and trace elements. They have topped the list of the like products in China and possess an effect of ridding coughs, phlegm and aphtha. They are both a seasonal food in winter and spring and a significant gift for friends and relatives.

临潼火晶柿子

临潼火晶柿子,因为果实色红如火,果面光泽似水晶而得名。陕西柿子树的栽培十分广泛,但火晶柿子品质最佳,是临潼特有的柿子品种。它的特点是:个小色红,晶莹光亮,皮薄无核,果肉蜜甜。

临潼火晶柿子含糖量高,除鲜食外,可酿酒或做醋,药用能治肠胃病、止血润便、降血压,同时还是良好的滋补品。用临潼火晶柿子和面粉做成的火晶柿子饼,绵软香甜,是西安的名小吃。

临潼火晶柿子每年都大量出口,深受国内外旅游者的赞誉。

The Fire-Crystal Persimmons

The persimmons grown in Lintong District look as red as fire and as clear as crystal, hence the name Fire-crystal Persimmons. Though persimmons are popular in Shaanxi, the Fire-crystal Persimmons—the local product in Lintong, rank No. 1 in quality. With thin peel and sweet pulp, they are small, fire red, crystal clear, and seedless.

Lintong Fire-crystal Persimmons can be used to make wine and vinegar despite their popularity as a fresh fruit. They can also help with stomach problems and constipation, stop bleeding, lower blood pressure for their medicinal property apart from their tonic effect. The pancakes made from the persimmons, soft and tasty, are very popular in Xi'an.

Being exported in large quantities, Lintong Fire-crystal Persimmons enjoy high reputation both at home and abroad.

黄桂柿子饼

黄桂柿子饼是西安特有的风味细点,采用临潼特产火晶柿子为原料,并配有面粉、桂花酱、玫瑰、桃仁、白糖等制成饼状,在石锅中烙烤至两面均呈金黄色即可。

关于黄桂柿子饼,民间流传一段轶闻。相传1644年,李自成在西安称王,即将带大军攻打北京。当时正值灾荒之年,临潼百姓就用当地特产的水晶柿子拌面粉烙成柿面饼,让士兵们在路上食用。由于这种饼抗饥耐饿,官兵食后,个个精神饱满,没有多长时间就攻下了北京城。从此,临潼人民每年秋季都要制作柿子饼,用来纪念李自成。后来经过西安厨师们不断的改进,发展成为现代的黄桂柿子饼。

西安饭庄制作的黄桂柿子饼已被列为"中华名小吃"。

The Persimmon Pancake

The Persimmon Pancake is a specialty in Xi'an. They are made of Lintong fire-crystal persimmon, wheat flour, osmanthus sauce, rose petals, walnuts and sugar. and then they are baked until golden colored on both sides.

Among the local people there is a story about the pancakes. In 1644, Li Tzucheng, a peasant rebel leader in the Ming Dynasty, occupied Xi'an and claimed himself king. When Li's army was setting off to attack Beijing, the capital city, the local people could provide them nothing but some pancakes due to the great famine in the year. Those pancakes were made of persimmons mixed with wheat flour, so they were fairly hungry-resistant. Every soldier felt energetic after eating them. As a result, Beijing was soon occupied. The local people in Lintong would make pancakes to commemorate Li Tzucheng ever since. Years of improvement have formed the cooking method of the pancakes we have today.

The Persimmon Pancakes made in Xi'an Restaurant has been listed among "Best Delicacies in China".

黄桂稠酒

  稠酒是西安地区名贵饮料之一。酒中加入桂花后，就成为"黄桂稠酒"。它不像一般酒那样澄清，类似豆浆而略带黏稠，所以古人也称"玉浆"。西安人后来把它叫作稠酒、甜酒、米酒。黄桂稠酒的特点是汁稠醇香、绵甜适口，有健胃、活血、止渴、润肺的功能，对促进食欲，增加热量有一定的作用。白酒放的时间越长越好喝，而稠酒因含糖质较多，易变酸，不便久存，所以越鲜越好。

  黄桂稠酒历史悠久，相传杨贵妃酷爱稠酒，"贵妃醉酒"就是喝的稠酒。诗圣杜甫"李白斗酒诗百篇，长安市上酒家眠"的诗里说的酒，据考证，也是指稠酒。稠酒因酒精含量低，仅15%左右，对身体有益无害，所以李白往往开怀畅饮。

The Rice Wine

  The Rice Wine is one of the famous drinks in Xi'an. Since sweet-scented osmanthus is added to the wine when it is made, it is called "Huanggui Rice Wine", which means "wine with osmanthus". It was once called "jade pulp" because it is white in color and thick as soybean milk. Later the local people called it "thick wine", "sweet wine" or "rice wine". Huanggui Rice Wine is thick, aromatic and delicious. It is characterized by the functions of invigorating stomach, stimulating blood circulation, quenching thirst and moistening lungs. It can also arouse appetite, and increase temperature in the human body. As for common wines, the longer they are kept, the more aromatic they would become, but the Rice Wine cannot be kept for a long time since it contains much sugar.

  The Rice Wine boasts a long history. It is said to be the favorite of Yang Yuhuan, concubine of Emperor Xuan Zong of Tang Dynasty. In the famous opera "Lady Yang Gets Drunk", the wine she drinks is Huanggui Wine. Du Fu, a famous Tang-Dynasty poet, once described Li Bai's craziness for the wine as "Li Bai can compose dozens of poems after he drinks wine. He often sleeps in the inns at the market in Chang'an". Research has proved that the wine mentioned in the poem is also rice wine. Containing a low percentage of alcohol, approximately 15%, the rice wine causes no harm to human body, so that Li Bai dared to drink as much as he could.

水晶饼

水晶饼是陕西传统名特糕点之一，已有 800 年的历史。新中国成立后，多次被国家商业部、陕西省商业厅授予优质产品称号。

始于宋代的水晶饼是一种酥皮点心。相传北宋时期，有一年寇准从京都回到故乡下邽郿县（今渭南市下邽镇）探亲，适逢其五十大寿，亲朋们送来寿桃、面花、寿匾，表示祝贺。为了酬谢大家的情意，寇准特设宴款待。酒过三巡，手下人捧进一个精致的盒子，寇准打开一看，里面装着 50 个晶莹透明、如同水晶石一般的点心，点心上面放着一张红纸，工整地写着一首诗："公有水晶目，又有水晶心；能辨忠与奸，清白不染尘。"落款是"渭北老叟"。后来，寇准的家厨也仿照其样式做出了此种点心，寇准取名"水晶饼"，一直沿用至今。这种饼当时就很有名，曾与燕窝、银耳、金花火腿齐名。元代，水晶饼就已经远销到北京、天津等地。

约在 19 世纪后期，水晶饼的制作技艺传入古城西安，由位于西大街南广济街口的德懋恭食品店引进继承，制作技艺不断改进提高，成为秦式糕点之首。

The Crystal Cakes

The Crystal cakes are traditional Shaanxi pastry bearing a 800-year history. They have been praised as "high-quality food" by the National Business Ministry and Shaanxi Provincial Business Department.

Legend has it that in the Northern Song Dynasty, Kou Zhun, the famous clean official, once went back to his hometown from Beijing. It happened to be his fiftieth birthday. So his friends and relatives brought peaches, steamed bread, and inscribed wooden boards for his birthday celebration. During the course of the banquet, a servant brought in an delicate wooden box in which Mr. Kou found 50 crystal cakes. The red paper sheet that covered the cakes read: "Penetrating are your eyes, and pure is your heart; being able to tell the loyal from the wicked, you are upright from the start." The name of the sender was "an old man from Weibei". Later, Mr. Kou's chef learned its cooking technique. The name "Crystal Cakes" given by Mr. Kou is still in use today. The assorted cakes share the same fame with edible bird's nest, white wood fungus and Jinhua ham. In the Yuan Dynasty, such pancakes could be found in the markets in Beijing and Tianjin.

Then in late 19th century, the cooking technique was introduced to Xi'an. Demaogong Bakery in Xi'an gave it some improvement and made the pancakes the most favorite pastry among the people in Shaanxi Province.

临潼石榴

石榴原产中亚,相传西汉张骞出使西域时引入中国,先在长安御花园和帝王离宫临潼温泉宫栽植。经过2000年的繁殖和人工培育,现在,虽然石榴在全国各地都有栽培,但最负盛名者仍属临潼石榴。临潼石榴品种多达50多种,产量高达1000多万公斤,居全国之首,是西安市传统出口产品,在东南亚和港澳地区久负盛名。临潼石榴分为酸、甜两种,均色红个大,汁多皮薄。临潼石榴不但是美味鲜果,还是很好的中药材,具有驱虫杀菌、帮助消化、止痢治泻等作用。

Pomegranates

Pomegranates were originally grown in Central Asia. It is said that they were introduced to China by Zhang Qian when he was sent to the Western Regions as an envoy in the Western Han Dynasty. They were first grown in the imperial gardens in Chang'an and in the Hot Spring Palace in Lintong. Through 2,000 years of propagation and cultivation, pomegranates are now grown all over the country. But Lintong pomegranates are the most famous. With as many as 50 varieties and an output of over 10,000,000 kilograms, the Pomegranates in Lintong is the lead in China and they are the traditional export products of Xi'an, which have been popular in Southeast Asia and Hong Kong as well as Macao for a long time. There are two kinds of Lintong Pomegranates: sweet and sour. Both of them are juicy, red, and big with thin peel. The pomegranates have medicinal value while they serve as fresh fruit. They have curative effect on bacterial dysentery and diarrhea. They can function as anathematic and bactericide, and can help with digestion as well.

中华猕猴桃

中华猕猴桃又叫阳桃,因为都是从中国引种的,中外遍称"中华猕猴桃"。

中华猕猴桃历史悠久,在中国有两三千年的栽培历史。中国16世纪杰出的医学家李时珍编著的《本草纲目》指出:"其形如梨,其色如桃,而猕猴喜食,故有其名。"

中华猕猴桃滋味酸甜,含有丰富的维生素C、氨基酸和多种矿物质,除食用外,具有滋补强身等功效,享有"世界珍果"之美称。

陕西省中华猕猴桃年产量居全国之首,且色泽鲜艳,品质优良。陕西省出口的猕猴桃鲜果、果汁、果酱等在国际市场上颇受欢迎。

The Kiwi Fruits

With the nickname Yang Tao, the kiwi fruit, originated in China, is well-known in the world.

The Chinese kiwi fruit was grown in China as early as 2,000 to 3,000 years ago. It is described in *Compendium of Materia Medica* written by the renowned doctor Li Shizhen in the 16th century as "With the shape of pears and color of peaches, this fruit is named Mihou Tao (macaque peaches) because it is the favorite fruit of macaques".

The kiwi fruit tastes sweet and sour, and is rich in Vitamin C, amino acid and other mineral substances. It is reputed as "the valuable fruit in the world", because it is not only edible but also nutritious.

The output of the kiwi fruit in Shaanxi, with gloss and good quality, ranks No. 1 in China. The export products such as the kiwi fruit, juice, and jam from Shaanxi are very popular at the international market.

陕南核桃

核桃原产伊朗和阿富汗,张骞出使西域时带回中国。陕南地区普种核桃,以商洛核桃最为有名,栽种数量最多。商洛核桃果大、壳薄、不夹心,年产量全国第一。

核桃富含蛋白质、钙、磷、铁和多种维生素,长期食用可降低胆固醇,润肺止喘,补脑健神。

The Walnuts in Southern Shaanxi

Walnuts, originally grown in Iran and Afghanistan, were introduced into China by Zhang Qian, an envoy who was sent to the Western Regions in the Western Han Dynasty. Though they are widely grown in Southern Shaanxi, the walnuts grown in Shangluo are big, thin-shelled and loose-kernelled, and enjoy the fame in quality and quantity. The annual production comes in the first place in the country.

Walnuts abound in protein, calcium, phosphor, iron and many other vitamins. Taken constantly they can decrease cholesterol, moistenlangs, relieve asthma, mourish brains and lift spirits.

陕西青茶

陕西青茶属于绿茶,产于陕南的紫阳、西乡、安康、岚皋、汉阴等县。陕西青茶除了含有咖啡因、茶碱等以外,还含有人体所需的微量元素,尤其是所含硒元素最多,所以陕西青茶又被称为富硒茶。

茶的饮用、栽培、制作及药用最早开始于四川、云南、贵州,而后传入陕西秦岭和淮河地区。8世纪时,唐朝学者陆羽撰写了我国第一部也是世界上第一部茶叶专著《茶经》,系统地阐述了唐代以前我国劳动人民种茶、制茶、煮茶及饮茶的历史,其中记述了当时陕南巴山山区已成为全国七大茶区中的"山南区"的一部分,以后又逐渐扩大到汉江南北。

The Shaanxi Green Tea

The green tea is produced in Tzuyang, Xixiang, Ankang, Langao and Hanyin in the Southern part of Shaanxi Province. Apart from caffeine and alkali, the tea also contains some trace elements that are essential to human health. Among these elements, selenium is the most in quantity, so the tea is also called "selenium-abundant tea".

The growing and consumption of tea started in Sichuan, Yunnan and Guizhou provinces. Later it was introduced to the Qinling mountainous region and Huaihe River valley. Ancient Chinese people's experience of growing, making and boiling of tea was recorded in *The Classic of Tea*, which was written by Luyu, a scholar in the Tang Dynasty, in 8th century. Back then the Bashan area in Southern Shaanxi had become part of the "Shannan District", one of the seven major tea production bases in China. This area expanded later to both sides of the Hanjiang River.

洋县黑米

黑米与普通大米相似，但形扁，其颜色乌黑有光泽.除了食用外，还有药疗价值。黑米主要用于煮粥，可以单独煮，也可以与芝麻、白果、银耳、红枣、冰糖等一起煮。粥色黑里透红，香甜可口。

因为洋县土质独特，所产黑米在过去一直被列为贡品，普通百姓难以品尝。现在，洋县黑米不但早已上了普通百姓的饭桌，同时还出口到国外。

The Black Rice

Similar to ordinary rice but flat and black, black rice is edible and of medicinal value. Black rice can be used to make porridge either alone or together with sesame, gingko, white wood fungus, dates and crystal sugar. The porridge looks dark red and tastes good.

The black rice grown in Yangxian County used to be the tribute in the past, for the soil there is unique. It was by no means for common people. However, it is now not only available on the table of the common people, but also exported overseas.

陕北红枣

红枣是陕北著名土特产。由于陕北土质独特，光照、气温、降雨量等自然条件适宜，因此所产红枣果大、肉厚、色红、味甜。红枣营养丰富，含多种维生素和矿物质，不但可以食用，还可入药，深受人们喜爱。

Dates/jujubee

The dates are the well-known local products of Northern Shaanxi. Thanks to the favorable natural conditions such as the unique soil, the sunshine, the temperature and the precipitation, the dates are big in size, thick in pulp, red in color and sweet in taste. With various vitamins and minerals dates are very popular for its rich nutrition. They are edible and have medicinal effect.

第十二部分　旅游纪念品

秦兵马俑复制品

随着秦兵马俑的发掘与展出，秦兵马俑复制品越来越成为中外游客想得到的纪念品和礼品，也成为一些企业、公共场所等提高声誉和档次的装饰品。秦兵马俑复制品之所以能够如此风靡，原因有三个。首先，复制品的造型忠于原物，无论是陶俑和陶马的姿态，还是发型、衣着、表情等细节，都完全依照兵马俑的原件。为了提高复制品的艺术品位，各种复制品均特邀文物和艺术部门的权威人士进行鉴定和修正，保证准确传达原俑的艺术精神。其次，为了满足消费者的不同需要，兵马俑的复制品规格大小齐全。既有适宜艺术馆、历史博物馆、工艺美术馆和大型饭店陈列的与原俑规格相同的大型俑，也有可供家庭和会客场所摆设装饰的1∶1和1∶4等规格的陶俑，满足了中外旅游者的需要。最后，兵马俑复制品的品种多样：既有将军俑，也有士兵俑；既有站姿俑，也有跪姿俑；既有人物俑，也有马俑。而且随着秦兵马俑发掘清理和整复工作的进展，复制品也将出现更多的新品种。

PART TWELVE　TOURIST SOUVENIRS

The Replica of Terra-Cotta Figures

After years of display since they were excavated, the Qin Terracotta Warriors and Horses become even more popular today. Their replicas are not only accepted as souvenirs and gifts by both Chinese and foreign tourists, but also accepted by enterprises and public organizations as decorations that can promote their reputation and better demonstrate their artistic tastes. There are probably three reasons for the popularity of these of Terra-Cotta figures. Firstly, the replicas of thess replicas are made strictly after the model of the real ones. And they resemble the real ones in almost every detail such as the postures, the hair style, the clothing and the facial features. In order to promote the artistic taste of the replicas, some experts were hired to examine and revise them so that the original artistic beauty can be sufficiently conveyed. Secondly, replicas are made of all sizes to meet the needs of different tourists. The ones of original size are suitable for displays in art galleries, history museums, art exhibition halls and big hotels. Life-sized or one-quarter-sized ones are suitable for decoration of family or guest receiving places. While the mini-sized ones are good portable gifts for both friends and relatives. Tourists of all nationalities can never fail to find the replicas of the right size they want. Thirdly, the replicas are made in a wide variety. There are general figures, soldier figures, standing soldiers and kneeling soldiers etc. Besides soldiers, there are also horse figures. With the progress of excavation and revision, a lot of replicas of new kinds will be available for tourists' choice.

唐三彩复制品

唐三彩是中国古代陶瓷艺术中一颗灿烂的明珠。由于它出现于唐代,又多用黄、绿、赭三种釉色,故名唐三彩。

西安作为唐代的都城,周围出土了大量的唐三彩器物,被誉为唐三彩的故乡。

唐三彩制品造型雄浑简练,生动传神;釉色相互溶渗,绚丽多彩。在唐代,唐三彩不但为达官贵人所珍爱,还远涉重洋,被运往日本、伊朗、埃及、意大利等国。

陕西继承唐代传统,恢复唐三彩的制作已有几十年的历史,拥有造型、配釉、烧窑等方面经验丰富的艺人,所制产品受到国内外人士的称赞。凡来陕西的旅游者,莫不以能得到一件唐三彩制品而为快事。将唐三彩陈设案头,能使室内洋溢出古色古香的东方艺术情趣。唐三彩还可作为高雅而珍贵的礼品用来馈赠亲友。

The Replicas of Tri-color Glazed Pottery

The tri-color glazed pottery, which is known as a splendid pearl in the art of ancient Chinese ceramics, originated in the Tang Dynasty. It is mainly a three-color glaze: yellow, green and brown, hence the name "tri-color glazed pottery of the Tang Dynasty".

Xi'an was the capital of the Tang Dynasty. It is also the home-town of tri-color glazed pottery. Large numbers of pottery wares have been unearthed from around the city.

The shapes of tri-color glazed pottery articles are bold, vivid and life-like, and the glazed colors are mutually-permeated, multifarious, gorgeous and fully expressive. They were treasured even at that time by the Tang people, and were shipped to Japan, Iran, Egypt, Italy and other countries across the ocean.

The traditional way of making tri-color glazed wares has been carried on in Shaanxi. The manufacture of these wares was resumed decades ago. Now Shaanxi Province boasts many artists and artisans with rich experience in modelling, glazing and baking. The products are spoken highly of by people both at home and abroad. All visitors to Shaanxi think it is a pleasure to have tri-color pottery items as souvenirs. If you put them on the desk in your room, the room will be permeated with the charms of Asian art. They are also elegant and valuable presents for your friends and relatives.

碑刻拓片

碑是古代记事、铭记、造像、装饰建筑物等的物凭。从柱础、门楣、石棺到石碑、画像石等，皆为珍贵艺术品，它们记录了古代的社会政治、经济、文化、科技、军事、艺术、民族往来、宗教活动等方面的情况。西安碑林收藏了从东汉到清诸朝代碑碣共3000余件，是我国书法名碑的荟萃之地。由于碑石常出自古代名书法家之手，其中如唐代大书法家颜真卿所写的《多宝塔》碑，柳公权所书的《玄秘塔》碑，怀素的"狂草"，欧阳询、褚遂良等大书法家的作品等，深爱书法爱好者的仰慕。

碑刻拓片是书法艺术爱好者研摹临习的法帖。拓片就是用纸墨在碑石上进行翻拓的图片，拓印出的文图与原碑石上的完全一样，常被文人墨客视为珍宝。

陕西省文物管理部门请拓碑高手对名碑拓印出少量拓片,工艺美术部门用碑石复制品进行数量较多的翻拓,作为旅游纪念品,这些碑刻拓片深受旅游者的欢迎。

The Rubbings of Stone Tablets

Stone tablets bear evidence to ancient records, inscriptions, statues and architectural decorations. From column bases, door frames, stone coffins to stone tablets and stone relievos, all of these objects are valuable because they reveal the facts of ancient politics, economy, culture, science and technology, military affairs, art, ethnical contact and religious activities. Over 3,000 stone tablets from the Eastern Han Dynasty through the Qing Dynasty are preserved in the Forest of Stone Tablets in Xi'an. Most of the tablets were created by the famous ancient calligraphers. The best examples are the "Tablet to Duobao Pagoda" by Yan Zhenqing, the "Tablet to Mysterious Padoga" by Liu Gongquan, works of cursive script by Monk Huai Su, and works of Ouyang Xun and Chu Suiliang. Therefore, they are always favored by calligraphy fans as copies for practice.

Rubbings are the copies of inscriptions on the stone tablets that are made with paper and Chinese ink. The rubbings are almost the same with the original pictures and calligraphy, so they are greatly cherished by men of letters.

The Shaanxi Relics Management authorities had some of the tablets rubbed by experts, but only in small amount. The institutions of applied art have copies of the original tablets made in order to make rubbings in large numbers. As souvenirs, the copies are also well received among tourists.

布贴绣

布贴绣在陕西民间流传已久。它既是布贴和手绣结合的工艺美术品,也是儿童的玩具和日用品。布贴绣有童帽、童鞋、套袖、耳枕等儿童用品,也有布老虎、布麒麟等摆设玩具。传说布老虎和布麒麟等可以避邪镇妖,给孩子带来平安与吉祥。

布贴绣以动物为题材,造型讲究夸张,色彩强调对比,具有鲜明的民间色彩,蕴含着农家妇女无限的深情。

The Applique Articles

The applique articles have been handed down among the people in Shaanxi for ages. The art and craft of applique and hand embroidery include children's toys and daily necessities including children's caps, shoes, over sleeves, ear-pillows. There are also cloth tigers, cloth-unicorns and other ornamental toys. It is said that cloth-tigers and unicorns have the power to exorcise evil spirits and bring good luck and fortune to children.

Using animals as popular subject matter, the applique articles are very exaggerated in shape with sharp contrasts in color. They are of exquisite workmanship and rich imagination, and display a kind of appeal with a simple and unaffected flavor. They are characterized by a distinctive folk style, and show the intense feelings of the country women.

凤翔彩泥偶

凤翔是陕西古城之一，古称雍州，秦始皇统一中国之前，秦人曾在此建都300多年。

凤翔彩泥偶是以当地胶泥和纸浆为材料，成形后加彩绘而成。它题材广泛，造型概括简练、大胆夸张，色彩强烈鲜明，具有浓郁的乡土气息，因而深受当地群众的欢迎。他们用彩泥偶作为儿童玩具和吉祥物。逢年过节，民间艺人手提担挑，从四面八方来到集市，把色彩绚丽的泥偶一字儿摆开，使节日集市显得更加红火热闹。

据文字记载，凤翔彩泥偶已有300多年的历史。但民间传说其历史更为久远，约产生于600多年以前。凤翔彩泥偶蕴含劳动人民质朴纯真的感情，体现了农民们高超的艺术创造才能，是地道的民间艺术。它不仅引起了艺术家们的特别注意，而且颇为国内外各界人士所喜爱。

The Painted Clay Figurines

Fengxiang, called Yongzhou in ancient times, was one of the ancient towns in Shaanxi Province. Before the First Qin Emperor unified China, the town had been the capital of the Qin Kingdom for over 300 years.

The figurine is made of local clay which is mixed with a pulp and is painted after it is shaped. The figurines appear in a variety of shapes which show a lot of simplicity, generality and exaggeration. They are brightly colored with strong local style, and well liked by the local people, who use them as toys and symbols of good fortune and happiness. Each time when the Lunar New Year draws near, local handicraftsmen carry the beautifully painted clayfigurines to the local market and set up stalls in meandering lines, which makes the country fair more florishing and exciting during the festival.

The craft of making the painted clayfigurines in Fengxiang has a recorded history of more than 300 years. According to the folklore, however, the figurines first appeared some 600 years ago. Combined with simple and sincere feelings of the people, the painted clayfigurines reflect the superb creativity in art of the peasants. They are typical articles of Chinese folk art that not only attract the attention of artists, but also appeal very much to people from all walks of life both at home and abroad.

附　录

关中八景

1. 华岳仙掌

西岳华山，是我国著名的五岳之一，位于陕西省华阴市城南，距西安以东120公里，南接秦岭，北瞰黄河，"远而望之若花状"，因为在中国古代，"花"与"华"通用，故有其名。华山有东、西、南、北、中五峰，即东峰朝阳、西峰莲花、中峰玉女、南峰落雁、北峰云台。南峰最高，海拔2160米。由北向南一路行去必经千尺幢、百尺峡、老君梨沟、上天梯、苍龙岭等绝险要道，可饱尝华山之险。此外，山上还有长空栈道、鹞子翻身等闻所未闻的险景。游人越过华山苍龙岭至将军石，便可清晰地观赏到华山东峰朝阳峰的仙掌崖，位于东石峰面东的崖壁上。大自然的风剥雨蚀在崖上造化了一面手掌形石纹，高数十米，五指分明，宛如一只巨人左手掌迹，形象生动逼真、蔚为壮观，人称华岳仙掌，被列为陕西著名的"关中八景"第一景。历代有关华岳仙掌的神话传说很多，其中一种说法为在上古时候，今山西境内的首阳山同华山相连使得黄河在此阻隔。黄河之神巨灵神悲悯人间疾苦就一手推华山，一手推首阳山，将两山推开一条峡谷，使得黄河水向东奔腾而去，被称为"仙掌"。

西岳华山奇险莫名，给每一个登临的游客以极深的感受。华山山势挺拔，登山路线紧贴岩壁而上，陡峭狭窄，步步惊心。由于修建道路难度太大，多年来只有一条路径可以上山，故有"自古华山一条路"之说。1996年建成登山索道，大大方便了游人，使普通游客也可在半日内游赏山顶主要景点。

2. 曲江流饮

曲江位于西安市南郊,北临大雁塔,是我国汉唐时期一座富丽堂皇、景色优美的开放式园林,园内奇花异草品种繁多,随四季争芳竞艳。两岸依地势连绵起伏建有云台亭榭、宫殿楼阁,为曲江优美的自然景致增添了几分人文之美。

在唐代政府选拔官员的科举考试中,进士考试是科举中最难的一科。除通过礼部每年春季举行的全国笔试外,还要经过几道测试才能踏上仕途。而举子们一旦中第,对这样一件关乎个人、门庭荣辱的大事,自然是要好好庆祝一番的,庆祝的形式就是曲江大会,即曲江宴,也称"杏园宴"。后来"杏园宴"逐渐演变为文人雅士们吟诵诗作的"文坛聚会"。盛会期间同时举行一系列趣味盎然的文娱活动,"曲江流饮"正是"文坛聚会"很风雅的一种行乐方式。每当唐代新科进士及第,总要在曲江赐宴。新科进士在这里乘兴作乐,放杯至盘上,放盘于曲流上,盘随水转,轻漂漫泛,转至谁前,谁就执杯畅饮,遂成一时盛事。"曲江流饮"由此得名。每逢春分、秋分及重要节日,城里的皇室贵族、达官显贵都会携家眷来此游赏,樽壶酒浆、笙歌画船,宴乐于曲江水上。优美的环境、丰富的人文气息也吸引了大批文人雅士吟诗作画。

据《全唐诗》记载,大诗人李白、杜甫、白居易、李商隐、刘禹锡等都曾到曲江一游,为世人留下许多脍炙人口的优美诗句。如今的曲江一带,依地势盘旋环绕建造了庞大的仿古建筑群,置身亭廊轩榭,不时有乐舞笙箫传来,依稀梦回到唐朝,令人产生恍如隔世之感。

3. 骊山晚照

骊山,是我国古今驰名的风景游览胜地,它距离西安以东30千米,属秦岭山脉的一个支脉,海拔1302米。山上长年覆盖四季常青的松树和柏树,使骊山看起来好似一匹青苍的骊驹。周秦汉唐以来,骊山成为历代帝王必造访之地。每当夕阳西下,落日的余晖给骊山重重地涂上一抹红霞,漫山皆红,层林尽染,其妖娆动人的自然风光,使人流连忘返。此情此景,又往往勾起人们对周幽王"烽火戏诸侯"的历史回忆。关于骊山还有许多传说和故事。在古代,这里是女娲(中国神话传说中一位创造人类的女性)为拯救世界炼石补天的地方。在秦朝,中国第一位皇帝秦始皇在骊山脚下修建了他的陵墓,以宏伟的兵马俑作为陪葬物。唐朝时,唐玄宗和他美丽的妃子杨玉环在那里写下了他们凄美动人的爱情故事。同时,骊山也见证了1936年的西安事变。除了苍翠秀雅的自然景色和动人的神话传说外,骊山上还建有许多古代独立的皇家宫殿和花园,以及具有疗养功能的温泉。这些都证明了骊山是古代帝王最钟爱的地方。

4. 灞柳风雪

"灞柳风雪"是"关中八景"之一，灞桥两岸，河滩宽阔，长桥跨河，垂柳依依，碧水蓝天，一望无垠。每当春意盎然、春风扑面之际，柳絮漫天飞扬，烟雾蒙蒙，宛如雪花，成了长安灞桥一大景致。因"柳"与"留"同音，表留恋不舍之情，久而久之，灞桥与灞柳成为乡思与离愁的代名词。灞桥之柳，与古长安植柳的传统有着密切的关系。长安周围多水、多川，很适宜柳的成活与生长，加之周、秦、汉、唐宫中，御道多植柳树，民间植柳也蔚然成风。

灞桥位于西安以东12公里处的灞河上，是东出西安的必经之地，也是一座颇有影响的古桥。它西临浐水，东接骊山，东南为白鹿原，北面为渭河平川。历史的车轮曾从这里一一碾过：秦穆公称霸一方，刘邦、项羽楚汉之争，大将军郭子仪平"安史之乱"，慈禧忌惮八国联军的铁骑逃往西安，震惊中外的"西安事变"……在史料典籍中，灞桥第一次横跨在灞水之上是在春秋时期。公元583年，隋文帝曾在秦汉桥之南，修建了"南桥"，后经过历代重修，长久保存了下来。唐朝时，在灞桥上设立驿站，人们多在此处迎宾送客，折柳相赠，依依话别。史籍载，"灞柳风雪"之说，始于明清之际，当时流传于民间的《关中八景》佚名诗中，就有"灞柳风雪扑满面"的诗句。"灞柳风雪"是灞桥风光的一部分，由于其景色宜人，年年吸引着四方的游客。加之在此远可眺山，近可戏水，历来是古城长安官民春游远足的好去处。

5. 雁塔晨钟

"雁塔晨钟"是指陕西省西安市城南荐福寺内的小雁塔及荐福寺钟楼内的古钟。清代每天清晨荐福寺寺内的僧人会定时敲钟，清脆悠扬的钟声响彻西安古城上空，数十里内都可听到。钟声清亮，塔影秀丽，在古城中别有一番韵味，因此小雁塔及其古钟即"雁塔晨钟"被列为"关中八景"之一。

荐福寺创建于唐代文明元年（公元684年），初名献福寺，是唐高宗逝后百日，唐睿宗李旦为其父"献福"而建立的佛教寺院，武则天天授元年（公元690年）改名为荐福寺。小雁塔修建于唐中宗执政期间（公元707年），塔形秀丽，挺拔玲珑，与位于西安南郊大慈恩寺内的大雁塔同是唐代长安城保留至今的两处重要标志性建筑。因规模较小，故称小雁塔，是唐朝精美的建筑艺术遗产。塔身为密檐式方形砖结构，初建时为15级，后受地震破坏，塔顶震坍，塔身破裂，剩下13级，现在看到的是1965年弥合裂缝以后的小雁塔。小雁塔由一块块的方砖砌制，而形成了整体的浑圆，取得了较好的建筑艺术效果，整个塔形显得凝重秀丽，给人以苗条、俊俏、舒展的美感，恰似一位亭亭玉立的淑女。

1300年前，这里是万众瞩目的寺院，是中外文化交流的中心。今天，小雁塔俯览了强国盛世的盛衰变迁，感受了博大高远的唐人情怀，承载了伟大时代的理想追求，更保存了唐代建筑的原始风貌，是全国保存至今难能可贵的原态古塔。当绚丽的晨曦、朝霞映衬出挺拔而秀美的塔影，当唤醒千年古都的宏大钟声在这里敲响时，光、影、声交织成了脍炙人口的绝美景观"雁塔晨钟"。

6. 咸阳古渡

咸阳古渡就是咸阳的渭河渡口，横贯关中的渭河，从古秦都咸阳旁边流过。据咸阳地方志记载，"咸阳古渡"建筑于明嘉靖年间，渡口处建有一座木桥，通陇通蜀，过客众多，为秦中第一渡。"咸阳古渡"为古长安通往西北甘肃和西南四川的咽喉要道，处于十分重要的地理位置。木桥遗址的发现，为研究明清时期西北地区的交通、经济、军事，以及渭河流域的桥梁建筑提供了一个重要的物证。李商隐有诗云："京华庸蜀三千里，送到咸阳见夕阳。"从长安城到咸阳桥，送行送出一天的路程，颇有送君千里的情谊。唐代诗人王维《送元二使安西》就是在此为朋友饯行所作："渭城朝雨浥轻尘，客舍青青柳色新，劝君更尽一杯酒，西出阳关无故人。"

咸阳古渡是古代丝绸之路的桥头堡，古渡遗址附近出土了大量文物，为人们研究当时的经济、文化、军事提供了重要的物证。丝绸之路也称为佛教之路，咸阳古渡遗址出土的大量隋唐佛像，为研究当时佛教文化活动以及中原和西域国家的佛教文化交流，提供了翔实的实物资料。

咸阳作为中国第一个封建王朝的国都，被世人熟知。这座古城背原面水，形势险要。其所背靠的原称为"北坂"或"毕原"。原下不远处滔滔渭水奔流东去，宛似一条游龙。这段渭河也就是关中东西大道的分界线，东来西往的人必须从这里渡过渭河，然后才能东出函谷，或向西踏上丝绸之路，于是也有了"咸阳古渡"。

7. 草堂烟雾

草堂寺位于西安市鄠邑区东南方草堂镇，景色秀丽，曾是佛教传入中国后的第一个国立译场，也是一座千年古刹。它之所以著名与鸠摩罗什有着很大的关系。鸠摩罗什是东晋时后秦高僧，著名的佛经翻译家。当时，后秦国王姚兴崇尚佛教，于弘始三年（公元401年）迎请龟兹高僧鸠摩罗什来长安，住逍遥园西明阁翻译佛典，后在园内建寺院，供罗什居住。由于鸠摩罗什译经场以草苫盖顶，故得名为"草堂寺"。

鄠邑区当地对草堂烟雾有两种说法：一种认为所谓的"草堂烟雾"就是指山岚水汽，因为草堂寺靠近终南山，而终南山沿线一带都属于热水带地区，地下都打出过温泉，每年秋冬时节水汽上升，形成薄雾，从西飘向东，看似仿佛都是从草堂寺溢出的，所以名为"草堂烟雾"；另一种说法是草堂寺曾是国立译经场，香火鼎盛，终日香火缭绕，形成烟雾飘在草堂寺上空。

其实，井内的地热是引起这股烟雾的真正原因。经省水文队等部门勘测，草堂寺近处有明显的地热异常，从临潼到眉县西汤峪的秦岭山前地带，存在一个地热田，开发前景十分广阔。每年秋冬的早晨，天气寒冷，空气潮湿，井内喷出的热气一时不易散失，和空中的水汽凝聚为一体，就生成这一罕见的景象。

8. 太白积雪

太白山是我国南北分水岭——秦岭山脉的主峰，横卧于陕西省眉县、太白县、周至县三县境内，距西安市区70公里。太白山主峰拔仙台是陕西省的制高点，海拔3767.2米，也是我国大陆的东半壁——东经105°以东地区的最高峰。"太白积雪"作为关中八景之一，是历代文人所赞美的胜景，早在北魏郦道元的《水经注》里就有记载："太白山南连武功山，于诸山最为秀杰，冬夏积雪，望之皑然。"这是"太白积雪"一词的最早出处。由于山高云淡、空气稀薄、气候寒冷，终年积雪不化，即使三伏盛暑，皑皑白雪，仍然莽莽天际银光四射，"太白积雪"，因其景致格外壮观美丽，被誉为关中八景之一。

太白山森林茂密，溪流潺潺，鸟兽繁多，景观迷人，拥有丰富的地质、自然资源，有绿色植物宝库和天然动物园之称，也是世界上少有的天然高山植物园和动物园。太白山森林公园内还有春秋战国时期王禅老祖修道的"鬼谷子洞"，相传为汉钟离、吕洞宾等八仙修行处"钟吕坪"，道教始祖老子骑牛过玄关路经汤峪休息的"青牛洞"，唐玄宗携杨贵妃游汤峪所建的"唐子城"，药王孙思邈上太白采药的栈道等遗址。森林公园入口处为汤峪温泉，唐代称"凤泉汤"。现有大泉三口，日出水400多吨，出口水温度60℃，对多种疾病有一定疗效。千百年来，被誉为太白山八景的红河丹崖、斜峪雄关、古枫函境、桃川曲流、斗母奇峰、平安云海、太白明珠、拔仙绝顶，正吸引着越来越多的海内外旅游者。

ADDEDUM

The Eight Famous Scenic Attractions in Central Shaanxi

1. Immortal's Palm Cliff of Mount Hua

With the Yellow River to the north and the Qinling Mountain Range to the south, Mount Hua stands in the south of Huayin County, 120 kilometers east of Xi'an. There are five peaks of Mount Hua: the Morning Sun Peak (the East Peak), the Lotus Flower Peak (the West Peak), the Jade Lady Peak (the Middle Peak), the Wild Goose-resting Peak (the South Peak) and the Cloudy Terrace Peak (the North Peak). These five peaks look very much like a lotus flower, hence the name of Mount Hua (Hua used here means flower in Chinese, for 华 and 花 are homophones). The South Peak, with an altitude of 2160 meters, is regarded as the monarch of Mount Hua because it is the highest peak among the five. Hiking through Mount Hua is very popular among backpackers. For many years most visitors have taken a traditional but efficient walking-ascending route. By taking this route, visitors can experience not only its danger, but also the major captivating scenic spots, like the Thousand-Foot Precipice, the Hundred-Foot Crevice, Laojun's Furrow, the Heavenward Ladder and the Blue Dragon Ridge, etc. There are also other impressive sights on the way to the summit, such as the Cliffside Plank Road, the Sparrows' Somersault Cliff, etc. Climbing from the Dragon Ridge to the General's Stone, visitors can see Immortal's Palm Cliff on the East Peak, ranked as the first of The Eight Scenic Attractions in Central Shaanxi. Its name comes from the natural rock veins of the cliff, which looks like a giant palm-print. There are many myths and legends about the sacred cliff. Legend has it that Mount Shouyang and Mount Hua were an huge mountain in ancient times, which blocked the Yellow River passage, causing devastating flood in the human world. Juling, the god of the Yellow River, managed to push the two mountains apart, and then the Yellow River found its way and flowed eastwards easily. Thus a giant palm was imprinted on cliff of the West Peak of Mount Hua.

As the saying goes "There has been only one path up Mount Hua since ancient times". Upon reaching the top, visitors can enjoy the awesome grandeur of these peaks. The peaks are peculiar; the cliffs are a lot more perilous. The sights make climbers tremble with fear, but gasp in admiration as if they were touring a fairyland. As the mountain's accessibility vastly improved with the completion of the cable car in 1996, visitors can enjoy the major scenic spots of Mount Hua in half a day.

2. The Drinking Feast at Qujiang

The Qujiang Pool is a relic park located in southeast Xi'an, with the Dayan Pagoda in its north. It was a magnificent and beautiful garden in the Tang Dynasty. There were many kinds of delicate flowers blooming all the year round, which look more graceful in emerald grass and bushes in the garden. Around the Qujiang Pool platforms, pavilions, and palaces are constructed according to rolling terrains, which endowed the natural scenic spots with artistic glamor.

In the imperial examination in feudal China, the successful graduates in the court exam would serve as officials in the royal government. For many scholars, the exam could change their life and bring them honor and crowning glory. The successful candidates of the imperial examination would be given banquets for celebration in the Apricot Garden, so the banquet was also called Apricot Garden Banquet. Later, the celebration gradually evolved into gatherings for literati and scholars to chant poems. During the grand meeting, a series of interesting recreational activities were held, among which The Drinking Feast at Qujiang (Wine drinking at Qujiang Pool) was most renowned. The graduates put wine in the cup on a tray, and then let it float on water. When the plate floating with moving water stopped in front of a particular person, he would compose a poem on the spot as it was required. This is literally called "The Drinking Feast at Qujiang". When spring equinox, autumn equinox and the important festivals came around, the royal aristocrats and dignitaries would come to the Pool with their families to enjoy wine, music, boating and feasting. The beautiful natural scenery and profound artistic charm also attracted a large number of literati and scholars to create poems and paintings.

According to *A complete Collection of Tang Poems*, great poets, like Li Bai, Du Fu, Bai Juyi, Li Shangyin, Liu Yuxi and many others, all visited this historical place, and wrote many well-known poems. Today, around Qujiang Park there are many man-made or archaized pavilions, towers, galleries, verandas and terraces with music reverberating in the air, which creates an illusion to visitors as if they were in the Tang Dynasty.

3. The Rosy Sunset Glow at Mount Li

Mount Li is a famous tourist resort located 30 kilometers east of Xi'an. The mountain is part of the Qinling mountain range and rises to a height of 1,302 meters above sea level. Evergreen pines and cypresses are found covering the entire mountain and made it resemble a black horse. Since Zhou, Qin, Han and Tang dynasties, Mount Li had been the place that many emperors would like to visit. Whenever the sun sets down in the west, the whole mountain is veiled in a rosy glow, coating layers of mountain ranges and dense woods in enchanting glamour, and attracting swarms of visitors to fully immerse themselves in the radiating glow. The beautiful natural scene reminds one of an event in history—Teasing the Marquess with Balefire. There are also many legends and stories about the mountain. In ancient times, it was the place where Nüwa (one who created human beings according to Chinese legend) smelt stone to patch the sky-hole in order to save the world. In the Qin Dynasty, the first emperor built his mausoleum at the foot of the mountain with the magnificent terracotta warriors and horses as the funeral artefacts. In the Tang Dynasty, Emperor Xuanzong and his beautiful concubine Yang Yuhuan composed their sorrowful yet moving love story there. The mountain also witnessed Xi'an Incident in 1936.

Apart from the natural scenery of verdant beauty as well as the fascinating legends and stories, there are many ancient detached royal palaces and gardens, thermo springs with medicinal effects. All these have proved that Mount Li gains the popularity with and favor of ancient emperors.

4. The Willow Catkins at Baqiao

The Baqiao Willow Catkins is one of The Eight Famous Attractions in Central Shaanxi. Both sides of the Bahe River are lined with rows upon rows of willow trees. The clear river water, the azure sky and the snow-white catkins form a fascinating scene. In every spring, when gentle breeze caressed willow trees and scudded over the sky, willow catkins began to dance gracefully in the air as if snowflakes were falling elegantly. In Chinese, 柳 and 留 are homophones, which share the same pronunciation of "Liu". 柳 means willow, while 留 means to beg somebody to stay behind. So the

Baqiao bridge and willow catkins are representative of one's reluctance and unwillingness to let friends go. In ancient times, there were many rivers around Chang'an (Xi'an today), which created favorable natural conditions for the growth of willows, so willows were planted along roads of the palace and country in Zhou, Qin, Han and Tang dynasties.

The Baqiao Bridge over the Bahe River is located 12 kilometers east of Xi'an. It is the only way out of Xi'an bound for east. It is also an influential ancient bridge as it connects the Chanhe River in the west, Mount Li in the east, Bailu Plateau in the southeast and the Weihe River Basin in the north. Bahe willows have witnessed the historical events in Chinese history, like the expansion of Qin in the reign of the Duke Mu, the battle between Liu Bang and Xiang Yu, Guo Ziyi's suppression of An Lushan Rebellion, Empress Dowager Cixi fleeing to Xi'an for fear of the Allied Forces of Eight Foreign Powers, and then the Xi'an Incident known both at home and abroad.... It is recorded in history books that the Bahe Bridge was originally built in the Spring and Autumn Period. In 583 AD, Emperor Wen of the Sui Dynasty built the South Bridge to the south of the Qin-Han Bridge, and later it was rebuilt in different dynasties, for which the bridge still stands high over the river. During the Tang Dynasty, a stage was set up close to the bridge to accommodate people on their journey. These men plucked willow twigs and gave them to friends as gifts upon parting from each other. As early as the Ming and Qing dynasties, there were poems to eulogize the spectacular scene of dancing Baqiao willow catkins. In addition, other beautiful scenes in Baoqiao borough also attracted visitors from all over the country all year round.

5. The Morning Bell Chime at Xiaoyan Pagoda

The Morning Bell Chime in the Xiaoyan Pagoda has been known as one of The Eight Famous Scenic Attractions in Central Shaanxi since ancient times. The Xiaoyan Pagoda and the bell are situated in the Jianfu Temple in the southern part of Xi'an. The bell is stricken every morning, and the sound was so resonant that it can be heard several miles away.

The temple was originally named Xianfu Temple, and it was built in 684 AD under the command of Li Dan (Emperor Rui Zong of Tang) in honor of his father Li Zhi—Emperor Gao Zong of the Tang Dynasty. It got its current name Jianfu Temple in 690 AD when Wu Zetian ascended the throne and became the only Empress in China. The

XiaoyanPagoda was initially built in 707 AD during the reign of Emperor Zhong Zong in the Tang Dynasty. With its exquisite construction, The Xiaoyan Pagoda and the Dayan Pagoda are the two iconic ancient buildings of the Tang Dynasty. The original pagoda had 15 stories and it survived over several earthquakes with only the two top stories slightly damaged, and 13 stories remained. The pagoda stands on a round base made from packed earth and it is believed that in the event of an earthquake, the tremor is evenly distributed by the base, hence its survival. The pagoda was repaired in 1965. The Xiaoyan Pagoda is a multi-eave and square brick structure which suggests the good workmanship and artistic style of the early Tang Dynasty. The whole pagoda looks dignified and magnificent, just like a graceful lady with a marvelous bearing.

1300 years ago, it was a temple that attracted much attention with its grandeur and was the center of cultural exchange between China and foreign countries. Today, the original style and featurism are well preserved, witnessing the decline of Tang from the prime, the lofty pursuit and achievement of Chinese monks in the great empire, and the dream of this new age. When the radiant morning sunlight is cast on the tower, and the ancient bell is stricken in the early morning, there comes the enchanting scene of glowing light, the elegant pagoda image and the resonating bell striking.

6. The Xianyang Ancient Ferry

The Xianayang ancient ferry is the ferry by which to cross the Weihe River at the Xianyang section. The Weihe River runs across the Guanzhong Plain. According to the Xianyang Local Chronicles, the ancient ferry was built in the Jiajing period of the Ming Dynasty. A bridge was constructed across the ferry and it connected Chang'an with Gansu province in the northwest and Sichuan Province in the southwest. As there were swarms of passengers passing through, the ferry was referred to as the First Ferry in the province. The discovery of the wooden bridge site at the ferry provides an important evidence for the study of transportation, economy, military affairs and bridge construction in the Weihe River basin in the northwest region during the Ming and Qing dynasties. Many poets like Li Shangyin and Wang Wei composed poems to eulogize or depict the ferry. They wrote many poetic works such as this one written by Li Shangyin, a well-known poet in the later Tang Dynasty. Here are the two stanzas from the poem:

Along the thorny passage out we set,

Till the ferry did we see the sunset.

This poem is about the poet seeing his friend off to the ferry where they parted reluctantly from each other. Though it took them a whole day to walk to the ferry, yet to them a day's walking distance seemed to be thousands of miles away. From this it can be seen that it is very symbolic of how great their ever-lasting friendship was. Another poem was composed by Wang Wei, a famous poet in the Tang Dynasty when the he held a farewell feast to his friend at the ferry. The poem goes like this:

The morning drizzle wetted the floating dust in the air,

The tender willow trees outside the inn are fresh and fair,

Oh, my dear friend, please have one more glass of wine,

For once going out west you will meet no friend so fine.

The ancient ferry was the bridgehead and a strategic stronghold along the Silk Road. A large number of cultural relics were unearthed near the ferry site and provide important material evidences for experts to study the economy, culture and military at that time. The Silk Road is also known as the Buddhism Road. A great number of Buddhist statues in the Sui and Tang dynasties unearthed at the site offer detailed physical information for the study of Buddhist cultural activities at that time and the Buddhist cultural exchanges between the Central Plain and the Western Regions.

As the capital of China's first feudal dynasty, Xianyang is well known all over the world. The ancient city has fascinating landscapes and fertile soil, for the Weihe River flows in its south and the tableland lies to its north. The river meanders like a swimming dragon eastwards. This section of the Weihe River is a dividing line in Guanzhong, setting the west and the east apart. In ancient times, passengers from various directions had to cross the river to embark on their journey eastwards out of Hangu Pass or initiate their journey westwards along the Silk Road.

7. The Mist at the Caotang Temple

The Caotang Temple or the Straw-thatched Temple is located in the Caotang Village to the south east of Huyi Borough of Xi'an. The temple became a sacred monastery since Abbe Kumarajiva, a Buddhist master, translated Buddhist scriptures here. From Qiuci of the present Xinjiang Uggur Autonomous Region, Kumarajiva was invited to Chang'an in 401 AD by Yao Xing, king of the later Qin, who showed great interest in

Buddhism. So kumarajiva was treated as the national master in Buddhism. As the temple where he did his translation of Buddhist scriptures was straw-roofed, it was named the Caotang temple or the Straw-thatched Temple.

There are two interpretations about the mist coming from the temple. One explanation takes the Temple Mist as the mountain vapor. This parlance bases its version on the fact that the Temple is situated near the Zhongnan Mountain, whose underground is a the geothermal water belt and there are many underground thermas. In the autumn and winter seasons every year the vapor rises into the air and forms a mist, floating from west to east as if it moves out of the temple, hence its name. The other parlance takes it that the Temple used to be the national scripture translation venue, where there were swarms of pilgrims who burnt joss sticks in the Temple, so mist of fog were formed in the air over the Temple.

Virtually, the real cause of the mist might be geothermal vapor as the Caotang Temple is close to Mount Zhongnan below which there is a hot spring belt according to the survey of provincial hydrologic authority. There is a geothermal field along the belt from Lintong to Meixian at the northern foot of Qinling Mountains. It has a good prospect of development. In autumn and winter every year, the weather is cold and air is damp. The thermal vapor from the well cannot be dispersed easily and the hot vapor is quickly condensed with the water vapor in the air to create this rare and spectacular scene. Thus, it is referred to as one of the Eight Scenic Attractions of Shaanxi province.

8. Snow on Mount Taibai

Mount Taibai is the main peak of the Qinling mountains—geographically a demarcation line between the north and the south of China. It lies at the junction of three counties: Meixian, Taibai and Zhouzhi, 70 kilometers west of Xi'an. The main peak, the Baxian Peak is the highest with an elevation of 3,767.2 meters. It is the commanding point in Shaanxi Province and also the highest mountain in Eastern China (east area of 105°E). The snow-capped peak of Taibai, one of The Eight Famous Scenic Attractions in Central Shaanxi, is highly eulogized by men of letters throughout the ages. As early as the Northern Wei Dynasty, it was recorded in *Commentary on the Waterways* by Li Daoyuan: "Mount Taibai is connected to Wugong Mountain in the south, and it is the most beautiful among all mountains. It is snow-capped in both winter and summer, so it looks silver white all year round." This is perhaps the earliest occurrence of the version "snow-capped Taibai". Due to the unique geological location and meteorological condition of the mountain—its height, light clouds, thin air and cold spell, the yearly accumulated snow never seems to thaw, even on dog days. The mountain looks silver white and glistens with snow covering the peaks. It is truly a spectacular vista, so it is regarded as one of "the Eight Scenic Wonders in Central Shaanxi".

Mount Taibai has its own distinguishing features: lush forests, gurgling streams, various birds and animals, charming landscapes, rich geological and natural resources, thus known as a botanic garden of alp exuberant plants and a natural zoo. Significantly, there are some historical relics in the Taibai Forest Park such as the Cave of Gui Guzi (a dwelling place for the master Wang Chan in the Period of Spring and Autumn and Warring States), the Zhonglü Terrace (the abode for Eight Immortals), the Black Ox Cave (where Lao Tzu, the Taoist originator, took a rest when passing through), the Tangzicheng built by Emperor Xuan Zong of the Tang Dynasty when visiting the Tang Ravine with his imperial concubine Yang Yuhuan and the trestle path along which Sun Simiao (a master of Chinese herbal medicine) went uphill to gather medical herbs. At the entrance of the Forest Park is the Tangyu Thermo-Spring known as "Fengquan Spring" in the Tang Dynasty. At present, there are three hot springs, with over 400 tons of water gushing out of the ground every day. The highest water temperature at the mouth of the spring is 60℃, and has a curative effect for many diseases. For thousands of years, the spectacular views of Mount Taibai have been attracting visitors both at home and aboard with its charm.

陕西珍禽异兽

1. 洋县朱鹮

素有"东方宝石"之称的珍禽朱鹮是世界上最濒危的鸟类,为国家一级保护动物。受环境恶化以及人类活动的影响,朱鹮种群数量急剧减少,在一些国家已消失殆尽。经我国鸟类学家考察,1981年5月在陕西洋县重新发现朱鹮种群,是世界上仅存的种群。它体长约为80厘米,体重1.8千克,通体白色,两翅、腹部及尾部以朱红色渲染,腿与爪也呈朱红色,喜欢栖息于浅涧和稻田中觅食水生昆虫，多成群结伴翱翔。由于朱鹮性格温顺，在我国民间它被视为吉祥的象征，被称为"吉祥之鸟"。

2. 佛坪大熊猫

陕西佛坪是大熊猫在地球最北缘的栖息地，野外分布密度居全国之首，被认定为秦岭亚种。陕西秦岭大熊猫与四川大熊猫形态上存在明显差异，四川亚种头长像熊，而秦岭亚种头圆像猫，更加可爱而漂亮，被誉为"国宝中的美人"。佛坪熊猫谷气候温和，冬无严寒，夏无酷暑，群山雄峙，风景如画，是秦岭大熊猫回归野性的理想天堂，被专家称为"野生大熊猫最有希望生存和繁衍的地方"。

3. 牛背梁羚牛

牛背梁国家森林公园孕育了丰富的珍稀濒危动植物，被誉为"天然动物园"，是我国唯一的国家级羚牛野生动物自然保护区。羚牛是国家一级保护动物，分为四个亚种，其中秦岭亚种是最漂亮的亚种，体形最大，长相最为威武，数量也最为稀少，通体白色间泛着金黄，也被称为金毛扭角羚。雄性和雌性都有粗大的角，体长约1.8米，成年雄性可达到2米以上。成年雄性体重200~300公斤，其毛色色泽依老幼而不同，老年个体为金黄色，幼体通体为灰棕色。羚牛与朱鹮、大熊猫、金丝猴共同被列为"秦岭四宝"。

4. 周至金丝猴

周至县双庙乡玉皇庙村坐落于秦岭高处的一个山坳里，三面环山，山上古木铺天盖地，金丝猴自然保护区坐落于此。金丝猴被列为国家一级保护动物。这里的金丝猴相貌奇特，面孔呈宝蓝色，鼻子朝天，人称它为"仰鼻猴"。其尾巴长度几乎与身体长度相当，肩背和前肢上的毛色呈现金色，背上最长的毛长达50多厘米，光亮如丝，故称金丝猴。它们大都活动在海拔1500~2500米的针阔叶混交林中，在树上行走、吃食、嬉戏、休息，过着典型的树上群栖生活。

5. 榆林红碱淖遗鸥

被誉为"湿地精灵"的遗鸥是全球最大的珍禽濒危鸟类，国家一级重点保护动物。直到20世纪20年代它才被人发现认知，发现时全球不足4000只。遗鸥属中型水禽，体长40厘米左右，喙和脚呈暗红色，前额扁平，头部纯黑，背部、肩部为淡灰色，腰部、尾羽和下体为白色。它们对繁殖地的选择近乎苛刻，只在干旱荒漠湖泊的湖心岛生育后代。每年夏季大约占全球90%以上的遗鸥会光临红碱淖。红碱淖上烟波浩渺，波光粼粼，融草原风光与江南泽国景象于一体，是它们理想的避暑天堂。

Rare Birds and Animals of Shaanxi Province

1. Ibises in Yangxian County

Ibises or crested ibises, known as "the Oriental Gem", are the most endangered birds in the world and are national first-class protected animals. The population of crested ibises, affected by environmental deterioration and human activities, has decreased dramatically and has become extinct in some countries. With the observation and investigation by Chinese ornithologists, the ibis population was rediscovered in May 1981 in Yangxian County, Shaanxi Province. It is the only remaining population in the world. The individual ibis is about 80 centimeters long and weighs 1.8 kilograms each. They are white with vermilion on its wings, abdomens and tails, and their legs and claws are also vermilion. They love to live in shallow streams and paddy-rice fields and feed on aquatic insects and fly in flocks. Because of their gentleness ibises are regarded as a symbol of good luck. That is why they are also called "auspicious birds".

2. Giant Pandas in Foping County

Foping is the habitat of giant pandas on the northernmost edge of the earth. The density of wild pandas in Foping is the highest in the country and they are recognized as the Qinling subspecies. There are obvious morphological differences between the Shaanxi Qinling Pandas and the Sichuan Pandas. The Sichuan subspecies has a bear-like head, while the Qinling subspecies has a cat-like head. The latter is more lovely and beautiful and is known as "the beauty in the national treasure". The Foping Panda Valley, with picturesque mountains surrounding it, is an ideal haven—a paradise with a mild climate without freezing winters or scorching summers—for pandas in the Qinling Mountains to return to the wild. Experts call it "the most ideal place for them to survive and reproduce".

3. Takins in Niubeiliang

Niubeiliang National Forest Park is rich in rare and endangered animals and plants (fauna and flora), known as the "natural zoo", and is the only national nature reserve for wild takins in China. Takins are national first-class protected animals and they are divided into four subspecy, of which the Qinling subspecy is the most beautiful one, the largest in size, the most formidable in appearance and the rarest in number. They are also known as golden-yellow antelopes with white bodies. Both males and females have strong horns, with a body length of about 1.8 meters, and adult males can grow to more than 2 meters. Adult males weigh 200-300 kg, and their hair color varies with to their ages. The aged individuals look golden yellow, and the baby takins are grayish brown. Takins, Crested Ibises, Giant Pandas and Golden-haired Monkeys are jointly listed as "the Four Treasures of the Qinling Mountains".

4. Golden-haired Monkeys in Zhouzhi County

Yuhuangmiao Village in Shuangmiao Township, Zhouzhi County, is located in a col surrounded by mountains on three sides and covered with ancient trees high up on the Qinling Mountains. The nature reserve for golden-haired monkeys is just located there. They are the national first-class protected rare animals. The golden-haired or the snub-nosed monkey in the Qinling Mountains has a peculiar appearance: its face is sapphire blue and its nose is upside down. That is why it is called the "nub-nosed monkey". The length of its tail is almost the same as that of its body. The fur color on their shoulders and forelimbs is golden. The longest fur on the back is more than 50 centimeters long and is as bright as silk, so it is also called golden-haired monkey. Most of them live in mixed coniferous and broad-leaved forests at an altitude of 1500-2500 meters. They walk, eat, play and rest on trees and live a typical arboreal life.

5. Relict Gulls at Red Alkaloid Lake in Yulin

Known as the "wetland fairy", relict gulls are the world's largest, rare and endangered birds, and are under national first-class protection. It was not until the 1920s that it was discovered and recognized, with fewer than 4,000 in the world. Relict gulls are medium-sized waterfowl with a body length of about 40 centimeters, dark red beak and feet, flat forehead, pure black head, light gray back and shoulder, and white waist, tail feather and lower body. Their adaptability is very limited, especially their selection of breeding places is highly restricted, and they only give birth to offspring in the central islet of arid desert lakes. About 90% of the world's relict gulls visit the Red Alkaloid Lake every summer, which, with its vast expanse of sparkling water, is an ideal summer sanctuary for them, presenting us with loess grassland scenes and the southern tropical landscapes.